Justice
for All

Promoting Social Equity in Public Administration

Edited by

Norman J. Johnson *and* James H. Svara

NATIONAL ACADEMY OF
PUBLIC ADMINISTRATION

TRANSFORMATIONAL TRENDS IN
GOVERNANCE AND DEMOCRACY

M.E.Sharpe
Armonk, New York
London, England

Library of Congress Cataloging-in-Publication Data

Justice for all : promoting social equity in public administration / edited by Norman J. Johnson,
James H. Svara.
    p. cm. — (Transformational trends in governance & democracy)
Includes bibliographical references and index.
ISBN 978-0-7656-3025-4 (cloth : alk. paper) — ISBN 978-0-7656-3026-1 (pbk. : alk. paper)
    1. Social justice—United States. 2. Social values—United States. 3. Equality—United
States. 4. United States—Economic policy—2009– 5. United States—Social policy—1993–
I. Johnson, Norman J. II. Svara, James H.

    HN65.J86 2011
    303.3′720973—dc22
                                          2010044470

Printed in the United States of America

Transformational Trends in Governance and Democracy

National Academy of Public Administration

Terry F. Buss, Series Editor

Modernizing Democracy:
Innovations in Citizen Participation
Edited by Terry F. Buss, F. Stevens Redburn, and Kristina Guo

Meeting the Challenge of 9/11:
Blueprints for More Effective Government
Edited by Thomas H. Stanton

Transforming Public Leadership for the 21st Century
Edited by Ricardo S. Morse, Terry F. Buss, and C. Morgan Kinghorn

Foreign Aid and Foreign Policy:
Lessons for the Next Half-Century
Edited by Louis A. Picard, Robert Groelsema, and Terry F. Buss

Performance Management and Budgeting:
How Governments can Learn From Experience
Edited by F. Stevens Redburn, Robert J. Shea, and Terry F. Buss

Reengineering Community Development for the 21st Century
Edited by Donna Fabiani and Terry F. Buss

Innovations in Public Leadership Development
Edited by Ricardo S. Morse and Terry F. Buss

Innovations in Human Resource Management: Getting the Public's Work
Done in the 21st Century
Edited by Hannah S. Sistare, Myra Howze Shiplett, and Terry F. Buss

Expanding Access to Health Care: A Management Approach
Edited by Terry F. Buss and Paul N. Van de Water

Justice for All: Promoting Social Equity in Public Administration
Edited by Norman J. Johnson and James H. Svara

About the Academy

The National Academy of Public Administration is an independent, nonprofit organization chartered by Congress to identify emerging issues of governance and to help federal, state, and local governments improve their performance. The Academy's mission is to provide "trusted advice"—advice that is objective, timely, and actionable—on all issues of public service and management. The unique source of the Academy's expertise is its membership, including more than 650 current and former cabinet officers, members of Congress, governors, mayors, legislators, jurists, business executives, public managers, and scholars who are elected as fellows because of their distinguished contribution to the field of public administration through scholarship, civic activism, or government service. Participation in the Academy's work is a requisite of membership, and the fellows offer their experience and knowledge voluntarily.

The Academy is proud to join with M.E. Sharpe, Inc., to bring readers this and other volumes in a series of edited works addressing current major public management and public policy issues.

The opinions expressed in these writings are those of the authors and do not necessarily reflect the views of the Academy. To access Academy reports, please visit our Web site at www.napawash.org.

To Philip Rutledge,
whose life was devoted to advancing social equity.

Contents

Acknowledgments

This book draws on the ten years of work by the Social Equity Panel of the National Academy of Public Administration (NAPA). The panel consists of over 250 people in public organizations and universities who are committed to understanding and advancing social equity. The members include both NAPA fellows and associate members. The lively exchanges at monthly panel meetings combine the face-to-face exchange of participants in Washington and many other people who connect to the meeting by telephone.

The group regularly organizes several panel sessions each year at the major public affairs organizations—the American Society for Public Administration, the National Association of Schools of Public Affairs and Administration, and the Association for Public Policy Analysis and Management—as well as special panels at other organizations including the International City/County Management Association. Countless members of the panel have stepped forward to raise the visibility of the social equity issue and make it a regular part of the discussions carried on in practitioner and academic associations.

The panel has been guided by imaginative and dedicated leaders. Phil Rutledge was the first chair of the panel. He was succeeded by Costis Toregas from 2005 to 2007. Blue Wooldridge has been chair since 2008. All have been highly effective at keeping the large and loose organization focused and moving forward. The panel has been ably assisted by staff members at NAPA. In the introduction we describe the reports prepared by the panel with major contributions from George Frederickson, Charles Washington, and members of the initial coordinating committee —Bill Hansell, vice chair; Gail Christopher, Valerie Lemmie, Sy Murray, and Costis Toregas.

In the preparation of this volume, we thank all the contributors for their efforts. Terry Buss, a contributor and former staff member at NAPA who is executive director and Distinguished Professor of Public Policy at Carnegie Mellon University in Australia, shepherded us through the process of preparing the manuscript and working with the publisher. Harry Briggs at M.E. Sharpe offered guidance in the publishing process and thoughtful feedback about our topic. Daniel Ledbetter, a doctoral student in the Ph.D. program in Public Affairs at the University of Texas at Dallas, prepared the final manuscript for publication. He combined his high-level organizing and editing skills with his interest in social equity and a deep knowledge of public administration.

We acknowledge our profound debt to Philip Rutledge and share his words in the Introduction. This book is dedicated to him.

Introduction

This is an appropriate time to reconsider the record of achieving social equity in the United States. With the election of Barack Obama, an African American, as president (and his nomination over the final contender who was a woman), we added significantly to the drive toward perfecting our constitutional democracy. Hopefully this breakthrough will make it possible to recognize that acknowledging progress does not undercut the need to continue the work of making the union more perfect. There is still much work to do, Obama's election notwithstanding. His election is an opportunity to pursue more aggressively the justice-for-all agenda.

The essays in this volume were selected to serve as foundational stones to support the twenty-first-century efforts to ensure justice for all. These efforts will reflect the governance of our nation, states, and local governments in combination with decisions and delivery of services by nongovernmental organizations. The union was marred and flawed at the nation's founding. Inequality was built into the organizational fabric when these founders were unable to wrestle to the ground the issues of slavery and exclusion. In the words of then candidate Obama, the Constitution was "ultimately unfinished." These issues were left to American generations to come. Each succeeding generation has been expected to contribute to making the union more perfect. This beginning structural flaw has been partially remedied, but the consequences of what former Secretary of State Condoleezza Rice called the American "birth defect" remain to this day and take new forms fueled by complexity, expanding diversity, and globalization.[1] These factors generate vertical differentiation and heterogeneity in an underlying cycle that constantly distributes and redistributes opportunities, resources, and outcomes to our citizens and the other residents who continue to enter American society. We have long been committed to preserving liberty and securing justice for all, but we have fallen short of achieving these ends, and achieving equality has been a continuing challenge. This book seeks to develop the shared understanding and commitment among those who work for the people as public servants on how to add to perfection of our union and encompass more in the circle of justice.

This book will attempt to capture what has been learned, to provide a foundation for public officials to use in building an expanded commitment to equity and an action plan for promoting it. Beyond public officials, this volume seeks to inform observers of public affairs, citizen activists, and the general public about social equity's place in American society in the past, present, and future. Engaging the public is intended to spark an enlarged conversation on what it will take to achieve our highest ideals as a society grounded in justice for all. The essays examine the current state of equality in the key sectors of the United States and identify crucial issues—some longstanding and others expressed in today's headlines—that must be confronted if social equity is to be promoted. Hopefully it will serve as a primer to advance social equity while acknowledging the complexity of the concept and the many obstacles that stand in the way of achieving an equitable society that assures justice for all.

Social Equity Panel of the National Academy of Public Administration

Early in the new millennium, in February 2000, the Board of Trustees of the National Academy of Public Administration approved the creation of the Standing Panel on Social Equity and appointed Philip Rutledge as its chair. Phil had been the primary advocate for the creation of the panel and the increased attention to social equity that it was intended to foster. He coalesced a group of leaders in practice and research who "have invested much of our careers in trying to bring a better sense of fairness, justice, and equity to the field of public administration" (Rutledge 2002, 391). He worked with the energy and creativity he brought to all the tasks that were important to him until his sudden death in January 2007. The panel was expected to:

A. review and evaluate developments in public administration that have to do with critical matters in social equity and governance and provide guidance to the Academy on those issues,
B. initiate or sponsor educational meetings to communicate with the public administration community and the fellows of the Academy on social equity issues in public administration,
C. prepare papers for public release on social equity and governance,
D. serve as a forum where fellows interact on issues of social equity and governance,
E. serve as a means of identifying ideas, issues, and projects in social equity and governance, and
F. provide or recommend witnesses and/or draft or review testimony for congressional hearings related to social equity and governance.

With the exception of point F, the panel has engaged in all of these activities. The initial meeting of the Standing Panel on Social Equity was held at the spring 2000 meeting of the fellows of the Academy. A first draft of an Issue Paper and Work Plan for the Standing Panel on Social Equity was prepared in October 2000, with George Frederickson as the principal author.[2] The initial coordinating committee members in addition to Rutledge, chair, and Frederickson, were Bill Hansell, vice chair; Gail Christopher, Valerie Lemmie, Sy Murray, and Costis Toregas.

The first chapter of this book owes a debt to the Issue Paper, but it reflects as well the work of the panel in the ensuing eight years and what we have learned in the process. A lively discussion among practitioners and scholars about a topic of mutual interest has been a regular but somewhat diffuse exchange of ideas organized around monthly meetings of the panel and one or more sessions each year at meetings of professional associations in public administration along with a meeting once a year where an intense examination of the topic occurs. These Leadership Conferences have been held in Indianapolis, Dallas, Cincinnati, Cleveland, Omaha, Richmond, Phoenix, and Newark. At each, members of the panel, other scholars, and leaders from the community hosting the meeting have made presentations and engaged in discussions about the state of social equity and how to advance it. In addition to face-to-face meetings and conference calls, the panel has helped to foster writings that have appeared in the *Journal of Public Administration Education*. The panel also produced in 2005 a Call to Action intended to draw forth commitment from individual administrators and scholars and to serve as the basis for shared activities among major associations of public professions, although there has been little formal response to this point. The National Academy of Public Administration (NAPA) itself has recognized the importance of social equity as the third pillar of public administration—along with effectiveness and efficiency/economy. NAPA is committed to advancing social equity in all its activities as it does with effectiveness and efficiency/economy.

Based on a careful review of the tradition of public administration and drawing on extensive deliberations among its members, the Standing Panel on Social Equity of the National Academy of Public Administration defines social equity in public administration as follows:

> The fair, just, and equitable management of all institutions serving the public directly or by contract, and the fair, just, and equitable distribution of public services, and implementation of public policy, and the commitment to promote fairness, justice, and equity in the formation of public policy (Standing Panel on Social Equity, 2000).

This definition and the concepts of fairness, justice, and equity will be analyzed in depth throughout chapter one.

Insights of Phil Rutledge: Founder of the Standing Panel on Social Equity

Although Phil Rutledge is not here, his words from the Donald Stone Lecture at the 2002 conference of the American Society for Public Administration set the tone for the Social Equity Panel and created a framework we will attempt to fill.

Some Unfinished Business in Public Administration

Issues of social equity have not always been at the forefront of the attention of the founders of either our profession or its organizational instruments like ASPA, NAPA, and NASPAA[3]—but social equity has always been implicit in both the language and the philosophy of their founding fathers. Just as equality for minorities and women was not foremost in the minds of the white male slaveholders who wrote our Declaration of Independence and the U.S. Constitution, the philosophy and values they promulgated in those documents made possible the tremendous gains we have made in social equity over the past 200 years. . . .

It is now time to adapt the social equity concepts, so well defined for us by our public administration scholars, into modules that the practitioners among us can use on the streets and in the neighborhoods, as well as in the bureaucracies. . . .

Although the issue was joined some 35 years ago, the profession still does not have good answers or acceptable strategies for policy implementation. A major weakness has been our failure as a profession to develop the quantitative tools, indicators, and benchmarks to define objectives and measure progress in the pursuit of social equity. This deficiency may be second only to our failure to marshal the will and commitment within our professional ranks to move social equity front and center among our national concerns.

Phil Rutledge (2002)

Introduction to the Book

The book is divided into three sections: context and background of social equity, measuring social equity, leadership, outreach, and organizational development to advance social equity.

Context and Background

The first chapter, written by the editors, examines the concept of social equity, how it has developed, and how it can be measured in terms of access, procedural fairness, quality, and outcomes. It is followed by chapters that stretch back in time and survey the global scene at the present time.

In Chapter 2, Sallyanne Payton offers a penetrating analysis of the differential treatment of whites and blacks (and in time other groups that do not trace their roots to Northern Europe) in American society. She was originally asked to write a chapter on the Constitution and social equity and then when other responsibilities dominated her schedule, we asked her to write a short commentary on this topic. What she has provided instead is a provocative reexamination of the narrative of the slow movement of African Americans from slavery to freedom and the continuing struggle to expand equality. She recounts instead a fundamental disjuncture between the constitutional and public policy principles that have advanced the "ideal of the self-governing, enterprising, educated white man" and the counter principles and policies that have restricted the prospects for "free persons of color" not just in the Jim Crow era but in post–World War II urban development and up to the present time.

In Chapter 3, Bárbara Robles examines the historical roots of inequity in income and wealth in the United States drawing from *The Color of Wealth* published in 2006. She broadens the themes developed by Payton to consider a wider range of minority groups and a broader array of governmental activities. Public policies that affect income and the accumulation of resources have not been equally applied nor had the same impact on all ethnic and racial groups. Some groups have been advantaged—until recently whites—while others have suffered from laws that put them at an economic disadvantage or limited their capacity to accumulate wealth. In addition, private actions condoned or not by governmental officials subjected racial and ethnic minorities to personal attacks and destruction of property.

Chapter 4 by Terry F. Buss and Usama Ahmed may strike the reader as odd in its content and placement. Its importance is the description of social equity issues at the present time in various places in the world. The authors' vignettes of inequity now resurrect aspects of the American history of inequity rooted in its "original sin." The raw urgency of these current stories reminds us of the difficulties American society has faced and the detours and regressions it has experienced in the long effort to create a more perfect union. What happens in many countries today is often foreshadowed by occurrences in the United States over its history extending almost to—and many would contend up to—today. Gaps in social equity are an important part of the world described by Thomas Friedman (2008) as hot, flat, and crowded.

Edward L. Glaeser, Matthew Resseger, and Kristina Tobio analyze the sources of inequality across urban regions and the policy options for addressing it in Chapter 5. Inequality—the disparity between income groups—has harmful effects but is often associated with growth. Indeed, an increase in inequality may accompany growth if it produces an influx of people with high skill and income and also attracts low-skill workers seeking employment. The authors assess both national and local policy options to reduce inequality. An aggressive policy of tax-based redistribution that takes from the rich and gives to the poor may be an option at the national level (although American values and governmental arrangements make the adoption of European social welfare policies unlikely). At the local level, such policies would likely lead to emigration of the prosperous and an influx of the poor. Improving the education of the least fortunate seems to be the most promising policy for reducing inequality and supporting development.

The examination of the meaning and context of social equity is completed in Chapter 6 by Samuel L. Myers Jr. He traces the development of affirmative action programs in the 1970s and 1980s, and their replacement with a "diversity" strategy in the last decade of the twentieth century. Although advocates of diversity have commonly linked diversity with social and economic benefits—the efficiency case—Myers identifies a number of weaknesses or unknowns in this argument. The case for expanding racial, ethnic, and gender representativeness in public organizations should rest on social equity grounds rather than relying on benefits that may not be realized or may accrue to nonminority staff members.

Measuring Social Equity

Four chapters measure social equity in divergent areas of public policy and service delivery. Richard W. Hug has tackled the complex and changing issue of social equity in health care in Chapter 7. There is a fundamental shortcoming in access to care in the system that has evolved through 2008. The over 46 million people uninsured is a well-known figure, but nearly two-thirds of American adults, or 116 million people, are underinsured, have difficulty paying medical bills, or have problems getting care because of costs. There continue to be many indicators of lower quality health care received by blacks and Hispanics, although some improvements have also been documented. Minorities have experienced less fairness in being referred to specialists or receiving patient-centered care. From an outcomes perspective, the United States continues to demonstrate dramatic differences in morbidity and mortality among different racial, ethic, and income groups.

The record of criminal justice agencies in providing equitable service and incorporating equity in their data reporting is the focus of Chapter 8 by James R. Brunet. These agencies are actively involved in performance measurement and routinely present reports on crime levels, response and case processing times, and recidivism rates. Their performance measure systems tend to focus on measures of workload, efficiency, and effectiveness. The performance measures largely exclude, however, an agency's progress in promoting social equity. Little is known from the agencies themselves about disparities in the distribution and quality of criminal justice services delivered to different citizen groups. Outside organizations measure the performance of criminal justice agencies and sometimes present evidence of disparities. Despite perceptions, studies do not document consistent evidence of racial profiling in traffic enforcement. Racial differences are more evident, however, in the interactions of police and citizens after a traffic stop is made, in incarceration rates, in the quality of representation, and other aspects of the criminal justice system.

Chapter 9 by Leanna Stiefel, Amy Ellen Schwartz, and Ingrid Gould Ellen addresses a topic that seldom appears in the public administration literature. The essay received the Douglas Wilder Award in 2008 for the Best Paper on Social Equity presented by Virginia Commonwealth University. This is an effort to build a crosswalk from the silo of research on educational performance to the field of public administration. This chapter points out that there are huge gaps in educational performance that undo the efforts at access and process equity described in this volume. Although these test score gaps are explained in part by racial and ethnic differences in poverty rates and differences in English proficiency, an even more important determinant of the race gap in any year is the performance of students in prior years, which is lower for black and Hispanic students. Put simply, much of the race gap "this year" is explained by the race gap "last year," a factor beyond the influence of this year's schools and teachers. These students start off behind, and the gap becomes larger over time. The adverse impact of this failure to close the gap is huge for the individual and his family, the city, the region, the state, and the nation's economy.

Finally, in Chapter 10, Sylvester Murray and Mark D. Hertko assess issues of environmental justice in land use planning. Past approaches by local officials have left some communities, often people of color or low-income communities, without adequate protection for health and welfare, and in some cases have deprived citizens of opportunities for effective civic engagement. A legacy of actions that left citizens without meaningful involvement in decisions affecting their health, environment, and neighborhoods requires current public officials and administrators to conduct the business of land use planning and zoning with the goal of environmental justice in the forefront of their minds.

Leadership, Outreach, and Organizational Development

The final section presents four perspectives on how social equity can be promoted at a time when there are breakthroughs in advancing equality along with new kinds of obstacles and resistance. How does social equity survive as the "new kid" in the public policy square? What behavioral science theory and practice informs the development of leadership strategies? These are the ideas that underpin Chapter 11 by Kristen Norman-Major and Blue Wooldridge. Here the reader meets framing theory as a central idea that shapes how various audiences respond to appeals for social equity and to policy entrepreneurs as key actors driving the likely success of social equity in practice. In some policy disputes, there is a clear battle over how the issue is framed with a number of competing approaches, as has been evident in the debate over health, but often the response to a proposal is shaped by its initial framing, for example, economic arguments versus addressing the problems of discrimination. Although social equity advocates may not want to abandon a social justice rationale or risk having to make compromises by engaging policy entrepreneurs from business, dooming important policy actions through a lack of awareness is not acceptable in the twenty-first century. Building a more perfect union requires flexible strategies and broader coalitions in the nuanced, complex society that America has become.

Susan T. Gooden reports on an agency that refuses to act like the "cowards" who avoid talking about race identified by U.S. Attorney General Eric Holder (2009). Overcoming that reluctance potentially opens up a great deal of emotional baggage, but it is necessary if racial issues are going to be confronted and resolved. The welfare department of Wisconsin is the unit of analysis in Chapter 12. Its leaders wanted to know if the interactions between street-level bureaucrats and clients contributed to the disparate imposition of sanctions. To get a handle on the subject, an internal review and monitoring committee was established to guide this fact-finding effort and obviously to insulate it from the sabotage activities of the "cowards" who do not want to confront sensitive racial issues. This work provides a solid roadmap in terms of methodology and process to launch the recommended study journey.

Chapter 13 by Susan T. Gooden and Blue Wooldridge, which received the National Association of Schools of Public Affairs and Administration award in 2008 for the best article of the year in the *Journal of Public Affairs Education*, explores how to strengthen understanding of the formal and informal personnel policies and practices that can promote or impede social equity. The authors make the case that social equity should guide all components of human resource management, and they give special emphasis to the handling of job analysis, recruitment, and selection. Both formal and informal personnel policies and practices affect how each component is handled. Decisions are shaped by both formal policies and informal practices, especially the "HR dialogues" that express how officials work their way to conclusions about what to do. Gooden and Wooldridge advise readers concerning how to recognize when these behind-closed-doors conversations undercut the intent of law and policy and how to use these informal exchanges to promote social equity.

The final chapter, by the editors, summarizes the book and issues a "call to action" on social equity for administrators in public and nonprofit organizations, elected officials, and the public at large. Our country is making progress in creating a more perfect union, but each significant step forward creates new sources of resistance and encourages some to argue that we have gone far enough (or too far). Public servants have a special responsibility to argue that more must be done and to find ways to use their position and discretionary authority to be agents of social equity. Building a more perfect union demands nothing less.

Notes

1. Secretary Rice used this term in a speech in 2005 in Birmingham commemorating the 1963 church bombing there and commented that "when the Founding Fathers said, 'We the people,' they didn't mean many of us," www.usembassy.org.uk/gb030.html (accessed June 2009). She repeated the phrase in March 2008 after candidate Barack Obama's speech on race in America: " . . . Black Americans were a founding population. Europeans and Africans came here and founded this country together. Europeans by choice and Africans in chains and that's . . . not a very pretty reality of our founding. I think that particular birth defect makes it hard for us to confront it, hard for us to talk about it and hard for us to realize that it has continuing relevance for who we are today," www.diversityinc.com/public/3347.cfm (accessed June 2009).

2. Standing Panel on Social Equity, Issue Paper and Work Plan, National Academy of Public Administration, October 2000.

3. American Society for Public Administration, National Academy of Public Administration, and National Association of Schools of Public Affairs and Administration.

References

Friedman, Thomas L. 2008. *Hot, Flat, and Crowded is Classic. New York*: Farrar, Straus & Giroux.

Holder, Eric. 2009. Remarks as prepared for delivery at the Department of Justice African American History Month Program, February 18, xx.

Rutledge, Philip. 2002. "Some Unfinished Business in Public Administration. *Public Administration Review* 62, no. 4 (July/August): 390–94.

Standing Panel on Social Equity. 2000. Issue Paper and Work Plan. National Academy of Public Administration (October).

Justice
for All

Part I
Context and Background

1

Social Equity in American Society and Public Administration

Norman J. Johnson and James H. Svara

Social equity and the related values of equality and fairness have been central themes in American history. They are powerful ideals but they have been challenged and for a time overshadowed by other values. To explore the boundaries and possibilities of social equity in the present, it is necessary to examine its historical and conceptual foundations. The discussion can then turn to matters of definition and measurement.

The Idea of Social Equity

Social equity refers to the promotion of equality in a society with deep social and economic disparities. It embodies the goal that the members of all social groups will have the same prospects for success and the same opportunity to be protected from the adversities of life. Although the conditions and success of individuals will vary greatly, in a socially equitable society, these differences are not strongly linked to membership in groups defined by characteristics such as ethnicity, race, or gender. Class, or more generally socioeconomic status, is associated with differing levels of resources, but should not be linked to differences in the availability of basic public services nor to the quality of those services. The United States faces critical issues in the fair, just, and equitable formation and implementation of public policy, distribution of public services, and management of the organizations that do the work of the public.

In the initial Issue Paper and Work Plan in 2000, the Academy's Standing Panel on Social Equity in governance issued this statement, which still guides its work.

> As in our past, there are at present serious problems of fairness, justice, and equality in the United States. We are not as fair, as just, or as equal as we should be, and public administration cannot say that these problems belong only to lawmakers. They are our problems too. Over the years public administration has contributed much to a more equitable, a more fair, and a more just America. We have much more to contribute. (Standing Panel 2008, 8)

In addition, the economic underpinnings to encourage widespread political participation are missing, and there are continuing and possibly growing differences in the capacity to influence public officials. The report of the Task Force on Inequality and American Democracy (2004, 1) of the American Political Science Association puts it this way:

> Our country's ideals of equal citizenship and responsive government may be undergoing threat in an era of persistent and rising inequality. Disparities of income, wealth, and access to opportunity are growing more sharply in the United States than in many other nations, and gaps between races and ethnic groups persist. Progress toward realizing American ideals of democracy may have stalled, and in some arenas reversed.

The persistence of shortcomings does not mean that American society has not made progress in overcoming inequality over its history, but there are serious problems that must still be confronted.

People who serve the public in government and nonprofit organizations have a special responsibility to make certain that there is "justice for all." In an era of "new governance" and blurred boundaries between sectors (Kettl 2002), efforts by public agencies to promote equity will increasingly include partnerships between government and citizen groups, nonprofit organizations, and businesses. Individual administrators and the public administration community must recognize that social equity problems persist and that public administrators should take action to alleviate and correct these problems as they develop, analyze, manage, and deliver public programs. Throughout this chapter, the term public administration is used broadly to include not only the policies and management of governmental and jurisdictional agencies, but also the work of nonprofit, voluntary, nongovernmental, and contract organizations with public purposes and engaged in public work.

In countless ways over a myriad of programs, many public administrators are addressing equity needs to a greater or lesser extent, but many do not. Despite a widespread recognition that administrators should be committed to social equity, the concept and the practices that advance social equity are still not well understood or universally embraced. Some administrators define their responsibilities narrowly and do not stress social equity or incorporate its principles into their practice. Some may take actions that inadvertently contradict social equity out of a lack of awareness, a lack of sensitivity, or bias, and some may discriminate based on prejudice. It does not make sense in political or managerial terms to allow this to happen in the face of an ever-wider acceptance of the idea that social equity is essential to our survival as a society on this continent and on this planet.[1]

The Contribution of Public Administrators

Public administrators carry out and help to shape the work of governance in their positions in government, nonprofit organizations, and as private deliverers of public services. They exercise discretion in implementing the law and delivering services, because the law is seldom so clear, so precise, so evident that we know how to apply it in one concrete case and subsequent versions of that case. Justice requires that administrators have the flexibility and judgment to provide individualized attention within the framework of law and policy (Cooper 2002, 303–4). Woodrow Wilson (1887), often mistakenly associated with a strict separation of politics and administration, was broadly concerned with "how the law should be administered" (198) not only with "speed, and without friction" but also with "enlightenment [and] with equity" (213). He also argued that administrators have "large powers and unhampered discretion" in carrying out their responsibilities in the governmental process. Frank Goodnow, (ibid) the architect of American public administration, observed that in the administrative process, "much must be left to official discretion, since what is demanded of the officers is not the doing of a concrete thing, but the exercise of judgment" (1900, 81). As they exercise discretion, make judgments, implement policy, deliver services, and manage public resources, they have the opportunity to take actions that advance or impede social equity.

Furthermore, public administrators are partners with elected leaders in our system of democratic self-government. Based on their commitment to the public interest, their knowledge and experience, and their extensive interaction with citizens, public administrators advise elected officials and make recommendations about policy. Although this policy advisory role has become more obvious in the past fifty years, it has always been a central role filled by administrators.[2] It is critically important that the officials responsible for carrying out the laws and policies provide their perspectives about what is equitable public policy. All public officials are obligated to uphold the Constitution, to respect the constitutional rights of all citizens, and to advance the principles embodied in the Constitution (Rosenbloom and Carroll 1990). Along with citizens, they have their responsibility to make the union more perfect (Wamsley 1990).

As in our past, there are at present serious problems of fairness, justice, and equality in the United States. We are not as fair, as just, or as equal as we should be, and public administration cannot say that these problems belong only to lawmakers. Often problems are identified and policies are recommended by administrators. Furthermore, given the nature of American political values and the incremental expansion of justice and equality, advances often occur through administrative actions within the existing policy framework rather than dramatic policy change. Over the years public administrators have contributed much to the creation of a society that is more equitable, more fair, and more just. And they have much more to contribute to social equity in American life both in the formulation of policy and in its execution.

This chapter sets the stage for the essays that follow. We start by considering two great conceptual and moral challenges in American society. One of these is a widely recognized but a continuing challenge: how do we understand equality and the past and current failures to achieve it? The second has not received as much attention in the public administration literature on social equity. This is the tension between the values of equality and freedom. Although it is a factor that underlies public policy debates, it is often not explicitly recognized. When we confront the question of why we have not done more to promote equality, the answer has often included some effort to preserve freedom or protect competition. It is not enough to contrast the "good" of equality with the "bad" of inequality. In the United States, to a greater extent than in many other societies, it is necessary to come to terms with the competing "goods" of equality and freedom. Administrators must be cognizant of the obligation to protect freedom as they seek to advance equality. The remaining sections of the chapter examine how public administrators balance the responsibility to act with democratic and legal constraints, how equity draws upon fairness and justice, and how social equity can be defined and measured.

History and Significance of Equality

The ideal of equality is one of the central values in American culture, but achieving equality has been a struggle. Rhetorically, equality is the defining feature that justified our formation as a separate, self-governing society. The Declaration of Independence set forth the "self-evident" principle "that all men are created equal, that they are endowed by their creator with certain unalienable rights, that among these are life, liberty and the pursuit of happiness." Time and again over our history, advancing equality would be the rallying cry for efforts to correct abuse and reform the political process. Frederickson (2010, 50) sums up the overarching importance of this value:

> So it is that the ideal of equality touches our emotions. All these aspects of equality—protest, hope, and faith, infused with emotion—came together in an August afternoon over almost a half century ago when Martin Luther King, Jr., spoke to a multitude at the Lincoln Memorial, repeatedly returning to the phrase: "I have a dream."

King's words made it clear that the promise of America was not yet its reality. Fairness and justice have been contested.

In the founding period and early decades of the new republic, there were obvious limitations to fairness and justice and practices that contradicted the commitment to equality. These included the treatment of the indigenous population, the forced introduction of people seized in Africa, the legally enshrined institution of slavery, the disenfranchisement of women, and many others.[3] Despite these contradictions, the manifestations of equality were so widespread in American society that de Tocqueville would offer this observation in 1831:

> Among the novel objects that attracted my attention during my stay in the United States, nothing struck me more forcibly than the general equality of conditions. I readily discovered the prodigious influence which this primary fact exercises on the whole course of society, by giving a certain direction to public opinion, and a certain tenor to the laws; by imparting new maxims to the governing powers, and peculiar habits to the governed.[4] (1956, 3)

Equality of conditions, in contrast to inherited systems of rank and privilege in Europe, were remarkable. A kind of equality of opportunity was available in the relative openness of the society for white men and in the option to move to the frontier and start a new life. Coexisting with these conditions, however, were deep disparities based on wealth, class, gender, and race. These disparities would not be remarkable to Tocqueville; equality to the extent it was found would have been.

At the time of Tocqueville's travels, forced relocation of Indians was taking place under the provisions of the Indian Removal Act of 1830, beginning with the Choctaws in Mississippi. Although the removal of the Cherokee from north Georgia was temporarily delayed by the Supreme Court, President Jackson found a way to appear to treat the Cherokee as a sovereign nation—by securing a treaty with a small minority of the tribe that agreed to move to a new location. In this case, the rule of law was used creatively and cynically to undermine a community and force its relocation to the so-called Indian country of Oklahoma with terrible suffering and loss of life.

The dispute over the extension of slavery led to a civil war less than a century after winning independence. President Lincoln took the controversial action during the war of freeing the slaves in the slaveholding states. In a fundamental sense, the civil war was a second founding, and the constitutional principles were reasserted and expanded (Hargrove 1998). The United States as a society was henceforth to be "dedicated to the proposition that all men are created equal."

The post–Civil War amendments rectified the "birth defects" in the Constitution regarding slavery and race. The Thirteenth Amendment abolished slavery in the United States and its territories. In the Fourteenth Amendment, equality was explicitly enshrined in the Constitution:

> nor shall any state deprive any person of life, liberty, or property without due process of law; nor deny to any person within its jurisdiction the equal protection of the laws.

The Fifteenth Amendment declared that the right to vote "shall not be denied or abridged by the United States or by any State on account of race, color, or previous condition of servitude." In the postwar period, there was an ambitious but flawed commitment to social equity in the Freedmen's Bureau, but it ended in 1872, and the compromise of 1877 resolving the disputed presidential election of 1876 ended reconstruction and protections for African Americans in the South and generally everywhere else in America.

The commitment to participation by African Americans was short-lived and always contested. Equality was redefined and aligned with the separation of races enforced by law in the states of the Confederacy and typically enforced by social practices in the rest of the country. In the South, disenfranchisement, economic exploitation, and social repression were fully established in the Jim Crow laws. There was systematic use of the legal system to channel black men into forced labor for industries, mines, plantations, and government (Blackmon 2008). The postwar period also witnessed an expanded assault on Native Americans, the exclusion of Mexicans from full participation in what was once their own country, and severe restrictions on Orientals.

In the late nineteenth century, the story of the Pledge of Allegiance offers a glimpse of prevailing attitudes. It was drafted in 1892 as a project of the state superintendents of education in the National Education Association to celebrate the quadricentennial Columbus Day in 1892 in public schools. The principal author was Francis Bellamy, cousin of the socialist author Edward Bellamy. His pledge included the phrase "liberty and justice for all." According to John Baer (1992), Bellamy considered placing the word "equality" in the pledge, but knew that the state superintendents of education on his committee were against equality for women and African Americans. In light of prevailing conditions, even the affirmation of "justice for all" did not mean the same justice for all groups in American society. In the twentieth century, issues of racial injustice did not recede. The Swedish scholar Gunnar Myrdal (1944) documented the continuing racial injustice and unequal conditions of blacks and whites in *An American Dilemma.*

The Supreme Court decision *Brown v. Board of Education* (1954) finally affirmed the legal principle that the standard of equality must be the same for all groups. In response to Brown, Dwight Eisenhower chose to uphold the rule of law by sending the 101st Airborne to Little Rock to execute the order that put the Little Rock nine into the all-white and segregated Central High School. His actions affirmed the Supreme Court decision in contrast to Jackson's efforts to undermine the intent of the decision asserting the sovereignty of the Cherokee. These two fundamentally different strategies to executing the rule of law represent different responses to the recurring challenge to form a more perfect union—the first found a legal basis to preserve an imperfection, and the second started the process of eliminating the principle and the practice of separate but equal.

At these and other critical turning points in American history, the decision is made by leaders and citizens whether to address the prevailing expressions and underlying causes of inequality or to leave them to future generations to resolve. The contradiction between the founding ideals and the reality of conditions existing at any given time does not mean that the founders were hypocrites and that we as a society are opposed to change. The ideals are aspirational, and each generation must make its own choices about whether and to what extent it will contribute to moving toward these ideals. We are all involved in the continuing process to create a more perfect union. Candidate Barack Obama described it in this way:

> [W]ords on a parchment would not be enough to deliver slaves from bondage, or provide men and women of every color and creed their full rights and obligations as citizens of the United States. What would be needed were Americans in successive generations who were willing to do their part—through protests and struggle, on the streets and in the courts, through a civil war and civil disobedience and always at great risk—to narrow that gap between the promise of our ideals and the reality of their time.[5]

Administrators as well must deal with the continuing discrepancy between the ideal and reality of equality. Despite the long-standing commitment to fairness as an administrative principle, administrators must be humbled by the realization that they contributed to the discrepancy and in many places helped to institute inequality in the past by enforcing discriminatory laws and using their broad discretion to advance exclusionary social mores (Smith 2002). According to Payton (Chapter 2 in this volume), they also developed a system of federal, state, and local laws and regulations that tended to confine blacks to segregated areas and to limit their opportunities outside minority organizations.

Freedom as a Value and Its Relationship to Equality and Justice

The Constitution originally gave more attention to protecting liberty than ensuring equality. Although it embodied the ideal of equal citizenship under the law, the Constitution did not mention equality. The Preamble calls for promoting the general welfare but not explicitly the welfare of all people. In comparison, Article I protects contracts and reflects the "relationship between secure property arrangements and authentic human freedom" recognized by the founders (Rohr 1989, 226–27). Basic freedoms are protected in the first ten amendments to the Constitution, including the Fifth Amendment, which requires due process:

> No person shall . . . be deprived of life, liberty, or property, without due process of law; nor shall private property be taken for public use, without just compensation.

The requirement of due process is essential to protecting fairness, and in time "no person" would be interpreted to apply equally to all. Explicit protection of equality, however, was not added to the Constitution until the Fourteenth Amendment, as noted above.

In his commentary on American society and reflections on developments in Europe, Tocqueville identified the "tension between freedom and equality" (Rohr 1989, 217). He was concerned that enforcing equality would stifle freedom of expression and weaken democracy. In Tocqueville's (1956, 303) words,

> [Equality] every day renders the exercise of the free agency of man less useful and less frequent; it circumscribes the will within a narrower range and gradually robs a man of all the uses of himself. The principle of equality has prepared men for these things; it has predisposed men to endure them and often to look on them as benefits.

He feared that the tyranny of the majority can lead to the imposition of an equality that opposes expression of difference.

Free speech and freedom of choice can be at odds with equality. Rohr (1989, 217–21) notes the contest between freedom of expression and equal treatment of all persons in his examination of the Supreme Court decision *Bob Jones University v. United States*. The free exercise of religion as reflected in the university's prohibition of interracial dating based on biblical sources was pitted against antidiscrimination laws. The court would not accept the discriminatory practice and removed the university's tax exempt status. At the present time, Patrick Buchanan (2007) objects to new efforts to limit discrimination in hiring based on sexual preference in the name of freedom:

> Civil rights laws restrict freedom. Men are told they will face disgrace, fines, ruin if they act on their beliefs in deciding whom they will hire, whom they will serve in a bar or restaurant, or to whom they wish to sell or rent their homes.

Protecting minority groups from discrimination may have implications for the freedom of others.

Others argue that freedom and equality are incompatible because free competition contributes to economic inequality and equality restricts free enterprise. Philosophers Will and Ariel Durant (1968, 20) observe that it is naive to unify freedom and equality in utopian visions, "for freedom and equality are sworn and everlasting enemies, and when one prevails the other dies." Mortimer Adler (1981) contends that the only equality favored by conservatives is equality of opportunity so that all can compete equally. Measures to equalize conditions or outcomes are anathema to conservatives. Historian Erwin Hargrove (1998, ch. 3) stresses the importance of individualism—a value closely related to freedom—in American political culture, and contends that it has always predominated in contests with equality. In his view, the central debate in American political discourse is not between individualism and equality (in Hargrove's terminology, "radical egalitarianism," which has never had mainstream support), but rather between two versions of individualism:

- *Economic* individualism that seeks to protect freedom and competition.
- *Democratic* individualism that seeks to redress social inequalities that result from economic individualism that might undermine democratic processes.

In the political discourse between parties and ideological camps, equality is not promoted as an end in itself in the United States but as a means to sustain democracy and offset the excesses of the market. Equality may also be stressed as an antidote to negative themes in American culture: racism, sexual inequality, ethnic prejudice, nativism, and religious intolerance. Still, efforts to expand equality may be blocked by defense of freedom or individualism. These countering views are expressed in the policy debate in areas such as affirmative action, progressive taxation, and access to medical care.

In the tension between freedom and equality, Adler suggests that a third great idea can serve as a mediator. Everyone should have as much freedom and equality as justice allows and no more than that (Adler 1981, 138). He argues that whereas there can be too much freedom and too much equality, there can never be too much justice in a society.

An important factor that affects how Americans feel about justice is a long-standing acceptance of the idea that groups differ in their worthiness. Some groups or individuals with certain characteristics may not be considered worthy of receiving a full measure of justice. In the view of Abel and Sementelli (2007, 35–36), attitudes have shifted over time and the society has broadened its acceptance of formerly marginalized or excluded groups, but there has been a tendency to exclude certain groups from full protection of the law or full access to rights and benefits. It has been possible to be committed to liberty, equality, and justice for those inside the established circle of acceptance. Some would argue that those outside the circle do not deserve the same treatment, and such attitudes have allowed some groups to be oppressed and excluded up to our time. Abel and Sementelli argue that justice is a complex, contested concept that has many possible meanings and reflects the prevailing community of interest at any given time. An alternate view is that justice is a standard with accepted meaning that can be used to assess the quality and extent of justice available to all persons regardless of and in conflict with the prevailing standard.

Building on these ideas, a set of definitions can be offered to guide our discussion.

Freedom

Freedom means that each individual is able to make any choice, and no individual is limited in what he/she can choose by membership in a group. Our respect for freedom and individualism means that there should be no restrictions on competition so long as actions do not restrict the ability of some one else to compete. John Rawls in his *A Theory of Justice* (1971, 302) derived this first principle of justice: "Each person is to have an equal right to the most extensive total system of equal basic liberty compatible with a similar system of liberty for all." The most serious historical violations of equal treatment in American society have involved denying freedom to significant groups of Americans. In this sense, freedom and equality are intrinsically bound, as Rawls asserts. Freedom must be available equally to all if it is to have any meaning. President Lyndon Johnson asserted this logic in his commencement speech at Howard University setting forth the philosophy of the War on Poverty: "Freedom is the right to share, share fully and equally, in American society—to vote, to hold a job, to enter a public place, to go to school. It is the right to be treated in every part of our national life as a person equal in dignity and promise to all others."

Equality

Equality means that each individual is treated in the same way as others. There is no favoritism or arbitrary denial of rights to life, liberty, or the pursuit of happiness regardless of the group to which one belongs. In the view of some, equality also requires that all groups have at least minimally acceptable resources needed to exercise freedom (Adler 1981), and that the outcomes for all groups are within an acceptable range of variation. Wide disparities in outcomes might be a signal of unequal treatment or evidence for a lack of minimal resources.

Fairness

Fairness means that all should be treated consistently following the same standards and procedures without bias or favoritism.

Justice

Justice means that all are treated fairly and get what they deserve. In Adler's view (1981), justice is the condition when everyone has as much freedom and equality as is fair without undermining the freedom or equality of others. Justice also requires that individuals can obtain a remedy if freedom or equality is denied. This view of justice can be applied to a broad array of situations that administrators encounter, but administrators may also have to confront situations in which the meaning of justice is unclear and contested. In the past, differential treatment of racial minorities was accepted, and at the present time there is debate over the treatment of undocumented immigrants or "enemy combatants." In dealing with these "exceptional" cases, determining the answer to the question "what treatment do these persons deserve?" will include not only fixed standards but also the "realities of power differences, of persuasion, and of symbolism" in a process that should include active contributions from public administrators (Abel and Sementelli 2007, 112).

Understanding the U.S. Record on Equality

To conclude the consideration of the conceptual and historical foundations of social equity, it is useful to assess the performance of the United States compared to that of other countries in sharing resources across the population. Equality may be viewed as the relatively homogeneous distribution of income that is produced in modern societies by policies that redistribute resources from the wealthy to the poor in economies that provide compensation in a relatively uniform way. Inequality refers to the disparity between rich and poor, and it can be measured by the Gini coefficient. In cross-national comparisons of equality, the United States ranks 94 out of 138 countries included in analysis conducted by the Central Intelligence Agency (2009). It is less equal than all the countries of Western and Eastern Europe as well as Canada, Australia, and New Zealand. There is a widespread perception that inequality has become worse in the United States and even that the rich are getting richer and the poor are getting poorer. This pattern was found comparing the incomes of high- and low-income groups between 1979 and 1993. The gap narrowed a bit during the 1990s, and both groups moved up. From 2000 to 2006, the gap increased again, although not as much as in the 1990s (Haskins 2009). Over the entire period from 1979 to 2006, however, the income of the wealthiest 5 percent of the population increased by almost 50 percent whereas the income of the lowest 20 percent of the population increased by only 10 percent. Compared to other countries of the Organization for Economic Cooperation and Development (OECD), the United States is third from the worst level of income disparity with average incomes of the richest 10 percent more than fifteen times greater than the poorest 10 percent. In addition, it has the third highest proportion of persons who are poor (OECD 2008).

There are social, political, and historical factors that shape the degree of inequality in a country. The United States is less equal in part because of a relatively greater emphasis on freedom than equality in its political values, as noted previously, whereas the emphasis tends to be reversed in European countries. Edward Glaeser (2005) attributes America's low level of redistribution and greater degree of inequality to two factors: ethnic heterogeneity and political institutions. Cross-national comparisons show that inequality increases with greater racial and ethnic diversity in the population. In addition, the governmental institutions used in the United States—federalism, separation of powers, and majoritarian election rules—all serve to constrain the adoption of redistributional policies in comparison with unitary states, unified authority as in parliamentary systems, and proportional representation. In Europe, the adoption of these institutions together with the ascendancy of leftist parties, and the approval of government-supported social welfare policies can all be traced to the political and social upheaval produced by World War I. In Glaeser's view (2005, 17), "the European welfare state is, in many cases, built on political institutions which are the legacy of the chaos and defeats of 1918."

The difference in political orientation, in turn, supports different opinions about the poor and social mobility. A three in five majority of Americans believe that the poor are lazy and have plenty of opportunities, whereas a similar majority of Europeans believe that the poor are trapped by an unfair economic system. The differences in attitudes cannot be explained by differences in mobility rates or hours worked among the poor themselves. Instead, Glaeser (2005, 18) argues "beliefs about income mobility and inequality reflect indoctrination and the political success of the right in the U.S. and the left in Europe, more than they do anything about reality." Even the left in America justifies their policies in terms that stress individualism rather than an explicit commitment to equality.

There is substantial economic mobility in the United States, although our record does not match our self-image. In a major study comparing the income distribution of parents and adult children (reported in Haskins 2009; see Table 1.1), some of the next generation move up, especially if they have a college education.

For example, among children from the lowest income quintile, 14 percent move into the top two quintiles if they lack a higher degree compared to 41 percent who do have a degree but grew up in the poorest families. Still, with higher family income, the prospects that children will be in the top income group increases without or with a college education.

Table 1.1

How Income of Adult Children (without and with college degree) **Compares to Parents' Income**

Adult children's income quintile	Parents' income quintile				
	Bottom	Second	Middle	Fourth	Top
Children without college degree					
Top	5	6	13	16	23
Fourth	9	17	16	31	20
Middle	19	25	23	24	21
Second	23	24	28	19	20
Bottom	45	29	21	10	18
Children with college degree					
Top	19	23	40	42	54
Fourth	22	24	19	33	27
Middle	21	29	23	12	9
Second	22	21	12	10	9
Bottom	16	13	6	4	2

Source: Adapted from Haskins 2009, Figure 3.

Although the American myth is that ours is a land of opportunity where anyone can succeed because of greater freedom and less government redistribution of income, the United States (along with the United Kingdom) actually lags behind France, Germany, and Sweden, Canada, Finland, Norway, and Denmark in the relationship between the income of fathers and sons. Because the incomes of sons are closer to fathers in the United States, there is less economic mobility than in other industrialized countries (Haskins 2009). If you start out poor or rich, there is a greater likelihood than in other industrialized countries that you will wind up poor or rich.

The United States is unlikely ever to develop a comprehensive welfare state as found in many European countries. At our core we are a free market society. The constant influx of foreign immigrants reduces the inclination to share resources and increases the difficulty of sustaining political unity among the relatively disadvantaged. Prevailing political values that stress individualism and competition tend to constrain the scale of measures to address needs and redistribute income. Furthermore, over the course of American history, governmental policies that have tended to build wealth have been primarily available to whites, whereas policies that have had the effect of limiting the accumulation of wealth or even stripping wealth have been targeted at Native Americans and racial/ethnic minorities (Lui et al. 2006). The United States is likely to continue to be a country in which the commitment to equality and justice for all will be an aspirational goal in competition with other values. Large (and probably growing) amounts of income transfer payments will continue, along with opposition to creating a social welfare "system."[6] The aspiration of equality will coexist with the reality of substantial inequality of condition related not only to class but also to ethnic, racial, and gender identity. The gap between aspiration and reality is being narrowed as we continue to build a more perfect union, but the process is likely to be incremental as it has been in the past with occasional breakthroughs that add major new programs to the policy mix.

The American political system rooted in the constitutional order established more than 200 years ago and transformed through amendments, court decisions, and new policies has advanced freedom, justice, and equality. Americans have acted, although belatedly, to support equal protection and to forbid discrimination. It is generally agreed that the exercise of freedom by some cannot extend to the denial of freedom to others.[7] The needs of certain categories of the population have been recognized—the elderly, children in poor families, the extremely poor, and the handicapped. There is not a full-scale acceptance of the principle of providing consistently to all groups those resources necessary to the exercise of freedom. As a consequence, many of the efforts to advance social equity will come from public administrators acting within the current policy framework rather than by large-scale changes in public policy. Health care is the major current debate over whether full access to an essential service will be provided to all Americans.

Equalization (or egalitarianism) involves an expansive definition of equality that seeks to ensure a basic level of resources for all or outcomes within an acceptable range of variation. This form of equality runs up against the commitment to freedom, and sparks fly from the tension between the two. Equalization as opposed to equal protection and equal treatment must meet stringent tests when it is attempted. For example, using race as a classification is subject to "strict judicial scrutiny" (Rohr 1989, 134–35). The government must show that there is a "compelling state interest" to justify the classification, for example, in affirmative action, and that there is "no alternative means" to accomplish the state interest. Stated differently, government policies must incorporate the "least restrictive means" to accomplish the purpose of advancing equality. Rosenbloom (2005, 248) observes that constitutional equal protection "requires race and ethnicity based public policies to be 'narrowly tailored,' which in turn mandates that applicants for public university education (and other public benefits) be given 'individualized consideration'" (*Gratz v. Bollinger*, No. 02–516 [2003]; majority slip opinion, 26–27). The recent *Ricci* decision that upheld the validity of test results for firefighters in New Haven, even though no minority candidates were determined to be in the highest qualified group for promotion, narrowed the grounds for using disparate impact as the basis for disqualifying a selection process. Disparate results alone do not invalidate a selection standard or process. Thus, efforts to promote equality and to eliminate discriminatory practices must be sensitive to both freedom and equal treatment.

Defining Social Equity

The efficient, effective, and impartial delivery of services and management of government agencies characterized much of the early reasoning in American public administration. An ethic of fairness for individuals within the law was combined with an emphasis on effectiveness and management efficiency and economy. Administrators may have assumed that the effects of good management, efficiency, and economy would be evenly and fairly distributed among the population, but they operated under a partial definition of equality that often permitted individuals in a group to be treated in the same way but groups to be treated differently. Gradually, beginning in the 1950s with the recognition in legal philosophy that the provision of separate institutions and programs led to unequal treatment, it came to be understood that there is a social dimension to fairness that had been too long ignored. The civil rights movement challenged laws and administrative practices that discriminated against minorities, and the women's movement challenged gender bias. Policy initiatives based on the recognition of widespread poverty sought to redistribute some resources and expand the political participation of the poor. All contributed to making a more perfect union.

Furthermore, there was the growing awareness that public administration could not logically claim to be without responsibility for some practices that resulted in obvious unfairness or injustice. Armed with this understanding and challenged by a group of young scholars in the New Public Administration movement, there emerged an argument for a social equity ethic in public administration. Social equity took its place with efficiency, economy, and effectiveness as pillars of public administration.[8] A major textbook offers this summary of the emergence of social equity (Shafritz and Russell 2005, 436):

> . . . The ethical and equitable treatment of citizens by administrators is at the forefront of concerns in public agencies. Reinforced by changing public attitudes, the reinventing government movement and civil rights laws, the new public administration has triumphed after a quarter century. Now it is unthinkable (as well as illegal), for example, to deny someone welfare benefits because of their race or a job opportunity because of their sex. Social equity today does not have to be so much fought for by young radicals as administrated by managers of all ages.

Clearly social equity has moved to the center of the field of public administration, but the meaning is often not clear. There is a wide range of negative practices that are inconsistent with a commitment to social equity, but the positive practices that advance social equity are not as obvious. The concept is multifaceted but lacks coherence.

Based on a careful review of the tradition of public administration and drawing on extensive deliberations among its members, the standing panel on social equity of the National Academy of Public Administration (NAPA) defines social equity in public administration as follows:

> The fair, just and equitable management of all institutions serving the public directly or by contract, and the fair, just and equitable distribution of public services, and implementation of public policy, and the commitment to promote fairness, justice, and equity in the formation of public policy.

This definition encompasses the use of human and material resources within public organizations and organizations that do public work under contract, the interaction with citizens in the delivery of services and the implementation of public policy, and the monitoring of social and economic conditions by administrators and advice about policy options for elected officials.

There is a shortcoming in defining social equity in part as equitable. What does "equitable" mean, and what does it add to fairness and justice? Public administrators should be fair and just in their practices. In addition, engaging in "equitable" management, implementation, and service delivery and promoting equity in policy formulation implies commitment to *advance* fairness and justice and to *correct* instances of unfairness, inequality, and injustice.

The "social" aspect of equity means that public administrators are particularly attentive to differences in fairness and justice based on important social characteristics.[9] How far do we extend the commitment to treating all the same despite individual variation? Shafritz and Russell (2002, 395) claim that social equity is " . . . the principle that each citizen, regardless of economic resources or personal traits, deserves and has a right to be given equal treatment by the political system."[10] It is important to be more focused in the identification of characteristics that should not be the basis for different treatment. Rosenbloom (2005, 249) reminds us that strict adherence to equal treatment for all would mean that "public personnel systems and state universities would violate social equity by distinguishing between applicants who are intelligent and unintelligent, achievers and nonachievers, motivated and unmotivated, leaders and followers, honest and dishonest." The salient categories will change over time, but at present they include those characteristics that define personal identity such as race or ethnicity, gender, age, and gender orientation as well as characteristics that shape circumstances such as income, disability, or place of residence.[11]

In order to clarify and strengthen the definition of social equity, we would suggest adding this sentence to the panel's definition.

> Public administrators should seek to promote greater equality and to prevent and reduce inequality, unfairness, and injustice based on important social characteristics.

Public administrators should not only contribute to making the union more perfect moving forward, that effort should start with relentlessly attacking existing imperfections (Denhardt 2004, 105). In some instances, these changes can be made by administrators alone, for example, removing job qualifications that limit the hiring of women. Reducing the imperfections in health care will require contributions from public administration including policy recommendations, design of new delivery systems, and improved provision of existing services as well as contributions from elected officials, the private sector, and individual citizens.

Social equity action takes two approaches: treating people the same to promote fairness and equality and treating them differently to provide justice. It is the potentially contradictory nature of the two approaches that makes social equity complex and dynamic and requires that great care be taken in choosing and explaining social equity actions.

The simplest approach to social equity is the requirement to treat all persons the same and to overcome any differences in treatment based on membership in a group. This requirement is based on the logic of equality and applies to those areas in which all persons are fundamentally equal. This condition may appear to fly in the face of reason because we are all different in size, age, gender, race, talent, and energy. We may expect equality in the sense of being treated equally or having equal chances, but being equal in this way does not mean that we are all the same and should, therefore, be somehow entirely equal in our accomplishments, living conditions, and outcomes. Lincoln recognized this distinction in his consideration of the meaning of equality in the Declaration of Independence:

> the authors . . . did not intend to declare all men equal *in all respects*. They did not mean to say all were equal in color, size, intellect, moral development, or social capacity. They defined tolerable distinctness in what respects they did consider man created equal—equal in "certain inalienable rights, among which are life, liberty, and the pursuit of happiness" (Stern 1940, 422).

Similarly, Adler (1981, 165–69) argues that there are certain equalities to which all are entitled "by virtue of being human." As persons "equal in our humanity," all deserve the "equality of their dignity as persons." Furthermore, as human beings with the power of free choice, we must have an equal right to political liberty and participation. Since all human beings have the natural right to pursue happiness, all must have "that *sufficiency* of economic goods which is *enough* for living well—for making a good life." There will be differences in degree in the possession of economic goods, but there should not be a difference in kind—those who have versus those who do not have resources sufficient for a decent life.

Treating all equally means that we do not discriminate, and it means that a negative condition such as poverty or poor health is an individual characteristic resulting from one's own efforts and circumstances and not the result of membership in a group. If members of a group have low income because they are systematically denied jobs, or residents of a neighborhood are sick because they live downwind from a polluting factory, their problems can be remedied by treating and protecting them equally with other groups and other neighborhoods.

Ending all discrimination is not without opposition or controversy, both because it runs counter to the prejudicial attitudes that support it and also because it can be opposed on value grounds. As noted earlier, prohibiting certain actions limits the choices individuals can make. Proponents of antidiscrimination measures must consider when the group to be protected should have access to essential equality. They must also be prepared to make the case that the choices being restricted have the effect of limiting the exercise of freedom by those who are being discriminated against or diminishing their equality.

When assessing equality, an important question is the basis for comparison: are we comparing individuals, segments, or blocks? In many of our activities and characteristics, we are divided into social segments. A commitment to equality is often based on the logic of equality *within* a segment but not between the segments (Frederickson 1997). We expect to be treated equally *within* the segments that characterize our personal and occupational lives but generally recognize why our segment is not equal or the same as another segment. Virtually all of the institutions in which we work are organized hierarchically, and hierarchy is segmented equality. Five-star generals with comparable seniority are approximately equal to each other but hardly equal to privates first class. Merit systems are very elaborate forms of reconciliation of the principles of competence, qualifications, and experiences that presume to determine which of us has the greatest merit, and principles of equal pay, benefits, and working conditions within each segment. Equal pay for equal work is segmented equality. And there are endless such examples. The point is that one form of social equity is a socially constructed set of agreements as to what things are to be equal within a segment and what things are allowed to be unequal between segments. Less frequently, questions may arise about how much inequality should be accepted between segments, for example, the ratio of compensation of top executives to the average pay of workers. These social agreements change through time as we sort through issues of fairness.

The principles of block equality call for equality between blocks, a block being a broad grouping of people, for example, all women or all African Americans. Under conditions of block equality all women, as a block, would be approximately equal to all men as a block. Many contemporary debates involve the conflict between the logic of individual equality and the logic of block equality and attempts to increase equality between blocks. Affirmative action policies, contract set-aside policies, comparable worth policies, and many other similar policies are designed to make one block—all persons of color, all women—more nearly equal to another block. Methods such as these take us out of the approach of treating all individuals in the same way and have been restricted in their application.

In the second major approach to social equity, people are treated differently in order to promote justice. This is the core traditional meaning of the term. According to Philip Cooper (2000, 62), "equity is, in a sense, the deliberately unequal treatment of some people before the law for some very limited purposes where equal application would be unjust."[12] The Bible tells us "the poor ye shall always have among you," and we know that variations among people will not be eliminated. The way that we treat the poor of our day, however, goes to the heart of the continuing effort to treat the birth defects in our society and meet the founding aspirations. The poor, the disabled, the unemployed may be provided by government with certain benefits to address their basic needs that are not available to persons who do not share their condition. Rawls's second principle is that "social and economic inequalities are to be arranged so that they are to the greatest benefit of the least advantaged." People may also be treated differently in order to equalize resources, such as progressive taxation that is based on the ability to pay. These compensatory benefits or services for a group with special needs as well as redistributive programs that transfer wealth from the rich to the poor increase equality, but they can produce other blemishes and social strains. They may contradict our commitment to individualism, self-reliance, and competition. When people are treated differently, it is necessary to justify the differential treatment and any direct or indirect restrictions on the freedoms of others. How we explain the logic of equity based on differentiation is critical. Some individuals and members of certain groups need special assistance in order to be more likely to have a chance to compete on equal terms.

Following the principle of using differential treatment to reduce inequality, government should not take actions that increase disparities or produce unfair consequences. Introducing service fees should not deprive low-income persons of services. Budget cutbacks should not reduce services for the disadvantaged disproportionate to the cuts for other groups. Outsourcing of government activities or service delivery should not impose more costs on the employees of contractors, for example, by eliminating their benefits. If government is going to advance fairness, justice, and equality in society, it should not take actions that have the opposite effect.

Measuring Social Equity

For a number of reasons, it is important to measure the extent and impact of social equity in the work of public organizations. Measures help to specify more precisely what equity is and how it is possible to systematically examine when and how equity is being achieved. A committee of the Social Equity Panel of the National Academy of Public Administration has created four criteria for measuring equity: procedural fairness, access, quality, and outcomes.

Procedural Fairness

Procedural fairness involves examination of problems or issues in procedural rights (due process), treatment in a procedural sense (equal protection), and the application of eligibility criteria (equal rights) for existing policies and programs. The fairness criterion includes examination of fairness in management practices involving areas such as hiring, promotion, and award of contracts. A commitment to procedural fairness is integral to administrative values: public administrators have an ethical and legal obligation to ensure that constitutional rights are protected. Practices such as failure to provide due process before relocating low-income families as part of an urban renewal project, using racial profiling to identify suspects, or unfairly denying benefits to a person who meets eligibility criteria all raise obvious equity issues.

Access

Access—distributional equity—involves a review of current policies, services, and practices to determine the level of access to services/benefits and analysis of reasons for unequal access. Alternative distributional principles may be used to promote equity: (1) simple equality, (2) differentiated equality, (3) targeted intervention, and (4) redistribution. Access concerns who receives benefits or services. Equity can be examined empirically—do all persons receive the same service and the same quality service (as opposed to the procedural question of whether all are treated the same according to distributional standards in an existing program or policy)—or normatively—should there be a policy commitment to providing the same level of service to all?

If there are gaps in equality of access, what approach should be taken, if any, to address inequality? As discussed earlier, if one does not pursue equal distribution, the other approaches are guided by the principle of using unequal treatment to promote a fairer distribution of resources in society by benefiting those who are disadvantaged. There are a wide variety of programs that offer a form of differentiated equality based on recipients, meeting eligibility criteria that direct benefits to low-income or minority persons. Targeted intervention is similar, with an emphasis on geographical areas in which low-income people reside, for example, inner-city health clinics. Finally, certain programs have an explicit commitment to redistribution of resources as a policy purpose, although it is not necessarily the only purpose. Temporary Assistance to Needy Families is redistributive with the primary objective of moving the recipients of assistance into regular jobs. Medicaid offsets the disadvantage in access to health care for low-income persons.

Quality

Quality—process equity—involves a review of the level of consistency in the quality of existing services delivered to groups and individuals. Process equity requires consistency in the nature of services delivered to groups and individuals regardless of the distributional criterion that is used. For example, is garbage pickup the same in quality, extent of spillage or missed cans, in all neighborhoods? Do children in inner-city schools have teachers with the same qualifications as those in suburban schools? Does health care under Medicaid match prevailing standards of quality? Presumably, a commitment to equity entails a commitment to equal quality.

Outcomes

Outcomes involve an examination of whether policies and programs have the same impact for all groups and individuals served. Regardless of the approach to distribution and the consistency of quality, there is not necessarily a commitment to an equal level of accomplishment or outcomes. This approach represents a shift in focus from procedures and inputs to outputs and results. The results approach examines social and economic conditions and then asks why different outcomes occur, for example, achievement gaps in schools or differences in life expectancy based on income or race. Equal results equity might conceivably require that resources be allocated until the *same results* are achieved. This is the most demanding standard of equity and could involve an essentially open-ended commitment of resources. Part of the difficulty of achieving equal results is that government action is not the sole determinant of social outcomes. Social and economic conditions, for example, poverty, that are broader than the policy problem being examined may explain the differences in outcomes in education or health. Furthermore, individual behavior is often a critical element in explaining social outcomes. Still, a critical issue in consideration of equity at this level is how much inequality is acceptable and to what extent government can and should intervene to reduce the inequality in results. Group differences in outcomes are usually a signal that there are short-comings in access, due process, or quality. Actions may be required to eliminate unequal treatment or interventions may be needed to provide special assistance to those who have fallen behind.

Conclusion

In the past half century, there has been widespread acceptance of the idea that public administrators are obligated to promote greater equality in society and to prevent and reduce inequality, unfairness, and injustice based on the many social groups into which our diverse population is divided. This obligation applies to those who work in public service positions in governmental and nongovernment organizations. This is an essential normative requirement for the broad and multifaceted field of public administration because the field exists to advance the public interest and to support the democratic process. There may be government administrators or party functionaries in authoritarian governments who carry out the dictates of superior officers, but administrators who arise from and serve the people have different values. All persons must be able to participate and have the opportunity to influence the direction and conduct of public-serving organizations. The public cannot be segmented into the favored (as opposed to more successful) and the slighted (or the mistreated or even oppressed) if the public interest is to have any meaning. Looking forward, public administrators should be committed to the fairness, justice, and equality in policy formation, delivery of services, and management of public organizations. This approach will help to prevent a society in which treatment, access, quality, and results are segmented by class, race, ethnicity, gender, or other significant social characteristics. At the same time, it is important to dismantle the accumulated social disparities and the factors that can perpetuate them.

Notes

1. For example, the International City/County Management Association (Willis 2006) includes social equity in its definition of sustainability.

2. For reviews of the development of the field, see Lynn (2001) and Svara (2001).

3. Sallyanne Payton argues in the next chapter that freedom and equality of opportunity were the ideal for white men, many of whom escaped from a condition of indentured servitude. Black people not only were originally enslaved but also have been treated according to a set of principles that restrict freedom and deny equality.

4. Tocqueville did not include slavery in his description of equality. He opposed slavery but largely ignored it in his account. Although slavery was an American institution, he recognized that it was not democratic "and it was the portrait of democracy that I wanted to paint." He offered examples of American society from the North and West because he did not consider the South to be democratic (Gershman 1976, 469).

5. Speech by presidential candidate Barack Obama in Philadelphia, March 18, 2008.

6. Haskins (2009) estimates that the United States expends about $162 billion in grants, loans, and tax breaks as student aid for disadvantaged children, $600 billion in antipoverty programs, and through Medicaid, Medicare, and health assistance for poor children essentially equalizes per person spending on health care across the income spectrum.

7. The same issue arises regarding the emerging value of sustainability that entails a commitment to intergenerational equity as well as recognition of the natural limits of the earth. Presumably, the exercise of freedom should not extend to the destruction of resources needed for future generations to thrive, but achieving the right balance between freedom and sustainability will be contentious.

8. Frederickson (1980) referred to efficiency and economy as pillars and omitted effectiveness and suggested that equity should be added. In making a commitment to advance social equity in 2005, NAPA referred to equity as a pillar along with efficiency, economy, and effectiveness (Svara and Brunet 2004, 2005).

9. Rosenbloom (2005, 248) warns against confounding social equity and equity and argues that many discussions ignore that "constitutional procedural due process is overwhelmingly an *individual* right, not one that protects large groups from unfair deprivation of liberty or property by government."

10. In the next edition of their book, Shafritz and Russell (2005, 465) dropped the phrase "regardless of economic resources or personal traits."

11. For example, equal employment laws do prohibit discrimination or disparate treatment to group characteristics: Title VII of the Civil Rights Act of 1964, as amended, prohibits discrimination on the basis of race, color, religion, sex (including pregnancy and sexual harassment) or national origin. Title I and Title V of the Americans with Disabilities Act of 1990 apply to employees with disabilities. The Age Discrimination in Employment Act of 1967, as amended, protects applicants and employees forty years of age or older from discrimination. The Equal Pay Act of 1963, as amended, prohibits sex discrimination in payment of wages to women and men performing substantially equal work.

12. Cooper (2000, 62) notes that confusion has been created in public administration because the term is used "incorrectly to have the same meaning as equality." Similarly, Denhardt (2004, 105) argues that "in contrast to equal treatment for all, equity proposes that benefits be greater for those most disadvantaged."

References

Abel, Charles F., and Arthur J. Sementelli. 2007. *Justice and Public Administration*. Tuscaloosa: University of Alabama Press.

Adler, Mortimer J. 1981. *Six Great Ideas*. New York: Collier Books.

Baer, John W. 1992. "The Pledge of Allegiance: A Short History." Available at http://history. vineyard.net/pledge.htm (accessed June 14, 2008).

Blackmon, Douglas A. 2008. *Slavery by Another Name: The Re-enslavement of Black Americans from the Civil War to World War II*. New York: Doubleday.

Bob Jones University v. United States. 1983, 461 U.S. 574.

Brown v. Board of Education of Topeka. 1954. 347 U.S. 483.

Buchanan, Patrick J. 2007. "Freedom Versus Equality." November 22. Available at www. townhall.com/columnists/column.aspx?UrlTitle=freedom_vs_equality&Comments=true&ns=PatrickJBuchanan&dt=11/22/2007&page=2 (accessed June 14, 2008).

Central Intelligence Agency. 2009. The World Factbook: Distribution of Family Income—Gini Index. Available at www.cia.gov/library/publications/the-world-factbook/fields/2172. html (accessed November 16, 2009).

Cooper, Philip S. 2000. *Public Law and Public Administration*. 3d ed. Itasca, IL: F.E. Peacock.

Denhardt, Robert B. 2004. *Theories of Public Organizations*. 3d ed. Belmont, CA: Thomson Wadsworth.

Durant, Will, and Ariel Durant. 1968. *The Lessons of History*. New York: Simon and Schuster.

Frederickson, H. George. 1980. *New Public Administration*. University: University of Alabama Press.

———. 1997. *The Spirit of Public Administration*. San Francisco: Jossey-Bass.

———. 2010. *Social Equity and Public Administration*. Armonk, NY: M.E. Sharpe.

Gershman, Sally. 1976. "Alexis de Tocqueville and Slavery." *French Historical Studies* 9: 467–83.

Glaeser, Edward L. 2005. "Inequality." Discussion Paper Number 2078. Cambridge, MA: Harvard University, July. Available at http://post.economics.harvard.edu/hier/2005papers/2005list.html (accessed May 19, 2007).

Goodnow, Frank J. 1900. *Politics and Administration*. New York: Macmillan.

Hargrove, Erwin C. 1998. *The President as Leader*. Lawrence: University Press of Kansas.

Haskins, Ron. 2009. "Getting Ahead in America." *National Affairs*, no. 1 (Fall). Available at http://nationalaffairs.com/publications/detail/getting-ahead-in-america (accessed October 7, 2009).

Kettl, Donald F. 2002. *The Transformation of Governance: Public Administration for Twenty-First Century America*. Baltimore: Johns Hopkins University Press.

Lui, Meizhu, Bárbara Robles, Betsy Leondar-Wright, Rose Brewer, and Rebecca Adamson. 2006. *The Color of Money*. New York: The New Press.

Lynn, Lawrence Jr. 2001. "The Myth of the Bureaucratic Paradigm: What Traditional Public Administration Really Stood For." *Public Administration Review* 61: 144–60.

Myrdal, Gunnar. 1944. *An American Dilemma: The Negro Problem and Modern Democracy*. New York: Harper and Bros.

Organization for Economic Cooperation and Development (OECD). 2008. "Are We Growing Unequal?" Available at www.oecd.org/dataoecd/48/56/41494435.pdf (accessed January 15, 2010).

Rawls, John. 1971. *A Theory of Justice*. Cambridge, MA: Harvard University Press.

Rohr, John A. 1989. *Ethics for Bureaucrats*. 2d ed. New York: Marcel Dekker.

Rosenbloom, David H. 2005. "Taking Social Equity Seriously in MPA Education." *Journal of Public Affairs Education* 11: 247–52.

Rosenbloom, David H., and James D. Carroll. 1990. *Toward Constitutional Competence: A Casebook for Public Administrators*. Englewood Cliffs, NJ: Prentice Hall.

Shafritz, Jay M., and E.W. Russell. 2002. *Introducing Public Administration.* 3d ed. New York: Longman.
———. 2005. *Introducing Public Administration.* 4th ed. New York: Pearson Longman.
Smith, J. Douglas. 2002. *Managing White Supremacy: Race, Politics, and Citizenship in Jim Crow Virginia.* Chapel Hill and London: University of North Carolina Press.
Standing Panel on Social Equity. 2000. Issue Paper and Work Plan. National Academy of Public Administration (October).
Stern, Philip Van Doren, ed. 1940. *The Life and Writings of Abraham Lincoln.* New York: Modern Library.
Svara, James H. 2001. "The Myth of the Dichotomy: Complementarity of Politics and Administration in the Past and Future of Public Administration." *Public Administration Review* 61: 176–83.
Svara, James H., and James R. Brunet. 2004. "Filling in the Skeletal Pillar: Addressing Social Equity in Introductory Courses in Public Administration." *Journal of Public Affairs Education* 10: 99–109.
———. 2005. "Social Equity Is a Pillar of Public Administration." *Journal of Public Affairs Education* 11: 253–58.
Task Force on Inequality and American Democracy. 2004. "American Democracy in an Age of Rising Inequality." Washington, DC: American Political Science Association. Available at www.apsanet.org/imgtest/taskforcereport.pdf (accessed November 15, 2009).
Tocqueville, Alexis de. 1956. *Democracy in America,* ed. Richard D. Heffner. New York: Mentor Books.
Wamsley, Gary L., Robert N. Bacher, Charles T. Goodsell, Philip S. Kronenberg, John A. Rohr, Camilla M. Stivers, Orion F. White, and James F. Wolf. 1990. *Refounding Public Administration.* Newbury Park, CA: Sage Publications.
Willis, Michael. 2006. "Sustainability: The Issue of Our Age, and a Concern for Local Government." *Public Management* 88, no. 7 (August).
Wilson, Woodrow. 1887. "The Study of Administration." *Political Science Quarterly* 2 (June): 197–222.

2

Two Governments: Commentary

Sallyanne Payton

This chapter began as an account of the constitutional underpinnings of the idea of social equity. Superficially, this might seem to be an easy task: a reference to the Declaration of Independence, a short trot through the antislavery movement and the Civil War culminating in the Thirteenth, Fourteenth, and Fifteenth Amendments to the United States Constitution, a lament for the undermining of those amendments after the end of Reconstruction, pained outrage over Jim Crow, an expression of satisfaction that the country began in good faith to rectify its errors as a result of the civil rights movement, and a recapitulation of the past forty years of progress in legislation, constitutional law, and social practice, culminating in the election of President Barack Obama, who is the emblem of America's capacity for change and redemption. That is the story the State Department likes to tell the world, and it moves smoothly into support for the idea that the Constitution of the United States has social equity—that is, a commitment to treating all American citizens as equally worthy regardless, as they say, of "race, color, or creed"—as a bedrock value from which there are now only temporary and unfortunate lapses deplored by all persons of goodwill and rectified promptly by the operation of enlightened public policy and a just and efficient legal system. Right?

Not exactly. Not even close.

Let us start with the Constitution. The U.S. Constitution as originally enacted is silent on matters of social organization or even principles of government administration. It does not create the society; it only creates the federal government, which is only one piece of the governance system. The purpose of the Constitution was to "form a more perfect Union, provide for the general welfare, and secure the blessings of liberty to ourselves and our posterity," by revamping the structure and function of the federal government, which as it existed under the Articles of Confederation was not equal to its tasks. "Liberty" is not defined; it is what flourishes by default where arbitrary power does not reach. This concept accounts for why the Constitution is designed to prevent the concentration of power within a republican form of government that itself is a rejection of hereditary monarchy and aristocracy, the twin sources of arbitrary power. Republican self-governance

26

secured by separated powers is the constitutional invention the efficacy of which America hoped to demonstrate.

The two other pillars of the constitutional order, not mentioned in the document because they are to be achieved by mechanisms other than the federal government itself, were:

(a) the rule of law, or justice, which meant, functionally, that the white inhabitants of the new American republic had the rights of Englishmen amplified by the elimination of various forms of arbitrary privilege, and might look, for protection of these legal rights, to a professionalized, independent judiciary; and

(b) opportunity for individuals, which would result from measures to be taken by state courts and legislatures:

   (i) eliminating the legal privileges that would have accompanied the now-forbidden titled nobility;

   (ii) declining to create new privileges and monopolies that would constrain economic activity (e.g., guilds and monopolies); and

   (iii) adopting positive policies of using the powers of government to favor the development of the people through education, property ownership, infrastructure development, and other measures that would make the American people capable of personal independence and collective self-government.

Finally, because the new nation would be owned and operated by its (untitled, unprivileged) people, the purpose of government would be to serve the people, whose interests constituted the "general welfare," to help them achieve their potential, and through their achievement to grow into a mighty nation that would take its place among the great nations of the world, indeed be a beacon to them and to their people.

Because the framers of the Constitution believed that the rights of individuals under the common law were sufficiently protected by the states and the people, and by the structural provisions of the Constitution that were intended to render the federal government harmless, the constitutional document is spare, containing no substantive protection for particular legal rights of individuals. This lack was the source of opposition to ratification, and stimulated enactment of the first ten amendments (the "Bill of Rights") in the first Congress.

Free White Men

We will leave aside for the moment the anomaly of slavery, which is protected in the Constitution, and the question of Native Americans, who are barely mentioned, and focus instead on the implications of this document for what it meant to be a free white man, that person being the prototypical American. Indeed, it is not inaccurate to say that the purpose of the American project as it came into focus throughout the eighteenth century was to create this free, self-governing, "enterprising," independent man who would, in cooperation with his fellows, create a new civilization. He came in a range of characteristic types who engaged in characteristic exploits demonstrating practical mastery of their environments. He was Benjamin Franklin, arriving penniless in Philadelphia and figuring out how to become wealthy and influential. He was George Washington, symbol of America's victory over the British and of republican virtue manifested in public service and personal rectitude, creating a new idea of political leadership. He was Daniel Boone, explorer, frontiersman, businessman, opening up the frontier to civilized settlement. He was Andrew Jackson, a flinty, folksy commander, impatient with refinement. He was Meriwether Lewis, mapping out the expansion of the nation.

Most important, where the American went, his support system followed. Great effects could be produced from the combination of enterprising ingenuity, land, and capital. The first explorer might send home news and description; the engine of capital development produced land speculators, settlers, crops, manufacturing. Towns sprang up. Newspapers and books came, delivered by the United States Post Office, whose need to move the mail produced a market for transportation, and created a communications infrastructure that made it possible for states as far removed as Kentucky, Missouri, and Kansas to develop educated leadership. The countryside became a market for manufactured goods that were produced in new cities. This made it possible for the free white man to get some land, and enough capital to finance his farm or his business, and things would sprout.

Achieving this national vitality required a commitment to equality among white men, since it was not likely that the best-bred sons of Yale- or Harvard-educated clergymen and merchants—who could claim to be the "meritocracy" promoted by the Federalists—would be the ones to open up the frontier or found new enterprises in the new lands in the Old Northwest Territory or the Louisiana Purchase. The enterprising man was just as likely to be an illiterate Scots-Irish Revolutionary War veteran coming out of an Appalachian log cabin built on land on which his family had been squatting for three generations (see Morgan 1975). It was impossible to predict who would emerge from the new American mass, so opportunity had to be available to all. A transformation in ideas about property and rights thus occurred that cannot be attributed to clashes of interests as commonly understood. It was conceptually simple: the exalted idea of "the people" as expressed in the Constitution was grafted onto the utilitarian idea of "the public," as it had existed historically in the law of duties of public and private officials. Under English common law, for example, a blacksmith working on the king's highway had to serve equally all customers who presented themselves for service and could pay the price, which itself had to be just and reasonable. A nobleman who owned a ferry franchise had to maintain the ferry in good condition and provide passage for all who needed to use the service. This duty was enforced in the king's court, or, with more draconian potential penalties (e.g., excommunication), in the ecclesiastical courts before the Reformation. It was this body of law that led to Mr. Madison's duty to make sure that Mr. Marbury got his commission, since Mr. Madison had no discretion in the matter, his function of delivering signed commissions being merely "ministerial."

The American innovation in this body of law was to make the idea of "the public" trump property interests of all types, on the premise that no one had a privilege to do harm to the public interest. With the rejection of hereditary monarchy and aristocracy came hostility in general to claims of privilege, and the judicial upholding of various forms of public regulation, mainly at the local level, designed to protect the access of ordinary people to essential resources. This change formed the basis of judicial extensions of the law of nuisance and eminent domain and judicial endorsement of many uses of the police power throughout the nineteenth century (Novak 1996).

What we see in the early American republic, therefore, is a steady equalization of access to resources, both by curtailing privileges and by positive grant (e.g., giving away or selling at very low prices the public domain). We see an effort to make white people independent in order to make them conform to Jefferson's idea of the independent yeoman farmer. In addition, there is a major push for education, coming mainly out of the Protestant church communities, since being able to read the Bible is a religious obligation of Protestants. Small colleges designed to produce Protestant clergy spring up to match the move of the population to the west, as do some major institutions. Oberlin College was founded in 1833, the University of Michigan in 1817. These institutions, outposts of the northeastern culture, were intended to send civilization along with the population as it moved into the wilderness (Wood 1991).

Because the national expansion effort required investment, credit was made available for farmers and businesses through state banks that produced recurring panics and persistent calls for rationalization of the banking industry, and resistance based on objections to centralization of authority. This problem produced Andrew Jackson's crisis of the Second Bank of the United States. The point is that there would not have been such a conflagration over banking had there been no banking. In fact, there was an enormous amount of banking and credit creation. The year 1837 marks a turning point in the American economy because of the Panic of 1837 and the resulting railroad consolidation.

Meanwhile, there was a great deal of work to be done in building America that was not being done by people who were aiming for independence and education. That work was done by slaves and servants, the latter term encompassing not only the "indentured" servants but also the people now euphemistically called "employees," then called "hired help." Although all the whites became "free" as of the time of the founding of the republic, none of these people, being under the control of their masters/employers, was regarded as "independent" within the meaning of the republican ideology. Being an employee, however, was a condition that could be overcome by sustained effort and reflected on a person's origins more than his character. America as a land of opportunity made the most difference precisely for people who had the initiative to work their way up into independence.

Slavery, the most decisive and irreversible form of unfree status, was widespread in the colonial period, including in the North. But the real problem was not the existence of unfree status, because that could be undone and the previously unfree whites would be allowed to join the free white population and take advantage, even without stigma, of their new status as members of the "public" entitled to be treated equally, to have access to land, and education, and so forth. The real problem was the presence of black people, whether enslaved or not. And the conceptual challenge, which has not been resolved down to this very day in the year 2010, is how to think about the black person who is not a slave.

The conventional method of discussing the treatment of the "free people of color" is to rail against the system that did not treat them as white, always comparing their status in some particular respect to that of the free whites, who are (correctly) viewed as the standard for determining the operational meaning of the status of "free." Likewise, complaints against contemporary racial segregation compare the situation of segregated and discriminated-against blacks with the situation of the whites, who are treated in a manner rooted in the ideal of the self-governing, enterprising, educated white man. I take a different approach in this chapter. Having reviewed the entire history of the treatment of the free blacks before the Civil War, then the post-slavery black populations in both the South and the North, and then the segregated black populations down to the present day, I observe that there are more continuities than discontinuities across time, space, and circumstance. This suggests the existence of a group of principles, rather like the principles that determine the treatment of the white population, but in reverse. If there is an ideal white man, is there also an ideal black man who fits into the same system? If so, what would be the characteristics of that ideal? If there is no ideal, then what are the principles that animate the treatment of the African Americans who are the successors to the category of "free persons of color"? I do not pretend to have answers to these questions, partly because the situation since World War II has been in flux in many ways. But I do suggest that looking at racial segregation as an organized social practice with an institutional structure and principles makes it easier to see what is happening and why.

Not a Member of the Public

When white men with disabilities denoting unfree status had those disabilities removed, the white men became free in all senses of the term. A man might subsequently become unfree again, but that would be as the result of a separate transaction. So if one gained release from indenture but subsequently was imprisoned for debt and compelled to work off the debt, that was a separate piece of business, and one was subject to the debt slavery as a result of one's own action, not as the result of some residual assumption of unfreedom that followed one throughout life. There were no colonial or early American statutes that imposed restrictions on persons who had formerly been indentured servants. Indeed, a substantial fraction of all white Americans came as indentured servants, which is part of the reason why the idea of a "free people" in a "free" nation was embraced so fervently. Former indentured servants who were white blended into "the public" without difficulty.

Not so with a formerly enslaved black person who became free. Such a person would find that "freedom" for "free blacks" was a highly regulated state, loaded with legislated disabilities. These disabilities changed over time, but mainly in the direction of becoming more harsh and restrictive, suggesting the intensification of a systemic logic. The most important point of this analysis, however, is to note that these restrictions were not random but were designed specifically to prevent black men from attaining the independence, property ownership, and education that the system was attempting to provide to white men who would take the opportunity to acquire them. A number of states prohibited black people from owning property. Attempts to educate free blacks were met with resistance and violence: white mobs burned down black (private, non-tax-supported) schools in several places. Over time, all the states prohibited black men from voting even where they met the property and education qualifications. And the blacks were progressively barred from skilled occupations, being over time relegated to unskilled labor at the insistence of the growing white working class that qualified to assimilate to the ideal of the true American and that, most immediately, qualified for the vote. These developments were discouraging and demoralizing to the free blacks, who were in effect being told that they were not to be allowed on the path to becoming Americans.

A deliberate strategy of creating a class of adult men as unlike as possible as the ideal men of the society will necessarily entail a need for constant vigilance and effort, because the innate tendencies of the society will be against it. As the Enlightenment philosophers observed in asserting the existence of what they called "the natural sociability of human beings," people will generally attempt to do nice things for people with whom they are in contact. Therefore a system of regulating black people to prevent them from acquiring money, property, education, and a self-confidence consistent with being a free person in a free society required regulation as well of the white people, who might be tempted to stray individually and to convey to the blacks within their circles certain assets that had to be reserved for whites. In the antebellum South, it was particularly important to disable black people from inheriting or acquiring property. This had the effect of preventing white property owners from conveying property to their black relatives. The antebellum will contests discussed by Susanna Blumenthal (2006) provide a window onto the world of outraged white relatives trying to prevent the transfer of what they regard as white family assets to their deceased relatives' mulatto mistresses and children. Prohibitions on manumission in place were also designed in part to prevent the emergence of a propertied, well-connected mulatto class that might threaten the slavery-based order of the South. The southern and border states also enacted laws against teaching slaves to read, another transfer of cultural competence and capacity that would be threatening to the order.

There were also prohibitions on interracial marriage, which would tend to produce mulatto children raised by a white parent and therefore familiar with white culture. Such people would be likely to be impatient with the existing order. The attempt to keep all the blacks, enslaved and "free," ignorant and incompetent intensified after the Haitian revolution and the rise of the abolitionist movement, which affirmatively proclaimed its belief in racial equality.

The rest of the history of the Black Codes is well-known and need not be repeated here. After the Haitian revolution, control and surveillance of all black people was imperative, and forestalling revolt by punishing the independent-minded was likewise regarded as urgent.

Fast forward, then, through the antislavery movement, Civil War, and Reconstruction, in which it was discovered that many of the aforementioned measures had not worked as well as might have been expected, and a literate, competent black middle class was found to have been created. The abolitionists had also been at work in the South during Reconstruction, and a number of colleges and universities for black people had been established and were turning out graduates who were becoming teachers, physicians, and other types of professionals in professions from which blacks were not barred.

The game now changed. But it changed for everyone, because in the 1860s and 1870s, Europe and America became obsessed with the theme of the decline of the West and the rise of the colored peoples, a problem with which their racial policies were closely engaged until the end of World War II. Now the northern cities were being flooded with immigrants from southern and eastern Europe who were coming to work in industry. The northern European theorists reinvented themselves as "Nordics" and "Aryans" and relegated the immigrants, all classified as Caucasian or white within the meaning of the Immigration Act of 1790, to the not-quite-white categories of "Mediterranean" and "Alpine." This had the effect of intensifying the panic, because it reduced the number of people in the world who counted as "white." The immigrants were also overwhelmingly Catholic, and for the most part did not conform to the image of the intrepid farmer or enterprising mechanic. The Ideal American model, together with its cultural and financial infrastructure, fell apart and disintegrated into the politics of resentment documented by Richard Hofstadter (1955) in *The Age of Reform*. In any event, the frontier was declared dead in 1890, and the new problem was how to manage the cities. The northern European Protestant group, which was moving into corporate management and the professions, was now living in the cities, which were tumbling into chaos because of overcrowding and poor municipal management. Their Progressive Movement resulted from the pressure to deal with the slums, the immigrants, the urban political machines, the new tasteless and predatory rich, and the growing sense that America was losing its status as a beacon to the world because it could not manage industrialization as well as England or Germany. Socialism beckoned, not least because it envisions an economy run with a management structure and can be used to create a state organized on scientific administrative principles.

At this point, the South triumphantly explained to the world that it had the solution to the problem of managing nonwhites in urban areas, which is strict segregation of residential areas and places of public accommodation, coupled with uncompromising occupational segregation. This idea was not entirely new, but it became relentless. It was Jim Crow, a logic of apartheid that proved appealing not only to the North but to other countries taking up imperialism or finding themselves with shrinking white ruling classes. Jim Crow became part of the mainstream American racial management strategy, somewhat moderated outside of the South, but recognizable wherever it was used. It was during this period that nearly every major American city segregated its public transportation, so that all black people were humiliated on every contact with the transportation system and were reminded that they were not part of "the public" but rather a nuisance from which "the public" was entitled to be protected. This system was resisted by the streetcar and railroad carriers mainly because of the expense of maintaining dual facilities, not on principle. Black professional women were barred from the first-class cars.

In the North, the core of the apartheid strategy was the planning map because it coordinated, silently, the efforts of many institutions. The profession of urban planning grew up around the idea of segregating uses, allowing everything to bloom in its place, but preventing the weeds, so to speak, from overwhelming the beautiful places and spaces, which were to be planned to stir the soul, refresh the senses, provide the relief of contact with nature (e.g., Central Park and other amenities).

So where were black people in this system? Any black occupancy was sufficient to tag a neighborhood as "blighted," which in turn was sufficient to signal that resources were to be withdrawn from that neighborhood. There was close cooperation between the city planners and the real estate industry: black people were to be crammed into a few neighborhoods, effectively cordoned off from the rest of the city. Rents would rise in these areas, which would make them attractive to predatory landlords. These would be the only neighborhoods in which blacks would be allowed to buy houses, and because they were slated for deterioration, the houses of the black homeowners would decline in value rather than rise over time, thereby preventing their use for purposes of capital accumulation. The net result would be the enrichment of slum landlords and the impoverishment of the emerging black middle class. If what a college education bought for a black person was a government job in one of the social service bureaucracies for which black professionals were needed, and a house in one of these neighborhoods, there would be no reason to fear that the black middle class would rise economically beyond what the wage rate would provide for ordinary sustainment. And, of course, the neighborhood schools would be segregated and deprived, thereby making escape difficult. Or escape, if it occurred, would be to one of the black colleges, which would renew the cycle of segregation and progressive falling behind the white middle class. One more thing: designating a neighborhood as "blighted" meant that banks would not lend to make repairs and renovations. So a middle-class, well-employed homeowner who had paid off his house would discover that he could not renovate his kitchen, or fix his roof, except out of current income, because he would not be able to get a loan on his house in order to repair it.

Fast forward, again, to the immediate postwar era and the creation of the federal housing programs that built the suburbs. The Federal Housing Administration (FHA) explicitly refused to guarantee loans on houses in mixed neighborhoods. So a developer who sold a house to a black person would jeopardize his ability to get financing for the entire subdivision. He did not dare offend the FHA, which by this simple policy coordinated the segregation of the suburbs all over the country (FHA 1938). By this time most of the better housing in the country, built after 1920, also had restrictive covenants forbidding ownership or occupancy by non-Caucasians, so the FHA policy had the effect of encouraging developers to include those covenants in the original deeds to the first buyers. The *Shelley v. Kraemer* case (1948), making the restrictive covenants judicially unenforceable, did not eliminate their force in practice, as they had the backing of the Real Estate Boards.

Shelley v. Kraemer did, however, encourage the real estate industry to look at the pent-up demand for good housing among the black middle class, which was allowed to escape to better neighborhoods contiguous to existing areas of black occupancy. This accounts for why the current configuration of black neighborhoods includes both lower-income and quite beautiful neighborhoods, contiguous to each other.

By the 1960s, the results of this kind of disinvestment were being felt in cities all over the country, and there were efforts to change policy. By this time, policy was being created centrally and explicitly, in organizations such as RAND and the Urban Institute (Metzger 2000). The riots had occurred in the areas that had been redlined in accordance with the policies set forth above. Now the question was how to salvage the situation, and one important strategy was to disperse the poor. Unfortunately, the policy entailed further impoverishment of the black middle class, since part of the strategy was to drive down real estate prices in neighborhoods slated for renewal so that property acquisition would be cheaper. The homeowners in those neighborhoods were black working and middle class. They were now to cope with further adverse wealth and neighborhood effects, not to mention further deterioration of the schools and other public facilities. And deindustrialization was in progress, making jobs for black men increasingly scarce. The bright spot was that their children were to be offered affirmative action programs. What about the black upper middle class? It is still hypersegregated, still allowed to live in areas where home values are at best stable. Many cities are more segregated now than they were in the 1930s.

If you look at this story with an eye toward observing continuities and looking for explanations, there is much here that links the current situation to the Black Codes. Perhaps we should look at how to modify regulatory policy, which is articulate, published policy and not a myth or a random speculation, rather than treat every disadvantage as though it were disconnected from all the rest and is something that just happened to happen.

References

Blumenthal, Susanna L. 2006. "The Deviance of the Will: Policing the Bounds of Testamentary Freedom in Nineteenth-Century America." *Harvard Law Review* 119, no. 4 (February): 959–1034.

Federal Housing Administration (FHA). 1938. *Underwriting Manual.* Washington, DC: U.S. Government Printing Office.

Hofstadter, Richard. 1955. *The Age of Reform.* New York: Vintage Books.

Metzger, John T. 2000. "Planned Abandonment: The Neighborhood Life-Cycle Theory and National Urban Policy. *Housing Policy Debate* 11, no. 1: 7–40.

Morgan, Edmund S. 1975. *American Slavery, American Freedom: The Ordeal of Colonial Virginia.* New York: Norton.

Novak, William J. 1996. *The People's Welfare: Law and Regulation in Nineteenth-Century America.* Chapel Hill: University of North Carolina Press.

Shelley v. Kraemer. 1948. 334 U.S. 1.

Wood, Forrest G. 1991. *The Arrogance of Faith: Christianity and Race in America from the Colonial Era to the Twentieth Century.* Boston: Northeastern University Press.

3

Historical and Policy Dimensions of Inequity in Income and Wealth

Bárbara J. Robles

Nation building has moved to the forefront of our current domestic and foreign policy discussions as we continue to move further into the twenty-first century. We are reminded that nations have historical legacies and that nation building is much more than physical structures and participatory voting. Nation building also requires good governance and national values promoting the public good. Trusted government coupled with value-oriented civic participation cultivates political will in neighborhoods, communities, municipalities, and states, and results in a strong national commonwealth.

Historically, nation building in the United States rested on federal and state policies passed legislatively and enacted administratively culminating in economic prosperity for some communities and a chronic state of social inequity for "other" communities. Even as diverse groups and communities participated in the building of the nation, not all were allowed equal participation in economic prosperity, public governance, policy formulation, and legislative input. The historical consequences of communities' being left out of involvement in economic markets and social integration produced strains on public administration at the local, state, and federal levels that are still with us today. We see the tensions between the "haves" and the "have-nots" during episodes of slow economic growth and rapid acceleration in unemployment, which fuel expanding demand for public services. Each episode in our country's history of big and small, long and short economic downturns, also offers an opportunity to review our advances in restructuring and revitalizing "good governance" in the public sector and formulating "policies" that mobilize our diverse assets and reframe our collective well-being. We face such a juncture today.

New policies require new partnerships, collective political will, and coalition building between the public sector, the third (nonprofit/nongovernmental organizations) sector, and the private sector. Knowing what policies we employed in the past and the intentional and unintentional consequences those policies created are crucial lessons that help guide us in the design of more socially inclusive, broad-based policies. This chapter chronicles the legacies of income and wealth inequality stemming from our past nation-building policies and legislation.

Historical Legacies of Income and Wealth Inequities

Understanding why the United States continues to lag behind other industrial countries in income and wealth inequality requires us to examine the political choices and legislated policies that were deliberately meant to reward specific citizens with particular ethnic and racial characteristics as well as those governmental policies that were intended to redress inequities between diverse populations. Two factors remain at the forefront of a deep understanding of why chronic inequalities have lingered and why they continue to elude resolution: (1) historical forces that drove economic arrangements worldwide, and (2) colonial perspectives that morphed over time into institutionalized societal acceptance.

Clearly, these factors have implications for domestic public administration and good governance especially given the historical roots of nation building in the United States, where diverse immigrant populations (freely arriving and those forced as well as the encounters with indigenous populations) have contributed to national economic productivity and prosperity. Our urban and rural communities indicate a continued growing diversity that requires innovative public administration planning and inclusive community initiatives to meet the challenges of current and future domestic economic restructuring and global change. Table 3.1 provides a historical chronology of policies that benefited and hindered our diverse communities in efforts to build individual and collective wealth. A closer look at the impact these policies have had on specific communities of color provides us with a deeper understanding of why growing inequality and an escalating wealth divide remain so intractable and require bold governance and future-oriented policies to reverse (Lui et al. 2006).

Native Americans

Hollywood has provided generations of Americans with a persistent one-dimensional perspective of the role of Native Americans in the founding of the United States. This popular media-driven history has left mainstream America with little reality-based understanding of how history, government policies, and current economic conditions, domestic and global, have impacted reservations and urban Indian populations. Reviewing the historical record of U.S. treaty making with indigenous tribes encountered in the exploration, settlement, and subsequent western expansion of the United States depicts a dismal record of policies enacted and reversed when not overlooked and ignored by branches of the federal government.

The early period between the 1500s and the early 1800s brought both Spanish and English colonizers into contact with indigenous tribes in North America. Because boundaries and borders are socially constructed and subject to political will and military encounters, land was claimed and settled by the newly arrived colonizers that had two lasting and continuing bases for contested ownership:

Table 3.1

Chronology of Government Policies and Communities Impacted

Communities Impacted	Wealth-Building Policies	Communities Impacted	Wealth-Stripping Policies
White/European American	Pre-1776: Land Grants to Colonists	Native American	Colonial Period: Indian Land Wars
White/European American	1790: Naturalization Act	African American	1787: Slavery in Constitution
White/European American	1849: Gold Rush Land Claims	Hispanic American	1824: Monroe Doctrine
White/European American	1853: Preemptive Acts	Native American	1830: Indian Removal Act
White/European American	1862 to early 20th century: Homestead Acts	Hispanic American	1845–1848: Mexican War and 1845–1848 to early 20th century: Mexican Land Loss
African American	1865, 1868: 13th and 14th Amendments to the Constitution	Asian American	1849: Foreign Miners Tax
White/European American	Mid-1870s to early 20th century: Open Door to European Immigrants	African American	1850: Fugitive Slave Law
White/European American	1913: Home Mortgage Interest Deduction	Asian American	1853–1952: Asian Denial of Naturalization
Native American	1934: Indian Reorganization Act	African American	Post–Civil War to 1964: Jim Crow Laws
White/European American	1935 to early 21st century: New Deal Legislation: Federal Housing Loans, Social Security, Labor Rights	Asian American	1882 to late 1930s: Chinese Exclusion Act & Other Asian Exclusion Acts
White/European American	1944: GI Bill	Native American	1887 Allotment Act
Asian American	1952: Asian Naturalization Act	Hawaiian and Pacific Islander	1893: Hawai'i Annexed
Communities of Color	1952: Social Security Coverage for Farm Labor & Domestic Workers	African American	1896: Plessy (Segregation Legal)

Group	Policy	Group	Event
African American	1954: *Brown vs. Topeka Board of Education* (end of segregation)	Hispanic American	1898: Annexation of Puerto Rico
Hispanic American	1962: Cuban Refugee Assistance Act	Filipino and Pacific Islander	1898: Annexation of Philippines
Communities of Color	1964–1980s and early 21st century: War on Poverty Legislation: Civil Rights, Voter Rights, Affirmative Action, OEO Programs	Asian American	1913 to late 20th century: Alien Land Laws
Communities of Color	1977: Community Reinvestment Act	Immigrants & Communities of Color	1919 to early 21st century: English Only Laws
Communities of Color	1986: Amnesty for Immigrants	Hispanic American	1930s (Great Depression) & 1954 (Operation Wetback): Deportation of Mexicans & Mexican Americans (U.S. Citizens)
Asian American	1988: Japanese Reparations	African American/Communities of Color	1935: FHA Redlining
Middle & Upper Class	1997: Tax Cuts for Asset Owners	Asian American	1942–1945: Japanese Internment Camps
Affluent Taxpayers	2001: Economic Security and Worker Assistance Act	Native American	1953: Tribal Termination
		Native American	1968: Tribal Taxation

Source: Based on data in Meizhu Lui et al., *The Color of Wealth: The Story Behind the U.S. Racial Wealth Divide* (New York: New Press, 2006).

(1) land used for settlement and cultivation, and (2) land historically used by indigenous populations for survival purposes.

Access to land led to the period in American history known as the Indian Wars and to the ultimate enactment of several federal and state laws during the 1800s: the creation of the Bureau of Indian Affairs (1824) giving the Department of the Interior the management of tribal lands, the Indian Removal Act of 1830, the California Preemptive Act of 1853, the Homestead Act of 1862, and the Pacific Railway Act of 1862, culminating with "individual property ownership" acts that were meant to transfer a "private or individual" ownership culture to indigenous populations such as the General Allotment Act of 1887 (also known as the Dawes Act), the Curtis Act of 1898 (allotment of Oklahoma lands), and the Burke Act of 1906. What most of these legislative enactments accomplished was an easier "legal" avenue for property transfers from Native Americans to developers and white settlers wanting farming and ranching lands as well as escalating land loss due to property tax nonpayment to states that allowed wholesale foreclosures.

At issue is the collision between two cultural worldviews: (1) a private property paradigm based on the primacy of the individual's right to own private property and prosper, and (2) a communal and natural environment tradition based on tribal cohesion and long-run stewardship of land and natural resources. The loss of land ownership and rights by Native Americans was more consequential than a simple bill-of-sale exchange between two individual property owners with similar Western views of landownership and land use. For the indigenous populations of the United States, the loss of land both as the base of tribal homes and the ranging/hunting lands, was a complete deconstruction of cultural cohesion and tribal survival. During this period of colonization continuing into the early twentieth century with the Indian Reorganization Act of 1934 (IRA), the indigenous population of the Americas declined substantially.

The IRA of 1934 was part of the New Deal congressional legislation that provided for extended land trust periods allowing tribes reacquisition of lands, and, in theory, allowed more autonomous tribal governance. In addition, the act included the ability for tribes to craft corporate business charters thereby promoting economic development on reservations independent of the Bureau of Indian Affairs (BIA). In practice, the BIA retained oversight and veto power over important management and land use issues facing tribal governments (Lui et al. 2006).

In the space of a century, legislated wealth-stripping policies were established that have had grave repercussions for Native Americans on and off reservation lands: the loss of land-based and abundant natural resource economic arrangements and the repression of traditional cultural capital through forced assimilation. Many tribes retained their cultural customs, unique languages, and land-stewardship traditions, which can be viewed in retrospect as asset-enhancing for the United States. One such example of a communal asset-enhancement for the nation was the importance of the Navajo Code Talkers during World War II in the Pacific theater.[1]

After the end of World War II, attempts to end the federal government relationship with tribes including trust management and federal benefits to tribes by inducing complete integration of Native Americans into mainstream society led to the "Termination Period." With the passage of House Concurrent Resolution No. 108 and Public Law 280 (1953), tribal termination began in earnest and in retrospect appears driven more by economic considerations and less by the stated goal of social integration. During this period, 109 bands and tribes were terminated with the surrender of over 20 million acres of tribal trust lands and the loss of federal services such as health, education, and housing.[2]

Since the 1980s, tribes have been balancing two contradictory issues: (1) federal legislation that was enacted to encourage reservation-based economic activities, and (2) state governments seeking to increase their budgetary revenue by taxing income streams generated by tribal gaming revenues. The conflicting issues become even more pronounced during economic downturns. As tribes comply with the existing laws both at the state and federal levels, the asset sharing of tribes with local economies in the form of employment of nontribal members, donations to local charities, and direct funding of local government operations bring full circle the asset-building interrelatedness of tribes as sovereign governments and U.S. local, state, and federal governments.

Adamson (2003) labels the periods of U.S. tribal history in terms of asset and wealth gains and losses:

- Asset stewardship—prior to the arrival of colonists;
- Asset exchange—treaties signed with colonizers where land was exchanged for promised legal rights and sovereignty;
- Asset theft—treaties broken and promises unfulfilled during expansionism;
- Asset extraction—federal management of mineral and natural resource leases on tribal lands; and
- Asset mismanagement—overlaps with asset extraction and culminates in tribal land abuse, sacred site violation, and failure of the Department of Interior to account for tribal trust fund accruals.

A remaining issue regarding tribal capacity to generate and retain assets and wealth continues to elude the mainstream public: not all tribes are casino rich. The unfortunate perpetuation of media images focusing on either gaming wealth of tribes or extreme poverty of particular reservations does not bring us closer to a balanced understanding of policies that have created legacies of wealth inequality among Native Americans. What is still left to address is the asset-based knowledge maintained by tribes concerning the future stewardship of our country's remaining natural resources. We have yet to acknowledge the potential wealth-enhancing cultural traditions that tribes embody in the form of green knowledge, medicinal lore, and natural resource conservation. Tribal cultural capital represents a national treasure and provides us with a blueprint for twenty-first-century sustainable, resource-based wealth-building initiatives. Tracing the history of the various enactments and judicial rulings on tribal ownership of assets leaves no doubt about how political will and social change played a decisive role in past confiscation of Native American assets and is clearly tied to the future wealth-generating capacities of indigenous peoples residing within the United States.

African Americans

The wealth accrual of landed slave owners (the ownership of slaves as assets) in the forging of the United States as a nation is one of the earliest forms of workers' wealth transferred to European settlers/land owners. The codified legal definition of slavery was overturned in the United States only after a civil war and various amendments to the Constitution. However, legislated deconstruction of an egregious government-sanctioned policy does not automatically correct social conventions and established economic arrangements.

The legacy of slavery, the Civil War, and subsequent Jim Crow laws spanning the early colonial period up to the mid-twentieth century created an entrenched social and economic compact leading to passive public policies and a social culture of unexamined exclusion. The emergence of economic and political structures that routinely overlooked the constrained choices pertaining to employment, limited access to markets, and restricted civic participation by African Americans has proved difficult to eradicate. Despite the short-lived enactment of progressive policies during the period of Reconstruction with the creation of the Freedman's Bureau and redistribution of land (forty acres and a mule) to provide economic opportunities for former slaves, the political backlash following Reconstruction that ushered in the establishment of Jim Crow laws initiated a cycle of indebtedness among African Americans (Conley 1999; Oliver and Shapiro 1995). This was especially harmful for African American sharecroppers and subsistence farmers. Farming was the one economic activity that led directly to land ownership and the possibility of intergenerational inheritance for African Americans with knowledge of harvest cycles and crop production.

Even with limited social and economic opportunities and participation available to the African American community, many nurtured businesses and farms and managed to prosper in various areas of the country. Such prosperity brought with it an emerging merchant and business leadership within segregated African American communities. Unfortunately, these corners of African American economic prosperity also induced resentment by surrounding white communities, which heightened racial tensions and produced episodic razing of black businesses and communities. Between 1919 and 1925, African American communities in Detroit, Chicago, Pittsburgh, and St. Louis experienced heightened mob violence and massive property damage. The most virulent of these attacks occurred in Tulsa, Oklahoma (1921), with the destruction of "Black Wall Street" and in Rosewood, Florida (1923), with the burning of an entire black community (Lui et al. 2006). There are countless community oral histories of the wealth and asset destruction in black neighborhoods that are only now being documented and publicly retold.

As land and business ownership were severely restricted, so too was the ability to secure work for many African Americans. Marable (2000, 142–43) indicates that as early as 1865, a "person of color" was required to obtain a $100 one-year license in order to engage in "artisan, mechanic, shopkeeper, or any other trade or business" activity while no such license or time-defined fee was required of whites. Furthermore, avenues to public service employment were also restricted:

> During Reconstruction, blacks had begun to get jobs in local government—the same road to advancement white immigrants would use a few decades later— but the "white reaction" in the 1870s put an end to black public employment.[3] (Lui et al. 2006, 84)

The "great" migration of African Americans from the South to other areas in the nation became increasingly visible during World War I, accelerating during the Great Depression and continuing after World War II. Blackmon (2008) chronicles the persistent "slavery" aspects of life for African Americans in the Deep South between the end of Reconstruction and the end of World War II. The historical record of those days can be recovered; yet, what it illuminates is not a saga of full integration into political and economic participation for the freed men and women, but rather a local governance structure in collusion with local businesses and family plantation owners in need of "serfs and peons" for no-wage labor.

The escalation of the prison system in the South as a holding pen for African American men (and to a lesser degree, women) of working age was supported and stoked by local sheriffs and deputies whose complicity and silence were bought with "finder fees" and "commissions." That local government colluded with local land holders and regional businesses in need of labor speaks to the continuation of embedded Southern sociopolitical beliefs; that no federal retribution or rectification occurred attests to a national failing and mythologizing of the U.S. Constitution as "symbolism" but not as law.

It was not a grassroots movement that ended this "informal slavery" system but rather the advent of World War II and the fear of enemy propaganda stirring up massive disaffection among the "left-behind and unfairly treated" African American citizens in the United States that led the Department of Justice (a federal agency) to apply the seventy-year-old legislatively ratified Thirteenth and Fourteenth Amendments to state and local "debt slavery" and "involuntary peonage" economic systems of the South in court. Ultimately, the entire U.S. federal criminal code was overhauled after World War II, explicitly accounting for involuntary servitude, with Congress finally passing legislation in 1951 directly making any form of slavery a crime (Blackmon 2008, 375–84).

The African American diaspora out of the South was closely aligned with waves of employment opportunities generated by the federal government as well as episodic economic boom cycles. This migration dynamic increased the diversity of

Figure 3.1   **Convict wagons used in the early twentieth century in the South to transport and house African Americans working on roads, lumberyards, chain gangs, and farms** (Blackmon 2008).

Source: www.shorpy.com/node/427?size=_original (accessed November 30, 2009).

the cities and regions of the Northeast and Midwest as well as the West. Due to restrictions on community real estate covenants, urban inner city concentrations of African Americans occurred with a corresponding exodus of whites to the suburbs and adjacent metro areas. The tax base implication of such stark residential housing "choices" created a legacy of constrained funding for educational opportunities for inner-city African American children. With the decline of the manufacturing base in many of the "Rust Belt" cities, the loss in employment opportunities created a "reverse black migration" to the South that accelerated in the last decade of the twentieth century.

Perhaps the most enduring, misguided U.S. policy that prevented families from acquiring wealth-building capacity and hindered intergenerational transfers of wealth was educational segregation. We know that many returning World War II African American veterans were denied their right to participate in the GI Bill. The historical ruling of the Supreme Court in 1954, *Brown v. Board of Education of Topeka*, engendered immediate local and regional resistance and decades of slow implementation nationwide. Ultimately, the expansion of educational opportunities for African Americans continues to be hindered by the local property tax–public education financing arrangement that prevails in most states and municipal governments.

Outlawing the poll tax in 1964 under the Twenty-Fourth Amendment to the Constitution and passing the Voting Rights Act of 1965 increased the political participation of the African American community in various levels of municipal, state, and federal government. However, the slow-to-change nature of the entrenched social legacy of segregation induced an economic apartheid and a racialized view of poverty that, despite legislation to eradicate discriminatory economic practices, continues to engender double-digit unemployment rates for the African American community in the United States. The most powerful tool African Americans have used to promote their civic participation in U.S. society and in economic activities has been the voting booth. African Americans vote at rates that are substantially higher than other ethnic-racial communities: " . . . Blacks are at least as likely, if not more likely, to vote as Whites" (Gaither and Newburger 2000, 4). Exercising the right to vote has provided an important platform for change and for securing a voice in the political debates concerning policies that impact a variety of civil and economic justice issues.

The legacy of the programs enacted during the Great Depression and revisited during the War on Poverty years indicates that federal government leadership at the executive, congressional, and judicial levels has been the "keeper of the flame" for expanding equal opportunities for marginalized minority communities. An additional aspect of the progressive advances in both the exercise of civil rights and the continued economic progress of the African American community has been its own homegrown production of leaders via its triumvirate institutions: (1) historically black colleges, (2) the black church, and (3) mutual aid societies (now known as nonprofit or third sector organizations). Without these important and instrumental African American community institutions advocating for full civic participation and equal economic opportunities, many of the governmental policies that have contributed to wealth erosion would not have been mitigated and reversed.

Latinos/Hispanic Americans

The Latino presence in the United States has a complex historical and immigrant dynamic that continues undiminished in the twenty-first century. Although considered a monolithic group under the umbrella term of "Latino/Hispanic," the Latino community in the United States hails from a variety of countries with unique cultural legacies, and each group arrived in the United States with varying immigrant experiences. Central to the historical relationship between the United States and its southern neighbors is the persistent legacy of Manifest Destiny and the Monroe Doctrine. Both of these political agendas have become part and parcel of institutionalized policy attitudes toward Latinos in the United States irrespective of their being eleventh-generation Americans or recently arrived.

Spanish, French, and British colonizers were among the first explorers to the New World.[4] As Spain claimed the southern Western Hemisphere, having arrived as part of the first wave of explorers in 1492 and quickly establishing colonies and exploration routes, the British colonists arrived at the end of the fifteenth century and the beginning of the sixteenth century to establish permanent colonies on the eastern seaboard of the United States with the founding of Jamestown (1607). During this same period, French colonizers had a smaller but strategic presence on the southeastern seaboard, the Gulf of Mexico, and Canada. Given the competing colonizers' economic interests, the encounters among Old World stakeholders led to various conflicts on the New World shores. In New Spain, which included parts of the southern United States and the western portion of the United States to the tip of South America, the Spanish colonizers mixed with the indigenous populations and quickly awarded land grants to ruling nobles of New Spain in order to establish permanent outposts in present-day New Mexico, Arizona, Texas, and California. Thus, the presence of Spanish-origin peoples (with an ethnic, mixed-race legacy) in the United States has complex colonizing roots with similar economic interests to those of the British and French colonizers as well as claim to lands that were originally Native American.

From these early colonial beginnings and territorial disputes, the United States acquired the Louisiana Territories (which the French had ceded to Spain in 1762 and then reacquired from Spain in 1800).[5] With the advent of the U.S.-Mexican War (1845–48), the remaining portion of Spanish territories in the southwestern United States was acquired along with Mexican citizens who automatically became U.S. citizens through the territory acquisition and ratified peace treaty (the Treaty of Guadalupe Hidalgo).

The Spanish-American War of 1898 was a direct outcome of the Monroe Doctrine applied toward Spain's influence in the Caribbean and cemented Teddy Roosevelt's political career as he led his "Rough Riders" to victory in Cuba. Although Cuba maintained its independence from Spain and the United States, shortly after the Spanish-American War, Puerto Rico, along with Guam, became permanent U.S. commonwealths.[6] The special relationship conferred by commonwealth status extends U.S. citizenship to residents of these U.S. protectorates.[7] From this special relationship, Puerto Ricans have historically practiced transnational family and community activities by moving between the U.S. mainland and the island as economic cycles dictate. Cubans have migrated to the U.S. mainland in varying waves since the Spanish-American War but are singularly remembered for their island exodus during the Castro led revolution of 1953–59. The bulk of Cuban refugees arrived in the United States during the years 1959–62. Our most progressive immigration policies at the federal level were enacted during this period, leading to a rapid economic integration of Cuban refugees.[8]

In 1924, the U.S. Border Patrol was created, although mounted inspectors had been assigned to the southwestern border as early as 1904. Between 1929 and 1935, massive deportations of Mexicans, Mexican Americans (legal U.S. citizens and native-born citizens), and their families occurred as a result of the severity of the Great Depression and subsequent, anti-immigrant sentiment. As the U.S. Congress debated and then passed the Social Security Act of 1933, it disallowed coverage for farm workers, laborers, housemaids, and others in the service sectors. A large majority of Latino and African American workers were in occupations not covered by the Social Security Act. The legacy of this egregious policy that punishes domestic and field workers remains with us today; countless families with live-in maids and nannies do not pay social security taxes for their household "help." The political vetting process that includes financial disclosures such as employers' payment (or lack of payment) of social security taxes for maids, nannies, and groundskeepers has ruined political aspirations. Yet, enforcement of this particular policy is toothless, with the consequence of jeopardizing retirement security via Social Security for Latino and other racial-ethnic domestic and fieldworkers. This lack of enforcement of codified labor laws results in working families' bearing a double burden: economic support of their elders (who formerly toiled in fields and as domestics) while attempting to secure an economic future for their offspring.

During World War II, the strict U.S. immigration policy toward Latin America reversed itself with the passage and implementation of the Bracero Program.[9] Many farm workers were recruited in Mexico and transported to the United States to work in agricultural industries: the fields and cannery processing. The program only recently, through litigation, finally compensated former *Braceros* residing in Mexico and in the United States for their withheld social security taxes in the form of retirement settlements. Many died prior to the resolution of this long-standing dispute and never received old-age compensation for their participation in the Bracero Program.

A second wave of deportations targeted at southwestern Mexican-looking peoples began in 1954 under Operation Wetback during the Eisenhower administration. The term "wetback" arose from the mode of crossing the Rio Grande River, which demarcates a portion of the southern border between Mexico and the United States. Again, Mexican Americans (native born) were caught in the roundups and deported not to the Mexican side of the border but to the interior of Mexico with the expressed U.S. policy of increasing the difficulty of traveling north. Estimates of the deportations of Mexican Americans and Mexican nationals range from 500,000 to 1.8 million people and families (Dillon 2006). Between the Depression deportations and Operation Wetback, no cost estimates of lost land, property, or businesses have been calculated. We do know that targeted "ethnic/racial" profiling ensnares native-born Hispanics along with unauthorized, undocumented Hispanics.

The Civil Rights movement of the mid-1960s and the legislation from President Johnson's Great Society and the War on Poverty spurred a growing political movement for social and economic justice among Latino students and community-based organizations nationwide. During the late 1960s, striking farm workers organized by Cesar Chavez and Dolores Huerta in California and later throughout the Southwest brought national attention to the working conditions of Latino migrant farm workers (U.S. born and foreign born). Working conditions in the produce industry such as the use of DDT and other toxic pesticides, the lack of sanitary portable outhouses, and most important, and perhaps most significantly for economic well-being, the lack of minimum wage coverage and health and retirement benefits for agricultural and migrant farm workers were exposed.

The legacy of racial-ethnic conflicts among the "Anglo and Spanish-origin colonizers" in North America creates a present-day ambivalent narrative for both groups. The Latino community in the United States displays the diversity of racial characteristics of its colonial past and suffers the consequences that the "color line" has on economic mobility (Darity and Myers 1998). Studies indicate that black and indigenous-looking Latinos fare worse in labor market outcomes than do more European-looking Latinos (controlling for English language ability) (Darity et al. 2002; Gomez 2000). Policies that attempt to remedy past discrimination such as Affirmative Action have become controversial, and for many "divisive," amid a growing immigration backlash. Present-day economic stagnation has given rise to a focus on the costs of immigration (Vélez-Ibañez 2004) and not the long-term benefits that accrue to local, state, and federal government sales taxes and revenues through economic activity and market participation.

Asian Americans

Like Latinos, the Asian American diaspora in the United States is driven by histori-cal legacies and new waves of immigrant arrivals and has the equal problematic of being viewed as a monolithic community. Unlike Latinos, the media and govern-ment data-driven image of the Asian American as the "model minority" obscures the disaggregated reality of the Asian American experience in the United States. Asians, as defined by the Census Bureau, are peoples with origins in the Far East, Southeast Asia, or the Indian subcontinent, which includes Cambodia, China, India, Japan, Korea, Pakistan, the Philippine Islands, Malaysia, Thailand, and Viet Nam. Clearly, the umbrella of Asian American accounts for a diverse community rich in language assets and cultural bridge capacity but enumerated and often analyzed as if their immigration experience was a shared reality.

Lui et al. (2006) maps out the three historical waves of immigration of Asian Americans to the United States: early to mid-1800s to mid-1900s, 1941 to 1965, and 1965 to the twenty-first century. Each immigrant wave also chronicles the episodes of American foreign policy and conflicts abroad that created a variety of immigration experiences for the Asian community in the United States. For example, the early Chinese immigrants arrived during the Gold Rush period in California and the need for manual labor in North America that traces out the construction of rail lines. Vietnamese and Cambodian immigrants arrived during and after the Viet Nam War as refugees (this includes the Hmong and Chinese-ethnic Vietnamese) with a variety of urban and rural legacies.

The 1790 Naturalization Law created no pathway for citizenship for nonwhite immigrants (only free white persons qualified), including Asians, although many attempted to gain "white status" through the U.S. court system only to be defined "nonwhite legally" while still being counted as white racially. The Fourteenth Amendment of 1868 grants citizenship to all people born in the United States, and thus, children of immigrant Asians were allowed protection by the rule of law while naturalization laws that would also have granted protection to nonwhite im-migrants were denied. Indeed, naturalization rights for foreign-born Asians were not granted until after World War II.

During the late 1800s, the Chinese were singled out more so than other Asians by excluding the emigration of Chinese women under the Page Law of 1875, effectively denying Chinese male immigrants a family life and the possibility of wealth accumulation through extended family networks. Antimiscegenation laws equally ruled out interethnic/racial marriages on a state-by-state basis. These laws remained in effect until 1967 (Lui et al. 2006).

Because of the West Coast's proximity to the Asian mainland, most Asian Americans arrived in California and settled along the West Coast states. During World War II, the Asian community West Coast density and the Pearl Harbor bombings changed the dynamic of the history of the United States as an "immigrant friendly" country via the judicial and legislative systems with Executive Order 9066. Rounding up approximately 120,000 Japanese families into thirteen "detention" camps throughout the United States (see Figure 3.2) amounted to a community wealth loss estimated at $4–5 billion (in 1999 real dollars) for Japanese Americans. The Civil Liberties Act of 1988 provided "redress" for this wealth loss via reparations to remaining relocation camp inmates of $20,000 per internee at a total cost of $1.6 billion (1992 real dollars). More meaningful was the formal U.S. government apology to the Japanese American community over the government sanctioned loss of their civil rights during World War II.

The Alien Land Laws of 1913 (not repealed until 1948) precluded the nonwhite, foreign-born unable to qualify for naturalization from acquiring and owning land. Thus, asset and wealth building often occurred after the birth of native-born children in whose name land and assets could be registered. The desire for economic betterment is a fundamental compelling force in immigrant communities in the United States. As an aggregated community, Asian Americans have the strongest educational participation and attainment rates for both native and foreign-born members compared to all other U.S. communities. The Asian American community's contribution to U.S. economic progress and prosperity is a chronicle of immigrant ambition and determination.

Asian communities have enriched the United States through cultural exchange, and participation in labor markets and the military. They have also contributed as producers, workers, and consumers, to continual economic growth as well as to technological innovation. Asian Americans have also brought additional multilingual and cultural assets to U.S. businesses and diplomacy during a period of rapid globalization. The continual waves of immigration become a resource for Asian American communities and, consequently, for the United States. For example, many Asian American families retain close ties with their extended family in their countries of origin. This allows continual learning of cultural mannerisms and nuances by U.S.-born Asians, which gives them marketable assets that can then be translated into premium wages in a variety of U.S. occupations in the private and public sectors. This is a form of wealth and asset building in Asian American communities that has not been identified as a benefit and resource to U.S. economic markets and institutions. Indeed, all high-density immigrant communities in the United States display rich cultural lega-

50

Figure 3.2 Sites in the United States Associated with the Relocation of Japanese Americans During World War II

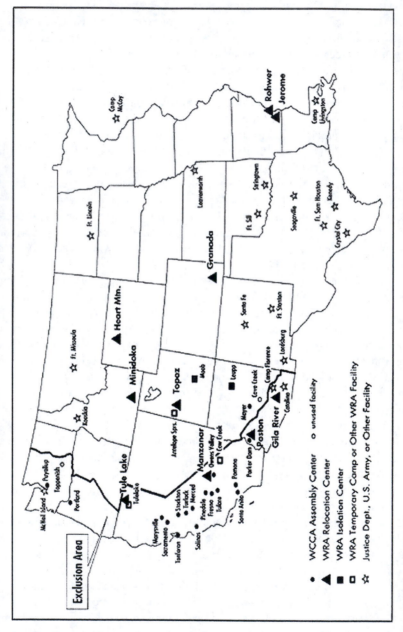

Source: Burton et al. (2000). www.nps.gov/history/history/online_books/anthropology74/ce1.htm (accessed November 30, 2009).

cies and continue providing intergenerational cultural capital in terms of language assets and cultural navigation knowledge, contributing to a labor force that is better prepared to meet the global challenges of tomorrow.

Future Prospects for Social and Economic Justice: Challenges and Opportunities

The historic election of November 2008 has engendered great hope as well as great anxiety over our economic future as a global stakeholder. The first decade of the twenty-first century ushered in several significant changes in America's narrative, bringing about a historic inflection point in our trajectory as a global stakeholder: (1) a politically engaged youth–technology interface, (2) undisciplined and excessive capitalism, (3) an abdication of governmental regulatory oversight, (4) an aging infrastructure, and (5) a visibly changing demographic base. Despite the enormous challenges ahead brought on by the confluence of such singular events, we also have a window of opportunity to undertake significant strides in revitalizing our nation's neglected communities. By forging a renewal of public service dedication and inclusive public administration, we have citizen support to undertake innovative approaches to good governance through inclusive community participation in strengthening the public trust through transparency and accountability.

The deep wealth divide historically concentrated in left-behind communities of color has rapidly spread to large portions of the aspiring middle class of all U.S. populations. In recommitting to an inclusive economic prosperity for all, we can remedy the decline in economic opportunities through increased educational access with linkages to employment that offers a living wage. Government policymakers at local, state, and federal levels can contribute to wealth and asset building in distressed and faltering communities through an inclusive partnering process with community-based organizations, our K–16 education system, and our private sector enterprises, large and small.

Small Business and Entrepreneurship

An important source of tax revenues can be had from incorporating informal entrepreneurial activities and self-employment behaviors into mainstream markets. These activities are present in our communities, especially our communities of color, but are not fully documented in local, state, or national databases. Families can benefit from establishing formal relationships with private and public sector institutions facilitated by third-sector, nongovernmental organizations long established in communities of color that can serve as bridge entities. Community wealth and asset-building activities can continue to occur below the "formal" radar or can be brought into the mainstream via trusted community-based organizations serving low-income and working poor communities. Examples of such informal entrepreneurship are weekend mechanics, home-based food preparation sold in public venues during seasonal religious and cultural holidays, informal elderly care, informal child care, and the persistence of the "nanny problem" where domestic workers are paid in cash and cannot access family supports such as the Earned Income Tax Credit during tax-filing season since they have no paper trail of having earned self-employed income during the previous year.

Public administration that recognizes the opportunities to cultivate inclusive partnerships with community stakeholders and highly trusted community organizations serving hard to reach communities can enlarge their future public servant talent pool and create pathways to permanent community outreach. By partnering with nonprofit youth entrepreneurship, microbusiness programs serving women and minorities, city and municipal community initiatives, and economic development agencies can capture new revenue sources while also bringing left-behind entrepreneurs into the mainstream.

Education for the Twenty-First Century

Income-generating activities and behaviors that engender a legacy of continued wealth accumulation have historically centered on ownership of tangible assets such as land, a home, or a business. Our current economic environment has taught us that intangible wealth and knowledge assets are of equal importance. These include the capacity to invest in acquiring human capital in the form of an education leading to professional or status degrees, being entrepreneurial, owning inventions and patents, exercising the right to vote, and the ability to join professional, community, and religious organizations (expanding social capital). Public administration cooperative learning programs anchored in municipal and state governments can promote an apprentice program that engenders a public service spirit in aspiring junior high, high school, community college, and university students. Additionally, senior professionals can prove to be an additional source of "learning" mentors and facilitators by harnessing their experience as past public servants and agency officials. Such a "hands-on" cooperative program brings an inclusion message to communities and actively recruits community participation in public service.

The Presidential Management Fellows Program is a good template to reproduce at the high school, community college, and undergraduate university levels. What would be different with these programs would be the "cooperative" learning component focused on building a public service youth local government corps. This type of program starts early and employs a "buddy/mentoring"-type system that places a youth trainee in a city agency. The youth-trainee placement rotates with a different staff member one day a week throughout the school year while the youth earn school credit. This allows youth the length of time to acclimate to an agency division while also exposing them to all the different levels of staff career placement while not overly taxing the division with the usual labor-intensive time allocation directed at training a new employee. The key to success here is that during the summer the "cooperative training component" of the program accelerates by placing each intern with a "mentor/cooperative trainer" for the entire summer. The rotation during the school year has provided the youth with sufficient knowledge to choose a placement that would expand their knowledge set and would be "overseen" by an experienced public servant.

In order to coordinate such a citywide program, for cities large and small, a program for retired or part-time public servants donating their time once a week or providing informal seminars to the youth trainees focused on personal "narratives" of lifelong public service could contribute to preparing youth trainees for their placements with city agencies. Such a program would serve two purposes: (1) act as a feeder and early "boot camp" for the youth placement program during the year, and (2) be a "subject-oriented" cooperative learning partnership between youth and senior public officials. During the "boot camp" a "product deliverable" in the form of video–voice or photo–voice "oral histories" of the senior public servants' public service years would be a cohort project. Some examples are: chronicling particular advances in public services instituted during the senior public servants' tenure with the local government/agency, and documenting renovations of neighborhoods, new public spaces, or economic development areas. By engaging youth in understanding their city's history and the important role public servants' play in the sustainability and delivery of public services to the wider community, we cultivate a spirit of public service and community advocacy in our youth.

Public Service and Public Administration: The Pathway to Inclusive Economic Security

The task before us is to reconceptualize community and family wealth generation with sustainability based on good governance of our public institutions that directly cultivate the diverse assets from each community. We can strike a balance between individual prosperity and shared prosperity by revitalizing our public institutions to reflect our plural heritage. Without our diverse "national assets" embodied in the cultural capital and multilanguage fluency that are vital characteristics of our cities, metro areas, regions, and states, the United States cannot sustain its competitive edge in global markets. By harnessing the nation's demographic changes and anchoring our recovery and revitalization initiatives on the pluralistic dynamism and diverse assets of our citizenry, we can permanently reverse the wealth gap and begin to forge a more inclusive blueprint for our future national well-being.

Notes

1. A comprehensive cost assessment of the prolongation of the war in the Pacific theater has not to my knowledge been undertaken. It would be an important contribution to understanding the impact of the use of a language asset in reducing the associated costs to the United States in both lives saved and cost savings in terms of supplies and deployment outlays. In addition to Navajo being used in World War II, Hopi and other Indian languages were used as well (oral history of Hopi tribe member).

2. Some tribes that were terminated during this period have been reinstated, but the economic consequences of loss of tribal status were never addressed (Lui et al. 2006).

3. Carnoy (1994, 162).

4. Recent archaeological evidence suggests the presence of Nordic explorers on the North American northeastern seaboard (Newfoundland, Lief Eriksson) in the early 1000s.

5. The land purchased contained all of present-day Arkansas, Missouri, Iowa, Oklahoma, Kansas, Nebraska, portions of Minnesota, most of North Dakota, nearly all of South Dakota, northeastern New Mexico, the areas of Montana, Wyoming, and Colorado east of the Continental Divide, and Louisiana west of the Mississippi River. The Louisiana Purchase also contained land that would eventually become parts of Alberta and Saskatchewan.

6. The Philippines were also included in the Spanish-American War but sought their independence and the Philippine-American War (1899–1913) resulted in the U.S. annexation of the Philippines until the end of World War II when the Philippines gained their independence.

7. The United States also confers citizenship to inhabitants of the U.S. Virgin Islands since 1927, having purchased the islands from Denmark in 1917.

8. The Cuban refugees emigrating to the United States and Puerto Rico during this time were heavily weighted toward the affluent and middle-income class, with significant human capital and merchant class capacities.

9. This guest-worker program derives its name from the Spanish term *brazo* (arm). Guest workers were meant to lend their "arms" (labor) to the U.S. agriculture and food-processing industries.

References

Adamson, Rebecca. 2003. "Land Rich and Dirt Poor: The Story of Indian Assets." *Indian Country Today (Lakota Times),* September 10. Available at http://64.225.252.249/ln/documents/Adamson_LandRich_jb3.pdf (accessed November 30, 2009).

Blackmon, Douglas A. 2008. *Slavery by Another Name: The Re-enslavement of Black Americans from the Civil War to World War II.* New York: Anchor Books.

Burton, J.; M. Farrell; F. Lord; and R. Lord. 2000. "Confinement and Ethnicity: An Overview of World War II Japanese American Relocation Camps." National Park Service, U.S. Government. Available at www.nps.gov/history/history/online_books/anthropology74/ce1.htm (accessed March 10, 2009).

Carnoy, M. 1994. *Faded Dreams: The Politics and Economics of Race in America.* New York: Cambridge University Press.

Conley, Dalton. 1999. *Being Black, Living in the Red: Race, Wealth, and Social Policy in America.* Berkeley: University of California Press.

Darity, W. Jr., Derrick Hamilton, and J. Dietrich 2002. "Passing on Blackness: Latinos, Race, and Earnings in the USA." *Applied Economics Letters* 9: 847–53.

Darity, W. Jr., and S. Myers Jr. 1998. *Persistent Disparity: Race and Economic Inequality in the United States since 1945.* Northampton, MA: Edward Elgar.

Dillon, John. 2006. "How Eisenhower Solved Illegal Border Crossings from Mexico." *Christian Science Monitor,* July 6. Available at www.csmonitor.com/2006/0706/p09s01-coop.html (accessed April 10, 2009).

Gaither, A., and E. Newburger. 2000. Population Division, U.S. Census Bureau, Powerpoint Based on Population Division working paper no. 44 (June 2000) and Table A-1. Reported Voting and Registration by Race, Hispanic Origin, Sex and Age Groups: November 1964 to 1998.

Gomez, C. 2000. "The Continual Significance of Skin Color: An Exploratory Study of Latinos in the Northeast." *Hispanic Journal of Behavioral Sciences* 22, no. 1 (February): 94–103.

Lui, M.; B. Robles; B. Leondar-Wright; R. Brewer; and R. Adamson. 2006. *The Color of Wealth: The Story Behind the U.S. Racial Wealth Divide.* New York: New Press.

Marable, M. 2000. *How Capitalism Underdeveloped Black America: Problems in Race, Political Economy, and Society.* Boston: South End Press.

Oliver, Melvin L., and Thomas M. Shapiro. 1995. *Black Wealth/White Wealth: A New Perspective on Racial Inequality.* New York: Routledge.

Vélez-Ibañez, C. 2004. "Regions of Refuge in the United States: Issues, Problems, and Concerns for the Future of Mexican-Origin Populations in the United States. *Human Organization* 63, no.1: 1–20.

4

Social Equity and Development

Terry F. Buss and Usama Ahmed

Coming generations will learn equality from poverty.

—Khalil Gibran, Lebanese philosopher

People in developing countries oppressed because of their religion, class, race, ethnicity, and the like were, until quite recently, "invisible," to borrow Ralph Ellison's term (2002). This invisibility is similar for the oppressed in the American story. Cable news operating globally, cell phones, satellites, and the Internet operating twenty-four hours daily, seven days a week, link even the remotest corners of the planet. The modern media enable us to see America yesterday in today's stories drawn from around the globe, particularly in developing countries. We seldom stop, however, to realize that it does match many aspects of the American reality at various stages of our development painful though that reality may currently be. Progress often appears to be slow and uneven as in our own program of building a more perfect union.

This chapter begins by offering widely accepted definitions for social equity and social exclusion. Next, the chapter discusses the negative impacts of insufficiently addressing or foolishly promoting inequity or exclusion. Then, the chapter looks at the different appearances of inequity and exclusion across the developing world, some of which parallel the American experience. Finally, the chapter reports on the different ways international organizations, donors, nongovernmental organizations, and developing countries themselves have promoted social equity agendas.

Social Equity and Exclusion in a Development Context

Social equity in the developing world has many meanings, but the most widely accepted definition in use comes from the World Bank. "[Social] equity means equal access to the *opportunities* that allow people to pursue a life of their own choosing and to avoid extreme deprivations in outcomes"—that is, equality in "rights, resources and voice" (World Bank 2006, 2). "Equality of rights refers to equality under the law, whether customary or statutory. Equality of resources refers to equality of opportunity, including equality of access to human capital investments and other productive resources and to markets. Equality of voice captures the ability to influence and contribute to the political discourse and the development process" (International Monetary Fund [IMF] 2007, 106).

The failure to achieve social equity, taken in a development context, also has many meanings, hence the concept of social exclusion is in wide use. "Social exclusion describes a process by which certain groups are systematically disadvantaged because they are discriminated against on the basis of their ethnicity, race, religion, sexual orientation, caste, descent, gender, age, disability, HIV status, migrant status or where they live. Discrimination occurs in public institutions, such as the legal system or in education and health service systems, as well as social institutions like the household" (Department for International Development 2005, 3). The Inter-American Development Bank (IADB) refers to those excluded simply as "outsiders" (Marquez et al. 2007).

In a highly influential book, *Freedom as Development*, Nobel Prize winner Amartya Sen (1999), expands the notion of social exclusion to include the notion of "functionings" (Marquez et al. 2007, 5).

> Social exclusion is an inefficient and dysfunctional dynamic social, political, and economic process whereby individuals and groups are denied access to opportunities and quality services to live productive lives outside poverty.
>
> . . . [T]hose social, political, and economic processes of societies limit the functionings of certain individuals or groups, resulting in their diminished well-being.
>
> . . . Functionings is different from the concept of opportunities, in that functionings refer to the social interactions and exchanges in which individuals or groups engage in order to achieve a certain outcome, rather than to the ability (exercised or not) to engage in those interactions; it is different from the concept of capabilities in that functionings refer to a particular realization of the (unobservable) set of capabilities.

Figure 4.1 illustrates these concepts.

Costs of Not Addressing Social Equity Are High

Attainment of social equity, or eliminating social exclusion, in societies, appropriately, has often been justified on moral or ethical grounds, and this is the case in the development literature as well. But morality and ethics notwithstanding, there are four powerful political, social, and economic reasons for achieving social equity as a national and international goal.

1. Social exclusion causes or deepens poverty among the oppressed, and reduces social capital and welfare for the population

Surely it should be obvious that an entire society is less well off when large numbers of people are marginalized or excluded. Excluded groups contribute less to build-

Figure 4.1   **Capabilities, Functionings, and Opportunities**

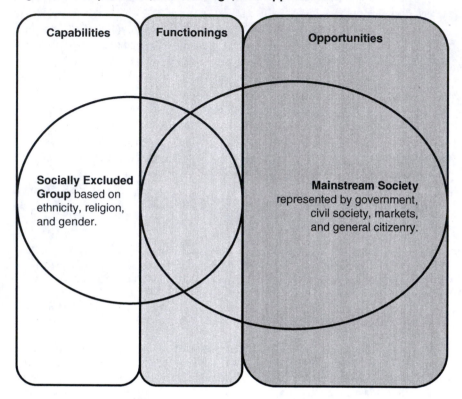

ing wealth in society because they produce and consume less. Excluded groups often require public subsidies just to keep themselves afloat. If excluded groups are belligerent about their exclusion, then additional societal costs are incurred in holding them down—more crime, more police, and more prisons. Operating parallel societies—two school systems, for example—to promote exclusion is costly. Even though costs of exclusion are large, enough people are willing to have less wealth so they can feed their hate or disdain for others. And, of course, there are those who benefit from discrimination because they are unable to compete on their own or too lazy to do so.

2. Exclusion may cause an upswing in violent crime, threatening economic growth and political stability

Besides draining the exchequer, social exclusion is also an economic deadweight retarding growth because of the increase in violent crime it causes. The inequality/ violence nexus has been observed throughout most of the developing world—Latin

America and the Caribbean, Sub-Saharan Africa, the Middle East, and Asia as well as the former Soviet bloc. Such crime restricts access to employment and social services. Economic potential is stifled by "raising the risks and costs involved in economic activity, for example through forcing businesses to spend more on protection, encouraging emigration, and deterring the development of a tourist industry" (World Bank 2006, 3). Social inequality and the violent crime it causes threaten democracy and the benefits associated with it, such as peace and stability. Nascent democracies are especially endangered—both their birth and life span are determined by levels of social inequality and the political conflict they portend.

3. Societies practicing social exclusion may experience violent uprisings among the oppressed

Violence may take place on a much larger scale than on the street corner. Many civil wars, revolts, guerrilla movements, ethnic cleansing, genocide, and violence on a large scale in developing countries, as illustrated by the cases below, have their origins in social exclusion policies or practices (see especially Bodea and Elbadawi 2007). Once violence is unleashed, it can extend for years, even centuries. Unfortunately, "scapegoating" tactics are the most common last resort for governments clinging to power. They must perpetuate violence and discrimination to survive. Unfortunately, governments in developing countries often seem to consolidate and maintain power by targeting groups that pose a threat—usually imaginary—to the social order. So, some governments stay in power perpetuating violence and discrimination because they cannot sustain themselves without this.

4. Violent uprisings in one developing country often spill over into others

In 2010, East Central Africa is yet again ablaze with regional conflict, much of it stemming from tribal, racial, and ethnic cleavages, many originating in colonial times. Hundreds of thousands have been killed and millions have been displaced. Somalia remains in the throes of civil war among its government, warlords, and Islamists, with an occupying force of Ethiopians and an African Union force of Ugandans. Eritreans and Ethiopians continue to be at odds, ostensibly over a border dispute. Kenya is in the midst of tribal violence, and some say on the verge of civil war. The Islamic government in Sudan, in what former Secretary of State Colin Powell characterized as a genocide, has been systematically killing and expelling the population in Darfur mostly by supporting paramilitary groups. Chad, a neighboring country to Sudan, is battling rebel groups based in Sudan. Sudan is supporting the Lords Resistance Army in northern Uganda, a war displacing millions. The Central African Republic (CAR), bordering Chad, Sudan, and Congo, has found itself embroiled in conflict. The previous CAR government came to power in a coup supported by Congolese and Libyan rebels. This government was overthrown by rebels supported by Chadian mercenaries. Chad now supports hundreds of thousands of refugees from Sudan and CAR. Rwanda and the Congo have been struggling with large rebel units representing both the Tutsi and Hutu tribes fighting in the Congo in a continuation of tribal conflicts in Rwanda and Burundi. The international community clearly has a stake in eliminating exclusionary practices for economic and political reasons, if not ethical ones.

Appearances of Social Exclusion and Inequality

Developing countries—and developed ones for that matter—are awash with exclusionary practices that marginalize legions of people, denying them full benefits of membership in society. In preparing this chapter over a period of months in 2008–9, numerous and varied social exclusionary practices—most long-standing—were easy to find in the news media. Here is a sampling. Unhappily, they represent only the tip of the iceberg.

Gender Impacts

Gender as a social equity issue is common in most, if not all, developing countries (IMF 2007). Women tend to have fewer legal rights than men. Women cannot own property as individuals. Women are subjected to violence and abuse. Wife beating is not illegal in many places. Women are relegated to work in the home, having been denied education or employment opportunities. Women may not hold public office. And women can simply be discarded through neglect and in extreme cases exploited through human trafficking.

Missing Girls

The ultimate form of social exclusion is the killing of unwanted members of society. In many developing countries, girls are eliminated by prenatal gender selection, abortion, or infanticide through murder or neglect. India and China appear to be the worst offenders, although these practices are common enough across Africa and Asia. Although there is great disagreement about the accuracy and meaning of the "missing girl" figures, there seems to be consensus that a major problem exists. A leading British medical journal, the *Lancet,* estimates the loss of about 10 million potential female births in India over the past twenty years (India: Missing Girls 2007). In New Delhi, there are only 814 girls born for every 1,000 boys. In China, according to the International Planned Parenthood Federation, there are nearly 7 million abortions annually, of which 70 percent are females (Ten Million Missing Chinese Girls? 2007). In India and China, females are much less desirable than males in that females constitute a "financial burden"—dowries for those who marry or unwed daughters who remain at home—on their families. In China, it is official policy for families to have only one child, hence the large number of abortions. The Chinese government estimates that since the promulgation of its one-child policy in the 1980s, 400 million births have been prevented. Those violating the policy can be heavily fined or worse. A paradox: in the case of both countries, the shortage of girls means there are many more men searching for many fewer women as marriage partners.

Pakistan

In most developing countries, gender inequity results from weak enforcement rather than biases within the law itself. Pakistan faces both problems. They originate in social and cultural mores postcoded in literal interpretations of Islamic law, where they find legitimacy and resilience. Marital rape has not been criminalized. The Citizenship Act of 1951 excludes foreign men married to Pakistani women, as well as their children, from citizenship eligibility. The Law of Evidence of 1984 halves the value of a woman's testimony in cases of financial transactions. The Hudood Ordinance of 1979 requires four adult male Muslims of good repute as witnesses of the actual rape or a confession from the rapist himself before the offense can be proved. When rape is not established, the victim herself can be charged with, and sentenced for, adultery. According to the Human Rights Commission of Pakistan, honor killings of women who refuse arranged marriages, seek divorce, commit adultery, or are suspected of any other acts that "dishonor" the family or clan, have increased from 271 in 2006 to 636 in 2007 (61 victims being under the age of eighteen). Offenders enjoy immunity through the waiver of retribution by the victim's heirs, or monetary compensation to them, who are in most cases the male relatives behind the killings. These gaps have not been addressed by legal reforms—such as the Criminal Law Amendment of 2004 and the Protection of Women Act of 2006—despite the severe opposition they faced from conservative political groups in Pakistan. Nilofar Bakhtiar, the minister for Women's Development, who championed these reforms, was herself recently ousted from office over a controversial skydiving incident in France, where she allegedly hugged her instructor. This is telling of the difficulties in Pakistan faced by women who are victimized by the law, and by women trying to change it.

Race/Ethnicity

Apartheid—a state-sponsored, legal form of social exclusion—characteristic of South Africa before the fall of the Afrikaner government in 1994, for many, is the first thing that comes to mind when thinking about racial discrimination in developing countries. Basically, colonists of Dutch and British descent, in an effort to protect their way of life, excluded indigenous peoples. Secret police and the army were developed to segregate people of color, then to deprive them of the means to advance and prosper. South Africa was one large ghetto with a few wealthy core cities reserved for whites. But there are numerous other countries employing these tactics, among them America at an earlier time.

Darfur

Darfur is a region in western Sudan. In 2003, a civil war broke out between the Sudanese army and Arab Islamists, on the one side, and rebels, including non-Arabs and non-Islamists, on the other. Although the war has been portrayed by some as religious in origin, many experts place the cause on the gradual encroachment of Arab Islamists—seeking better pastures—into non-Arab lands. The Sudanese government supports Arab Islamist militias—*Janjaweed*—who terrorize villages they wish to expropriate. Estimates are that 200,000–500,000 people have been killed and another 2.5 million have been displaced.

Haiti

Haiti is, and has for 200 years, been one of the most racist of countries (Buss 2008a). Since Haiti's founding in 1804 from a successful slave revolt, a mulatto class—descendants of black African slaves and French colonists—has systematically taken control of the country's economics and politics, exploiting Haitian blacks who comprise 95 percent or more of the population. The mulatto class so doggedly pursued its own self-aggrandizement at the expense of the vast black majority that it made Haiti the poorest country in the Western Hemisphere; it ranked among the poorest Sub-Saharan African countries. Three-fourths of Haitians live on $2 or less a day. Only 10 percent have electrical service. Some 95 percent work in the underground economy. Life expectancy is fifty-three years. Periodic revolts and revolutions by blacks have led only to the replacement of one group of oppressors for another.

Roma

The Roma—or Romani or Gypsies—are a racial/ethnic group of about 15 million present in many countries who have been the object of varying degrees of discrimination and exclusion. The Roma, a people migrated from India centuries ago, have a distinct culture and language, but have tended to adopt the religion of the countries in which they live, while maintaining a strict, traditional moral code of their own. In many countries, the Roma have become stereotyped as people who dwell on the margins of society, refusing to assimilate, and surviving by begging, petty crime, and illegal money changing. In Central Europe, state discrimination is widespread against them. Governments have channeled Roma children, for example, into Roma-only schools, or into "delinquent" or "special education" classes en masse. In Bulgaria (technically a transition economy/country), the Health Ministry tried to reduce Roma birthrates so they would not overwhelm other Bulgarians. Roma have a much higher incarceration rate than the general populations, in part because of their reputations with security forces. Ironically, the Roma have reportedly come under great discriminatory practices in Iraq with the fall of Saddam Hussein. In addition to targeting one another, Iraqi Sunni and Shiite Muslims have attacked the Roma.

Kurds

The Kurds are an ethnic group concentrated in the Iraq geographic region of Kurdistan, and in portions of Turkey, Iraq, Syria, and Iran, where they constitute majority populations. In Turkey, where they are the largest minority, their nationalist movement predates World War I and has historically prompted suppression by the government, which does not officially recognize any ethnic distinctions. Until 1991 it was illegal to publicize or broadcast in the Kurdish language. The relaxation was motivated by Turkish aspirations for European Union (EU) membership. Leyla Zana, the first Kurdish woman parliamentarian was jailed for fifteen years. Her offense was adding to her inaugural speech: "I shall struggle so that the Kurdish and Turkish peoples may live together in a democratic framework." In Iraq, Human Rights Watch, an advocacy group, estimates that Saddam's campaigns killed 50,000–100,000 and used mustard gas and nerve agents to target 40 Kurdish villages. Some 2,000 villages were destroyed during the Saddam regime. Post-Saddam, the Kurds have been termed by commentators such as Noam Chomsky as the "people in gravest danger," as future governments would not differ from their successors in Kurdish policy. In Syria, following a 1962 regional consensus, 120,000 Kurds were arbitrarily stripped of citizenship and termed aliens who could not be employed by the government, marry Syrian nationals, vote, own land, or relocate to another country because they lacked passports. The Kurdish language is banned, and Kurdish names cannot be registered for children or new businesses in a decades-old push for Arab nationalism. History though, is not without a sense of irony. Saladin, perhaps the most venerated military hero of Islam, the "deliverer of Jerusalem from Christian hands," was a Muslim Kurd.

Bolivia

Bolivia has perhaps the most politically successful Andean Indian movement. Evo Morales was elected president in 2006, and his supporters hold a majority of seats in the national assembly. Morales heads the Movement to Socialism Party, which seeks a communist society that would benefit Indians, who have been excluded for centuries. The movement is profoundly anti-American and somewhat anti-European, anticapitalistic, and prolegalization of cocaine for local consumption and export. Morales wants to nationalize industry, redistribute wealth, and modify the constitution to give himself much more power and longevity in office. Rather than work with the new opposition, international community, and foreign investors, Morales has chosen confrontation politics. In 2008, Morales began dismantling the antidrug trafficking and antiterrorist infrastructure developed in Bolivia by the United States. In 2007 and 2008, governance of the country remained deadlocked, unable to move forward (Bolivia: Revolution Postponed 2007). To complicate matters, Morales invited Hugo Chavez (Venezuela's strongman) and Fidel Castro (Cuba's long-serving leader) to aid him politically and financially. In 2009, Morales prevailed in a national referendum and has begun dismantling the constitution to favor Andean Indian interests.

Liberia

Liberia was founded in 1822 by the American Colonization Society, a group whose purpose was to repatriate American slaves back to Africa. In 1847, Liberia became the first free African Republic. Freed American slaves—"Americo-Liberians," seeing themselves as superior to indigenous African tribes in West Africa, soon took over the reins of government, making Liberia a one-party—True Whig Party—state for the next 160 years. Interestingly, the Americo-Liberians chose not to assimilate with other African peoples, preferring to maintain religious, cultural, and societal practices acquired in the antebellum South. In 1980, a successful military coup subdued the dominant Americo-Liberian class, plunging Liberia into two back-to-back civil wars, the last of which ended in 2003 with a U.S. military intervention. Some 250,000 people died during the period. Liberia elected a new president in 2006. Ellen Johnson-Sirleaf is seemingly restoring peace to the country.

Ethiopia

The Horn of Africa—comprising Ethiopia, Eritrea, Sudan, and Somalia—has experienced severe droughts that have devastated the people. In the 1980s, one of the worst droughts ever in the Horn was, as others had been in the past, blamed on acts of nature. But closer examination suggests that the drought was deliberately and wantonly exacerbated by the Marxist government in Ethiopia. The Marxist regime, seeing an opportunity to reduce ethnic and class opposition posed by Eritreans, perpetuated the drought to create famine.

Tribal Impact

Tribal affiliation, particularly in Sub-Saharan Africa, undergirds most social equity issues. Some scholars believe African tribes coexisted peacefully before the slave trade forced them to become much more protective of tribal members at risk of kidnapping. Other scholars believe European colonialists needed a way to dominate large portions of Africa, while employing relatively few white administrators and soldiers, so colonists and trading companies began to favor some tribes over others in an effort to divide and conquer the continent. These tactics were inherited by native governments who were suddenly charged with running newly minted states following the withdrawal of colonial powers. Vestiges of slavery and colonialism fuel much of the conflict in Africa as tribal differences are exploited by ruthless dictators, opportunists, and rebels. Following independence in the 1960s, Cold War and business interests also played on these cleavages for political and commercial gain. Rwanda and Kenya are foci for this illumination. There is an uncanny parallel with the plight of freed slaves in post–Civil War America and the legacy left behind today.

Rwanda

In 1994, in just 100 days, extremist Hutu tribes brutally murdered between 500,000 and 1,000,000 Tutsi and moderate Hutu tribesmen in an outright genocide. Although the predominance of Tutsis over Hutus in politics, economics, and class is complex, the Belgians exacerbated these by exploiting them to gain power in Rwanda after they acquired the country from the Germans in the 1919 Treaty of Versailles. The Belgians issued identity cards to Rwandans based on tribe, then proceeded to favor the Tutsis. A revolution by Hutus against Tutsis in 1959, in which they killed 20,000 and caused tens of thousands to flee, was the beginning of a long civil war and violent confrontation between the tribes. The Hutus emerged out of the conflict in control of Rwanda. Examples of discrimination against the Tutsis are numerous: in 1974, for example, Tutsis began to dominate the fields of medicine and education. The Hutu response was to force Tutsis to resign or go into exile. Some were murdered. Tutsi rebels spent thirty years organizing their comeback in base camps in Uganda. From then until 1993, Tutsi and Hutu factions tried to negotiate a political settlement. In 1994, things went terribly wrong: the genocide. In 1995, Tutsi rebels invaded, Rwanda defeating the Hutus. Rwandan Tutsis and Hutus now seem to be peacefully coexisting.

Kenya

Kenya was until recently a political/economic success story. President Mwai Kibaki, widely accredited for Kenya's economic miracle, won a highly disputed presidential election in December 2007. Kibaki's constituency consisted largely of the Kikuyu tribe, while his opponent, Raila Odinga, received support from the Luos, Kalenjins, and affiliated tribes. Odinga supporters, believing that Kibaki won the election through widespread fraud, began rioting and hunting down Kikuyu tribesmen. Some 1,500 people, mostly Kikuyus, were murdered by machete-wielding gangs in a few short days. Some 250,000 people have been displaced. The U.S. envoy to Kenya called the violence "ethnic cleansing" (Getterman 2008). The Luos-affiliated tribes had participated in the elections feeling that they could, for the first time, break the power exerted by the Kikuyu. Kikuyus were favored by the British in colonial times and eventually became the economic and political class, with the Luos relegated to lesser status. Kenya's instability has caused many foreign investors and international donors to become nervous about continuing to invest in the country, and other bordering nations, Sudan, Somalia, Ethiopia, and Uganda, with their own instability problems, have also become concerned.

Mauritania and Sudan

Slavery may seem anachronistic, but it continues to thrive in these places. While many in the developed world now suffer from "compassion fatigue" when it comes to Africa, modern-day slavery syndicates still have the power to shock and awe. The traditional chattel slavery (which builds on racial/ethnic/religious divisions embedded in social institutions reinforced by history) is practiced today in Mauritania, Sudan, and other North African countries. According to a year-long study by *Newsweek*, more than 100,000 descendants of slaves captured by Arabs and Berbers as far back as the twelfth century are still living as their property, despite being Muslims. The 1981 Abolition of Slavery Ordinance does not define slavery or the penalty for it, and the government investigated only five cases of slavery in 2007, with no reports of prosecutions or convictions. In Sudan, the slave trade has resurfaced following the civil war in Darfur mentioned earlier. Militias supported by the government raided non-Muslim villages in the South occupied mostly by the Dinka people, enslaving an estimated 11,000 people over twenty years until 2003, according to the Rift Valley Institute. The Sudanese criminal code is not universal in its prohibition of trafficking or slavery, and enforcement is minimal. No trafficker has ever been prosecuted. And the government's efforts toward prevention are minimal. While it is arguably commercial interests that drive it, slavery has been legitimized and so perpetuated by deep-rooted social inequity.

Religious Exclusion

Religious intolerance most affects social equity when a single religion dominates not only the social and spiritual spheres but also the political and economic spheres. Three cases illustrate this abuse.

Iraq

Shiites and Sunnis, the two main branches of Islam, have been in conflict since the religion's founding by Mohammed in the seventh century (although some scholars suggest the conflict between the two is much more recent). In Iraq under Saddam Hussein, the Sunni branch, representing the majority in all of Islam, was the favored sect even though they comprised only one-fifth of the Iraqi population. Military and government jobs were awarded to Sunnis, and party membership in the Baath Party was dominated by them. The Second Gulf War in 2003 changed the balance of power, with the Shiites now dominating the post-Saddam government. In Iraq, the issue is how to reconcile the two branches (three if the Kurds to the north are included). Sectarian violence is no small matter: tens of thousands of people have been killed by roving death squads, suicide bombers, and corrupt vigilante police and military.

Indonesia

Roots of the Aceh conflict lay in "imbalances in center-periphery relations and alienation of the Acehnese population from Jakarta." The central government did not recognize Aceh's unique history, culture, and religion or its role in securing Indonesian independence. The revenues from its natural resources fattened Jakarta's coffers but that largesse was seldom extended to the Achenese (Barron and Clark 2006, 1). An issue is that the Islamic population was folded into a largely Christian ethnic Chinese region—North Sumatra—in 1949 where much religious oppression occurred, exacerbated by unequal distribution of resources resulting from oil production. In 2003, Islamists were able to have Sharia Law recognized officially in a parallel system to that in Indonesia generally. Violent conflicts along ethnic, religious, and racial lines are ongoing. By 2004, 1.3 million had been displaced.

Saudi Arabia

The birthplace of a faith now 1.5 billion strong proves a poor model for social equity across religious boundaries. Islam is the official state religion, and the state's interpretation forms the basis of the legal system. Freedoms for non-Muslims are not recognized or protected in law, and remain severely restricted in practice. The same is true of Muslim sects such as Shias, Ahmediya, Sufis, summarily all denominations other than orthodox Wahhabism. Conversion by a Muslim to another religion is a capital offense. Anti-Jewish, anti-Christian, and anti-Shia rhetoric is common in sermons delivered by Sunni imams on the government payroll. State policy regarding women, immigrants, ethnic minorities, and political dissidents is modeled on similar lines.

Caste

Human Rights Watch summarizes the issue of caste and social equity on its Web site (2001).

> In much of Asia and parts of Africa, caste is the basis for the exclusion of groups by reason of their descent. [Caste is hereditary.] Over 250 million people worldwide continue to suffer under what is often a hidden apartheid of segregation, modern-day slavery, and other extreme forms of discrimination, exploitation, and violence. Caste imposes enormous obstacles to their full attainment of civil, political, economic, social, and cultural rights. . . . Caste systems throughout the world, also dominate in housing, marriage, and general social interaction—divisions that are reinforced through the practice and threat of social ostracism, economic boycotts, and even physical violence.

The Dalits or untouchables of South Asia—Nepal, Bangladesh, India, Sri Lanka, and Pakistan—and the Buraku people of Japan; the Osu of Nigeria's Igbo people;

and groups in Senegal and Mauritania are victims of caste discrimination. For example, Dalit children in India are forced to sit in the back of classrooms, are ignored by teachers, must eat separately from others, and have very high dropout rates (Wax 2008). In Yemen, where African Blacks—descendants of an Ethiopian army that invaded Yemen before 600 AD—are treated as the lowest class by Arabs. They are permitted to work only in garbage collection and street cleaning, receive no benefits even though they are employed by the government, and are subject to violent abuse by supervisors.

The storyline developed thus far might have been further extended if we included youths, gays, disabled persons, immigrants, and the rural poor. Their stories might have provided a more complete picture of the issues, but they would not change the basic picture here.

The Prosocial Equity Agenda in Developing Countries

International, multilateral, and bilateral aid, nongovernmental organizations, and individual countries all have a role to play in promoting social equity in the developing world. The bottom line in achieving success on the agenda is the extent to which governments value social equity and pursue it or the degree to which governments can be forced to adopt more equitable policies. There are numerous examples of both approaches in play at any given time internationally.

International Organizations

International organizations—primarily the United Nations—play a major role in social equity by setting international standards, disseminating information to improve policy and practice, and holding nations accountable.

United Nations

The United Nations (UN), for example, produces dizzying amounts of information offering guidance and best practices improving social equity. The UN Development Fund for Women (UNIFEM), established in 1976, periodically publishes a series of reports tying gender equality issues to aid effectiveness (UNIFEM 2010). There are eight UN-sponsored international conventions that define and protect human rights and in one way or another relate to social equity, such as the International Convention on the Protection of the Rights of All Migrant Workers and Members of Their Families, 1990. Others include:

- International Convention on the Elimination of All Forms of Racial Discrimination, 1965.
- International Covenant on Civil and Political Rights, 1966.

- International Covenant on Economic, Social and Cultural Rights, 1966.
- Convention on the Elimination of All Forms of Discrimination Against Women, 1979.
- Convention Against Torture and Other Cruel, Inhuman or Degrading Treatment or Punishment, 1984.
- Convention on the Rights of the Child, 1989.
- Convention on the Rights of Persons with Disabilities, 2007.

For the most part, international organizations hold nations accountable for social equity and exclusion through public exposure—ranking countries against social equity criteria. A major development accountability initiative is the Millennium Development Goals (MDG) program of the UN Development Programme (UNDP 2010). MDGs, eight in number, were adopted by the UN Millennium Summit in 2000 to encourage developing countries to quantify ambitious development goals, and then achieve them by 2015. Three of the MDGs are directly gender-related social equity issues, including:

- Promote gender equality and empower women (Goal 3),
- Reduce child mortality (Goal 4), and
- Improve maternal health (Goal 5).

Four specific targets under Goal 3 include concrete indicators of gender equity:

- Ratio of Girls to Boys in Primary, Secondary, and Tertiary Education
- Ratio of Literate Women to Men 15–24 years old
- Share of Women in Wage Employment in the Non-Agricultural Sector
- Proportion of Seats Held by Women in National Parliaments

The UN Development Programme also publishes reports on regions that have gender equity issues. A special 2005 issue of the *Arab Human Development Report* was subtitled *Towards the Rise of Women in the Arab World* (UNDP 2005). This report was viewed as quite courageous in that it attacked gender-related social equity head-on rather than avoiding it as had been done in past reports.

Others

The World Bank also promotes accountability in social equity by publishing special reports on the issues. In 2005, the World Bank (2006) devoted its entire annual *World Development Report* 2006 to equity and development. This report focused somewhat not only on women but also on social equity arising out of poverty. Likewise, the International Monetary Fund (2007) looked closely at MDGs and gender equality in fragile states in its *Global Monitoring Report: 2007*.

Although beyond the scope of this chapter, as noble as these efforts are, they make little difference among those developing countries whose governments do not heed them. In the end, the sovereignty of nations makes it difficult or impossible to enforce international standards where developing countries can opt out. Consider the classic cases of genocide in the past few years. In Rwanda, Sudan, Cambodia, and Iraq, the international community has done nothing (Power 2003). Only in the Balkans has the international community stepped in, and then with notable reluctance.

Bilateral and Multilateral Donors

Foreign aid in all its forms—loans, grants, technical assistance, debt forgiveness— offers huge leverage over developing countries, which depend on it to develop and prosper. Bilateral and multilateral donors are holding developing countries accountable for social practices and policies in exchange for foreign assistance. The Millennium Challenge Account (MCA) is arguably the most sophisticated foreign aid program reforming the behavior of developing countries (www.mca. gov). MCA is a new U.S. foreign assistance program that substantially departs from past aid practices (Buss 2008b). MCA requires that developing countries work toward and attain goals across a wide range of issues, including poverty reduction, democratization, free market practices, rule of law, human rights, and anticorruption, just to become eligible to submit proposals for assistance. Once a country submits a proposal, MCA consultants verify on the ground that the country has the procurement and financial management capacity to account for aid spending. They then provide funding in the form of grants in tranches after a country demonstrates progress on its approved projects. Funding ranges from $65 million to $700 million. Although the program was launched under the George W. Bush administration, President Barack Obama has continued support for MCA, requesting $1.4 billion in his budget request for 2010.

Eligibility standards to qualify to compete for MCA funding are infused with social equity requirements including:

- gender equality, equality of opportunity and freedom to travel, reside, work, marry, and determine whether or how many children to have.
- freedom from domination by the military, foreign powers, totalitarian parties, religious hierarchies, economic oligarchies, or any other powerful group in making personal political choices.
- the extent to which a government deliberately changes the country's ethnic composition to affect the political balance of power.
- respect for minority groups and protection of human rights.
- the degree to which the rural poor are able to enter into dialogue with government representatives and express their concerns and priorities (complete standards are available from Millenium Challenge Corporation, 2010).

Countries not achieving these standards across the board simply do not receive aid from MCA—a strong financial inducement for governments to pursue social equity.

Variations of this model are becoming increasingly popular in the UK's Department for International Development and the Canadian International Development Agency. The World Bank and its sister regional banks have weaker variations in their lending programs.

Again, those developing countries that value social exclusion over development are little influenced by foreign assistance. The military junta in Burma, where as many as 150,000 people lost their lives in a massive cyclone in 2008, refused foreign assistance because it preferred to keep the country isolated rather than save its people. The junta is a major violator of human rights.

Nongovernmental Organizations

Nongovernmental organizations (NGOs) play a variety of roles in promoting social equity in developing countries, including raising awareness of social equity issues, holding governments accountable for human rights abuses, empowering people to defend or attain their rights, and delivering programs that foster social equity.

Passage of the Republic of Ghana's domestic violence law, for example, illustrates the power of NGOs to effect change. It is common practice in Ghana to beat and violate women—wives, daughters, and house servants. Following intense lobbying by NGOs—International Federation of Women Lawyers, Gender Center, Women in Law and Development in Africa, and African Women Lawyers Association—a bill was finally introduced in 2002 after years of effort. The bill was not processed in the parliament until 2006, necessitating continuing NGO pressure. In 2007, the bill became law. NGOs seem to be most effective when they work in countries that are much more liberal politically than in dictatorships.

Pressuring governments with human rights abuse accusations is risky business for NGOs. More often than not, their workers are intimidated, imprisoned, or even murdered, and their organizations often are expelled from developing countries. Russia's President Putin expelled nearly all Western human rights organizations from Russia in 2007 because they were causing his administration such aggravation. President Mugabe of Zimbabwe did the same in 2008 when he apparently rigged elections to gain another term. And the Burma military junta imprisons those who speak out for human rights.

Governments

Greatly expanding the social equity agenda in developing countries likely depends on the strong will of the leadership in these countries to both recognize the need for change and execute it. This is not easy, considering that to promote social equity requires changing culture, religion, history, and beliefs that may have been ingrained for millennia. Nonetheless, some countries are trying to overcome barriers. In 2005, Central European governments came together to form the "Decade of Roma Inclusion 2005–2015" to work together to resolve human rights issues for the Roma (Decade of Roma Inclusion 2005–2015, 2010).

Taking It One Step Further

Social equity and social exclusion, as defined above, have led to a significant shift in policies and programs to achieve social equity for excluded groups at least in some places. Current thinking in development theory and practice is now moving from the predominant focus on "welfare" to a lesser tried one of "agency." The distinction is between socially excluded groups viewed as beneficiaries of the development process whose well-being it enhances—the welfare approach—and socially excluded groups viewed as agents of development, as movers and shapers of change that benefits themselves, others, and society as a whole as well—the agency approach (Hamadeh-Banerjee 2000, 7).

For agency to work, the most effective strategy includes facilitating the participation of once-excluded groups in positions of power, especially in the economic and political spheres, not to mention in households. But this participation must be fair, especially in the sense that rights, resources, and voice apply to everyone equally. A society that eliminates exclusionary practices, then, can expect much better economic growth, democracy, and development. Figure 4.2 offers a schematic tying these concepts together. In India, for example, excluded groups, especially women, are allocated places in regional assemblies so that they may participate in lawmaking. In South Africa, industries once white-owned and -operated now increasingly have black management in place through affirmative action programs. Again, it is not easy for those in power to give some of it up to excluded groups, but in the end, most forward thinkers already in power realize that everyone will be better off in a participatory society, not an exclusionary one.

This modern-day trot around the globe hopefully has given a glimpse of the equity and exclusion challenges similar to those that have been overcome (yet still need more work) here in America in its 200-year journey. The open question is whether these places can learn lessons from the American story as well as their own and keep marching toward social equity in a flat, crowded, hot public square (Friedman 2008). A strategy of one size fits all is not the goal. Each country must move in a way that is appropriate for its own conditions and developmental agenda. Still, equity and inclusion must be the ultimate goal.

Anyone browsing over the case examples of social exclusion and violence above might become discouraged about the prospects for achieving sustainable social equity in the developing world. Developing nations, as the United States once was, are in the end quite fragile—political, social, and economic institutions can easily be overturned by a committed few, and causes of social inequity and exclusion can be papered over but frequently not extinguished. Virtually

Figure 4.2 **Social Equity, Domains of Choice, and Economic Performance**

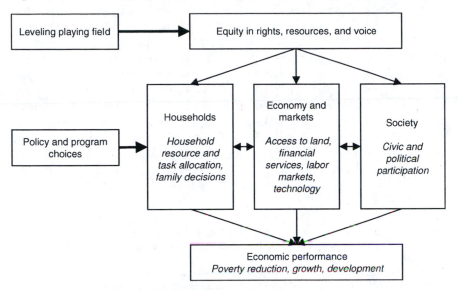

Source: Adapted from IMF (2007, 107).

overnight in Latin America, demagogues in Bolivia, Venezuela, Ecuador, Nicaragua, Honduras, and Argentina are systematically unraveling stability in their countries, exploiting yet again those things that have divided people, rather than seeking compromise and consensus. In Kenya, years of development evaporated in a matter of days when opposition forces refused to accept the results of a fraudulent election. Images of gangs wielding machetes were reminiscent of Rwanda's genocide in 1994.

Potential for renewed fragmentation lies just below the surface in many peaceful developing countries, threatening to erupt at any time. Peace in the Balkans ended when powerful actors in the international community aided the province of Kosovo to secede from Serbia. China faces an all-out revolt in Tibet as Tibetans seized the opportunity in the run up to the 2008 Olympic Games to protest the concerted effort by the Chinese government to end their way of life—"cultural genocide."

But there are rays of hope that things might change as they have in America's past. In South Africa, electric power companies are unable to meet demands for power. Rather than favor the rich (or whites) as was the case in the past, South Africa spreads power blackouts around the country on a rotational basis so that everyone shares the pain (Timberg 2008). Surprisingly, the rich and poor alike appear to see this as just. In Malaysia in March 2008, voters overturned the government's domination that imposed a quota system favoring the interests of the ethnic Malays, mostly Muslims and some Chinese and Indians (Trofimov 2008). And in Haiti, in

2006, excluded groups (which include about nine-tenths of society) successfully elected a new president, Rene Preval, who appears on his way to reconciling the country's most significant wrongs (Buss 2008a). The new millennium has seen women's suffrage being extended to four new Muslim majority countries, Bahrain (2002), Oman (2003), Kuwait (2005), and United Arab Emirates (2006). In the closing days of June, women along with men rose up in Iran. In Mauritania, the new antislavery law passed in August 2007 is hailed by activists as a historical first step, because it makes slave ownership a punishable offense. In India, there are signs of urban prosperity trickling down to the countryside: the government is now heavily investing in rural schools. Although many would like to see advances in social equity proceed at a rapid pace, it is far more likely that the wheels will turn slowly—but they will turn.

References

Barron, Patrick. 2006. "Decentralizing Inequality: Center-Periphery Relations, Local Governance, and Conflict in Aceh. Washington, DC: World Bank, Social Development Papers, no. 39.

Bodea, Christina, and Ibrahim A. Elbadawi. 2007. "Riots, Coups, and Civil War. Washington, DC: Macroeconomics and Growth Team, World Bank, Working Paper, no. 4397.

"Bolivia: Revolution Postponed." 2007. *Economist*, November 8.

Buss, Terry F. 2008a. *Haiti in the Balance: Why Foreign Aid to Haiti Has Failed and What to Do About It*. Washington, DC: Brookings Institution Press.

———. 2008b. "The Millennium Challenge Account: A New High Performance Program." In *Performance Management and Budgeting*, ed. F. Stevens Redburn, Robert Shea, and Terry F. Buss, 262–74. Armonk, NY: M.E. Sharpe.

"Decade of Roma Inclusion 2005–2015." 2010. Available at www.romadecade.org/index. php?content=1/ (accessed March 4, 2011).

Department for International Development (DFID). 2005. *Reducing Poverty by Tackling Social Exclusion*. London.

Ellison, Ralph. 2002. *The Invisible Man*. New York: Random House.

Friedman, Thomas. 2008. *Hot, Flat, and Crowded: Why We Need a Green Revolution—and How It Can Renew America*. New York: Farrar, Straus, and Giroux.

Getterman, Jeffrey. 2008. "U.S. Envoy Calls Some Kenya Violence Ethnic Cleansing." *New York Times*, January 31, A3.

Hamadeh-Banerjee, Lina. 2000. "Women's Agency in Governance." In *Women's Political Participation and Good Governance*, ed. UN Development Programme, 7–13. New York: UN Development Programme.

Human Rights Watch. 2001. "Caste Discrimination." New York. Available at www.hrw. org/reports2001/globalcast/.

"India: Missing Girls." 2007. *Frontline World* (PBS), April 24. Available at www.pbs.org/ frontlineworld/rough/2007/04/the_missing_gir.html (accessed February 8, 2008).

International Monetary Fund (IMF). 2007. *Global Monitoring Report: MDG—Confronting the Challenges of Gender Equality and Fragile States*. Washington, DC.

Marquez, Gustovo; Alberto Chong; Suzanne Duryea; Jacqueline Mazza; and Huga Nopo. 2007. *Outsiders*. Washington, DC: Inter-American Development Bank.

Millennium Challenge Corporation, 2010. Guide to the MCC Indicators and the Selection Process, Fiscal Year 2011. Available at http://www.mcc.gov/documents/reports/refer-ence-2010001040503-_fy11guidetotheindicators.pdf (accessed March 7, 2011).

Power, Stephanie. 2003. *A Problem from Hell*. New York: Harper.

Sen, Amartya. 1999. *Development as Freedom*. New York: Alfred Knopf.

"Ten Million Missing Chinese Girls?" 2007. *ReasonOnline*, January 25. Available at www. reason.com/blog/printer/118311.html (accessed February 8, 2008).

Timberg, Craig. 2008. "Rotating Power Outages an Equalizer in SA." *Washington Post*, Jan 20. http://www.washingtonpost.com/wp-dyn/content/article/2008/01/19/ AR2008011902590.html (accessed March 9, 2011).

Trofimov, Yaroslav. 2008. "Vote Rocks Malaysian Government." *Wall Street Journal*, March 10, 15.

United Nations. 2004. "Reduction of HIV/AIDS Related Employment Discrimination in Viet Nam." Hanoi: UN Country Team, June, Discussion Paper, no. 5.

United Nations Development Fund for Women (UNIFEM). 2010. "Materials." Available at www.unifem.org/materials/ (accessed February 8, 2011).

United Nations Development Programme (UNDP). 2005. *Arab Human Development Report: Toward the Rise of Women*. New York.

———. 2010. "Millennium Development Goals." Available at www.undp.org/mdg/ (accessed February 8, 2011).

Wax, Emily. 2008. "Overcoming Caste." *Washington Post*, January 20, A1, A20.

World Bank. 2006. *World Development Report: Equity and Development*. Washington, DC.

5

Urban Inequality

Edward L. Glaeser, Matthew Resseger, and Kristina Tobio

For the almost 2,500 years since Plato wrote that "any city however small, is in fact divided into two, one the city of the poor, the other of the rich," urban scholars have been struck by the remarkable amount of income inequality within dense cities (Wheeler 2005). While there is certainly plenty of rural inequality as well, the density of cities makes the contrast of rich and poor particularly striking. Indeed, there is a 44 percent correlation between inequality and density across those U.S. counties with more than one person per every two acres.[1]

The inequality of American metropolitan areas is particularly striking since the United States is more unequal than any comparable European country (Alesina and Glaeser 2004). Moreover, just as inequality within the United States has been rising since the 1970s, inequality in almost every metropolitan area has risen since 1980. In many cases, the increase in inequality has been considerable.

There are good reasons to be concerned about inequality. Many value systems treat inequality as undesirable in and of itself (e.g., Rawls 1972), yet there are also other correlates of inequality that suggest a highly unequal society might be problematic. For example, there is a negative correlation between economic growth and inequality across countries (Persson and Tabellini 1994). People who live in more unequal cities say that they are less happy (Luttmer 2005). Murder rates are higher in more unequal places (Daly, Wilson, and Vasdev 2001).

Yet it is not obvious that there are any easy ways to reduce inequality at the city level. After first discussing the measurement of inequality and some of the evidence on the impact of inequality, this chapter reviews the economic determinants of inequality at a local level. Pretax income inequality is generally understood as reflecting the distribution of skills in the population and the returns to skill. Over the past twenty-five years, economists have focused on the rise in the returns to skill, which itself reflects the impact of new technologies and globalization (see, e.g., Katz and Murphy 1992).

Inequality today does reflect more than just historical skill patterns. Many of the most unequal places got that way by attracting particularly large numbers of less skilled immigrants. This does not reflect badly on these communities. Those immigrants are presumably attracted to these areas because they provide economic opportunity and a socially comfortable milieu. The role that recent immigration plays in urban inequality reminds us that cities are, in part, unequal because they manage to attract both skilled and unskilled people, which is in many ways a reflection of urban strength.

The distribution of inequality across urban areas does not just reflect the distribution of skills; it also reflects the returns to skill. Highly skilled people are rewarded more in some places than in others. When skills are rewarded more strongly, then inequality increases. However, we understand little about why the returns to skill are steeper in some places than in others. The presence of industries that reward their most successful people well, such as computers or finance, has some ability to explain differences in the returns to skill across metropolitan areas. There is also a connection between the share of the population with college degrees and the returns to having a college degree. That fact, however, implies nothing about the direction of causality.

In the final section, we turn to the interaction between government policy and the level of inequality. At the national level, there are three possible channels that can be used to reduce the level of inequality. The first and most direct tool is taxes and redistribution. By directly taking money from the rich and giving it to the poor, after-tax income inequality can be reduced. There is no question that this type of policy can be effective at reducing inequality, although many economists have emphasized that there are numerous less attractive consequences of taxation, such as the reduction of the returns to innovation and effort. There are also good reasons to doubt that the American political system will suddenly swing and adopt a European welfare model.

The second tool for fighting inequality is industrial policy. By supporting industries, that pay their less skilled workers more, such as heavy manufacturing, it is often hoped that inequality can be reduced. However, there are many good reasons to think that this type of industrial policy is quite problematic. Subsidizing one industry means that the government is trying to pick winners, and it is not clear that the government is very good at that. Moreover, many of the beneficiaries of industrial policy will end up being the shareholders in the affected companies rather than low-wage workers. There are certainly good reasons to be skeptical about this type of policy even at the national level.

The third tool for fighting inequality is education policy. By spending resources on human capital, it is possible to make the distribution of human capital more equal. Certainly the higher levels of equality in European countries reflect, in part, the more equal distributions of skills within those nations. Moreover, people born into poor European families are more likely to exit poverty than comparable Americans. This high exit rate reflects the power of education to offer opportunity. However, the local administration of education within the U.S. inevitably means that national attempts to equalize the school distribution must interact with local governments.

In the second half of the final section, we turn from national policy to local

policy. Our first point is that even a strong egalitarian who desperately wishes for
equality at the national level may not approve of policies that create equality at the
local level. Increasing equality at the local level, while leaving national inequality
untouched, requires the sorting of likes with likes. Local equality is created if rich
people live with rich people and poor people live with poor people. Segregation by
income is another word for this kind of local equality and there are many reasons
to think that this type of segregation is to be avoided rather than pursued.

Our second point about local inequality is that attempts at income redistribution
can be far more problematic at the local level than they are at the national level.
When localities tax businesses and the rich to give to the poor, then the firms and
the wealthy can easily leave. The net result is not that the poor have more resources,
but instead that the poor do not have any neighbors who are more financially successful, which surely makes things worse. Mobility between places implies that
localities face a large barrier to any effective local redistribution.

Moving beyond local income redistribution to local industrial policy does not
lead to more hopeful conclusions. There are many reasons to think that local industrial policy is likely to be even less successful than national industrial policy.
Manufacturing has generally been correlated with urban decline over the past
thirty years (Glaeser, Scheinkman, and Shleifer 1995), which suggests that trying
to artificially augment the size of a city's manufacturing sector is unlikely to yield
attractive results. Localities survive by continually reinventing themselves. As it is
hard enough for sophisticated venture capitalists to wisely invest in the next new
thing, city officials are likely to be far worse at picking winners.

Localities do, however, have a natural role to play in any attempt to reduce
inequality. Changing the distribution of human capital will surely provide the best
means of reducing inequality in the long run. In the United States, school districts
are run at the local level, and this is likely to continue for the foreseeable future.
If America is going to have a more equal human capital distribution, then there
must be a more equal distribution of skills, which is likely to be achieved only by
improving the quality of education among the lowest performing schools.

Improving local schools provides a means of making the distribution of human
capital more equal, but it is doubtful that this can be achieved with only local resources. The problems facing troubled school districts are just too enormous to be
fixed independently. State governments and the federal government already transfer
resources across districts, and these transfers suggest a path toward a hybrid school
model that uses national resources and local management to reduce inequality in
cities and the country as a whole.

The Measurement of Inequality and Changes over Time

The data used in this chapter are taken from the 5 percent 1980 and 2000 Census
Integrated Public-Use Micro-Samples (IPUMS) (Ruggles et al. 2008). We use total
pretax household income as our measure of income. This means that one person

households and multiperson households are treated identically.[2] The Census top-codes income at $999,998 in 2000 and $75,000 in 1980. This top-coding causes our measures to understate the true amount of income inequality. The rise in the upper limit of measured income also means that standard measures of income inequality may well overstate the increase in inequality between 1980 and 2000.

The general measure of income inequality is the Gini coefficient, defined as

$1 - \dfrac{1}{\hat{y}} \int_y (1 - F(y))^2 dy$, where $\hat{y}$ is the mean income in the sample and $F(y)$ is the

share of the population with income levels less than y. This measure is the area between the forty-five-degree curve (which indicates perfect equality) and the Lorenz curve.[3] It ranges from zero (perfect equality) to one (all income is in the hands of one household). There are other attractive measures of inequality. Some of these, such as the share of income earned by the top 1 percent or 5 percent of the income distribution, are made difficult to use because of the top-coding of the U.S. Census. We are confident that other measures of income inequality are quite correlated with the Gini coefficient, so we adhere to this "industry standard" throughout the rest of the chapter.

We calculated Gini coefficients for 242 metropolitan areas in 1980 and a somewhat larger sample of metropolitan areas in 2000. Metropolitan areas are county or multicounty units defined by the U.S. Census. We have used the Census definition in each year instead of using a common county-level definition across decades.[4]

The most striking fact about inequality across America's metropolitan areas is that it is relatively large and rising. The average Gini coefficient across our sample of metropolitan areas is .44, which is roughly higher than the Gini coefficient in about 33 percent of the world's countries.[5] This fact is particularly striking since geographic subareas should generally be more equal than entire nations, as these subareas have residents who have sorted across space within a country.

Figure 5.1 graphs the Gini coefficient for 242 metropolitan areas estimated from the 1980 Census against the Gini coefficient from the 2006 American Community Survey, the most recent data available. For comparison, we also plot the forty-five-degree line. In every metropolitan area, except for Ocala, Florida, the Gini coefficient is higher today than it was twenty-six years ago. This rise parallels the increase in inequality in the country as a whole, which has been documented and analyzed in a rich literature (e.g., Katz and Murphy 1992).

Why has inequality been rising across American metropolitan areas? At the national level, economists have generally interpreted the rise in inequality as an increase in the returns to skill. Over the past thirty years, the wage difference between college graduates and high school dropouts has been rising steadily. Income heterogeneity within groups of people with similar educational levels has also been rising, and that has been interpreted as an increase in the returns to unmeasured human capital quality (Juhn, Murphy, and Pierce 1993).

Why has there been an increase in the returns to skill? Typically, the literature

Figure 5.1   **Gini Coefficient in 2006 and 1980**

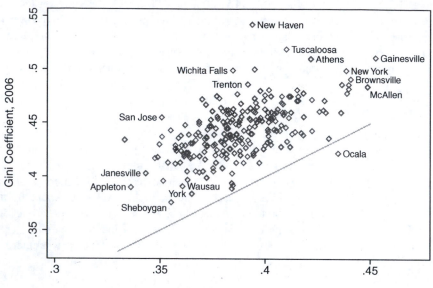

Gini Coefficient, 1980

Sources: 1980 Gini coefficients are calculated from the 5 percent Integrated Public Use Microdata Series (IPUMS) for 1980, at usa.ipums.org. 2006 Gini coefficients are from the 2006 American Community Survey.

Notes: The line shown is the forty-five-degree line, *not* a fitted regression. Only some data-points are labeled with their Metropolitan Statistical Area (MSA) names to aid readability.

has focused on new technologies such as computerization (e.g., Krueger 1993) or international trade. The trade hypothesis appeals to political advocates of protec-tionism, who argue that trade barriers will increase the wages paid to less-skilled American workers. However, many analyses of trade and inequality have suggested that globalization has played only a modest role in increasing inequality.

While increases in the returns to skill are the standard interpretation of changes in inequality over time, differences in the distribution of skills across space are at least as important in explaining differences in the level of inequality in urban areas. We will turn to these issues in the next section, but first note that the nature of urban inequality does seem to have changed somewhat over the past twenty-six years. Figure 5.2 shows the correlation between the Gini coefficient and family income in 1980. In that year, poverty and inequality went hand in hand. Metropolitan areas were unequal when they had a large number of poor people.

Figure 5.3 shows the same relationship for 2006. Today, inequality is much less correlated with low income levels. This shift represents a change in the nature of urban inequality. While in 1980 inequality was driven by the poorest Americans, today inequality is also driven by the number of very rich Americans. Because the

Figure 5.2   **Gini Coefficient and Log Median Family Income, 1980**

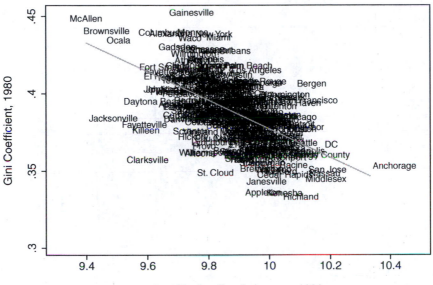

Sources: Gini coefficients are calculated using the 5 percent Integrated Public Use Microdata Series (IPUMS) for 1980, at usa.ipums.org. Median family income is from the 1980 Census.

rich have gotten so much richer over the past twenty-five years, the ability of the rich to drive local inequality figures has also become greater.

This very fact, though, should perhaps make public officials cautious about trying to reduce inequality at the local level. Inequality is driven, in part, by the number of wealthier people in a metropolitan area. Inequality could be reduced if wealthier Americans were to leave the area. Yet inducing an area's highest earning and highest taxpaying citizens to leave does not sound like a recipe for urban success. Few mayors are likely to think that their city will benefit if equality is increased by shedding high earners. Indeed, such urban leaders might consider the benefits of more wealthy taxpayers to be such that they seek to increase inequality by attracting the prosperous.

The Costs of Inequality

At the national level, there is an abundance of evidence suggesting that inequality carries costs. Glaeser (2005) summarizes this literature, which finds that more unequal places grow more slowly (e.g., Alesina and Rodrik 1994; Persson and Tabellini 1994). One interpretation of this fact is that political systems function less well in highly unequal places. These places may engage in redistributive efforts

Figure 5.3   **Relationship Between Gini Coefficient and Log Median Family Income, 2006**

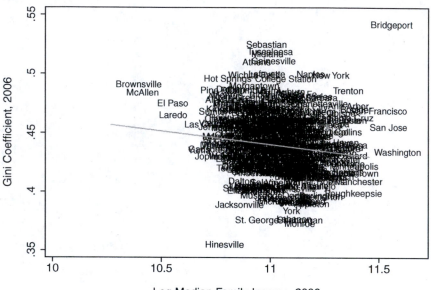

Log Median Family Income, 2006

Source: 2006 American Community Survey.

that reduce the incentives to invest or work hard. If this interpretation is correct, then it may not be inequality per se that is bad for economic growth, but rather the attempts to reduce inequality through government policies.

Alternatively, high levels of inequality may be associated with breakdowns in the rule of law. This hypothesis suggests that the super-rich have the resources to subvert justice (Glaeser, Scheinkman, and Shleifer 2003), which causes a breakdown in the legal order, which in turn reduces everyone's incentive to invest in human or physical capital. You and Khagram (2005) show an empirical connection between the level of inequality in a country and the level of corruption.

The link between inequality and corruption is just one example of a more pervasive correlation between inequality and crime. Fajnzylber, Lederman, and Loayza (2002), for example, show a correlation between country-level crime, particularly murder rates, and inequality. Daly, Wilson, and Vasdev (2001) also look at city-level data and show the connection between inequality and homicide. Figure 5.4 shows the positive correlation between murder rates and the Gini coefficient across metropolitan areas in 2000. There is a 35 percent correlation.

A final cost of inequality may be that people are just less happy in more unequal societies. Perhaps, the human tendency toward envy becomes more extreme when we live around people who are much wealthier than ourselves. Luttmer (2005) used

Figure 5.4   **Murder Rate and the Gini Coefficient, 2000**

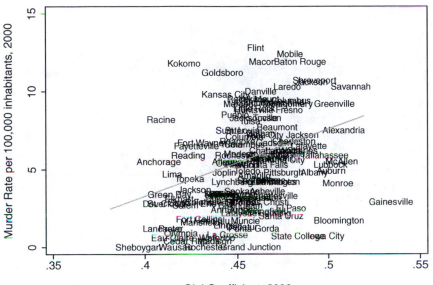

Gini Coefficient, 2000

Sources: Gini coefficients are calculated using the 5 percent Integrated Public Use Microdata Series (IPUMS) for 2000, at usa.ipums.org. Murder rates are from the FBI's Uniform Crime Reports.

self-reported happiness data and found that individuals do report themselves to be less happy when they live around people who are richer than themselves. Across metropolitan areas, inequality is strongly correlated with unhappiness (Glaeser, Resseger, and Tobio 2008).

While inequality certainly seems to have costs, the impact of metropolitan area economic success is less clear. Glaeser, Resseger, and Tobio (2008) look at the extent to which high levels of inequality, measured with the Gini coefficient, are negatively associated with metropolitan area growth in either population or income. When we do not control for the human capital distribution, we find that inequality is actually positively correlated with population growth and weakly negatively associated with growth. When we do control for the share of the population who have college and high school degrees, then inequality is negatively correlated with both population and income growth.

These findings essentially reflect the fact that education, specifically the share of the population with a college degree, is a very strong predictor of urban success, measured by either population growth or income growth (Glaeser and Saiz 2004). Figure 5.5 shows the correlation between share of the population with college degrees in 1980 and income growth since that date. Abundant quantities of college graduates are related to more inequality and faster growth. When we control for

Figure 5.5   **Median Income Growth and Initial Skill Level**

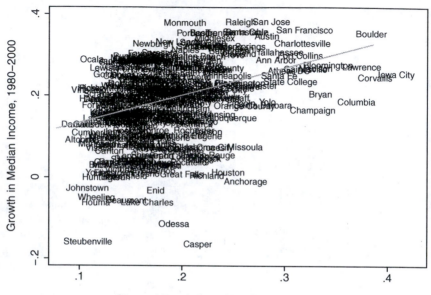

Source: 1980 and 2000 U.S. Census.

the tendency of skilled places to grow faster, then inequality does indeed appear to be negatively correlated with urban success.

These results therefore suggest that skill inequality is not particularly negatively associated with urban success. Places with lots of highly skilled people, which are more unequal as a result, have done extremely well over the past twenty-five years. The negative association between inequality and skills occurs only when we hold the skill distribution constant. We now turn to the causes of metropolitan-level inequality.

The Causes of Metropolitan Inequality

Labor economics views wages as returns on human capital (e.g., Becker 1964). Inequality in wages, or earnings, will therefore reflect inequality of human capital and the returns to human capital. One place may be more unequal than another either because it has a more unequal distribution of skills or because the returns to skill are higher in that place. In this section, we attempt to show that different levels of inequality across American metropolitan areas can be understood as reflecting, to a large extent, differences in the skill distribution across those areas. We also examine differences in returns to human capital.

There is a strong correlation between the inequality of an area and the human capital distribution in that area. A simple regression where the Gini coefficient is regressed on the share of adults over the age of twenty-five with college degrees and share of adults who are high school dropouts yields:

Gini coefficient = .63 + .22 * Share with BA + .29 * *Share without HS diploma*   (1)
$\qquad$ (.02) $\qquad$ (.02) $\qquad\qquad\qquad\qquad$ (.03)

Standard errors are in parentheses. There are 285 observations. The *r*-squared from this regression is 34 percent, meaning that these two coarse measures of human capital can explain a third of the variation in inequality across metropolitan areas.

Figure 5.6 shows this relationship graphically. Here we have regressed the Gini coefficient on the sum of the share of the population with college degrees and the share of the population who did not graduate from high school. This aggregate schooling measure can explain 32 percent of the variation in the Gini coefficient. The skill distribution explains a great deal of the variation in inequality across places.

The skill distribution may also be capturing some of the differences in returns to skill, if skilled people move to areas where the returns to skill are high. To address this possibility, we have calculated a Gini coefficient based only on human capital measures, which assumes that everyone is earning what people with their education levels earn on average in the nation. This modified Gini coefficient captures the degree of inequality implied only by the skill distribution, assuming that the returns to skill were the same everywhere. Glaeser, Resseger, and Tobio (2008) find that this measure can explain about one-third of the variation in the total Gini coefficient across space.

While this still leaves two-thirds of the variation in urban inequality unexplained, this skill-only Gini uses only the very coarsest measures of skill, without any controls for school quality or skills acquired outside of school. If we use occupations as a measure of skill, instead of years of schooling, we can explain almost three-quarters of the variation in the inequality across metropolitan areas. This may be an overstatement of the importance of the skill distribution, but it still suggests the tight link between workplace human capital and inequality.

Why do some places have so much more skill inequality than others? Researchers such as Simon and Nardinelli (1996) and Moretti (2004) have shown that skill levels are remarkably persistent over time. The occupation mix in the nineteenth century can explain skill levels today. Moretti shows that having a land grant college before 1940 explains which places are more skilled now.

Figure 5.7 shows the relationship between the share of the population who were college graduates in 1940 and the share of the population who were college graduates in the year 2000. The college share of the population in 1940 is able to explain more than 50 percent of the variation in the college share today, which implies that historical accidents still shape the skill composition of metropolitan areas. Measures of human capital from 1940 can explain a significant amount of the variation in inequality across metropolitan areas. While this permanence may

Figure 5.6   **Gini Coefficient and Sum of High School Dropouts and College Graduates, 2000**

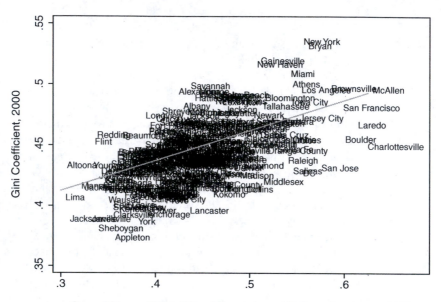

Sum of Share of High School Dropouts and College Graduates, 2000

Sources: Gini coefficients are calculated using the 5 percent Integrated Public Use Microdata Series (IPUMS) for 2000, at usa.ipums.org. Share of high school dropouts and college graduates is from the 2000 U.S. Census.

not be surprising, it suggests that any attempts to shift the skill distribution may take decades to have a discernible impact.

Nineteenth-century skill measures can also explain skills today. For example, the share of the population enrolled in college in 1850 can explain about one-tenth of the variation in the share of the adult population with college degrees today. Variables from 1850 can also explain a portion of the variation in the overall inequality measure (Glaeser, Resseger, and Tobio 2008).

Americans are an enormously mobile people. According to the 2006 American Community Survey, 7 percent of the U.S. population live in a different county or country than they did only one year ago, and 21 percent of the population live in a different county or country than they did five years ago. Given this mobility, it is somewhat surprising that education variables from 150 years ago are still able to explain the levels of inequality today. The key to understanding this puzzle is that skilled people have increasingly been migrating to places with more skilled people (Berry and Glaeser 2005). This fact is visible in Figure 5.7, which has a slope of three, meaning that as the share of adults with college degrees increases by 5 percent in 1940, the share of adults with college degrees goes up by 10 percent

Figure 5.7   **Share of Adults with College Degrees, 1940 and 2000**

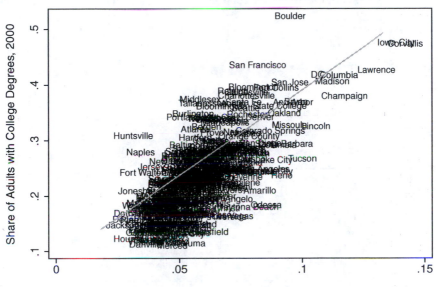

Source: Share of adults with college degrees in 2000 is from the 2000 U.S. Census. Share of adults with college degrees in 1940 is from Haines (2004).

in 2000. Since initial skills predict the growth in skills, we should not be surprised that these historical variables are so powerful.

We do not know why skilled people are increasingly migrating to places with more skilled people. We do know that the wage premium associated with being around skilled people is high and rising. This effect is often referred to as human capital spillovers, an expression which means that one person's skills enhance the skills of people who work nearby. We also know that skill premium increases with the level of human capital in the area, meaning that college graduates particularly benefit from working around other college graduates. The tendency of college graduates to move toward one another probably reflects the fact that their economic productivity rises from living near one another.

One variant of this hypothesis, advanced by Berry and Glaeser (2005), is that high human capital entrepreneurs increasingly innovate in ways that employ other highly skilled people. A century ago, Henry Ford's innovations created jobs for hundreds of thousands of less skilled Americans. Today, Bill Gates's innovations create many jobs for highly skilled software engineers. The increased tendency of skilled people to cluster together in particular industries supports the importance of this hypothesis.

The skill distribution, however, does not only reflect historical forces. Immigration, especially of less skilled workers, also predicts inequality.

Figure 5.8   **Relationship between Share of Adult HS Dropouts and Share of Hispanic Population, 2000**

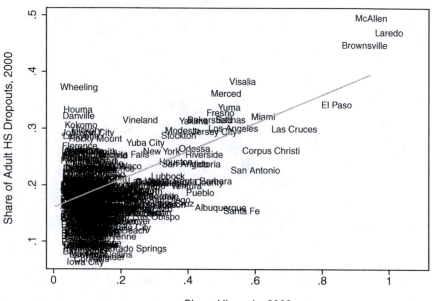

Source: 2000 U.S. Census.

Figure 5.8 shows the 57 percent correlation between the share of the population that is Hispanic and the share of the population without a high school degree. The correlation between percent Hispanic and the Gini coefficient is .25. Some of the most unequal places in America are close to the Mexican border; the correlation between Hispanic share and latitude is −.36.

The connection between inequality and Hispanic immigration emphasizes one of the problems with looking only at local inequality. When immigrants from poor countries come to the United States, the inequality of American cities may well increase at the same time that global inequality declines. If these immigrants earn more in the United States than they did in Mexico, then the world's poor are getting richer through immigration and global inequality is falling. Any attempt to decrease American inequality by reducing the flow of immigrants will only increase inequality worldwide.

Inequality does not just reflect differences in the skill distribution. There are also differences in the returns to skill across space. Figure 5.9 shows the 73 percent correlation between our estimated return to a college degree and the Gini coefficient across the 102 areas with more than 500,000 people. Places that pay a higher premium to college graduates are more unequal, both because they attract more skilled people and because skilled people earn high wages in those areas.

Figure 5.9   **Gini Coefficient and Returns to College, 2000**

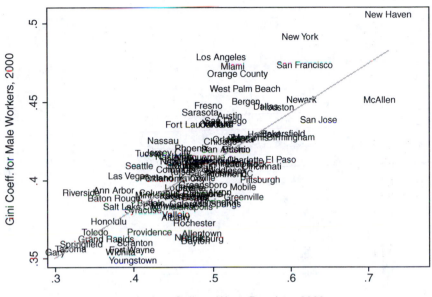

Log College Wage Premium, 2000

Source: Data are calculated using the 5 percent Integrated Public Use Microdata Series (IPUMS) for 2000, at usa.ipums.org.

A more sophisticated procedure is to calculate a Gini coefficient holding the human capital distribution constant across space, but to estimate different returns to skill in every metropolitan area. To do this, we run individual-level regressions for the entire United States allowing the returns to having a high school or college degree to differ across space. We then calculate a Gini coefficient for every metropolitan area, holding the skill distribution constant, but allowing the returns to skill to differ. We find that we can explain about half of the variation in inequality with our skills-constant Gini coefficient. This result emphasizes that inequality should be understood as reflecting both differences in the skill distribution and differences in the returns to skill.

Unfortunately, we know little about why the returns to human capital differ so much over space. Industrial concentration can explain some of this variation. For example, places with a greater concentration in finance or technology have higher returns to human capital. Figure 5.10 shows the correlation between the share of the population who work in the computer industry and the wage premium associated with having a college degree. This high-tech sector has yielded particularly strong returns to skilled workers, and areas that focus on new technology have higher levels of inequality as a result.

Figure 5.10   **Returns to Schooling and Share of Workers in Computers, 2000**

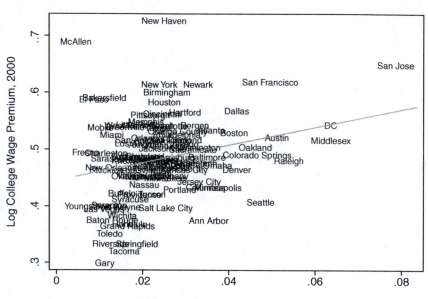

Source: Data are calculated using the 5 percent Integrated Public Use Microdata Series (IPUMS) for 2000, at usa.ipums.org.

There is also a strong correlation between the share of the population with college degrees and the returns to having a college degree, as shown in Figure 5.11. This fact might reflect human capital spillovers. The historical concentration of skilled people in an area may well be causing the productivity of skilled people in that area to rise. However, an alternative interpretation of this fact is that skilled people move to areas where the returns to skill are high. There is no obvious way to determine what is causing what, so this topic must remain an area for future research.

The levels of inequality in metropolitan areas reflect both the returns to skill and the distribution of skills. The returns to skill reflect the industries in an area, and other factors that we do not fully understand. The skill distribution reflects long-standing historical tendencies that have only been exacerbated by the tendency of skilled people to migrate near other skilled people. Inequality in skills is also higher in places that have attracted large numbers of Hispanic immigrants.

Government Policy

We now turn to the main focus of this chapter: the connection between government policy and inequality. We have, in fact, already touched on the role that government

Figure 5.11   Returns to College and the Percent of Residents with a College Degree, 2000

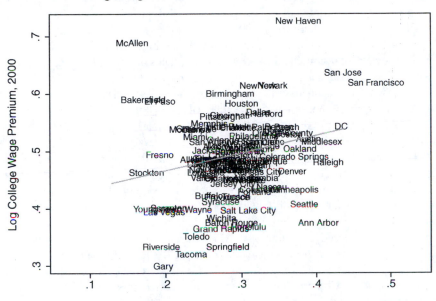

Source: Data are calculated using the 5 percent Integrated Public Use Microdata Series (IPUMS) for 2000, at usa.ipums.org.

policy can play in causing inequality. Immigration policy, for example, determines the flow of immigrants to American cities. Education policy helps determine the levels of skill in different metropolitan areas. We now turn to the ways in which governmental actions might reduce the level of inequality in American cities.

The previous discussion has emphasized that not all reductions in urban inequality are good and not all increases in inequality are bad. If an influx of highly talented entrepreneurs comes to a city, this may both increase employment and increase inequality. Many big city mayors would happily accept the rise in inequality in exchange for the extra economic health. Likewise, an increase in economic vitality in high-skilled industries may increase both inequality and income levels. Ideally, egalitarian policies would not significantly reduce economic growth.

We begin our discussion with national egalitarian policies and then turn to more local responses toward inequality.

National Policies Toward Income Inequality

There are three natural channels through which the national government can impact inequality. First, and most directly, the government can engage in taxes and redistribution. Second, the government can engage in industrial policy meant to strengthen those industries that increase the incomes of poorer Americans. Third, the government can attempt to equalize the skill distribution by improving the education level of the least fortunate.

At the national level, there is little doubt that taxing the rich and giving to the poor can create more equality. The robust welfare states in much of Europe illustrate that a heavy-handed state policy can reduce the gaps between rich and poor. Typically, these governments have higher tax rates on their wealthier citizens and then spend considerably more money, as a share of gross domestic product, on social services (Alesina and Glaeser 2004). The United States has followed a different path. Our redistributive policies have been far milder.

The typical discussion of large-scale national redistribution pits equality against economic efficiency. Certainly, there is a large economic literature suggesting that heavy tax rates and a generous welfare state can reduce work effort, innovation, and economic growth. There is still a robust debate on the magnitude of the effects of these policies, but ultimately economics cannot tell us whether there should be more or less tax-based redistribution in America. The optimal level of redistribution depends on how much Americans want to do for the less fortunate, and that is a question that is more the province of moral philosophy than economics. Certainly, the American track record does not suggest that Americans are eager to emulate the European model.

Regardless of what America should do, there is little evidence to suggest that Americans will adopt large-scale redistribution anytime soon. A combination of factors has historically led the United States away from a European-style welfare state. Alesina and Glaeser (2004) argue that the relatively modest American welfare state reflects the combination of American political institutions and racial fractionalization. Across countries, there is a strong negative connection between ethnic heterogeneity and the amount of social welfare spending. Voters seem to be much more enthusiastic about supporting redistribution if that redistribution helps people of their own race (Luttmer 2001). America has significantly more internal ethnic fractionalization than individual European countries, and this fact is one reason why the United States has historically had less redistribution.

American institutions also act to reduce the size of the welfare state. The American Constitution is actually much older than its continental European counterparts, and it was designed in the eighteenth century, in part, to check the power of government. For 220 years, it has served that function. By contrast, the majority of European constitutions were rewritten in the twentieth century, often in the wake of world wars when social democrats had the upper hand. As a result, these constitutions have institutions, such as proportional representation, that seem to empower left-wing parties. American majoritarianism and a strong system of checks and balances seem likely to limit redistribution for the foreseeable future.

Governments have also been attracted to industrial policies, such as protectionism, that can indirectly reduce inequality by supporting the demand for low-skilled labor. At the time that this chapter was written, the U.S. government contemplated significant aid to the automobile industry, justified in part by the possibility that such aid would ensure employment for industrial workers. In some cases, industrial policies may be more politically feasible than direct redistribution because such policies bring together labor unions and management, since both groups benefit from governmental support. The costs, of course, are borne by the diffuse group of U.S. taxpayers.

There are two good reasons, however, to be skeptical about such industrial policies. First, the benefits of such policies do not necessarily accrue strongly toward workers. While it is certainly true that low-cost loans to auto manufacturers will help auto workers, company shareholders and upper management will also reap the benefits from these policies. Some of the gains from the policy may also come to car buyers. Moreover, unionized automobile workers are hardly among the poorest Americans. While direct redistribution can target aid toward the poor, industrial policy benefits a wide range of individuals, only some of whom are at the bottom or middle level of the income distribution. If the goal is to increase equality, then economists have almost universally argued that doing so through the tax system, with programs like the Earned Income Tax Credit, is more efficient than targeting aid toward a particular industry.

Moreover, standard economic analysis raises significant doubts about whether the benefits of these policies outweigh the costs. In the case of a direct subsidy, taxpayers foot the bill in the form of higher tax liabilities. In the case of a protectionist tariff, the costs are borne by consumers. It is theoretically possible that tariff barriers can yield benefits for a country either because of learning-by-doing in an infant industry, or by changing the terms of trade. Yet the overwhelming share of economic research has argued that, in practice, trade barriers cost consumers more than they benefit producers.

Subsidies for specific industries generally move workers from more productive occupations to less productive occupations. There is a loss to the taxpayers and an efficiency loss from misallocated production. Does it really make sense to use tax dollars to essentially bribe workers to stay in the automobile industry if that industry is not able to compete on the global market?

The third public policy that can reduce inequality is to improve education for disadvantaged Americans. Investing in education does not generally have the adverse consequences for effort or investment that are the by-product of redistribution through the tax system. Investing in education is generally far more politically palatable in the United States than more direct redistribution. Moreover, if the human capital of the poor can be improved, then this will have a lasting impact on the wealth distribution that does not require constant redistribution throughout the lifecycle.

The economic literature on human capital spillovers also suggests that investing in education can create benefits for society as a whole. Economic growth at the country level is strongly linked to average years of schooling (see, e.g., Barro

1992). Many economists believe in the evidence of Rauch (1993) and Moretti (2004) showing the existence of human capital spillovers. If those spillovers exist, then private investments in education will be suboptimal, since private individuals would not internalize the benefits that their investment has on other workers.

Of course, investing in education does not always reduce inequality. If public investment in education in particular enhances the skills at the top end of the human capital distribution, then this investment will increase rather than decrease inequality. For example, Moretti (2004) shows that the presence of a land grant college in a metropolitan area prior to 1940 is positively correlated with the skill level of the area today. When we regress the area Gini coefficient on Moretti's land grant college indicator variable, controlling for area population, income, and the share of adults who are high school dropouts, we find a positive, but statistically insignificant, impact of land grant colleges on inequality. This effect disappears when we control for share of adults with college degrees, which implies that this variable (weakly) increases inequality because it increases the share of more skilled people.

If the aim is to decrease inequality, then it is necessary to invest in the education of the less fortunate. Increasing high school graduation rates, rather than college attendance, is more likely to reduce the level of inequality in society. We find a modest negative relationship between current high school enrollment rates and inequality when we control for area income and area population.[6] Indeed, many federal interventions into public education such as Head Start and No Child Left Behind have been particularly targeted toward the less advantaged in the hope that more education would reduce inequality.

While there is little doubt that skills determine income, and there is some political enthusiasm for improving the education of the less fortunate, it is less clear how to fix failing school systems. A long literature finds that student achievement is relatively independent of school spending. This finding may just reflect the fact that we spend more in troubled areas, but it is likely that just adding money will achieve little. Smaller class sizes have produced results (Krueger 1999), but this is an extremely expensive approach to the problem. Improving education may well be the most effective long-run means of reducing inequality, but it is not easy to improve education.

The problem of education reform is made even more difficult because education is itself administered at the local level. As a result, federal attempts at improving education must negotiate a highly heterogeneous nation where decisions are made at the very local level. One approach to this problem is to use federal aid to provide incentives to local schools, as in No Child Left Behind. A second approach is to directly provide federal programs that bypass local school authorities entirely, as in the case of Head Start. We now turn to local policies toward inequality.

Local Policies Toward Inequality

The best local policies are not the same as the best national policies. There is a whole host of issues created by the free mobility of people and firms across space.

The tendency of migration to respond to government policies means that local governments face limits (Peterson 1981) that are different from those faced by the federal government. In particular, many local attempts at redistribution can be completely counterproductive because taxpayers have an exit option.

At the national level, people may work or invest less when taxes rise, but they are unlikely to leave the country altogether. Limits on immigration mean that America does not attract all the world's poor when it has a more generous welfare state. However, at the local level, attempts to raise taxes to give to the poor can repel the rich and attract the less advantaged. The net result is a reduced tax base and increased segregation. Neither outcome is desirable.

There is a long economic literature suggesting that different local government policies have the ability to induce selective migration. For example, Borjas (1999) argues that heterogeneity in welfare policies across space has had a huge impact on the location patterns of less-skilled immigrants, and especially their tendency to locate in California. Blank (1988) also found that higher welfare levels impact the location decision of unmarried women with children. This type of effect can explain the poverty of East St. Louis, which traditionally had higher welfare payments because it lies on the Illinois side of the Mississippi River within the St. Louis metropolitan area.

Less work has been done on the impact of redistribution on the location decisions of the rich, but what evidence does exist supports the view that the wealthy are quite mobile and respond to attempts at redistribution. Certainly, within metropolitan areas, there are good reasons to think that the rich are sensitive to local tax rates and the bundle of local public goods. The strong tendency of richer people to live outside of city borders suggests that they are voting with their feet within certain areas. Haughwout et al. (2004) argue that these migration tendencies are quite strong and can mean that areas actually lose revenue by raising taxes. Feldstein and Wrobel (1998) argue that the migration elasticities are so strong that states cannot effectively redistribute income at all. This type of result supports the view that local governments can affect local inequality by moving people more than they can by classical redistribution.

It is possible that local tax policy could increase local inequality, but it is not obvious that such tools would enhance welfare. For example, the previous section suggested that much of the heterogeneity in income inequality across metropolitan areas was associated with differences in returns to skill. Localities could equalize local incomes by reducing the returns to skill through more redistributive taxation. Redistribution would both directly reduce inequality by giving from rich to poor, and indirectly reduce inequality by inducing wealthier people to leave the area. Few localities would actually find it attractive to increase equality by getting rid of the biggest taxpayers. While this migration effect might reduce inequality, if it eliminated the richest people in the city, there are many reasons to think that it would also hurt the area's economy.

Variants of industrial policy also exist at the local level. Sometimes localities are drawn toward subsidizing a particular type of industry, with public infrastructure such as a science park. In other cases, localities bid to try to attract a particular plant, or to try to keep a large employer from leaving. In most cases, these policies have little to do with inequality. When locales try to create a biotechnology cluster, they are trying to bring in high-earning workers who are more likely to increase inequality than to reduce it. Of course, this does not make such policies mistaken. While economists have typically been suspicious about attempts to micromanage industrial development, discussing the evidence on these policies is not the subject of this chapter.

Bidding for industrial plants is, however, often seen as a means of boosting demand for less-skilled labor, which can more properly be seen as an anti-inequality policy. Recent evidence by Greenstone and Moretti (2004) shows positive effects on wages in those localities that win bidding wars for million-dollar plants. However, these results can be interpreted only as indicating the benefits for the narrow set of localities that were in the bidding process to begin with. The findings do not suggest that older industrial towns, which typically were not in the bidding process, are likely to benefit from trying to retain manufacturing. After all, there are good reasons why manufacturing plants have been steadily leaving these places.

At the local level, just as at the national level, greater welfare gains would seem to be associated with policies that enhance the skills of the less fortunate. Improvements in school districts and reductions in the size of the criminal sector could have two possible benefits. First, they might increase the skill levels at the bottom end of the income distribution. Second, they might attract middle-income people into the area. Local policies that strengthen the bottom of the income distribution without targeting the top of the income distribution seem most likely to reduce income inequality without creating other problems.

However, while such policies might well be beneficial, local governments have again only a limited ability to make the nationwide skill distribution more equal. Areas with many poor parents have fewer resources with which to educate their children. These places have lower tax revenues, holding everything else constant, and also have less parental human capital on which to draw. The long-noted power of peers means that places with lower initial skill distributions inevitably have difficulty creating first-rate public schools.

The current structure of local public schooling creates incentives for middle-income people to leave big cities to get better schools for their children. The very rich, who send their children to private schools, and the poor remain. There could be welfare gains from an education system that keeps the advantages of choice and competition that are associated with the current system but that also reduces the incentive for middle-class parents to leave big cities.

This fact is the great challenge facing attempts to reduce inequality through schooling. Our schools are local, and localities have a great deal of trouble dealing with inequality. Poor places have fewer resources to allocate to their schools. Yet if there is going to be a more equal education distribution, then their schools must be improved. Creating equality in human capital requires the difficult co-operation of national-level education policy and schools that often operate at a very local level.

Conclusion

America is a land with much inequality, and our cities are places that are often particularly unequal. Urban inequality reflects both the distribution of skills and that returns to skill. The distribution of skills in urban areas reflects in part long-standing educational patterns, such as the presence of colleges in the area prior to 1940. In recent years, initial skill advantages have been exacerbated by a trend where skilled workers move to skilled places. Large flows of Hispanic immigrants are also correlated with a more unequal skill distribution.

There are also differences in the returns to skill across place. Higher returns to skill are associated with some industries, such as finance and computers. There are higher returns to skill in places that have more college graduates, but this may reflect the selection of college graduates into these places.

Inequality is a matter for concern. It is positively related to crime. There is a tendency for more unequal places to grow more slowly, once we control for the distribution of skills. Self-reported happiness is lower in more unequal places.

Yet there is only a limited set of policies that can effectively reduce inequality. At the national level, tax-based redistribution is a possibility, but at the local level, this type of redistribution can be quite counterproductive. When cities try to run local welfare states, the wealthy and businesses tend to flee. Local industrial policy is also likely to have a very limited ability to reduce inequality.

Education offers some hope of creating a more equal skill distribution, and more equal skills should eventually lead to a more equal income distribution. However, it is difficult to make the skill distribution more equal. Improving any school is hard, and it is particularly hard for the federal government to manage the nation's decentralized school system. Still, despite these difficulties, investing in human capital seems like the most promising road toward creating a more equal nation.

Notes

All three authors thank the Taubman Center for State and Local Government for financial support.

1. The relationship between inequality and density among America's many counties with extremely low density levels is quite weak.

2. Our income measures, like many in this literature, exclude non-income returns from capital ownership, such as the flow of services associated with owning a home.

3. If we let p denote $F(y)$, that is, the share of the population earning less than y, then the Lorenz curve plots the share of national income going to individuals earning less than $F^{-1}(p)$ as a function of p, that is, $\frac{1}{\hat{y}}\int_{y \le F^{-1}(p)} f(y)y\,dy$.

4. There are advantages and disadvantages that come from using a common county-based definition. A common county-based definition ensures that the geographic area in question does not change across years. However, if the Census's definition of a metropolitan area accurately captures the true labor market, then using a 1980 definition for 2000 or a 2000 definition for 1980 will lead to mismeasurement.

5. Gini coefficients are calculated by the World Bank for 126 countries (UNDP 2009).

6. This result may reflect the tendency of poverty to lead to low enrollment rates or the tendency of middle income people to move to areas with fewer dropouts or the ability of high school graduation to reduce inequality. We do not try to distinguish these hypotheses but just point out that correlations of this form suggest that education policy can surely impact inequality, both by its direct effect on the skill distribution and by shifting migration patterns.

References

Alesina, A., and E.L. Glaeser. 2004. *Fighting Poverty in the U.S. and Europe: A World of Difference.* New York: Oxford University Press.

Alesina, A., and D. Rodrik. 1994. "Distributive Politics and Economic Growth." *Quarterly Journal of Economics* 109, no. 2: 465–90.

Barro, R. 1992. "Human Capital and Economic Growth." *Proceedings, Federal Reserve Bank of Kansas City,* 199–230.

Becker, G.S. 1964. *Human Capital: A Theoretical and Empirical Analysis, with Special Reference to Education.* Chicago: University of Chicago Press.

Berry, C., and E.L. Glaeser. 2005. "The Divergence of Human Capital Levels Across Cities." *Papers in Regional Science* 84, no. 3: 407–44.

Blank, R.M. 1988. "The Effect of Welfare and Wage Levels on the Location Decisions of Female-Headed Households." *Journal of Urban Economics* 24, no. 2: 186–211.

Borjas, G.J. 1999. "Immigration and Welfare Magnets." *Journal of Labor Economics* 17, no. 4: 607–37.

Daly, M.; M. Wilson; and S. Vasdev. 2001. "Income Inequality and Homicide Rates in Canada and the United States." *Canadian Journal of Criminology,* 219–36.

Fajnzylber, P.; D. Lederman; and N. Loayza. 2002. "Inequality and Violent Crime." *Journal of Law and Economics* 45, no. 1: 1–40.

Feldstein, M., and M.V. Wrobel. 1998. "Can State Taxes Redistribute Income?" *Journal of Public Economics* 68, no. 3: 369–96.

Glaeser, E.L. 2005. "Inequality." *NBER Working Papers,* no. 11511 (July).

Glaeser, E.L., and A. Saiz. 2004. "The Rise of the Skilled City." *Brookings-Wharton Papers on Urban Affairs* 5: 47–94.

Glaeser, E.L.; M.G. Resseger; and K. Tobio. 2008. "Urban Inequality." *NBER Working Paper,* no. 14419.

Glaeser, E.L.; J. Scheinkman; and A. Shleifer. 1995. "Economic Growth in a Cross-Section of Cities." *Journal of Monetary Economics* 36, no. 1: 117–43.

———. 2003. "The Injustice of Inequality." *Journal of Monetary Economics* 50, no. 1: 199–222.

Greenstone, M., and E. Moretti. 2004. "Bidding for Industrial Plants: Does Winning a 'Million Dollar Plant' Increase Welfare?" *MIT Department of Economics Working Paper,* no. 04–39.

Haines, M.R. 2004. "Historical, Demographic, Economic, and Social Data: The United States, 1790–2000." Inter-University Consortium for Political and Social Data. Available at www.icpsr.umich.edu/cocoon/ICPSR/STUDY/02896.xml.

Haughwout, A.; R. Inman; S. Craig; and T. Luce. 2004. "Local Revenue Hills: Evidence from Four U.S. Cities." *Review of Economics and Statistics* 86, no. 2: 570–85.

Juhn, C.; K.M. Murphy; and B. Pierce. 1993. "Wage Inequality and the Rise in Returns to Skill." *Journal of Political Economy* 101, no. 3: 410–42.

Katz, L., and K. Murphy. 1992. "Changes in Relative Wages, 1963–1987: Supply and Demand Factors." *Quarterly Journal of Economics* 107, no. 1: 35–78.

Krueger, A.B. 1993. "How Computers Have Changed the Wage Structure: Evidence from Microdata, 1984–1989." *Quarterly Journal of Economics* 108, no. 1: 33–60.

———. 1999. "Experimental Estimates of Education Production Functions." *Quarterly Journal of Economics* 114, no. 2: 497–532.

Luttmer, E.F.P. 2001. "Group Loyalty and the Taste for Redistribution." *Journal of Political Economy* 109, no. 3: 500–528.

———. 2005. "Neighbors as Negatives: Relative Earnings and Well-Being." *Quarterly Journal of Economics* 120, no. 3: 963–1002.

Moretti, E. 2004. "Estimating the Social Return to Higher Education: Evidence from Cross-Sectional and Longitudinal Data.: *Journal of Econometrics* 121, no. 1–2: 175–212.

Peterson, P. 1981. *City Limits*. Chicago: University of Chicago Press.

Persson, T., and G. Tabellini. 1994. "Is Inequality Harmful for Growth?" *American Economic Review* 84, no. 3: 600–621.

Rauch, J.E. 1993. "Productivity Gains from Geographic Concentration of Human Capital: Evidence from the Cities." *Journal of Urban Economics* 34: 380–400.

Rawls, J. 1972. *A Theory of Justice*. Oxford: Clarendon Press.

Ruggles, S.; M. Sobek; T. Alexander; C. Fitch; A. Goeken; R. Hall; P.K. King; and M. Ronnander. 2008. "Integrated Public Use Microdata Series." Available at http://usa.ipums.org/usa/.

Simon, C.J., and C. Nardinelli. 1996. "The Talk of the Town: Human Capital, Information, and the Growth of English Cities, 1861 to 1961." *Explorations in Economic History* 33, no. 3: 384–413.

United Nations Development Programme (UNDP). 2009. "Demographic Trends." *Human Development Report 2009*. Available at http://hdrstats.undp.org/indicators/147.html.

Wheeler, C. 2005. "Cities, Skills, and Inequality." *Growth and Change* 36, no. 3: 329–53.

You, J. and S. Khagram. 2005. "A Comparative Study of Inequality and Corruption." *American Sociological Review* 70, no. 1: 136–57.

6

The Economics of Diversity

Samuel L. Myers, Jr.

Racial and ethnic economic inequality pervades many markets. In the labor market, there are persistent disparities in earnings and labor force participation (Darity and Myers 2000). In housing markets, there are wide racial and ethnic differences in ownership and access to mortgage lending (Ladd 1998; Munnell et al. 1996; Myers and Chan 1995; Myers and Chung 1996; Yinger 1986). In consumer credit markets, there are substantial differences in the terms of loans and approval rates between blacks and whites (Ards and Myers 2001; Hawley and Fujii 1991; Yinger 1998). In public procurement and contracting, where firms compete for federal, state, and local contracts worth billions of dollars for projects such as highway construction, there are huge disparities between white male-owned firms and women- and minority-owned business enterprises (Echaustegui et al. 1997; Myers and Chan 1996; Myers and Ha 2009). These racial and ethnic differences in market outcomes cannot be fully explained by differences in qualifications or human capital endowments alone.

There are also wide racial and ethnic differences in nonmarket and premarket outcomes. African Americans are 3 times more likely to be found in the criminal justice system than they are to be found in the overall population.[1] African American children are 1.6 times more likely to be found in child protective services[2] and 2 times more likely to be found in out-of-home placement than they are to be found in the overall population.[3] Moreover, in the education system there are wide disparities in important outcomes. African Americans are 3 times more likely to be suspended,[4] they are 1.8 more times likely to drop out,[5] and are less likely to graduate than are whites (48 percent vs. 65 percent).[6] Moreover, whereas the average math SAT score for whites is 536; the average for African Americans is 429.[7] In short, on a broad array of metrics, African Americans fare less well in markets and nonmarkets.

Over the past century, these and other instances of racial and ethnic inequality in American society have prompted distinct phases of direct public policy response. Each phase can be assessed based on equity and efficiency criteria. One phase might be called the desegregation phase; another might be called the equal opportunity phase. A next phase might be called the affirmative action phase, which was followed by an affirmative action retrenchment, post–civil rights phase. The current phase, a direct response to the affirmative action retrenchment era, might be called the "diversity phase," where "the case for diversity" is often understood to be a case for race and ethnic inclusiveness based on efficiency grounds.

Efficiency is understood broadly here to mean that a policy option produces net social benefits that exceed the net social benefits of all other alternatives. A looser and less precise notion of efficiency would require that a policy option produce social benefits that exceed its social costs.[8] While it is often difficult to measure social benefits and social costs, one rule of thumb for determining whether there are efficiency gains from a policy is to determine whether it is possible to make one group better off without making another group worse off. The "economic case for diversity" claims that diversity improves overall social welfare by making everyone better off.[9]

This chapter reviews the historical roots of the post–civil rights phase that is prevailing at the beginning of the twenty-first century and details the arguments for and against the diversity case. In particular, the literature exploring the relationship between ethnic diversity and economic development is juxtaposed against the literature on the putative impacts on majority group members from exposure to minorities in increasing the performance of majority members. Regardless of how attractive the case for diversity may be to supporters of affirmative action and equal opportunity, the economic arguments against it must at least be understood.

The central argument of this chapter is that one must be extremely cautious in embracing the "economic case for diversity" in the sense that the economics of diversity reveals contradictory indicators and outcomes. The putative efficiency impacts of diversity at the market level have rarely been formalized or operationalized. Even when evidence of majority group gains from diversity exists, the measured gains to the intended beneficiaries may be minimal. The case for diversity or population heterogeneity at the macro level is also suspect. Analysts point to the inverse relationship between national wealth and racial or ethnic diversity that stems from conflict and intergroup tensions. These economic arguments point to potentially harmful impacts of factors at the macrolevel that produce highly diverse populations. In short, the economic case for diversity hinges on demonstrating that there are net gains to nonminorities or that there are no net losses to society from diversity. Ironically, to date, not much empirical evidence has been fully marshaled to sustain the economic case for diversity.

Historical Underpinnings

The context of current policies intended to increase racial and ethnic diversity in markets is rooted historically in the legal status of African American slaves, indentured servants, and others deprived of basic protections under the law. Until the abolition of slavery, the ratification of the Fourteenth Amendment, and the guarantee of equal protection regardless of race, blacks were considered chattel and were denied rights that were constitutionally afforded to citizens.

> For many white Southerners, however, violence was still the surest means of keeping blacks politically impotent, and in countless communities blacks were not allowed, under penalties of severe reprisals, to show their faces in town on election day. (Franklin and Moss 2000, 282)

Gunnar Myrdal (1996) encapsulated the paradox of the American constitutional framework. The legal architecture and the constitutional guarantees of freedoms given to the American people set the United States apart from many other nations of the world. Yet, its denial of basic freedoms to a sizable portion of the population posed an ongoing dilemma long after slavery was abolished.

This historical legacy of slavery and the denial of equality under the law, even after Emancipation, are the backdrop for the post–World War II period that marshaled a sustained legal effort, undertaken in part by the NAACP Legal and Education Defense Fund and led by Charles Hamilton Houston and Thurgood Marshall (Higginbotham 2005; Myrdal 1996). The period, often called the Civil Rights Era, came at a pivotal economic period of low unemployment accompanied by a surge of migration from southern rural cities to northern industrial centers. The period also overlapped a transformation in technology and a change in labor demand (Noble 1986). The rapid migration of blacks to northern, urban inner cities following World War II combined with the rise of policy-induced suburban housing ownership by the white middle class reproduced in the North the very segregation that existed in the Jim Crow South (Lamb 2005). Efforts designed to eliminate the most blatant vestiges of slavery and segregation included both attempts to provide equality before the law and initiatives to dismantle racial discrimination and state-sponsored segregation. If the era from 1948 to 1989 is called the Civil Rights Era, then the era marked by major Supreme Court reversals beginning in 1989 might be termed the post–Civil Rights Era (Myers 1997).

Phases of the Post–World War II Civil Rights Policies

The entire post–World War II era of Civil Rights might be divided into five distinct phases (see Figure 6.1). The first phase might be termed the desegregation phase. It is during this period that the most vicious forms of *legal* separation of the races, codified and legitimized after the Civil War, were dismantled (Klarman 2007, chap. 3–5). The beginning of this phase rests largely with the *Brown v. Board of Education* (1954) decision by the U.S. Supreme Court that struck down the "separate but equal" doctrine of *Plessey v. Ferguson* (1896). Although the decision focused largely on schooling, its impacts were far-reaching due to the connection between quality schooling and labor markets (Donohue and Heckman 1991; Heckman 1990). The failure of this phase is evidenced by the fact that a half century after the ruling, public schools while no longer segregated by law were nonetheless segregated by housing patterns (Crowley 2006; Hartman and Squires 2006). Conspicuously, the policy of desegregation rested on equity grounds, with little or no attempt to make the case that racial segregation was inefficient.[10]

The passage of the Civil Rights Act of 1964 heralded the equal opportunity and antidiscrimination phase. The act banned segregation in public accommodations and discrimination in employment. The substance of the act was to make illegal discrimination in housing and labor markets in the quest for equal opportunity. The premise was that equal treatment would lead to equal results (Graham 1990).

Figure 6.1   **Five Phases of Post–World War II Civil Rights**

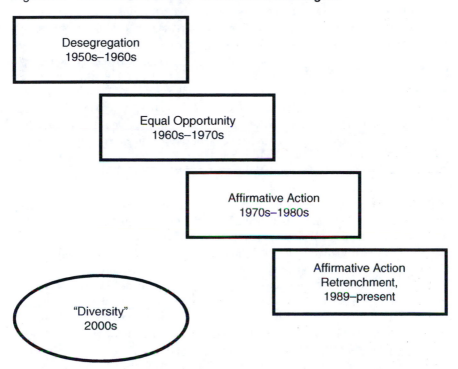

That there were wide racial gaps in earnings and incomes that could not be attributed solely to human capital differences suggested to many analysts that market discrimination was inefficient (Thurow 1969).

The next phase was officially marshaled in by Executive Order 11246 issued by Lyndon Johnson in 1965. It established the foundation for affirmative action in employment in the public and private sectors (Andorra 1998). A careful reading of the original executive order suggests that it was merely an advancement of antidiscrimination objectives (Anderson 1997). In practice, however, employers, colleges and universities, and government contracting and procurement offices rushed to implement affirmative action in ways that might at first glance be regarded as simplistic or mechanistic numerical repositioning. For example, following rules established by the Federal Transit Authority, state and local agencies receiving federal funds for highway and transportation projects established percentage goals for the allocation of funds to women- and minority-owned business enterprises. These numerical goals, often set with no penalty for noncompliance, nevertheless were characterized by critics as "quotas."[11] Arguably many affirmative action plans and timetables involved an expansion of opportunities for underrepresented groups to hear about and apply for openings, which widened recruitment efforts to attract larger pools of qualified candidates, as well as numerical goals and timetables. Some of these affirmative action efforts were in fact court ordered as remedies to specific instances of illegal discrimination. The rationale for these court orders was clearly based on equity considerations. The affirmative action in these cases was a redress or remedy for a prior wrong. Other efforts, however, were broad sweeping attempts to change the racial and ethnic composition of the workforce, higher education, and firms conducting business with public entities.[12] These efforts were only vaguely defined on efficiency grounds. Rather, they, too, were predicated upon equity considerations. It is these highly visible affirmative action efforts that prompted a broad challenge from alleged victims of affirmative action: whites generally, but white males in particular. The legal challenges were founded on the premise that the Fourteenth Amendment to the U.S. Constitution prohibited state actions that deprived any group—not just former slaves—of equal protection. The ideological framework upon which these cases arose was one of market efficiency. Why reduce employment of (better) qualified white males merely to redistribute employment outcomes? Plaintiffs in cases that reached the U.S. Supreme Court in one single transformative year, 1989, helped to set in place an unraveling of the entire affirmative action apparatus built up in the previous twenty-five years.

Illustrative of the reversal is the *City of Richmond v. Croson* (1989) case. In this instance, a white-owned plumbing supply company argued that the minority- and women-owned business set-aside program designed to rectify the underrepresentation of nonwhite firms among contractors in Richmond, the capital of the Confederacy during the Civil War, harmed non–minority-owned firms. *Croson*, indeed, argued that its efforts to comply with the affirmative action mandates of the City of Richmond were unsuccessful principally because of its inability to find "qualified" minority firms with which to subcontract. Pointedly, this is an efficiency argument against the city's affirmative action program. Associate Justice Sandra Day O'Connor, writing for the majority, while not denying that such race conscious set-asides were sometimes needed, pointed out that the City of Richmond had failed to prove a compelling state interest (remedying ongoing discrimination).

> 1. The city has failed to demonstrate a compelling governmental interest justifying the Plan, since the factual predicate supporting the Plan does not establish the type of identified past discrimination in the city's construction industry that would authorize race-based relief under the Fourteenth Amendment's Equal Protection Clause (498–506).

> 2. The Plan is not narrowly tailored to remedy the effects of prior discrimination, since it entitles a black, Hispanic, or Oriental entrepreneur from anywhere in the country to an absolute preference over other citizens based solely on their race. Although many of the barriers to minority participation in the construction industry relied upon by the city to justify the Plan appear to be race neutral, there is no evidence that the city considered using alternative, race-neutral means to increase minority participation in city contracting. (*City of Richmond v. Croson*)

It is clear from the wording of the *Croson* decision that a compelling state interest is required to justify a potentially inefficient market intervention. The implicit inefficiency is the award of contracts to minority firms when nonminority firms would have prevailed in the absence of the affirmative action policy. The phase following the 1989 Supreme Court decisions that severely challenged the constitutionality of affirmative action in many markets might be regarded as the Affirmative Action Retrenchment/Post-Civil Rights phase.

A major transformation was apparent in the 1995 California ballot initiative 209, which passed with 54 percent of the vote and which sought to eliminate affirmative action programs in all public contracts, at public state colleges and universities, and hiring within public state agencies. Constituents felt that the current affirmative action programs had become reverse discrimination. They argued that white men are harmed because less-qualified minorities are given an unfair advantage in the marketplace. Although constitutional challenges to Proposition 209 immediately emerged, the public outcry against affirmative action set in place other state initiatives and added creditability to efforts across the nation to eliminate affirmative action programs altogether.

Between 1992 and 1996, sixteen states faced similar ballot initiatives. From 1992 to 2000, twenty-nine states faced legislation banning affirmative action. Ards and Myers (1997, 2001) collected data on state ballot initiatives and legislative attempts to dismantle affirmative action from 1992 to 2000. The introduced bills range from those that eliminate all programs that give preferential treatment to individuals on the basis of race, sex, color, or ethnicity, to bills curbing race or other preferences in limited spheres of government activities, such as government contracting and procurement, admissions and scholarships to state institutions, and government employment. Altogether 108 anti-affirmative action in public employment bills were introduced; 113 anti-affirmative action in public contracting and procurement bills were introduced; and 107 anti-affirmative action in higher education bills were introduced. The most bills were introduced in California, South Carolina, Michigan, and Alabama. Only 8.5 percent of the bills made their way out of committee; only two bills actually passed (in Alaska banning affirmative action in fishery management). Although few of the anti-affirmative action bills introduced in the 1990s resulted in the formal dismantling of state affirmative action, the failed efforts served two interrelated purposes: these efforts highlighted the resolve to attack affirmative action programs even when there may be limited support from the executive branch or from other legislators, and the efforts provided widespread media attention that gave legitimacy to contemporaneous ballot initiatives.

What were the reasons for affirmative action retrenchment as measured by ballot initiatives and legislative attempts to dismantle affirmative action? Ards and Myers (1997, 2001) estimated logistic models to predict the probability that an anti-affirmative action ballot initiative appeared in a state between 1992 and 1996 and whether anti-affirmative action legislation was introduced, voted out of committee, or passed between 1992 and 2000. They controlled for measures of unemployment, shifts out of manufacturing, black–white income gaps, state employment, black elected officials, minority educational attainment, Democratic voting, percent of the voting age population registered, immigration, racial diversity, crime, and welfare.[13]

Factors that emerge as significant predictors of the probability of anti-affirmative action legislation are: black–white income inequality, black homeownership, percent retail and service firms, percent black, percent receiving welfare, urbanization, and education. Affirmative action retrenchment appears to rise when black income is lower relative to white income; when black homeownership is high; when retail and service firms are a smaller fraction of all businesses; when there are larger fractions of blacks and those on welfare in the population; and when the population is urbanized and with larger shares of high school graduates. In addition, ballot initiatives are more likely to be introduced in states with high nonwhite populations combined with high white male unemployment rates. These factors suggest that economic factors matter in affirmative action retrenchment efforts and that those factors that pose the greatest threat to white males translate more readily into ballot initiatives or legislative efforts to dismantle affirmative action.

Post-Affirmative Action

Many of the efforts of traditional civil rights organizations during the Affirmative Action Retrenchment phase were geared toward preventing the passage of ballot initiatives and thwarting legislative attempts to dismantle affirmative action. These efforts recognized the equity concerns of both (a) whether race-neutral policies were capable of redressing the legacy of inequality rooted in slavery, segregation, and historic discrimination and (b) whether the privilege afforded to white males should be balanced by advantages to women and minorities in order to level playing fields.

A dramatic shift in the thinking about affirmative action came about in the ensuing years. President Bill Clinton's argument that affirmative action should be mended but not ended and the rush within the federal government to enact policies and plans that produced greater diversity without creating harm to nonminority market participants signaled concerns about efficiency. In the face of cutbacks to, and elimination of, many affirmative action programs—even without court orders or legal challenges—the tone of policy discourse among advocates of minority and women's equal rights seemed to embrace the efficiency criteria that were the cornerstone of the dismantlement of affirmative action programs in the first place. The tone was that "diversity is good for business" or that diversity has broad social benefits that outweigh any individual costs incurred. Indeed, the argument was that nonminorities as a group benefited from diversity. This net-social-gain argument is the efficiency argument or the "economic case for diversity." The diversity case is both a case for inclusiveness beyond just race and ethnicity and also an argument against traditional affirmative action (Slack 1997).

The Economic Case for Diversity

The most compelling and articulate statement of the case for diversity, in particular the case for diversity in higher education and employment, comes from the October 16, 2000, Fortune 500 amicus brief filed on behalf of the defendants in *Gratz v. Bollinger* and *Grutter v. Bollinger*, which respectively challenge the University of Michigan's race-conscious admissions policies in the undergraduate school and in the law school. The joint amicus brief brought together multinational giants such as Microsoft, the Dow Chemical Company, General Mills, Kellogg, KPMG, and 3M to produce a stunning statement in defense of workplace diversity:

> In the opinion of *amici*, individuals who have been educated in a diverse setting are more likely to succeed, because they can make valuable contributions to the workforce in several important ways. *First*, a diverse group of individuals educated in a cross-cultural environment has the ability to facilitate unique and creative approaches to problem solving arising from the integration of different perspectives. *Second*, such individuals are better able to develop products and services that appeal to a variety of consumers and to market offerings in ways that appeal to these consumers. *Third*, a racially diverse group of managers with cross-cultural experience is better able to work with business partners, employees, and clientele in the United States and around the world. *Fourth*, individuals that have been educated in a diverse setting are likely to contribute to a positive work environment, by decreasing incidents of discrimination and stereotyping. *Finally*, an educational environment created by consideration of the potential promise of each applicant in light of his or her experiences and background is likely to produce the most talented possible workforce. (Brief of Amici Curiae 2000)

The central issue addressed is that a diverse workforce is good for business. This is sometimes called the business case for diversity. The business case for diversity asserts that a diverse workforce permits employers to hire and retain better qualified employees who in turn are more productive and innovative. The business case for diversity points to the need for a workforce that mirrors the diverse consumer base to which firms market. Minnesota-based 3M detailed these issues specifically in an appended statement in the amicus brief:

> Because it serves and works with an increasingly diverse group of communities in both the United States and around the world, 3M's future hinges upon its ability to attract, deploy, and maintain a diverse workforce capable of understanding, relating to, and satisfying the needs of its broad customer base. 3M invests heavily in research and development and is known widely as one of America's most innovative companies. As such, 3M has found that bringing together the collective talents and experiences of a diverse group of employees is necessary to develop creative approaches to problem solving, and to successfully market and sell its products to a wide range of communities. Time after time, 3M has found that input from employees who are members of the communities to which 3M markets and sells its products is crucial to ensuring that it can reach those communities in the most effective way. (Brief of Amici Curiae 2000)

A careful reading of the Fortune 500 submission reveals that the case made is one of a compelling state interest in promoting diversity and not necessarily a specific appeal to any particular method to achieve diversity. Moreover, little or no mention is made as to whether particular subgroups within a diverse population require or need greater intervention in order to attain the desired end of workplace diversity.

The actual details of the claims that a diverse workforce is necessary—if not sufficient—for achieving profitability in the global marketplace reside within a burgeoning literature in industrial relations and labor relations. Jonathan Leonard and David Levine (2006) review this literature and focus their empirical analysis on the effects of workplace diversity on labor turnover and productivity. Using longitudinal data from more than 800 similar workplaces, they show that low workplace diversity and employee isolation increase worker turnover. The specific impacts differ among race, gender, and age groups. They refute the hypothesis that workforce diversity retards stability.

The documentation of the efficiency case for diversity in higher education that underlies the case for diversity in employment comes principally from an expert report by Patricia Gurin in the *Grutter* and *Gratz* cases. After examining national institutional data, survey data, and classroom information, she found that:

> Students who experienced the most racial and ethnic diversity in classroom set-
> tings and in informal interactions with peers showed the greatest engagement
> in active thinking processes, growth in intellectual engagement and motivation,
> and growth in intellectual and academic skills. (Gurin 1999)

The Harvard Civil Rights Project in its amicus brief in *Gratz v. Bollinger* provides a summary of the social science literature that documents the positive impacts of diversity on student outcomes. They review the literature showing that (a) student body diversity improves classroom learning environments, (b) diverse learning environments promote critical thinking skills, and (c) cross-racial interaction has positive effects on retention, college satisfaction, self-confidence, interpersonal skills, and leadership (Brief of Amici Curiae 2001). These findings support the idea that diversity in educational and training environments improves educational and training outcomes.

Chang, Astin, and Kim (2004), using a national longitudinal data set on college stu-dents, note that diversity in student bodies produces cross-racial interactions for different groups and at different levels of student body diversity. Whereas cross-racial interaction is shown to produce improvements in cognitive outcomes, the primary beneficiaries of cross-racial interactions across all levels of diversity are white students.

Other areas that make the case for diversity include real estate markets and cor-porate boards. Real estate firms with greater diversity in their workforces capture larger shares of the diverse customer base (Bond, Seiler, and Seiler 2003). Firms with more diverse corporate boards have higher firm value (Carter, Simkins, and Simpson 2003).

The Economic Case Against Diversity

The economic case against diversity recognizes a trade-off between benefits and costs associated with diverse societies or workforces. This literature argues essentially that heterogeneity in populations has the potential to exacerbate existing ethnic hostilities and hatreds and thus to retard economic growth. In their review of this literature, Alesina and La Ferrara (2005) note:

> The potential costs of diversity are fairly evident. Conflict of preferences, racism, and prejudices often lead to policies that are at the same time odious and counterproductive for society as a whole. The oppression of minorities may lead to political unrest or even civil wars. But a diverse ethnic mix also brings about variety in abilities, experiences, and cultures that may be productive and may lead to innovation and creativity. (Alesina and La Ferrara 2005, 762)

In this view, the cost of diversity is conflict and inter-ethnic conflict, which must be balanced against the benefit associated with possible gains to productivity from a more heterogeneous population. The literature points to extensive examples—from Africa in particular—wherein these costs tend to outweigh the benefits (Easterly and Levine 1997). There is an important distinction in this literature between how advanced economies are able to resolve these conflicts and how ethnic fractionalization in less-developed economies may dominate the trade-off between the costs and benefits of diversity.

On balance, the economic case against diversity hinges on showing that these costs outweigh the benefits. Note the qualifier that Alesina and La Ferrara use in denoting the possible benefits of diversity: they say that a diverse mix *may* produce higher productivity and *may* generate innovation and creativity.

Part of the economic case against diversity derives from the organizational behavior literature on teams. When examining new product development, Ancona and Caldwell (1992) point out that engineers working alone may not be as successful as teams working with specialists from many disciplines. They write:

> As teams increasingly get called upon to do more complex tasks and to cross functional boundaries within the organization, conventional wisdom has suggested that teams be composed of more diverse members. (Ancona and Caldwell 1992, 321)

But Ancona and Caldwell (1992) also caution that there can be off-setting impacts of diverse product development teams:

> While it [diversity] does produce internal processes and external communications that facilitate performance, it also directly impedes performance. That is, overall the effect of diversity on performance is negative, even though some aspects of group work are enhanced. It may be that for these teams diversity brings more creativity to problem solving and product development, but it impedes implementation because there is less capability for teamwork than there is for homogeneous teams. (ibid.)

What specifically about group or team diversity might be inefficient, in the sense that it reduces productivity? One hypothesis is that it increases emotional conflict and that conflict impedes performance. Race and ethnic diversity in particular are believed to be sources of emotional conflict (Pelled, Xin, and Eisenhardt 1999).

At the macro level, the argument is that ethnic divisions—particularly in African countries—are associated with low rates of income growth and high rates of poverty. Of course, many of the most careful analysts of these patterns are quick to point out that it is not ethnic diversity itself that produces the tragic poverty in Africa, but rather the policies that arise from conflict-ridden, ethnically diverse populations that are responsible (Easterly and Levine 1997). It is polarization and civil conflict that produce the observed outcomes of retarded growth and poverty, not necessarily population heterogeneity alone (Montalvo and Reynal-Querol 2005).

Alesina and La Ferrara (2000) construct indexes of social capital that capture measures of trust, group membership, and civic participation. They show that there is a strong, inverse relationship between their social capital measures and community heterogeneity. In states such as Minnesota, North Dakota, Montana, Utah, and Wyoming where there is little racial diversity and low income inequality, there are high levels of social capital. In states such as Florida and Texas, which have higher levels of racial and ethnic diversity as well as greater income inequality, there are lower measures of social capital. Of the different types of heterogeneity (i.e., diversity), racial heterogeneity has the greatest impact on inhibiting the formation and transmission of social capital.

Robert Bates reviews the literature on the adverse impacts of ethnic diversity on instability and poverty in Africa. He summarizes the conventional wisdom:

> Those who study modem Africa commonly highlight three features: its poverty, its instability, and its ethnic diversity. Whether in lurid popularizations (e.g., Robert Kaplan 1994) or in social scientific research (e.g., William Easterly and Ross Levine 1997; but see also Paul Collier and A. Hoeffler 1998) scholars reason that Africa is poor because it is unstable and that its instability derives from its ethnic complexity. Ethnicity thus lies, it is held, at the root of Africa's development crisis. (Bates 2000, 131)

Although his critique challenges this view, the data he uses are limited and do not permit a full rejection of the underlying conventional wisdom. Paul Collier's World Bank study provides a more nuanced interpretation of the Easterly-Levine hypothesis concerning the adverse impacts of ethnic diversity on economic growth. He interacts the measure of ethnic fragmentation with measures of political dominance. He finds that in democratic societies ethnic diversity promotes economic growth, but in dictatorships fragmentation contributes to diminished growth (Collier 2000).

Another way of conceptualizing racial/ethnic diversity is to consider the blurring of traditional black–white boundaries. Bean and Leach (2005) report that states with the largest immigrant populations have the highest blurring of these traditional boundaries and represent greater racial and ethnic diversity. Patterns of multiracial identification occur more frequently in California, Florida, Hawaii, Illinois, Michigan, New Jersey, New York, Ohio, Texas, and Washington than in other parts of the United States. These states also have high immigrant populations. In states in the South with large black populations, or in the North with large white populations, multiracial categorization (i.e., greater racial or ethnic diversity) is lower.

The specific mechanism by which diversity produces adverse outcomes can come from other sources. Alesina, Baqir, and Easterly (1999) show that there are lower public expenditures in more diverse communities, perhaps, as Ferraro and Cummings (2007) argue, as a direct result of racial discrimination. Others have shown that lower public goods provision in ethnically diverse communities arises from the problem of enforcing sanctions through common community norms (Habyarimana et al. 2007). Lazear (1999) posits that the adverse outcomes derive from culture and language that inhibit communications within the firm. Using information on teams and within organizations, researchers have found that the gains to group performance from diversity can be offset by difficulties within groups to agree on strategies or difficulties in communicating with one another. On balance, then, the net effect of diversity on organizations depends in part on how and whether benefits outweigh costs.[14]

Few researchers have identified the time element in their analysis. A notable exception is Putnam, who argues that—at least for modern industrialized societies—the initial negative impacts of diversity ultimately are reversed once a society embraces the intrinsic value of the benefits from ethnic diversity. Putnam (2007) argues the important point that the ethnic diversity is prompted in industrial societies largely through immigration. Using the example of the United States, he argues that the infusion of diverse languages and cultures enriches society and even if there are short-term losses, in the long run net gains are likely to be sustained. This distinction, however, does not comment on whether populations *initially disadvantaged*, such as indigenous populations or former slaves, necessarily benefit or lose from immigration and thus diversity.

Conclusion

There are other cases to be made for diversity besides the economic one. For example, Mitchell Rice (2005) details and clarifies the substantive case for diversity in public sector employment as paramount for achieving democracy and a representative bureaucracy. These foundations for diversity clearly deserve as much merit as do the factors related to economic efficiency. In the Michigan case, the more uncontroverted evidence offered about diversity benefits referred to civic engagement and democratic participation rather than improved test score performance or heightened cognitive or problem-solving skills. Thus, the putative efficiency benefits associated with diversity might be less important than the general societal benefits from improved civic participation.

Nevertheless, the economic case for diversity hinges on a balancing of benefits and costs that are rarely assessed directly. Moreover, programs that purport to enhance and promote diversity are rarely evaluated or assessed based on these trade-offs of benefits and costs. When such assessments are made, more often than not they are done without the rigor of experimental or quasi-experimental designs that the National Science Foundation's Committee on Equal Opportunity in Science and Engineering (CEOSE) (2003, 2004) has recommended in its reports.

The contradictory evidence for and against the impacts of workforce diversity and classroom diversity on productivity may be explained in part by nonlinearities between diversity and performance outcomes. For example, in their study of problem-solving skills and group performance indicators, Terenzini et al. (2001) show that there are moderate levels of performance at low diversity levels that initially decline as diversity goes from the lowest levels to not-so-low levels. Then, as diversity increases beyond the low points, performance indicators increase. This positive relationship continues up until the very highest levels of diversity wherein diversity and performance move in opposite directions. The nonlinear relationship between diversity and performance may reflect the fact that in economic terms there exists some optimal level of diversity between the extremes of completely homogeneous groups to the other extreme wherein there is no critical mass of any group. Some researchers have attempted to compute what this optimal level of diversity would look like. Generally speaking, the optimal proportions, in democratic societies, are likely to be such that no one group dominates.[15]

Using the metaphor of biological diversity and the preservation of species, Weitzman (1992) postulates that there must exist a "diversity function" and that any good economic theory of diversity ought to consider the optimization role that diversity might play. If, as in ecological systems, diversity matters, so too should diversity matter in economic systems. This manner of thinking, however, which focuses almost exclusively on the efficiency of species within a larger ecosystem, may inadvertently lead analysts to rank groups according to their overall productivity, and they might ultimately conclude that at the optimal level of diversity the representation of certain less productive groups might be lower than it would be under other organizational schemes. Moreover, if the current productivity of specific groups is intricately linked to historic barriers and inequalities, it is difficult to know whether a model of "optimal diversity" would impede the ability of these groups to move into the mainstream of the economy and become productive contributors to society in the manner that the Fortune 500 amicus brief postulates. It is entirely possible that the "optimal" amount of diversity will vary across time as groups assimilate and the negative aspects of diversity become less apparent. Assimilation may also erode the creativity and innovation that is the cornerstone of the benefits to diversity, suggesting that at some point diversity no longer will produce huge net social benefits.

It is ironic that the key explanations provided by those who present evidence that the costs of diversity might exceed the potential benefits point to the strife, the conflict, the tensions, and the hostilities that arise from heterogeneous populations that face historic animosities. If in fact the purpose of race-conscious efforts is the equity goal to remedy and redress historic wrongs, then the fact that there are possibly efficiency-reducing redistributive impacts should be of no surprise. Ideally, of course, one would want to design remedies that are both efficient and equitable. But, if the cost of diversity is actually rooted in the ills that create bias, discrimination, and racism, perhaps the short-term costs that are attendant to creating more diverse communities can be justified based on longer-term transformations that reduce racism and discrimination. Furthermore, can we permit the opponents of inclusion to veto it by their hostility? If we must choose between efficiency and equity, do we not have to choose equity (narrowly tailored) based on constitutional grounds or principles of fairness and justice? Putnam argues that we can expect efficiency (or at least democracy) to rebound over time.

In summary, the economic case for diversity hinges on being able to show that the benefits of heterogeneous groups in the workforce or in the classroom exceed the costs associated with studying, living, and working outside of the comfortable, reassuring, and customary confines of homogeneous settings. While the evidence is mixed about the net social benefits of diversity, it is clear that the logic of diversity takes a significant turn away from the original purpose of affirmative action: to redress historic inequalities against specific groups, including African Americans harmed by the institution of slavery and state-supported segregation. Advocates for advancing the social and economic status of this group who shift attention and adopt the language of diversity run the risk of accepting policy proscriptions (e.g., about optimal levels of diversity) that enhance the well-being of majority group members without necessarily improving the relative economic well-being of the intended beneficiaries of the affirmative action policies that diversity programs replace. The calculus of net social benefits does not require that all groups benefit. It is important to note that the logic of the efficiency claims of diversity does not require that disadvantaged racial or ethnic minority group members gain or gain as much as majority group members. Efficiency, as it is commonly defined by economists, will prevail even if all of the net benefits accrue to the majority and none to the minority. It is precisely for this reason that advocates for reducing racial and ethnic economic inequality should be cautious about embracing "the efficiency case for diversity" without being attentive to the resulting distribution of outcomes that such a policy might produce.

Notes

1. Estimation based on Sabol and Couture (2008) and U.S. Census Bureau, Population Division (2008).

2. Estimation based on U.S. Department of Health and Human Services, Administration on Children, Youth, and Families (2008).

3. Estimation based on U.S. Department of Health and Human Services, Administration for Children and Families (2008) and U.S. Census Bureau, Population Division (2008).

4. Snyder, Dillow, and Hoffman (2008, Table 153. Number and percentage of students suspended from public elementary and secondary schools, by sex, race/ethnicity, and state: 2004).

5. Snyder, Dillow, and Hoffman (2008, Table 105. Percentage of high school dropouts among persons 16 through 24 years old [status dropout rate], by sex and race/ethnicity: Selected).

6. Snyder, Dillow, and Hoffman (2008, Table 8. Percentage of persons age 25 and over and 25 to 29, by race/ethnicity, years of school completed, and sex: Selected years, 1910 through 2007).

7. Snyder, Dillow, and Hoffman (2008, Table 131. SAT score averages of college-bound seniors, by race/ethnicity: Selected years, 1986–87 through 2005–6).

8. The broad definition here approximates the notion of pareto optimality, wherein an allocation cannot be achieved that makes one person better off without making another person worse off (Friedman 2002, 45). This conceptualization of efficient differs from cost effectiveness, wherein no other allocation exists that will lower costs. There is no single, commonly accepted definition of equity, although we will often use in this chapter the notion of "fairness" wherein no one group prefers an allocation other than its own (Baumol 1986, 15). The competing definitions of equity include equality (in outcomes or in opportunities) and procedural fairness.

9. Or, at least by making some groups better off without making other groups worse off.

10. Gary Becker (1971, 56) says: "Let us first examine discrimination by a factor, W, which is a perfect substitute for N. Each employer must pay a higher wage rate to a member of W if he is to work with N rather than with other W. An income-maximizing employer would never hire a mixed work force, since he would have to pay the W members of this force a larger wage rate than members of W working solely with other W's. He hires only W if W's rate is less than N's and only N if N's is less than W's. He is indifferent between hiring them if and only if their wage rates are equal. Both N and W can be employed (in different firms) only if each employer is indifferent between them. Therefore, if a perfect substitute for N has a taste for discrimination against N, market segregation rather than market discrimination results: a firm employs either teams of N or teams of W; W and N are not employed in the same work force."

11. See the review of myths about affirmative action as discussed by Fryer and Loury (2005).

12. In one of the best reviews of the benefits and costs of affirmative action, William Darity (2005) provides a comprehensive interactional comparison of who benefits and why.

13. The full set of factors in the ballot initiative model includes: percent change in median housing values, 1980–90; percent black owner-occupied housing; black–white per capita income ratio; Hispanic–white per capita income ratio; Asian–white per capita income ratio; percent change in state employment per 10,000 population; percent change in state employment earnings, 1986–92; state employment 1992 per 10,000 population; percentage change in average annual pay, 1979–89; percent change in state employment 1986–92; labor force participation rate for females; white male unemployment rate; disposable personal income per person, percent change 1990–93; labor force participation rate, males; percent retail trade of all nonfarm establishments; percent services of all nonfarm establishments; total black elected officials; total black statewide and federal elected officials; black federal, state, and local elected officials per 1000 blacks; black state and federal elected officials per 1,000 blacks; percent popular vote cast for Democratic candidate for president in 1992; the percent of the voting age population that was registered in 1992; the percent of the voting age population that voted in 1992; net international migration 1990–93; percent of the population that is sixty-five years old and over, 1993; percent change in crime 1981–91; percent change in crime 1986–91; percent of the population with greater than high school education; percent of the population with

college education; the percent of the population residing in a metropolitan area, 1992; the violent crime rate in 1991; percent nonwhite; ratio of net international migration, 1990–93 to population in 1993; percent black; percent college enrollment, among minorities 1991. There are significant differences between the affirmative action retrenchment states and the nonretrenchment states in many of the economic factors. Black homeownership is higher, black–white income ratios are lower, state employment is lower, and unemployment is higher in states with affirmative action retrenchment efforts.

14. Alesina and La Ferrara (2005, 766) write: "This trade-off also emerges from a number of recent studies on organization performance, surveyed among others by Jackson and Ruderman (1996), Katherine Williams and Charles O'Reilly (1998), and Orlando Richard, Kochan, and Amy McMillan-Capehart (2002). The majority of these studies rely on laboratory experiments to test the link between diversity and performance, and generally find a positive effect of racial and gender diversity on creativity and task completion. For example, O'Reilly, Williams, and Sigal Barsade (1997) analyze thirty-two project teams and find that more diversity leads to more conflict and less communication, but controlling for the latter it also leads to higher productivity."

15. Alessina and La Ferrara (2005, 770) write: " . . . [I]f a group is politically dominant, it may impose a type of government that restricts freedom of the minority. On the other hand, a more fractionalized society in which no group is dominant may end up with a constitution especially careful to defend the rights of minorities."

References

Alesina, Alberto F., and Eliana La Ferrara. 2000. "Participation in Heterogeneous Communities." *Quarterly Journal of Economics* 115, no. 3: 847–904.
———. 2005. "Ethnic Diversity and Economic Performance." *Journal of Economic Literature* 43, no. 3: 762–800.
Alesina, Alberto; Reza Baquir; and William Easterly. 1999. "Public Goods and Ethnic Divisions." *Quarterly Journal of Economics* 114, no. 4: 1243–84.
Ancona, Deborah Gladstein, and David F. Caldwell. 1992. "Demography and Design: Predictors of New Product Team Performance." *Organization Science* 3, no. 3: 321–41.
Anderson, Bernard E. 1997. "Affirmative Action Policy Under Executive Order 1146: A Retrospective View." In *Civil Rights and Race Relations in the Post Regan-Bush Era*, ed. Samuel L. Myers, 47–60. Westport, CT: Praeger.
Andorra, Bruno. 1998. "Affirmative Action in Employment: Background and Current Debate." *Congressional Research Service*. December 1.
Ards, Sheila D., and Samuel L. Myers. 1997. "The Political Economy of Affirmative Action Retrenchment." Paper prepared for the National Economic Association panel on the Political Economy of Affirmative Action Retrenchment, Allied Social Science Association Meetings. New Orleans, Louisiana.
———. 2001. "The Political Economy of Affirmative Action Retrenchment." Revised. Hubert Humphrey Institute of Public Affairs, University of Minnesota, Minneapolis.
Bates, Robert H. 2000. "Ethnicity and Development in Africa: A Reappraisal." *American Economic Review* 90, no. 2: 131–34.
Baumol, William J. 1986. *Superfairness: Applications and Theory*. Cambridge, MA: MIT Press.
Bean, Frank D., and Mark A. Leach. 2005. "Critical Disjuncture? The Culmination of Post–World War II Socio-demographic and Economic Trends in the United States." *Journal of Population Research* 22, no. 1: 63–78.
Becker, Gary. 1971. *The Economics of Discrimination*. 2d ed. Chicago: University of Chicago Press.

Bond, Michael T.; Vicky L. Seiler; and Michael J. Seiler. 2003. "The Effects of Multicultural Diversity in Real Estate Brokerage." *Journal of Real Estate Research* 25, no. 4: 529–42.

Brief of Amici Curiae. 2000. Steelcase, Inc., 3M, Bank One Corporation, Abbott Laboratories, E. I. Du Pont De Nemours & Co., Inc., The Dow Chemical Company, Eastman Kodak Company, Eli Lilly & Company, General Mills, Inc., Intel Corporation, Johnson & Johnson, Kellogg Company, KPMG International, Lucent Technologies, Inc., Microsoft Corporation, PPG Industries, Inc., The Procter & Gamble Company, Sara Lee Corporation, Texaco Inc., and TRW Inc. *Gratz et al. v. Bollinger; Grutter et al. v. Bollinger* (No. 97–75928, No. 97–75231). October 16.

Brief of Amici Curiae. 2001. The Civil Rights Project at Harvard University *Gratz et al. v. Bollinger et al., Patterson et al.* (Nos. 01–1333, 01–1416, 01–1418). May.

Carter, David A.; Betty J. Simkins; and W. Gary Simpson. 2003. "Corporate Governance, Board Diversity, and Firm Value." *Financial Review* 38, no. 1: 33–53.

Chang, Mitchell J.; Alexander W. Astin; and Dongbin Kim. 2004. "Cross-Racial Interaction Among Undergraduates: Some Consequences, Causes, and Patterns Research." *Higher Education* 45, no. 5: 529–53.

City of Richmond v. J.A. Croson Co., 488 U.S. 469 (1989).

Collier, Paul. 2000. "Ethnicity, Politics and Economic Performance." *Economics and Politics* 12, no. 3: 225–45.

Crowley, Sheila. 2006. "Where Is Home? Housing for Low Income People After the 2005 Hurricane." In *There Is no Such Thing as a Natural Disaster: Race, Class, and Hurricane Katrina,* ed. Chester Hartman and Gregory D. Squires, 121–66. New York: Routledge.

Darity, William A. Jr. 2005. "Affirmative Action in Comparative Perspective: Strategies to Combat Ethnic and Racial Exclusion Internationally." Sanford Institute of Public Policy, Duke University, Durham, NC.

Darity, William A. Jr., and Samuel L. Myers Jr. 2000. "Languishing in Inequality: Racial Disparities in Wealth and Earnings in the New Millennium." In *New Directions: African Americans in a Diversifying Nation,* ed. James Jackson, 86–118. Washington, DC: National Policy Association Report, no. 297.

Donohue, John, and James Heckman. 1991. "Continuous vs. Episodic Change: The Impact of Affirmative Action and Civil Rights Policy on the Economic Status of Blacks." *Journal of Economic Literature* 29, no. 4: 1603–43.

Easterly, William, and Ross Levine. 1997. "Africa's Growth Tragedy: Policies and Ethnic Divisions." *Quarterly Journal of Economics* 112, no. 4: 1203–50.

Echaustegui, Maria E.; Michael Fix; Pamela Loprest; Sarah C. Von der Lippe; and Douglas Wissoker. 1997. *Do Minority-Owned Businesses Get a Fair Share of Government Contracts?* Washington, DC: Urban Institute.

Ferraro, Paul J., and Ronald G. Cummings. 2007. "Cultural Diversity, Discrimination, and Economic Outcomes: An Experimental Analysis." *Economic Inquiry* 45, no. 2: 217–32.

Franklin, John Hope, and Alfred A. Moss Jr. 2000. *From Slavery to Freedom: A History of African Americans.* New York: Knopf.

Friedman, Lee S. 2002. *The Microeconomics of Public Policy Analysis.* Princeton, NJ: Princeton University Press.

Fryer, Roland, and Glenn C. Loury. 2005. "Affirmative Action in Winner-Take-All Markets." *Journal of Economic Inequality* 3, no. 3 (December): 263–80.

Graham, Hugh Davis. 1990. *The Civil Rights Era: Origins and Development of National Policy 1960–1972.* New York: Oxford University Press.

Gurin, Patricia. 1999. "The Compelling Need for Diversity in Education." Expert report prepared for the lawsuits Gratz and Hamacher v. Bollinger, Duderstadt, the University of Michigan, and the University of Michigan College of LS&A, U.S. District Court,

Eastern District of Michigan, Civil Action No. 97–75231; and Grutter v. Bollinger, Lehman, Shields, the University of Michigan and the University of Michigan Law School, U.S. District Court, Eastern District of Michigan, Civil Action No. 97–75928 (January).

Habyarimana, James; Macartan Humphreys; Daniel N. Posner; and Jeremy M. Weinstein. 2007. "Why Does Ethnic Diversity Undermine Public Goods Provision?" *American Political Science Review* 101, no. 4: 709–25.

Hartman, Chester, and Gregory D. Squires. 2006. *There Is No Such Thing as a Natural Disaster: Race, Class, and Hurricane Katrina.* New York: Routledge.

Hawley, Clifford B., and Edwin T. Fujii. 1991. "Discrimination in Consumer Credit Markets." *Eastern Economic Journal* 17, no. 1: 21–30.

Heckman, James. 1990. "The Central Role of the South in Accounting for the Economic Progress of Black Americans." *American Economic Review* 80, no. 2: 242–46.

Higginbotham, F. Michael. 2005. *Race Law: Cases, Commentary, and Questions.* Durham, NC: Carolina Academic Press.

Klarman, Michael J. 2007. *Brown v. Board of Education and the Civil Rights Movement.* New York: Oxford University Press.

Ladd, Helen F. 1998. "Evidence on Discrimination in Mortgage Lending." *Journal of Economic Perspectives* 12, no. 2: 41–62.

Lamb, Charles. 2005. *Housing Segregation in Suburban America Since 1960: Presidential and Judicial Politics.* Cambridge: Cambridge University Press.

Lazear, Edward P. 1999. "Culture and Language." *Journal of Political Economy* 107, no. 6: S95–126.

Leonard, Jonathan S., and David I. Levine. 2006. "The Effect of Diversity on Turnover: A Large Case Study." *Industrial and Labor Relations Review* 59, no. 4: 547–72.

Montalvo, Jose G., and Marta Reynal-Querol. 2005. "Ethnic Diversity and Economic Development." *Journal of Development Economics* 76, no. 2: 293–323.

Munnell, Alicia H.; Geoffrey M.B. Tootell; Lynn E. Browne; and James McEneaney. 1996. "Mortgage Lending in Boston: Interpreting HMDA Data." *American Economic Review* 86, no. 1: 25–53.

Myers, Samuel L. Jr., ed. 1997. *Civil Rights and Race Relations in the Post Reagan-Bush Era.* Westport, CT: Greenwood.

Myers, Samuel L. Jr., and Tsze Chan. 1995. "Racial Discrimination in Housing Markets: Accounting for Credit Risk." *Social Science Quarterly* 76, no. 3: 543–61.

———. 1996. "Who Benefits from Minority-Business Set-Asides? The Case of New Jersey." *Journal of Policy Analysis and Management* 15, no. 2: 202–25.

Myers, Samuel L. Jr., and Chanjin Chung. 1996. "Racial Differences in Home Ownership and Home Equity Among Pre-Retirement-aged Households." *Gerontologist* 36, no. 3: 350–60.

Myers, Samuel L. Jr., and Inhyuck Ha. 2009. "Estimation of Race Neutral Goals in Public Procurement and Contracting." *Applied Economics Letters* 16, no. 3: 251–56.

Myrdal, Gunnar. 1996. *An American Dilemma: The Negro Problem and Modern Democracy* (Black and African American Studies). Edison, NJ: Transaction.

National Science Foundation. Committee on Equal Opportunity in Science and Engineering (CEOSE). 2003. *2005–2006 Biennial Report to Congress.* April.

———. 2004. *The 1994–2003 Decennial & 2004 Biennial Report to Congress.* CEOSE 04–01. December.

Noble, David. 1986. *Forces of Production: A Social History of Industrial Automation.* New York: Oxford University Press.

Pelled, Lisa Hope; Katherine R. Xin; and Kathleen M. Eisenhardt. 1999. "Exploring the Black Box: An Analysis of Work Group Diversity, Conflict, and Performance." *Administrative Science Quarterly* 44, no. 1: 1–28.

Putnam, Robert D. 2007. "E Pluribus Unum: Diversity and Community in the Twenty-first Century—The 2006 Johan Skytte Prize Lecture." *Scandinavian Political Studies* 30, no. 2: 137–74.

Rice, Mitchell F. 2005. *Diversity and Public Administration: Theory, Issues, and Perspectives.* Armonk, NY: M.E. Sharpe.

Sabol, William J., and Heather Couture. 2008. *Prison Inmates at Midyear 2007.* Bureau of Justice Statistics. June. Available at http://bjs.ojp.usdoj.gov/index.cfm?ty=pbdetail&iid=840/ (accessed July 16, 2010).

Slack, James D. 1997. "From Affirmative Action to Full Spectrum Diversity in the American Workplace: Shifting the Organizational Paradigm." *Review of Public Personnel Administration* 17, no. 4: 75–87.

Snyder, T.D.; S.A. Dillow; and C.M. Hoffman. 2008. *Digest of Education Statistics 2007* (NCES 2008–022). Washington, DC: National Center for Education Statistics, Institute of Education Sciences, U.S. Department of Education. Available at http://nces.ed.gov/programs/digest/d07/ (accessed July 16, 2010).

Terenzini, Patrick T.; Alberto R. Cabrera; Carol L. Colbeck; Stefani A. Bjorklund; and John M. Parente. 2001. "Racial and Ethnic Diversity in the Classroom: Does It Promote Student Learning? *Journal of Higher Education* 72, no. 5: 509–31.

Thurow, Lester W. 1969. *Poverty and Discrimination.* Washington, DC: Brookings Institution.

U.S. Census Bureau. Population Division. 2008. *Annual Estimates of the Population by Sex, Race, and Hispanic Origin for the United States: April 1, 2000 to July 1, 2007* (NC-EST2007–03). May 1.

———. 2008. *Annual Estimates of the Black or African American Alone Population by Sex and Age for the United States: April 1, 2000 to July 1, 2007* (NC-EST2007–04-BA). May 1. Available at www.census.gov/popest/national/asrh/NC-EST2007-asrh.html (accessed July 16, 2010).

———. 2008. *Annual Estimates of the Population by Sex and Selected Age Groups for the United States: April 1, 2000 to July 1, 2007* (NC-EST2007–02). May 1. Available at www.census.gov/popest/national/asrh/NC-EST2007/NC-EST2007–02.xls (accessed July 16, 2010).

U.S. Department of Health and Human Services, Administration for Children and Families. 2008. *The AFCARS Report: Preliminary FY 2006 Estimates as of January 2008.* April. Available at www.acf.hhs.gov/programs/cb/stats_research/afcars/tar/report14.htm (accessed July 16, 2010).

U.S. Department of Health and Human Services, Administration on Children, Youth and Families. 2008. *Child Maltreatment 2006.* Washington, DC: U.S. Government Printing Office. Available at www.acf.hhs.gov/programs/cb/pubs/cm06/index.htm (accessed July 16, 2010).

Weitzman, Martin L. 1992. "On Diversity." *Quarterly Journal of Economics* 107, no. 2: 363–405.

Yinger, John. 1986. "Measuring Racial Discrimination with Fair Housing Audits: Caught in the Act." *American Economic Review* 76, no. 5: 881–93.

———. 1998. "Evidence on Discrimination in Consumer Markets." *Journal of Economic Perspectives* 12, no. 2: 23–40.

Part II
Measuring Social Equity

7

Social Equity, Health, and Health Care

Richard W. Hug

In March 2005, immediately following the Fourth Leadership Conference on Social Equity in Cleveland, the Committee on Social Equity Indicators and Measurements of the Standing Panel on Social Equity in Governance[1] (SEP) of the National Academy of Public Administration (NAPA) developed a plan to prepare a set of social equity indicators for the United States. The plan called for developing a "call to action" and two model social equity indicator chapters (on health and criminal justice) based on a set of definitions prepared by the committee. This chapter, on health and health care, is based on the four areas of social equity measurement identified by the committee:

A. Access and Distributional Equity—A review of access to and/or distribution of current policies and services.
B. Quality and Process Equity—Review of the level of consistency in the quality of existing services delivered to groups and individuals.
C. Procedural Fairness—Examination of problems or issues pertaining to groups of people in procedural rights, treatment in a procedural sense, and determination of eligibility within existing policies and programs.
D. Outcomes—Disparities in outcomes for population groups (e.g., by race or income).

Social Equity, Health Equity, and Health Disparities

In the United States, there is extensive governmental involvement in meeting health-care needs, but there is no commitment to universal care. Federal, state, and local governments are generally committed to ensuring that emergency care is available to all people and that the needs of the poor, the elderly, the disabled, and some children are addressed.[2] With this approach, there is a significant proportion of society that is "uncovered" and lacks access to continuing comprehensive health care.[3] In addition, unlike the approach taken in European democracies, there is little policy consideration given to dealing with the social determinants of health (Exworthy et al. 2006). This study considers both changes in policy and changes in performance within existing policy to address equity issues that are identified.

It recognizes the importance of initiatives outside the health-care system but, following the pattern of the debate in the United States, does not venture extensively into the realm of policies outside the health-care system.

The four-measure approach to measuring social equity in the health area proposed by the Research Committee of the Social Equity Panel is consistent with the public health approach to the topic, as it has emerged in that literature over the years. Following that tradition, Braveman and Gruskin define equity in health as

> the absence of systematic disparities in health (or in the major determinants of health) between social groups who have different levels of underlying social advantage/disadvantage—that is, different positions in a social hierarchy. Inequities in health systematically put groups of people who are already socially disadvantaged (for example, by being poor, female, and/or members of a disenfranchised racial, ethnic, or religious group) at further disadvantage with respect to their health; health is essential to well-being and to overcoming other effects of social disadvantage (Braveman and Gruskin 2003, 254).

Braveman and Gruskin include health *care* among the "major determinants of health." They also extend the analysis of health care to include "not only the receipt/utilization of health services but also to the allocation of health care resources, the financing of health care, and the quality of health care services" (ibid.). Among the major determinants they also list "household living conditions, conditions in communities and workplaces . . . (and) policies and programmes affecting any of these factors" (ibid.).

The four-part approach advanced by the Social Equity Panel calls for measurement and analysis of access to the health-care system, the distribution of benefits and burdens within the system, the fairness of procedures and processes within it, and the quality of the care provided within the health-care system. This approach, which will be used throughout the chapter, also extends to the health outcomes produced by the health-care system and the other major determinants of health described by Braveman and Gruskin.

Focusing on outcomes requires attention to public policies and practices outside the formal health-care system that are shown to be related to unacceptable differences in health outcomes.[4] Problems with basic nutrition and literacy, access to clean water and water treatment, and minimally adequate housing are particularly important health equity problems to be addressed by governments in developing countries. But there are parallels in more developed societies as evidenced by the recent efforts of European nations to pursue health equity by undertaking initiatives that go far beyond work with health-care systems (Acheson 1998; Exworthy et al. 2006; Wilkinson and Marmot 2003). The United Kingdom has adopted what they refer to as the "socioeconomic model of health and its inequalities." As a result of this approach, in their major document on this issue, the Acheson Report (Acheson 1998), only three of the thirty-nine recommendations to attack inequalities in health are directed to the British National Health Service.

In the United States, efforts to focus on the social and economic determinants of health have been considerably more limited.[5] In fact, health policy debates have tended to downplay even health-care access issues in favor of attention to concerns about cost and other matters. There has been, however, more recently, an effort to measure and study health disparities in the United States and a series of initiatives designed to reduce them. While the measurement effort does not completely parallel the approach suggested by the Standing Panel on Social Equity, the National Healthcare Disparities Reports (NHDR; AHRQ 2004–2007) address many of the issues raised by the social equity framework. At a minimum, the reports provide access to measures that are consistent with the framework. For that reason, measures from the NHDR form the basis of this chapter. The measures were chosen because they are collected regularly using well-established procedures and will, therefore, be easily updated. They also follow the approach suggested by Braveman and Gruskin by comparing the experience of the disadvantaged group to the group presumed to be advantaged—racial and ethnic groups compared to the white majority, the poor to the wealthy, and so on.[6]

While this chapter contains occasional efforts to address indicators of social conditions that lead to health disparities and possible remedies for those conditions, the bulk of what appears here is focused on the health-care delivery system. Other measures and remedies for those nondelivery system determinants of health can be found in the other chapters of this book.

Access and Distributional Equity

Indicators

The National Healthcare Disparities Reports have two major types of indicators—access and quality. Within each type there are several categories of measures. While many of the indicators in the access and quality sections of the NHDR match the similarly named categories of the SEP framework, some of the NHDR indicators belong more properly in the procedural fairness and outcome sections of the SEP framework. The sorting out of these issues is addressed in Appendix 7.1, which provides a "crosswalk" between NHDR and SEP categories.

There are two categories of NHDR access measures—facilitators and barriers to health care and health-care utilization. Indicators from those two categories form the basis for this section of measures. They will be addressed in turn here. A final part focuses on the NHDR's summary access measures.

Facilitators and Barriers to Health Care

Most discussions of facilitating entry to the U.S. health-care system begin with health insurance. Measures of health insurance (particularly for children and for those working full-time) will be addressed first, and followed by discussions of underinsurance and the importance of having a usual source of care.

Health Insurance

Modern democracies are generally committed to universal access to health-care services. Universal health insurance, available in virtually every other Western industrialized country (Commonwealth Fund 2008, 16), assures at least some form of access to the system. The latest data on health insurance in the United States show that large numbers of Americans remain uninsured. During the first half of 2007, more than 53 million Americans, about 21 percent of the population under age sixty-five, were uninsured (Roberts and Rhoades 2008).

Besides having large numbers of residents without health insurance, there are some large differences in the rates of coverage by age, gender, race/ethnicity, education, and income. These differences are in evidence regardless of working status. More than 12.5 million full-time workers were uninsured for the entire year in 2006 (Miller and Carroll 2009).

With regard to age, about 38 percent of all Americans aged nineteen to twenty-four were uninsured in 2007 compared to about 16 percent of those aged fifty-five to sixty-four. Almost 40 percent of all Hispanic/Latino males under age sixty-five were also uninsured compared to about 15 percent of white females (Roberts and Rhoades 2008, 4–5).

Table 7.1 shows some of the differences in coverage in greater detail. The table includes the relative rates of the minority group members' and lower-income persons' insurance coverage compared to the white majority and to the highest income category.[7]

Health insurance for children has been an important public policy issue for more than a decade. The latest figures show that while some progress has been made, there are still many children without health insurance. In 2007, there were 9.6 million uninsured children (aged zero to eighteen) in the United States—13 percent of all children—as compared with 11 percent in 2006. Of those children who were insured, almost a third (32.8 percent)—24.2 million children—had "public only" coverage. Since 1996, the number of uninsured and privately insured children has remained virtually constant. Public insurance programs, on the other hand, have grown rapidly. Public programs covered 13.8 million children in 1996. By 2007, there were 24.2 million children in those programs.

Table 7.1 shows that white children were more likely to be uninsured than African American children in 2007. This suggests that aggressive policy actions have been successful in reducing a long-standing disparity. For the previous four years, the rates for African American children averaged about two percentage points higher than whites. Rates for Latino children, on the other hand, have been consistently above 20 percent during this period—almost always more than twice the rate of whites (Roberts and Rhoades 2008).[8]

Latino adults did not fare as well as their children. The overall rate for Latinos (aged zero to sixty-five) stood at 37.2 percent in 2007—considerably more than twice the rate for whites. Among Latinos aged eighteen to sixty-five who were

Table 7.1

Health Insurance Coverage by Race/Ethnicity, Education, and Income, 2006 and 2007, and Rates of Uninsured Relative to Comparison Group

Health Insurance (% uninsured)	Race/Ethnicity		
	White	Black	Latino
Under age 18 (2007)	11.6	9.6	21.4
Ratio of Black and Latino to White		(0.83)	(1.84)
Under age 65 (2007)	16.7	21.1	37.2
Ratio of Black and Latino to White		(1.26)	(2.23)
Persons age 18–64 working full-time (2006)	9.1	13.8	32.6
Ratio of Black and Latino to White		(1.52)	(3.58)

	Education (in years)		
	Less than 12	12	12+
Persons age 18–64 working full-time (2006)	36.0	15.8	6.4
Ratio of lower education groups to 12+	(5.63)	(2.47)	

	Income (% of poverty level)			
	0–125	126–200	201–400	401+
Persons age 18–64 working full-time (2006)	40.8	32.7	15.2	4.2
Ratio of lower income groups to 401+	(9.71)	(7.79)	(3.62)	

Source: Medical Expenditure Panel Survey (MEPS), 2007, 2009

working full-time, almost a third (32.6 percent) were uninsured compared to less than 10 percent of whites (9.1 percent).

People with lower incomes and less education who worked full-time were also considerably more likely to be uninsured. For example, people working full-time who were earning less than 125 percent of the poverty level were about ten times (9.71) as likely to be uninsured as persons in the highest income category.

Underinsurance

Health-care researchers have documented the consequences of being *uninsured* for obtaining appropriate health care. Among other things, the uninsured are less likely to have a usual source of care, to get blood pressure and cholesterol checks, and to get cancer-screening tests. The Commonwealth Fund recently reported a study of these issues and also the nature, extent, and consequences of being underinsured (Collins et al. 2008). The researchers defined the underinsured as those who have health insurance but (1) have out-of-pocket health-care expenses of at least 10 percent of their incomes (5 percent for those with incomes less than 200 percent of poverty) or (2) have health plan deductibles of at least 5 percent of their incomes.

Figure 7.1   **Insurance and Underinsurance for Persons Aged Nineteen to Sixty-Four, by Income, 2007**

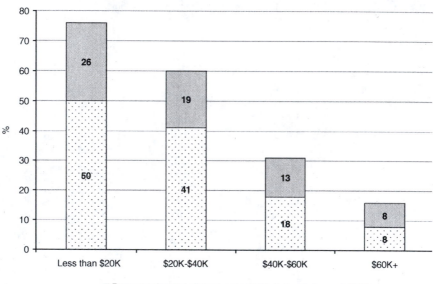

☐ Percent uninsured all year, ages 19-64, but underinsured, 2007
☒ Percent uninsured, ages 19-64, at some point in 2007

Source: Constructed from data in Collins et al. (2008), Table 1.

In 1983, the President's Commission for the Study of Ethical Problems in Medicine and Biomedical and Behavioral Research addressed the question of equitable access to health care. Their report concluded "society has a moral obligation to ensure that everyone has access to adequate care without being subject to excessive burdens" (22). The Commonwealth Fund study raises the issue of whether or not the current system has reached the point of imposing "excessive burdens."

The Commonwealth Fund has attempted to measure the extent and distribution of these "burdens." Figure 7.1 shows the estimates of the extent of "uninsurance" and underinsurance for 2007 by income.[9] More than three-fourths of all people aged nineteen to sixty-four with incomes less than $20,000 were either uninsured or underinsured compared with only 16 percent of those making $60,000 a year or more. The survey added additional questions about health-seeking behavior as well as insurance status, and the study concludes that the problems are widespread. The Commonwealth Fund study concluded that

> . . . in 2007, nearly two-thirds of (U.S.) adults, or 116 million people, were either uninsured for a time during the year, were underinsured, reported a problem paying medical bills, and/or said that they didn't get needed medical care because of costs. (viii)

Usual Source of Care

Getting into the health-care system and navigating properly is clearly associated with having a usual source of care. Health researchers have often pointed this out in great detail (Beal et al. 2007). Table 7.2 shows a list of "usual source" indicators from the NHDR.

Members of minority groups and people with lower incomes are uniformly more likely to lack a usual source of care (including when they have fair or poor health), more likely to use a clinic or hospital as a usual source, and more likely to report a financial cause for not having a usual source of care.

Utilization

Health-care utilization indicators have traditionally been employed to measure access to care. Because of the nature of the measures, however, and possible problems with interpretation, the authors of the NHDR reports have declined to make extensive use of them. While there may be some problems of interpretation, at least some measures of utilization are appropriate as indicators of access to care for the purposes of this report.

Table 7.3 shows a number of utilization measures that have been traditionally used to gauge access to care. The disparities noted in other access areas are apparent in these measures also. African American and Hispanic/Latino women are twice as likely as white women to fail to obtain prenatal care in the first trimester of their pregnancies. There are similar but less dramatic differences by race/ethnicity for children's dental visits, care for serious depression, and physician's office visits.

Dental visits for children and office visits are also more likely for those with higher incomes. More than twice as many children in poverty miss their yearly dental visits as compared with children in the highest income group.

Summary Access Measures

The 2004 NHDR authors identified thirty-one indicators of access for which they had measures by race/ethnicity and income data for both 2000 and 2001. They compared access of African Americans and Hispanics to whites and declared the groups' access worse than whites if the relative difference between the group's result and the result for whites was at least 10 percent and was statistically significant at the .05 level. Similarly, they compared the access of people in the lowest income group, less than 100 percent of poverty, with the access of people with incomes of 400 percent of poverty or more.

In that report, Hispanic/Latinos had access to care that was worse than whites on about 90 percent of all the access indicators. African Americans fared better and improved their standing relative to whites over the two years. By 2001 their access was worse than whites on only about a third of the indicators.

Table 7.2

Source of Care Measures, by Race/Ethnicity and Income/Poverty, and Rates Relative to the Appropriate Comparison Group, 2005 (in percent)

Source of care	Race/ethnicity			Income/poverty %			
	White	Black	Latino	Less than 100	100–199	200–399	400+
No usual source of care	10.6	14.2	23.1	21.9	18.6	12.8	7.7
		(1.34)	(2.18)	(2.84)	(2.42)	(1.66)	
Fair/poor health and no usual source of care	11.0	13.4	17.4	15.3	14.0	12.1	7.4
		(1.22)	(1.58)	(2.07)	(1.89)	(1.64)	
Hospital/clinic as usual source	14.2	21.3	25.6	29.6	22.3	16.2	10.9
		(1.84)	(1.80)	(2.72)	(2.05)	(1.49)	
No usual source—financial cause	11.6	14.8	22.1	24.9	20.5	14.4	5.6
		(1.28)	(1.91)	(4.45)	(3.66)	(2.57)	

Source: National Healthcare Disparities Report 2007.

Table 7.3

Utilization Measures, by Race/Ethnicity and Income/Poverty, 2004 and 2005, and Rates Relative to the Appropriate Comparison Group (in percent)

Utilization	Race/ethnicity			Income/poverty %			
	White	Black	Latino	Less than100	100–199	200–399	400+
Women not receiving prenatal care in first trimester (2004)	11.1	23.5 (2.12)	22.5 (2.03)	—	—	—	—
Children (aged 2–17) without a dental visit in past year (2004)	41.0	61.1 (1.49)	61.7 (1.50)	63.7 (2.08)	61.0 (1.99)	47.4 (1.55)	30.6
Age 18+ with serious depression and no care (2005)	30.2	43.6 (1.44)	49.2 (1.63)	—	—	—	—
Age 18+ without an office/outpatient visit in past year (2004)	21.7	36.4 (1.68)	42.4 (1.95)	33.3 (1.59)	31.9 (1.52)	28.6 (1.36)	21.0

Source: National Healthcare Disparities Reports, tables.

People in poverty had worse access relative to those with incomes greater than 400 percent of poverty for almost 90 percent (87.1 percent) of the access indicators.

The 2005 NHDR reduced the number of access indicators to eight facilitator and barrier "core report" measures[10] and five "utilization measures"; the 2006 NHDR dropped the utilization measures and reduced the facilitator and barrier measures to six.

By the time of the 2006 report, African American access was the same for four of the six measures while Hispanic/Latino access was the same for only one measure and the poor did not achieve the same access for any of the measures.

The 2007 NHDR chose to keep six core measures of access and to summarize the progress being made on the indicators by determining which measures were improving, which were the same, and which were worsening.[11] The idea was to track changes for the various populations as measured in 2000–2001 and 2004–5. Data were available for comparisons on five of the six measures. Figure 7.2 shows the results of the analysis.

While progress has been made on two indicators in the black vs. white comparison, there has been no progress for the poor, and progress on only one indicator for Hispanic/Latinos. On the other hand, disparities are worsening for the poor on three of the five indicators and on two each for African Americans and Hispanic/Latinos.

The authors of the 2007 NHDR summarized the results of the access indicators (and the quality measures addressed in subsequent sections) by noting three key themes:

- Overall, disparities in health-care quality and access are not getting smaller.
- Progress is being made, but many of the biggest gaps in quality and access have not been reduced.
- The problem of persistent uninsurance is a major barrier to reducing disparities (1).

Quality and Process Equity

The NHDR quality indicators form the basis for this section of the chapter. The NHDR defines "quality health care" as care that is effective, safe, timely, patient-centered, equitable, and efficient (2007, 21). The NHDR defines equitable care as "providing care that does not vary in quality because of personal characteristics such as gender, ethnicity, geographic location, and socioeconomic status" (21). Including equitable care as an element of quality reinforces it and warrants measurements of equity as part of internal quality control processes within the health-care system. It also justifies payment source incentives for equitable care and external processes that monitor equity in service delivery. The authors suggest that quality is measured through patient assessments, analysis of outcomes, and clinical performance measures. The NHDR indicators chosen for this section come from the NHDR quality categories of patient safety and effectiveness, and from the patient-

Figure 7.2   **2007 NHDR Summary Access Measures**

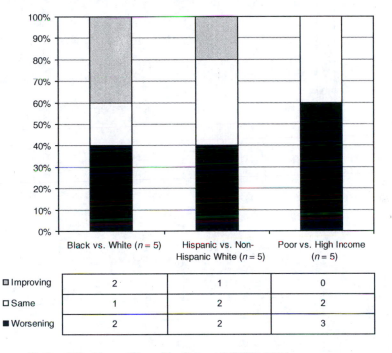

	Black vs. White (*n* = 5)	Hispanic vs. Non-Hispanic White (*n* = 5)	Poor vs. High Income (*n* = 5)
▨ Improving	2	1	0
□ Same	1	2	2
■ Worsening	2	2	3

Source: National Healthcare Disparities Report (NHDR) 2007.

provider communication category of access indicators. The section concludes with a discussion of the NHDR summary measures of quality of care.

Indicators

The quality indicators (Table 7.4) include items on disease management (diabetes and asthma), preventive care (vaccinations for children and adults), hospital care, and overall satisfaction with the care given by a provider. While some categories include measures on which there are no disparities, the overall pattern reflects the findings reported in the section on access to care.

Disease Management

For adults with diabetes, 16.3 percent of Hispanic/Latinos did not receive a hemo-globin A1C measurement in the past year as called for by good practice compared with 11.8 percent for African Americans and 6.5 percent for whites. People in poverty were almost twice as likely as those in the highest income category to have failed to receive A1C measurement (12.9 percent versus 6.6 percent).

Table 7.4

Quality Indicators and Rates Relative to the Appropriate Reference Group (in percent)

Quality indicator	Race/ethnicity			Income/poverty %			
	White	Black	Latino	Less than 100	100–199	200–399	400+
Disease management							
Adults with diabetes who did not have a hemoglobin A1C measurement in the past year (2004)	6.5	11.8 (1.82)	16.3 (2.51)	12.9 (1.95)	7.8 (1.18)	9.5 (1.44)	6.6
Hospital admissions for uncontrolled diabetes without complications per 100,000 adults (18+) (2004)	12.9	70.7 (5.48)	51.0 (3.95)				
Hospital admissions for asthma per 100,000 population age 18 and over (2004)	97.8	373.9 (3.82)	143.7 (1.47)				
Hospital admissions for asthma per 100,000 population under age 18 (2004)	91.1	304.1 (3.34)	177.9 (1.95)				
Disease prevention							
Children age 19–35 months who did not receive all vaccines (2005)	17.9	20.7 (1.16)	21.2 (1.18)	23.5 (1.74)	21.8 (1.62)	17.7 (1.31)	13.5
High-risk adults (18–64) who did not get flu vaccine in past year (2005)	21.4	19.6 (0.92)	19.3 (0.90)	19.5 (0.91)	19.9 (0.93)	21.3 (0.99)	21.5
Hospital care							
Decubitus ulcers (bedsores) per 1,000 discharges of length 5 days or more, ages 18 and over (2004)	24.3	36.0 (1.48)	27.2 (1.12)				
Selected infections due to medical care per 1,000 discharges (2004)	1.70	1.90 (1.12)	1.16 (0.68)				
Overall care quality							
Adults who rated the quality of their care less than seven on a ten-point scale (2004)	12.4	18.4 (1.48)	16.2 (1.31)	24.0 (2.35)	17.3 (1.70)	14.1 (1.38)	10.2
Children whose care was rated less than seven on a ten-point scale (2004)	5.0	9.2 (1.84)	7.0 (1.40)	11.4 (3.80)	6.9 (2.3)	6.0 (2.00)	3.0

Source: National Healthcare Disparities Report (NHDR) 2007.

Hospitalizations for uncontrolled diabetes without complications are generally considered to be failures of the health-care system to manage the disease and are therefore considered quality measures rather than access measures. Rates of admission for African Americans and Hispanic/Latino adults are five times and four times (respectively) the rates for whites.

Asthma hospitalizations show a similar pattern for adults and children by race/ethnicity. While differences between Hispanic/Latinos and whites are not as dramatic, African American adults are almost four times as likely as whites to be hospitalized for asthma.

Disease Prevention

Differences by race/ethnicity for childhood vaccinations and for flu vaccines for high-risk adults did not show the pattern found in the previous section. In fact, high-risk adults in the two minority groups were more likely to get their flu shots than whites. A distinct pattern of disparity by income was evident, however, for childhood vaccinations. Children in poverty were considerably less likely to have gotten all their shots than were those in the highest income category.

Hospital Care

The two measures selected for hospital care reveal a pattern similar to the disease prevention results. Hispanic/Latino patients are less likely to have infections due to medical care than whites or African Americans. On the other hand, whites are much less likely to have bed sores (decubitus ulcers) when they leave the hospital. On average, for each 1,000 discharges from stays of five days or more, 36.0 African Americans have bed sores compared to a rate of 24.3 for whites.

Overall Care Quality

Measures of overall care quality for adults and children show the classic pattern of disparities noted in several other categories reported. For both adults and children, members of minority groups and people in lower income groups report lower quality care. African Americans, for example, are about half again as likely as whites to rate their care at less than seven on a ten-point scale (18.4 percent versus 12.4 percent). For both adults and children the rates of poor care quality decline uniformly as income increases. For example, 24 percent of those in poverty report low quality care compared with only 10.2 percent of the highest income group.

NHDR Summary Measures of Quality

The final indicators of quality are summary measures produced for the 2007 NHDR report. In the 2004 NHDR, the authors counted the number of measures for which

African Americans and Hispanic/Latinos had lower quality care than whites. They made similar calculations for people in poverty relative to those with incomes at least 400 percent above the poverty line using the same criteria. As with the access measures, quality of care was considered lower if there was a relative difference of at least 10 percent and the results were statistically significant at the .05 level.

In the 2004 report there were thirty-eight measures for comparison between African Americans and whites, thirty-six measures for comparing Hispanic/Latinos to non-Hispanic whites, and twenty-two measures comparing the poor with the higher income group. The data for 2001 indicated that quality was lower for the poor on about 60 percent of the measures; lower for Hispanic/Latinos in almost 50 percent; and lower for African Americans on 68 percent of the measures.

As with the access measures, the 2007 NHDR notes that the number of measures of quality where disparities exist grew larger between 2000–2001 and 2004–5—the latest years for which comparisons were possible (2007, 2). The authors used seventeen core measures of quality (chosen for completeness of the demographic data) to determine which measures were improving, which were the same, and which were worsening.[12] Figure 7.3 shows the results of the analysis.

For all three comparisons shown above (and for two comparisons not reported here), the numbers of quality measures worsening or staying the same outnumbered the number of measures on which there was improvement. Of particular note is the income category in which seven of the seventeen measures worsened over the period.

Procedural Equity

Two issues come to mind when the topic is procedural equity in health and health care: civil rights enforcement and the experience of consumers within managed-care organizations.

Teitelbaum (2005) recently reviewed the history of civil rights and health care. He points out that "separate but equal" hospital facilities were legal until 1963 and that major change in the segregation of hospitals did not take place until the passage of the Civil Rights Act of 1964 and the implementation of the federal Medicare and Medicaid programs beginning in 1965. To receive reimbursement under Medicare and Medicaid, hospitals were required to comply with Title VI of the Civil Rights Act. That meant desegregating all operations in time for the July 1966 implementation of Medicare. Teitelbaum (2005), Smith (2005a), and others have written about the remarkable transformation that took place in a few short months (and in some cases, overnight) during that era. They have also pointed out that physicians were exempted from enforcement of the Civil Rights Act by classifying Medicare Part B payments as direct assistance to individuals rather than financial assistance to physicians. The result, they argue, is that the Civil Rights Act had an enormous, immediate effect on the provision of hospital care but that its effects in recent years have been more limited. Smith (2005b) citing Bach and

Figure 7.3   **Changes in Selected NHDR Core Quality Measures, 2000–2001 to 2004–2005**

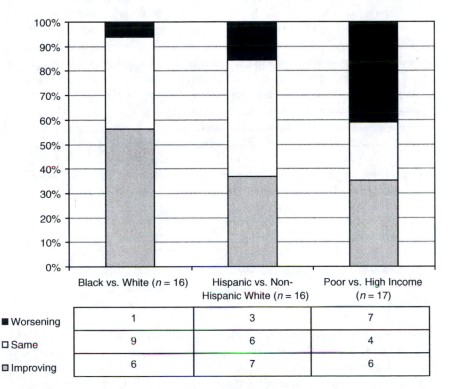

	Black vs. White (*n* = 16)	Hispanic vs. Non-Hispanic White (*n* = 16)	Poor vs. High Income (*n* = 17)
■ Worsening	1	3	7
□ Same	9	6	4
▣ Improving	6	7	6

Source: National Healthcare Disparities Report (NHDR) 2007.

others (2004), argues that primary care for blacks today is "separate and unequal." Smith (2005a, 2005b) argues that the tools to have an impact on the provision of health care by physicians (individually or through managed-care organizations) have been in place for many years but that the political will has been lacking.

Title VI certification processes begun in the 1960s required the collection of the type of data that were needed to ensure that health-care facilities were not segregated. Smith (2005a) notes that there have been no special data collection efforts and no testing programs to monitor discrimination in health care as there have been in areas of education, housing, and employment. Data such as these would normally provide the indicators that would be needed to monitor procedural equity in health care. Since they are not available, it will be necessary to use the less precise, less direct measures available in the NHDR.

In the late 1990s, managed-care organizations came under fire for allegedly denying medically necessary services to patients in the name of controlling costs. The result was a series of class action lawsuits and a movement to establish a Patient's

Bill of Rights to ensure that needed services are provided. Bloche and Studdert (2004) reviewed this area of procedural equity and concluded that federal courts and state regulators had "remade the rules of the medical marketplace" in response to the challenges posed by the more drastic cost-cutting practices of managed-care organizations. They argue that the lawsuits and bad publicity surrounding the practices caused the industry to back down from its more aggressive approaches. The combination of investor concerns about legal risks, Supreme Court decisions allowing more regulation at the state level, and the regulations themselves resulted in a reduction of concerns by consumers about whether or not they could get the care they needed from managed-care organizations. State legislatures have imposed procedural and substantive constraints on preauthorization review, independent reviews of coverage denials, protections for doctors who appeal coverage denials, and other requirements related to procedural equity within health-care organizations. One could imagine a series of indicators built on such items. In practice, however, the measures are simply not available and it will be necessary again to use the less direct NHDR measures.

On another front, Perez (2003, 662) notes that over 90 percent of African American doctors believe that managed-care organizations discriminate against them in contracting. But, as noted earlier, there is no formal data-gathering system or procedure to validate this point of view.

Indicators

One of the most important aspects of procedural equity within the health-care system has to do with the extent to which patients are referred for more specialized care. Two measures of referrals to specialists in the first group of procedural equity indicators, one for children and one for adults, are highlighted here. Measures of the extent to which the various groups receive patient-centered care and some measures of the process of applying for and receiving a kidney transplant complete the section. All are addressed in Table 7.5.

Referrals to Specialists

Table 7.5 shows that the pattern is the same for both children and adults when it comes to needed referrals to specialists. Hispanic/Latino adults and children were considerably more likely to report difficulties than their white counterparts. About 60 percent more Latino adults and about 25 percent more Latino children had problems getting referrals for needed specialty care. African American adults fared little better, with about 50 percent more than whites reporting problems.

Lower-income patients were uniformly more likely to have difficulties with referrals when compared to people with higher incomes (400 percent of poverty and higher). Almost 40 percent of adults in poverty who needed a specialist reported difficulties in getting care. Children in lower income families were 55–68 percent more likely to have problems than children in the highest income group.

Table 7.5

Indicators of Procedural Equity and Rates Relative to the Appropriate Reference Group, 2004 (in percent)

Procedural equity indicators	Race/ethnicity			Income/poverty %			
	White	Black	Latino	Less than 100	100–199	200–399	400+
Referrals to specialists							
Adults with problems getting referred to a specialist	23.9	34.8 (1.46)	38.6 (1.62)	38.0 (1.57)	29.2 (1.21)	26.9 (1.11)	24.2
Children with problems getting referred to a specialist	21.9	24.7 (1.13)	27.2 (1.24)	26.5 (1.58)	28.3 (1.68)	26.1 (1.55)	16.8
Indicators of patient-centered care							
Adults whose providers sometimes or never showed respect for what they had to say	7.3	8.2 (1.12)	9.1 (1.25)	13.9 (2.31)	9.1 (1.52)	8.1 (1.35)	6.0
Adults whose providers sometimes or never explained things in a way they could understand	7.3	10.8 (1.48)	12.1 (1.66)	14.7 (2.33)	10.4 (1.65)	8.5 (1.35)	6.3
Composite score: adults not receiving patient-centered care	8.7	11.0 (1.26)	12.2 (1.40)	15.8 (2.08)	11.0 (1.45)	9.8 (1.29)	7.6
Composite score: children not receiving patient-centered care	4.8	6.3 (1.31)	7.9 (1.65)	9.1 (3.03)	7.5 (2.5)	5.4 (1.80)	3.0
Kidney transplants							
Dialysis patients registered on the waiting list for transplantation (2003)	17.5	10.9 (0.62)	14.4 (0.82)				
Persons receiving a kidney transplant within three years of renal failure (2001)	26.9	9.1 (0.34)	14.9 (0.55)				

Source: National Healthcare Disparities Reports.

Patient-Centered Care

Indicators of patient-centered care focus on whether or not providers show respect for their patients, listen to them carefully, explain things in ways that the patient can understand, and spend enough time with them. Table 7.5 includes separate measures for providers' showing of respect and for explaining things for adults and composite measures of patient-centered care for both adults and children. For the composite measures, patients are determined to have received patient-centered care only when none of the four questions (respect, listening, explaining, and spending time) is answered with "sometimes" or "never."

For all four measures, the pattern of responses is identical across income status and race/ethnicity. On all the measures, African Americans were more likely than whites to have experienced problems. The differences ranged from 12 percent for the respect question to 48 percent for the question about explaining things. Latino patients experienced even more problems than African Americans on all the questions. Their differences from whites ranged from 25 percent for the respect question to 66 percent on the question about explaining things.

For all four measures, patient-centered care was consistently more likely as income increased. For all the measures, people in poverty were more than twice as likely to have missed out on patient-centered care. Poor children were three times as likely. For the composite score for adults, 15.8 percent of the poor did not get patient-centered care compared to only 7.6 percent of the highest income category.

Kidney Transplants

The final set of procedural equity measures focuses on the process of obtaining a kidney transplant. In 2003, 17.5 percent of all white dialysis patients were on the waiting list for a kidney transplant compared to 10.9 percent for African Americans and 14.4 percent for Hispanic/Latinos. The figures for actual transplants within three years of renal failure showed even greater disparities by race/ethnicity.

Outcome Equity

Former Surgeon General David Satcher (2005) and his research colleagues recently posed the question "What if we were equal?" with regard to black-white mortality rates. His question and answer provide background for the discussion of health equity outcomes. Satcher et al. (2005) report that in 2000 there were 83,369 excess deaths in the African American population. They calculated this value by applying the age-specific mortality rates of the white population to the black population and comparing them to the actual age-specific mortality rates for blacks. This outcome measure summarizes the impact of differences between blacks and whites in health care and all the other determinants of health.

The three previous sections have focused on determinants of health that are located, for the most part, within the health-care system itself or at least within the health policy establishment. When the question of overall health outcomes is addressed, however, the discussion extends beyond the health-care system to other areas of policy and administration that are within the province of public administrators.

Outcomes reflect the "bottom line" goals when it comes to health disparities, whether they are due to problems of access to care, problems of quality within the health-care system itself, or are due to "the adverse social and economic conditions faced by people of color in their own communities" (Lavizzo-Mourey 2005). In the foreword to a special issue of *Health Affairs* devoted to racial and ethnic disparities, Lavizzo-Mourey and her colleagues (2005) refer to this as the "triple whammy" (access, quality of care, and adverse social and economic conditions) confronting communities of color in the United States. And, putting the various determinants of health in perspective, they point out that it is

> widely known that less than one-quarter of our health status is attributable to health care; rather our health—or lack thereof—is primarily determined by social factors such as unhealthy health practices, poverty, unemployment and underemployment, racism and discrimination, housing, transportation, and other neighborhood environmental conditions. (Lavizzo-Mourey et al. 2005, 314)

In the same issue of *Health Affairs*, David Williams and Pamela Braboy Jackson (2005) highlight some of these non–health-care determinants. They write about "pathways" linking race, socioeconomic status (SES), and health. They note the association of education with homicide rates, and income with cancer and heart disease mortality. They point out that many problematic "health practices" are patterned along racial and SES lines—dietary behavior, physical activity, tobacco use, and alcohol abuse. These practices, they argue, are important risk factors for chronic diseases such as coronary heart disease and cancer (327). They also note the link between race and SES to exposure to chronic stressors in the environment (328). They point out that chronic exposure to psychosocial stressors is associated with altered physiological functioning, "which may increase risks for a broad range of health conditions" (ibid).

Williams and Jackson highlight the role of residential segregation and neighborhood quality in the overall picture. They argue that residential segregation is the central mechanism by which racial and ethnic economic inequality has been created and reinforced in the United States (328). They argue that it achieves this status by controlling access to education and employment opportunities. Problems in these areas lead, in turn, to neighborhood conditions (concentrated poverty, high unemployment, low wage rates, female-headed households, and low social control) that result in higher rates of homicide and other violent behavior. The perception of neighborhood safety, in turn, is linked to decreased opportunities for physical activity. Other neighborhood factors including differences in the availability of nutritious foods and aggressive marketing of tobacco and alcohol round out the array of "other" determinants of health that adversely affect the health of racial and ethnic minority citizens of the United States.

While it is well known that many of the gains in morbidity and mortality over the past century are due to improvements in sanitation and related public-health matters, efforts to reduce disparities in the United States are still mostly focused on the health-care system. One exception may be the effort to reduce disparities in cancer death by identifying differences in the larger historical, geographic, sociocultural, economic, and political contexts (Williams and Jackson 2005). This is in sharp contrast with public policy in Europe and throughout the industrialized world. The United Kingdom, for example, focuses on housing and child poverty interventions to address health inequality (Exworthy et al. 2006).[13]

Kawachi, Daniels, and Robinson (2005) join Isaacs and Schroeder (2004) in noting that in the widely cited *Health, United States, 2003,* only eight of the fifty-eight trend tables on "health status and determinants" contained data on socioeconomic status while fifty-seven contained information on race. This lack of data is reflected in the outcome tables that follow.

Indicators

Since many of the key outcome indicators are not available by socioeconomic status, the indicators presented will focus mainly on differences by race/ethnicity and by gender. Proposed new data-gathering efforts will likely expand reporting in this area over time.

Following Satcher and his colleagues (2005), the treatment will begin with black–white mortality rates and ratios for males and females by age and over time.

Mitchell Wong and his colleagues (2002; cited by Satcher et al. 2005) have pointed out that more than 50 percent of the disparities in years of life lost by racial minorities are due to cardiovascular disease, AIDS, and diabetes. Because of this, special attention will be given these diseases. Other sections will feature infant and maternal health outcomes and cancer.

Black–White Standardized Mortality Rates (SMR)

Satcher and his colleagues use standardized mortality rates (i.e., the age-specific death rates for African Americans divided by the comparable rate for whites) to show mortality patterns and arrive at their figures for "excess deaths" among African Americans. They point out that the SMR for all African Americans was 1.472 in 1960 and 1.412 in 2000. This means that African Americans suffered 47.2 percent more deaths than whites in 1960 and 41.2 percent more deaths in 2000. Satcher notes that the SMR for African American females started higher than the rate for males but has declined over the four-decade period. The SMR for African American males, on the other hand, has increased over time.[14]

Figure 7.4   **Selected Maternal and Infant Health Measures, 2004**

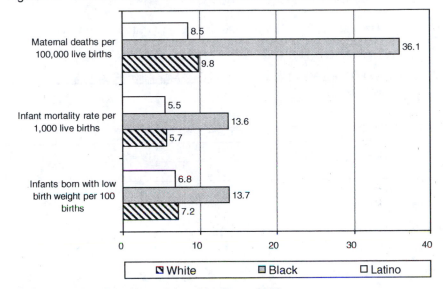

Source: National Healthcare Disparities Report 2007.

Maternal and Infant Health

Figure 7.4 shows low birth weight, infant mortality, and maternal death rates by race/ethnicity. The pattern is similar for all three measures: African Americans have strikingly higher rates for all three measures, with Hispanic/Latino rates very close to the rates for whites except for maternal deaths. For African Americans, infant mortality rates are more than twice those of whites while maternal deaths are more than three times the rates of whites and four times the rates of Hispanic/Latino mothers.

These rates have resisted major programmatic efforts over the past two decades. Research has suggested that differences persist even among better-educated and more affluent African Americans (David and Collins 2007; Singh and Yu 1995) leading some to conclude that the differences are related to the stress associated with minority group status (Jones 2000). Collins and David and their colleagues have reported adverse birth outcomes for black women exposed to neighborhood violence (1997), other unsatisfactory aspects of their residential environment and stressful life events (1998), and exposure to interpersonal racial discrimination (2004). Barnes (2008) confirmed this point of view with her focus groups and in-depth interviews with well-educated African American women.

Heart Disease and Cancer

Table 7.6 shows the mortality rates for the various forms of heart disease and cancer along with the ratio of the rates of the minority population to the majority (white)

Table 7.6

Heart Disease and Cancer Mortality Outcomes and Rates Relative to the White Population, 2005 (deaths per 100,000 people)

Outcome indicators	Race/ethnicity		
	White	Black	Latino
Heart disease—mortality			
Ischemic heart disease	145.2	173.7	118.0
		(1.20)	(0.81)
Major cardiovascular diseases	274.5	373.9	207.2
		(1.36)	(0.75)
Acute myocardial infarction	49.7	58.5	40.4
		(1.18)	(0.81)
Hypertensive heart disease	8.0	24.4	7.2
		(3.05)	(0.90)
Cancer—mortality			
Colorectal cancer	17.2	25.2	12.4
		(1.47)	(0.72)
Breast cancer (females)	24.0	33.5	15.0
		(1.40)	(0.63)
Prostate cancer (males)	22.8	54.1	18.5
		(2.37)	(0.81)
All cancers	187.0	226.8	122.8
		(1.21)	(0.66)

Source: National Vital Statistics Reports.

population. The pattern for all the measures of heart disease and all the cancer figures is the same: African Americans have the highest rates in each category followed by whites. In all of the measures Hispanic/Latinos have the lowest death rates.

For heart disease, African American rates range from about 20 percent greater than whites (for acute myocardial infarctions and ischemic heart disease) to three times the white death rate (for hypertensive heart disease). Latino rates are about 20 percent lower for acute myocardial infarctions and ischemic heart disease and about 10 percent lower for hypertensive heart disease.[15]

African American cancer rates are at least 40 percent higher for colorectal and breast cancer and are more than twice as large as white rates for prostate cancer. Cancer death rates for Hispanic/Latinos range from 20 percent to 40 percent lower than whites.

Stroke, Renal Failure, HIV/AIDS, and Diabetes

Table 7.7 shows selected mortality and other outcomes for stroke, renal failure, HIV/AIDS, and diabetes. As before, the rates for African Americans are highest

Table 7.7

Stroke, Renal Failure, HIV/AIDS, and Diabetes Outcomes and Rates Relative to the White Population, 2005 (deaths per 100,000 people)

Outcome indicators	Race/ethnicity		
	White	Black	Latino
Other diseases—mortality			
Stroke	45.0	66.3 (1.47)	35.7 (0.79)
Renal failure	12.6	29.6 (2.35)	11.6 (0.92)
HIV infection	1.9	18.5 (9.74)	3.9 (2.05)
Other outcomes			
New AIDS cases over age 12	7.5	75.0 (10.0)	26.4 (3.52)
Hospital admissions for long-term complications of diabetes (2004)	91.5	338.2 (3.70)	257.7 (2.82)
Hospital admissions for short-term complications of diabetes (2004)	46.0	154.3 (3.35)	55.7 (1.21)

Source: National Healthcare Disparity Reports and National Vital Statistics Reports.

in all of the categories. Differences between African American and white rates are particularly large for new AIDS cases and deaths from HIV/AIDS (about ten times greater) but they are also great for diabetes admissions (more than three times greater) and for renal failure (more than twice as great).

Hispanic/Latino rates for these measures do not uniformly follow the pattern established in the previous table. Only mortality rates for stroke and renal failure are lower than whites. Rates for new HIV cases and deaths, while not reaching the levels for African Americans, are still more than twice the rates for whites. Hispanic/Latinos also have relatively high rates for diabetes admissions.[16]

Initiatives

Two prestigious research groups, from the RAND Corporation and from Brandeis University, have examined the literature on initiatives to reduce health disparities and have come to somewhat discouraging conclusions. The Brandeis group set out to find "best practices" in the field but concluded that it was not yet possible to assign the title because of the paucity of adequately researched interventions. They preferred, instead, to write about "promising practices" (McDonough et al. 2004).

Former Surgeon General David Satcher and his colleagues, after noting that there were more than 83,000 excess deaths among African Americans each year, acknowledged the difficulty involved in dealing with health disparities.

> The interrelatedness of personal health behavior, social determinants, neighborhood ecology, provider bias, structural inequities, and institutionalized racism suggests that eliminating disparities will require large-scale, multidimensional, community participatory interventions focused explicitly on health disparities for specific population groups, as well as on broader dimensions of social equality and economic justice. (Satcher et al. 2005, 463)

Dr. Louis Sullivan, former secretary of the U.S. Department of Health and Human Services, expressed a similar view (2005) while attempting to set priorities for reducing disparities.

Nevertheless, despite these caveats, the literature suggests many plausible approaches consistent with the social equity view espoused here.[17] The four-part social equity framework outlined here provides a loose structure for the discussion. No attempt is made in what follows to provide an exhaustive review of possible initiatives. Rather, the attempt is focused on a sample of items suggested by the previous discussion.

Access/Distribution

Initiatives in the area of access and distribution of health-care services tend to begin with the federal and state governments. Initiatives associated with the Medicare and Medicaid programs and the State Child Health Insurance Program (SCHIP) are particularly prominent in these discussions.

The National Academy of Social Insurance recently organized a panel to review the role of the Medicare program in reducing racial and ethnic health disparities (Vladeck, Van de Water, and Eichner 2006). Their final report, released in October 2006, advocates the use of the Medicare program to:

> Increase the access of underserved minority beneficiaries to health care by promoting programs that provide supplementary coverage, improving access to providers, and expanding educational and outreach activities (2).

Their report also identifies initiatives related to the quality of clinical care, education of health professionals, and the responsibility of individual and institutional providers to reduce health disparities. Most important for public administrators, the report argues for establishing performance standards in this arena for the Center for Medicare and Medicaid Services (CMS), for enhancing the organizational structure of CMS to support the reduction of disparities, and for addressing disparities as a civil rights compliance issue (3). The authors note that most of their recommendations could be implemented by CMS using current statutory authority. They point out, however, that most of their recommendations would require additional Medicare spending.

Experts generally agree that some of the disparities in health care by race/ethnicity can be accounted for by differences in the levels of health insurance. However, because of the complexity of the analysis involved, it is difficult to determine the impact of eliminating disparities in coverage. Lillie-Blanton and Hoffman (2005) reviewed four studies that addressed this issue directly and concluded that equalizing health insurance coverage by race/ethnicity would eliminate about a third of the variation in access to a usual source of care, one of the keys to providing the opportunity for high-quality overall care.

Clearly, expansions of public health-insurance programs at the state and federal level and other strategies for reducing the numbers of uninsured are critical elements in any strategy to reduce disparities (Frist 2005; Kennedy 2005; Shone et al. 2005). And while the case is often made that expanding health insurance coverage will not be enough (Rosenbaum and Teitelbaum 2005; Smedley, Stith, and Nelson 2003), there are other measures that can be taken to improve health-insurance coverage within the existing structure of public health-insurance benefits.

Summer and Mann (2006) used Medicaid and the State Children's Health Insurance Program (SCHIP) to explore one aspect of this issue. They focused specifically on "churning"—the phenomenon of individuals losing and regaining coverage under a public health-insurance program in a short period of time. They found that instability in coverage under public health-insurance programs affected millions of children and families each year with serious consequences for health-care delivery and costs. They noted, for example, that in Virginia, over an eighteen-month period, about a third of the children enrolled in Medicaid or SCHIP lost their coverage at some point.

Quality—Quality Improvement Processes

Lurie, Jung, and Lavizzo-Mourey (2005) have argued that there are many federal policy levers for improving quality in the U.S. health-care system. They argue that federal and state health-care financing programs can and should use their buying power to require the collection of the data needed to identify disparities, enforce standards of cultural competence, and demand that providers monitor and reduce disparities in the provision of care.

A recent report from the Institute on Medicine (2006), *Performance Measurement: Accelerating Improvement*, argues, however, that a strong national system for performance measurement and reporting is unlikely to emerge from the current approach to quality improvement efforts. The report calls for the establishment of a strong new independent board, the National Quality Coordination Board (NQCB), housed in the Department of Health and Human Services and reporting directly to the secretary. Besides providing information that is useful for accountability purposes and quality improvement efforts, the NQCB would be responsible for providing information about population health:

... for stakeholders making decisions about access to services (e.g. public insurance benefits and coverage); those involved in community wide programs and efforts to address racial and ethnic disparities and promote healthy behaviors; and public officials responsible for disease surveillance and health protection. (Institute on Medicine 2006, 6)

The report "strongly advocates"

... collection of performance measures addressing health care services at the individual level, allowing for aggregation to various levels of providers, geographic regions, and demographics. The critical issue in measuring racial, ethnic, or socioeconomic disparities is the need for data aggregation and reporting systems that can provide this stratification when sample sizes are large enough to yield reliable estimates. (99)

The Standing Panel on Social Equity of the National Academy of Public Administration (NAPA) should give particular attention to this initiative since it is consistent with the purposes of the group and with the panel's chosen strategy to advance social equity. NAPA should consider holding hearings on the proposal, giving formal support to it if appropriate, and offering its expertise to develop the equity measures still needed to address the gaps in performance measurement identified in the report. The social equity framework adopted by the panel (and this chapter) should be useful in providing this assistance if NAPA chooses to offer it.

Procedural Equity

The section on procedural equity indicators focused on civil rights approaches to eliminating past disparities in health care and on the challenges to procedural equity posed by the practices of managed-care organizations. Here, the focus will be on civil rights approaches to addressing disparities.

As suggested above, expansion of health-insurance coverage would eliminate about a third of the racial/ethnic disparities in access to primary care. Rosenbaum and Teitelbaum (2005) argue that major procedural reforms are also needed. They note that the quality of care measures highlighted in *Unequal Treatment* (Smedley, Stith, and Nelson 2003) were documented for those who had gained access to the health-care system.

From a public policy standpoint, reducing disparities requires a formal and enforceable scheme that promotes accountability toward discrete sub-groups of patients as well as the overall population. Such a scheme would act as a lever for advancing reforms that otherwise might languish, and whose importance can be obscured by the aggregated results of generalized improvement activities. (141)

Teitelbaum (2005) recently reviewed the history of health care and civil rights. He acknowledged the success of the civil rights approach in desegregating hospitals in the mid-1960s but followed Smith (2005a) in arguing that civil rights enforcement impacts since then have been very limited. Teitelbaum points out, for example, that managed-care organizations:

> . . . may avoid setting up contracts in particular service areas altogether, or only sell its products to Medicare, but not Medicaid, in certain areas; or, they may maintain segregated provider networks even within a single service area. (Teitelbaum 2005, S2–29)

One promising development using the existing civil rights approach has been proposed in the area of limited English proficiency (Brach, Fraser, and Paez 2005; Ku and Flores 2005). Both the Clinton and Bush administrations have supported an effort to develop regulations to delineate provider obligations to meet the needs of those who cannot communicate effectively in English in a health-care setting. Some even believe that the approach taken regarding language competency can serve as an effective model for civil rights enforcement action in other important areas (Rosenbaum and Teitelbaum 2005).

As in the other initiative areas, effective initiatives addressing procedural equity begin with data gathering. David Barton Smith (2005a) makes the most compelling case for more effective data gathering in the civil rights arena. He points out that the Home Mortgage Disclosure Act of 1975 was needed to monitor discrimination in mortgage lending and that federal testing tools were (and are) needed to monitor discrimination in employment and housing. Smith argues that the public-reporting requirement implemented for home mortgages is needed in the health-care field particularly on the issue of physician compliance with Title VI of the Civil Rights Act: There has never been a lack of regulatory authority to require such collection and reporting; it has always been a lack of political will." (Smith 2005b, 323)

The areas to be covered would include data collection and analysis of health care to identify possible racial and ethnic disparities in diagnosis and treatment. The information would also be useful in determining who is accessing health services, the health status of different populations, utilization rates of services, and the effectiveness of public health interventions among different racial and ethnic groups (Smith 2005b, 323).

Outcomes

Over the past twenty years, research on disparate outcomes by race/ethnicity—of both morbidity and mortality—has led to numerous specific programmatic efforts to reduce disparities. Atrash and Hunter (2006) recently provided some examples of these efforts. The Health Resources and Services Administration's (HRSA) Minority Management Development Program focuses on developing skilled minority group managers in the managed-care industry. HRSA also operates the Health Disparities Collaborative, an organization focused on working with groups of primary-care providers to assure the delivery of high-quality care to patients with chronic conditions.

The Agency for Healthcare Research and Quality (AHRQ) has funded nine Excellence Centers to Eliminate Ethnic/Racial Disparities (EXCEED), which focus on understanding causes of disparities and ways to eliminate them. The Centers for Medicare and Medicaid Services (CMS) support two programs designed to increase the numbers of African American and Hispanic health researchers and their ability to design and carry out research and evaluation projects related to health initiatives in minority communities. The National Institutes of Health (NIH) also have programs focused on recruiting and training minority group researchers. The Centers for Disease Control and Prevention (CDC) operate the Racial and Ethnic Approaches to Community Health (REACH) program to reduce or eliminate health disparities. Specific projects concentrate on the operation of cancer registries and programs focused on prevention or early detection of cancer in minority groups. Atrash and Hunter (2006) mention two community interventions as being particularly successful, a diabetes program in South Carolina and the CDC's Childhood Immunization Initiative.

The diabetes program was successful in encouraging patients to engage in physical activity, improve their eating habits, and pay more attention to controlling their disease. In three years the program was able to eliminate the gap between blacks and whites in A1C testing. The CDC used a variety of strategies to boost immunizations in minority communities following a 1989–91 measles epidemic that affected minority children at four to seven times the rate of whites. By increasing funding for public-health departments, operating public-information campaigns, encouraging local immunization action plans, and providing free vaccines for uninsured and underinsured children, the CDC was able to increase the overall immunization rates for all children and virtually eliminate the gap in coverage between whites and minority groups.

In recent years a number of communities have mounted special efforts to address health disparities on several fronts at the local level. The efforts of two communities, Boston and Omaha, are reviewed briefly here.[18]

In Boston, the effort began in the spring of 2005 with Mayor Thomas Menino's Task Force on Racial and Ethnic Health Disparities. The goals of the Task Force were to improve the ability of the area to measure disparities; to build the capacity in communities and institutions to respond to the problem; to promote innovative practices in accessing care, diversifying the workforce, and creating public policy change; and to raise public awareness of health disparities. By 2007, the group had awarded thirty-three one-year grants to local organizations to undertake projects related to the goals articulated. In addition, quality improvement efforts focused on disparities were launched at several hospitals in the region and new regulations were promulgated requiring the hospitals in the region to provide the data required to prepare detailed maps of health-care access and utilization. Among other things, project funds also helped to develop new patient navigation models and provide cultural competency and antiracism trainings for hundreds of health professionals in the area. Boston's new Center for Health Equity and Social Justice now incorporates the area's REACH U.S. project and the work of the Task Force.

In another move with implications for health disparities and access to care, Mayor Menino recently established a Task Force on Improving Primary Care in the city. The Task force report noted that while health-care reform in Massachusetts had increased the number of insured patients and that while Boston is home to outstanding medical institutions, an adequate supply of primary-care providers was needed to assure that health-care costs would not rise and quality of care suffer.

In Omaha, the local effort has been facilitated by the University of Nebraska Medical Center's Center for Reducing Health Disparities. Besides addressing its research goals, the strategic plan of the unit details its efforts to reduce disparities in Omaha by engaging local partners in service and health-education efforts. The plan lists thirty-two specific collaborative efforts with the local partners scheduled for 2008–9, including health fairs and screenings, tobacco education initiatives, HIV/AIDS awareness activities, and similar such programs, all targeted on the minority communities in Omaha.

Conclusion

While researchers remain guarded about interventions to address health disparities, public administrators and social equity policy advocates have developed a large number of promising approaches to measuring the problem. For example, Amal Trevedi and his colleagues (2005) recently reported on their evaluation of state minority health efforts. It matches the four areas of equity measurement recommended by NAPA. They developed a scorecard of state performance based on four elements: (1) the health-insurance gap—the difference in coverage between low-income minorities and low-income whites, (2) the diversity of the physician workforce in the state, (3) the presence of a federally recognized State Office of Minority Health, and (4) the number of race/ethnicity categories in the state's vital-statistics system. They concluded that there was widespread variation in the performance of the states on all four measures.

There are developments that affect the attention to social equity in health, including the new administration in Washington, research on the links between social equity in non–health-care arenas, and the presence of thousands of dedicated social-equity-seeking professionals and advocates. Progress in reducing disparities in the near term seems likely despite the economic difficulties faced by the country. The Task Force on Improving Primary Care in Boston reminds us that the outcome of the national debate on health-care reform does not address all the issues in achieving social equity. Expanding health-insurance coverage does not guarantee the availability of services or that health care of equal quality is provided in a procedurally fair way. Continued action in all four areas of social equity measurement will continue to be required.

Update: The Patient Protection and Affordable Care Act of 2010

The Patient Protection and Affordable Care Act of 2010 (Affordable Care Act), the U.S. health-care reform legislation, does not contain the term "social equity." The word "equity," in its justice or fairness meaning, appears only two times, and forms of the word "disparity" appear only occasionally in the 906-page law. In its list of the major purposes of the legislation, the Obama administration includes a social equity goal, access, as a major aim but the other two purposes are related to overall costs and affordability. Despite this, there can be no doubt that the legislation has enormous potential for making large changes in the social equity measures of health and health care in the United States reported here.

Access

As a result of the Affordable Care Act, by 2019 the proportion of Americans covered by health insurance will move from the current 83 percent to 94 percent with 32 million newly insured people. People with incomes below the poverty level and up to 133 percent of poverty will be eligible for Medicaid in 2014, and those with incomes up to 400 percent of poverty will be eligible for subsidies limiting their health insurance premium costs to between 3 percent and 9.5 percent of their family incomes (Davis 2010a). The White House recently noted that about nine million uninsured Latinos, the minority group with the least coverage, would be eligible for health-insurance coverage (White House 2010). The act also addresses the problem of underinsurance by mandating minimum levels of services covered under new health-insurance policies along with limits on premiums and copayments.

The Affordable Care Act also provides for greater access to recommended preventive care and cancer screening by mandating that they be provided without cost-sharing by the patient in new health-insurance policies. States will get incentives to provide the same services without cost-sharing under their Medicaid programs. Medicare will provide a similar cost-sharing-free benefit along with an annual wellness visit. Provisions in the act will also outlaw "gender rating" by insurance companies, thereby reducing an important barrier to prenatal care for low-income women (Davis 2010a).

The act also strengthens access by supporting an $11 billion expansion of community health centers in medically underserved areas. It also has other provisions (e.g., educational loan assistance) that will improve primary-care service capacity in those areas.

Quality

The Affordable Care Act does not establish the National Quality Coordination Board described earlier in the chapter, but it does follow through on some of the ideas of those who proposed it. Section 4302 of the act requires the secretary to collect detailed demographic data in all federally funded "health care or public health program, activity, or survey" conducted or funded beginning in 2012. To the extent practicable, the secretary is to collect

- sufficient data to generate statistically reliable estimates by racial, ethnic, gender, primary language, and disability status subgroups for applicants, recipients, or participants using, if needed, statistical oversamples of these subpopulations; and
- any other demographic data as deemed appropriate by the Secretary regarding health disparities.

Requiring the collection of the appropriate data is the first step in the process of using the considerable spending leverage of the federal government to assure quality of care. High-quality care means no variation in treatment associated with any demographic characteristic. In short, no disparities. When this process is fully implemented, organizations that fail to deliver on this standard will put their federal funding at risk.

Besides requiring the collection of data to improve the monitoring of differences in quality in health-care services by demographic categories, the act has a number of provisions that should improve the overall quality of care provided to all who access the system. Taken together, these provisions will move the health-care system in the direction of delivering "more patient-centered, accessible, and coordinated care" (Davis 2010b). The provisions include funding of "patient-centered medical homes," incentives to implement electronic medical records, financial rewards to doctors and hospitals for providing higher quality care and achieving better outcomes, and better public information about the quality of physicians, hospitals, and health plans. Other provisions that contribute to providing equal quality in health care include the availability of grants for training health-care providers in culturally appropriate care, more funding and scholarships for disadvantaged and minority students to enhance the diversity of the workforce, and the requirement that the insurance exchanges created under the law provide explanations of the plans that are "culturally and linguistically appropriate" (Families USA 2010).

Procedural Equity

Section 1557 of the Affordable Care Act makes it clear that the provisions of Title VI of the Civil Rights Act of 1964, Title IX of the Education Amendments of 1972, Section 504 of the Rehabilitation Act of 1973, and the Age Discrimination Act of 1975 apply to the health-care providers and others funded under the act. As noted in the case of quality assurance approaches, efforts to pursue procedural remedies have been thwarted by a lack of good data. There is reason to believe that the availability of better data in the health-care field may eventually have the impact that the availability of detailed home mortgage data has had on discriminatory lending practices.

Outcomes

Achieving more equitable outcomes in the health arena will depend in part on the numbers of publicly supported eyes that are watching. The Affordable Care Act moves in that direction by creating a deputy assistant secretary for Minority Health who will report directly to the secretary of the Department of Health and Human Services (DHHS). The act also adds offices of Minority Health to all the major health agencies within DHHS (CDC, HRSA, SAMHSA, AHRQ, FDA, and CMMS). In addition, the act upgrades the National Center on Minority Health and Health Disparities to institute status within the National Institutes of Health. Taken together, these steps will increase the ability of the federal government to use the leverage to eliminate disparities provided by other provisions of the act.

The Affordable Care Act also provides additional funding for community-based prevention initiatives focused on chronic diseases and community-based approaches to eliminating disparities. These approaches will be consistent with a national prevention and wellness strategy to be developed as a result of the legislation (Families USA 2010).

Finally, in recognition of the fact that improvements in the health-care system cannot totally eliminate differences in health outcomes, the act promotes the use of health impact assessments for analyzing the effect of the built environment on health outcomes.

Clearly, the Affordable Care Act will forever alter the health-care landscape of the United States. It remains to be seen, however, whether its provisions that facilitate making health and health care more equitable will have their intended effects. As always, it will depend upon the ability and energy of the country's public servants and the goodwill of the American people.

Appendix 7.1

The NHDR – SEP Crosswalk

The National Healthcare Disparities Reports (NHDR) have most of the indicators needed for the work of the National Academy of Public Administration's Standing Panel on Social Equity in Governance (SEP). The organization of the various measurement categories in the NHDR has changed slightly since the original list in the 2004 report.

There are two measurement domains in the 2007 NHDR (Agency for Healthcare Research and Quality 2008) indicators, access and quality. Within each measurement domain there are several categories and subcategories of indicators that are appropriate for the various indicators proposed here. Some of the choices made in assigning the NHDR categories and subcategories to SEP measurement categories are detailed in the tables below. It is clear that some of the NHDR measures could be included in more than one SEP category. There are some cases in which NHDR quality measures are listed as SEP access measures (e.g., screening and usual source of care measures). In addition, there are situations in which analysts might reasonably disagree on the appropriate categories. For example, are higher numbers of hospitalizations for asthma among African Americans an indicator of poorer quality of care in managing the disease or a measure of less favorable outcomes (or even a sign of superior access)? Similar arguments arise with regard to diabetes management. Also, do measures of the respect providers show to patients and effective communication with patients belong in the quality category or in procedural fairness (as indicated below) since they are concerned with the interaction between the patient and the service system? At some point it is necessary to acknowledge the possibility of assignment to a different category and move forward with the analysis. While there may be some debate about where they might be placed, all of the NHDR measures clearly belong in the four-part SEP framework.

NHDR 2007 – SEP Crosswalk: Overview

NHDR Category	NHDR Sub-category	Measure Type	Example	SEP Category
Quality	Effectiveness	Prevention	Screening for breast cancer	Quality / Access
		Treatment	Treatment for depression	Quality / Outcome
		Management	Receipt of recommended services for diabetes	Quality / Outcome
	Patient Safety	—	Adverse drug reaction in hospital	Quality
	Timeliness	—	Getting care for illness or injury as soon as wanted	Quality / Access
	Patient Centeredness	—	Composite: provider-patient communication	Procedural Fairness
Access	Facilitators and Barriers to Health Care	Health Insurance Coverage	Persons with health insurance coverage	Access
		Usual Source of Care	Person has a specific source of ongoing care?	Access
		Patient Perceptions of Need (difficulties in obtaining care after need is established)	Persons who delayed needed health care	Access / Procedural Fairness
	Health Care Utilization	—	Dental visit in the past year	Access

155

NHDR – SEP Crosswalk: NHDR Quality Measures Used

NHDR Category	NHDR Sub-category	Measure Type	Measure	SEP Category
Quality	Effectiveness	Cancer	*Colorectal cancer—deaths per 100,000—2005	Outcome
			*Breast cancer—deaths per 100,000 females—2005	Outcome
			*Prostate cancer—deaths per 100,000 males—2005	Outcome
			*All cancers—deaths per 100,000—2005	Outcome
		Diabetes	Percent of adults with diabetes who did not have a hemoglobin A1C measurement in the past year—2004	Quality
			Hospital admissions for uncontrolled diabetes without complications per 100,000 adults (18+)—2004	Quality
			Hospital admissions for long-term complications of diabetes per 100,000—2004	Outcome
			Hospital admissions for short-term complications of diabetes per 100,000—2004	Outcome
		Heart Disease	*Ischemic heart disease—deaths per 100,000—2005	Outcome
			*Major cardiovascular diseases—deaths per 100K—2005	Outcome
			*Acute myocardial infarction—deaths per 100K—2005	Outcome
			*Hypertensive heart disease—deaths per 100K—2005	Outcome
		HIV / AIDS	New AIDS cases per 100,000 over age 12—2005	Outcome
			HIV-infection—deaths per 100,000—2005	Outcome

156

NHDR – SEP Crosswalk: NHDR Quality Measures Used *(continued)*

NHDR Category	NHDR Sub-category	Measure Type	Measure	SEP Category
		Maternal and Child Health	Percent of infants born with low birth weight (less than 2500 grams)—2004—by mother's ethnicity	Outcome
			Infant mortality rate per 1,000 live births—2004	Outcome
			Maternal deaths per 100,000 live births—2004	Outcome
			Percent of children age 19-35 months who did not receive all vaccines—2005	Quality
			Percent of pregnant women not receiving prenatal care in first trimester—2004	Access
			Percent of children (2–17) without dental visit in past year—2004	Access

*This measure is from the National Vital Statistics Report (NVSR), not the NHDR.

NHDR – SEP Crosswalk: NHDR Quality Measures Used *(continued)*

NHDR Category	NHDR Sub-category	Measure Type	Measure	SEP Category
Quality	Effectiveness	End Stage Renal Disease	Percent of Persons receiving a kidney transplant within three years of renal failure—2001	Procedural Fairness
			Percent of dialysis patients registered on the waiting list for transplantation—2003	Procedural Fairness
			Renal Failure—deaths per 100,000—2005	Outcome
		Respiratory and Other Diseases	High risk adults (18-64) who did not get flu vaccine in past year—2005	Quality
			Hospital admissions for asthma per 100,000 population age 18 and over—2004	Quality
			Hospital admissions for asthma per 100,000 population under age 18—2004	Quality
			Percent of persons aged 18+ with serious depression and no care—2004	Access
			*Stroke—deaths per 100,000—2005	Outcome
	Patient Safety	—	Selected infections due to medical care per 1,000 discharges—2004	Quality
			Decubitus ulcers (pressure sores) per 1,000 discharges of length five days or more, age 18 and over	Quality

(continued)

158

NHDR – SEP Crosswalk: NHDR Quality Measures Used *(continued)*

NHDR Category	NHDR Sub-category	Measure Type	Measure	SEP Category
	Patient Centeredness	—	Composite score—adults not receiving patient-centered care—2004	Procedural Fairness
			Composite score—children not receiving patient-centered care—2004	Procedural Fairness
			Adults whose providers sometimes or never showed respect for what they had to say—2004	Procedural Fairness
			Adults whose providers sometimes or never explained things in a way they could understand—2004	Procedural Fairness

*This measure is from the National Vital Statistics Report not the NHDR.

NHDR – SEP Crosswalk: NHDR Access Measures Used

NHDR Category	NHDR Sub-category	Measure Type	Measures	SEP Category
Access	Facilitators and Barriers to Health Care	Health Insurance Coverage	Percent uninsured—under age 18, by race / ethnicity—2007	Access
			Percent uninsured—under age 65, by race / ethnicity, 2007	Access
			Percent uninsured—ages 18-64—working full-time, by race / ethnicity—2006	Access
			Percent uninsured—ages 18-64—working full-time, by education—2006	Access
			Percent uninsured—ages 18-64—working full-time, by income / poverty status—2006	Access
		Usual Source of Care	Percent with no usual source of care—2005	Access
			Percent with fair/poor health and no usual source of care—2005	Access
			Percent hospital / clinic as usual source—2005	Access
			Percent with no usual source – financial cause—2005	Access
		Patient Perceptions of Need (difficulties in obtaining care after need is established)	Percent of adults with problems getting referred to a specialist—2004	Procedural Fairness
			Percent of children with problems getting referred to a specialist—2004	Procedural Fairness
		Patient-Provider Communication	Percent of adults who rated their health care less than seven on a ten-point scale—2004	Quality
			Percent of children whose health care was rated less than 7 on a ten-point scale—2004	Quality
	Health Care Utilization	—	Percent of persons aged 18+ without an office /out-patient visit in past year—2004	Access

Notes

1. NAPA's Standing Panel on Social Equity in Governance is usually referred to as the "Social Equity Panel" or SEP.

2. There is also the presumption that certain public-health services are provided for the benefit of all citizens. Public-health services, however, will not be addressed in this report.

3. There are several major surveys that attempt to measure the rates of health insurance in the U.S. population. For a review of the various methods see "Understanding Estimates of the Uninsured: Putting the Differences in Context" (U.S. Department of Health and Human Services 2005) and/or *Comparing Federal Government Surveys that Count Uninsured People in America* (Robert Wood Johnson Foundation 2006).

4. Exworthy and his colleagues (2006) cite Adler et al. (1993) and McGinnis, Williams-Russo, and Knickman (2002) in arguing that only 10–15 percent of the variation in health outcomes is due to health care.

5. There is some evidence that this pattern is beginning to change, however. Researcher Nancy Krieger (2007) recently pointedly reminded epidemiologists that they could not afford to ignore poverty in their work. Also, a recent issue of *Health Affairs*, a major health-policy journal, called for expanding the focus of policy considerations with regard to disparities (Robinson 2008). It noted the launching, by the Robert Wood Johnson Foundation, of the "first independent, nonpartisan health commission to consider solutions outside the medical care system for reducing health disparities and improving America's health" (319); www.commissiononhealth.org.

6. This chapter does not address a number of important social equity and health concerns detailed in the National Health Disparities Reports (NHDR) prepared annually by the Agency for Healthcare Reserach and Quality (available at http://www.ahrq.gov/qual/measurix.htm). The health concerns of Asian and Pacific Islanders, Native Americans, and some "priority" populations—women, the elderly, residents of rural and other medically underserved geographic areas, and individuals with special health-care needs—are given little attention here. Space and time limitations also precluded detailed discussion of international aspects of social equity and health (Braveman and Gruskin 2003; Daniels et al. 2000), promising new measurement approaches (Gibbs et al. 2006; Schoen et al. 2006); controversy over the NHDR reports (Exworthy et al. 2006); beliefs of the public (Harvard School of Public Health 2005) and some practitioners (Altman and Lillie-Blanton 2003) with regard to health disparities; local measurement strategies (Exworthy et al. 2006); and a host of other important issues.

7. For example, 21.4 percent of Latinos under age eighteen are uninsured compared to 11.6 percent of whites. The relative rate for Latinos is, therefore, 21.4/11.6, or 1.84. Latino children are 1.84 times as likely as white children to be uninsured. This approach will be used in tables throughout the chapter.

8. For further discussion of health insurance for children, differences in coverage by geography, and related issues, see *Going Without: America's Uninsured Children* (SHADAC and Urban Institute 2005), a Robert Wood Johnson Foundation Report and/or the full version of this chapter on the SEP Web site.

9. The Commonwealth Fund conducts a biennial health insurance survey. Their results are similar, but not identical, to the results of the 2007 Medical Expenditures Panel Survey. See endnote 3 for further details.

10. This was done, in part, by introducing composite measures—measures that combined several indicators into a single index of access. This relatively recent development, to choose a smaller group of indicators and some composite indicators, and to vigorously and rigorously track progress is consistent with the purposes of the Social Equity Panel's measurement project. It should be monitored closely by the SEP as it proceeds.

11. "Improving" refers to the population reference group difference becoming smaller at a rate greater than 1 percent per year. "Worsening" refers to the difference becoming larger at a rate greater than 1 percent per year.

12. As with access measures, "improving" refers to the population reference group difference becoming smaller at a rate greater than 1 percent per year. "Worsening" refers to the difference becoming larger at a rate greater than 1 percent per year.

13. For a more detailed discussion of this and related issues, research on inequality and health, and notes on class as the "ignored determinant" of health, see Kawachi, Daniels, and Robinson (2005) and Exworthy et al. (2006).

14. Between 1960 and 2000, the SMR for African American females went from 1.607 to 1.342. For African American males the comparable figures were 1.376 and 1.487.

15. Experts attribute the lower mortality rates of Hispanic/Latinos to (1) lower death rates at the older ages, (2) underreporting of Hispanic origin, (3) the healthy migrant effect (immigrants are selected for their health and robustness), and (4) the "salmon bias" (returning to the country of origin when ill or dying) (Kung et al., 2008, 4).

16. Hospital admissions for uncontrolled diabetes are listed as indicators of quality of care—in managing the disease. Admissions for short- and long-term complications are included here as outcomes—the impact of diabetes on the population over time.

17. In one of the most recent efforts (Schotthauer et al. 2008) to address the issue of effective actions to reduce disparities, a team from the Robert Wood Johnson Foundation simply listed the types of interventions that were being proposed in the latest round of the foundation's "Finding Answers" grant applications: patient or provider education (57 percent), community health workers (25 percent), integrated health care (24 percent), and cultural modification (24 percent). They concluded their report with a series of important future research questions.

18. Information about these efforts was gathered from Web sites focused on their activities: www.bphc.org/CHESJ/Pages/default.aspx; www.unmc.edu/publichealth/healthdisparity/healthdisparities.htm.

References

Acheson, D. 1998. *Independent Inquiry into Inequalities in Health (The Acheson Report).* London: Stationery Office.

Adler, N.E.; W.T. Boyce; M.A. Chesney; S. Folkman; and S.L. Syme. 1993. "Socioeconomic Inequalities in Health: No Easy Solution." *Journal of the American Medical Association* 269, no. 24: 3140–45.

Agency for Healthcare Research and Quality. 2008. *National Healthcare Disparities Report 2007.* U.S. Department of Health and Human Services. http://www.ahrq.gov/qual/nhdr07/nhdr07.pdf (accessed February 28, 2011).

Altman, D., and M. Lillie-Blanton. 2003. "Racial/Ethnic Disparities in Medical Care." *British Medical Journal USA* 3: 300–301.

Atrash, H.K., and M.D. Hunter. 2006. "Health Disparities in the United States: A Continuing Challenge." In *Multicultural Medicine and Health Disparities*, ed. D. Satcher and R.J. Pamies, 3–31. New York: McGraw Hill.

Barnes, G.L. 2008. "Perspectives of African-American Women on Infant Mortality." *Social Work in Health Care* 47, no. 3: 293–305.

Beal, A.C.; M.M. Doty; S.E. Hernandez; K.K. Shea; and K. Davis. 2007. "Closing the Divide: How Medical Homes Promote Equity in Health Care: Results from the Commonwealth Fund 2006 Health Care Quality Survey." Commonwealth Fund, June 2007.

Bloche, M.G., and D.M. Studdert. 2004. "A Quiet Revolution: Law as an Agent of Health System Change." *Health Affairs* 23, no. 2: 29–42.

Brach, C.; I. Fraser; and K. Paez. 2005. "Crossing the Language Chasm." *Health Affairs* 24, no. 2: 424–34.

Braveman P. and S. Gruskin. 2003. "Defining Equity in Health." *Journal of Epidemiology and Community Health* 57, no. 4: 254–58 (April 2003).

Collins, J.W. Jr., and R.J. David. 1997. "Urban Violence and African-American Pregnancy Outcome: An Ecologic Study." *Ethnicity and Disease* 7: 184–90.

Collins, J.W. Jr.; R.J. David; A. Handler; S. Wall; and S. Andes. 2004. "Very Low Birth Weight in African-American Infants: The Role of Maternal Exposure to Interpersonal Racial Discrimination." *American Journal of Public Health* 94: 2132–38.

Collins, J.W. Jr.; R.J. David; R. Symons; A. Handler; S. Wall; and S. Andes. 1998. "American Mothers' Perception of Their Residential Environment, Stressful Life Events, and Very Low Birth Weight." *Epidemiology* 9: 286–89.

Collins, S.R., J.L. Kriss, M.M. Doty, and S.D. Rustgi. 2008. *Losing Ground: How the Loss of Adequate Health Insurance Is Burdening Working Families: Findings from the Commonwealth Fund Biennial Health Insurance Surveys, 2001–2007.* Washington, DC: The Commonwealth Fund, August.

Commonwealth Fund. 2008. *Why Not the Best? Results from the National Scorecard on U.S. Health System Performance, 2008.* The Commonwealth Fund Commission on a High Performance Health System, July 2008.

Daniels, N.; J. Bryant; R.A. Castano; O.G. Dantes; K.S. Khan; and S. Pannarunothai. 2000. "Benchmarks of Fairness for Health Care Reform: A Policy Tool for Developing Countries." *Bulletin of the World Health Organization* 78, no. 6: 740–50.

David, R., and J.W. Collins Jr. 2007. "Disparities in Infant Mortality: What's Genetics Got to Do with It? *American Journal of Public Health* 97, no. 7: 1191–97.

Davis, K. 2010a. "Who Is Helped by Health Reform?" Commonwealth Fund Blog, June 17. Available at www.commonwealthfund.org/~/media/Files/Publications/Blog/Davis_Blog_June_2010_617.pdf (accessed July 15, 2010).

———. 2010b. "How Will the Health Care System Change Under Health Care Reform?" Commonwealth Fund Blog, June 29. Available at www.commonwealthfund.org/Content/Blog/How-Will-the-Health-Care-System-Change.aspx (accessed July 15, 2010).

Exworthy, M.; A. Bindman; H.T.O., Davies; and A.E. Washington. 2006. "Evidence into Policy and Practice? Measuring the Progress of U.S. and U.K. Policies to Tackle Disparities and Inequalities in U.S. Health and U.K. Health and Health Care." *Milbank Quarterly* 84, no. 1: 75–109.

Families USA. 2010. "Reducing Racial and Ethnic Health Disparities: Key Health Equity Provisions." Talking About Health Care Reform, March. Available at www.familiesusa.org/assets/pdfs/health-reform/reducing-racial-disparities-2010.pdf (accessed July 15, 2010).

Frist, W.H. 2005. "Overcoming Disparities in U.S. Health Care." *Health Affairs* 24, no. 2: 445–51.

Gibbs, B.; L. Nsiah-Jefferson; M.D. McHugh; A.N. Trivedi; and D. Prothrow-Stith. 2006. "Reducing Racial and Ethnic Health Disparities: Exploring an Outcome-Oriented Agenda for Research and Policy." *Journal of Health Politics, Policy, and Law* 31, no. 1: 185–218.

Harvard School of Public Health. 2005. *Americans' Views of Disparities in Health Care.* Boston.

Institute of Medicine (IOM) Committee on Redesigning Health Insurance Performance and Performance Improvement Programs. 2006. *Performance Measurement: Accelerating Improvement.* Washington, DC.

Isaacs, S.L., and S.A. Schroeder. 2004. "Class—The Ignored Determinant of the Nation's Health." *New England Journal of Medicine* 351, no. 11: 1137–42.

Jones, C.P. 2000. "Levels of Racism: A Theoretic Framework and a Gardener's Tale." *American Journal of Public Health* 90, no. 7: 1212–15.

Kawachi, I.; N. Daniels; and D. Robinson. 2005. "Health Disparities by Race and Class: Why Both Matter." *Health Affairs* 24, no. 2: 343–52.

Kennedy, E.M. 2005. "The Role of the Federal Government in Eliminating Health Disparities." *Health Affairs* 24, no. 2: 452–58.

Krieger, N. 2007. "Why Epidemiologists Cannot Afford to Ignore Poverty." *Epidemiology*
18(6): 658–663.

Ku, L., and G. Flores. 2005. "Pay Now or Pay Later: Providing Interpreter Services in Health
Care." *Health Affairs* 24, no. 2: 435–44.

Kung, H-C. D.L. Hoyert, J.Xu, and S.L. Murphy. 2008. *Deaths: Final Data for 2005*. National Vital Statistics Reports; Volume 56, number 10. Hyattsville, MD: National Center
for Health Statistics.

Lavizzo-Mourey, R.; W.C. Richardson; R.K. Ross; and J.W. Rowe. 2005. "A Tale of Two
Cities." *Health Affairs* 24, no. 2: 313–15.

Lillie-Blanton, M., and C. Hoffman. 2005. "The Role of Health Insurance Coverage in Reducing Racial/Ethnic Disparities in Health Care." *Health Affairs* 24, no. 2: 398–408.

Lurie, N.; M. Jung; and R. Lavizzo-Mourey. 2005. "Disparities and Quality Improvement:
Federal Policy Levers." *Health Affairs* 24, no. 2: 354–64.

McDonough, J.E., B.K. Gibbs, J.L. Scott-Harris, Karl Kronebusch, Amanda M. Navarro,
and Kimá Taylor. 2004. *A State Policy Agenda to Eliminate Racial and Ethnic Health
Disparities*. The Commonwealth Fund, June 2004.

McGinnis, J.M.; P. Williams-Russo; and J. Knickman. 2002. "The Case for More Active
Attention to Health Promotion." *Health Affairs* 21, no. 2: 78–93.

Medical Expenditures Panel Survey, 2007. "The Uninsured in America, First Half of 2006:
Estimates for the U.S. Civilian Noninstitutionalzed Population under Age 65." *Statistical Brief #171*. Rockville, MD: Agency for Healthcare Research and Quality (June).
http://www.meps.ahrq.gov/mepsweb/data_files/publications/st171/stat171.pdf (accessed
March 17, 2011).

———. 2009. "Health Insurance Status of Full Time Workers by Demographic and Employer
Characteristics." *Statistical Brief #234*. Rockville, MD: Agency for Healthcare Research
and Quality (January). http://www.meps.ahrq.gov/mepsweb/data_files/publications/st234/
stat234.shtml (accessed March 17, 2011).

Miller, G. E., and W. A. Carroll. 2009. *Health Insurance Status of Full Time Workers by
Demographic and Employer Characteristics, 2006*. Statistical Brief #234. Rockville,
MD: Agency for Healthcare Research and Quality. (January)

Perez, T.E. 2003. "The Civil Rights Dimension of Racial and Ethnic Disparities in Health
Status." In *Unequal Treatment: Confronting Racial and Ethnic Disparities in Health
Care*, ed. B.D. Smedley, A.Y. Stith, and A.R. Nelson, 626–63. Washington, DC: National
Academies Press.

President's Commission for the Study of Ethical Problems in Medicine and Biomedical
and Behavioral Research. 1983. *Securing Access to Health Care*. Washington, DC: US
Government Printing Office.

Robert Wood Johnson Foundation. 2006. *Comparing Federal Government Surveys that
Count Uninsured People in America*. Washington, DC.

Roberts, M. and Jeffrey A. Rhoades. 2008. *The Uninsured in America, First Half of 2007:
Estimates for the US Civilian Noninstitutionalized Population Under Age 65*. Statistical
Brief #215. Agency for Healthcare Research and Quality. (August)

Robinson, J.C. Rockville, MD: 2008. "Disparities in Health: Expanding the Focus." *Health
Affairs* 27: 318–319.

Rosenbaum, S., and J. Teitelbaum. 2005. "Addressing Racial Inequality in Health Care."
In *Policy Challenges in Modern Health Care*, ed. D. Mechanic, L.B. Rogert and D.C.
Colby, 135–47. Piscataway, NJ: Rutgers University Press.

Satcher, D.; G.E. Fryer Jr.; J. McCann; A. Troutman; S.H. Woolf; and G. Rust. 2005. "What
if We Were Equal? A Comparison of the Black-White Mortality Gap in 1960 and 2000."
Health Affairs 24, no. 2: 459–64.

Schlotthauer, A. E., A. Badler, S.C. Cook, D.J. Pérez, and M.H. Chin. 2008. *Health Affairs* 27: 568–73.

Schoen, C.; K. Davis; S.K.H. How; and S.C. Schoenbaum. 2006. "U.S. Health System Performance: A National Scorecard." *Health Affairs*-Web Exclusive: W457–W475 http://content.healthaffairs.org/content/25/6/w457.full.pdf+html.

Shone, L.P., A.W. Dick, J.D. Klein, J. Zwanziger, and P.G. Szilagyi. 2005. "Reduction in Racial and Ethnic Disparities after Enrollment in the State Children's Health Insurance Program." *Pediatrics* 115(6):e698–e705.

Singh, G.K, and S.M. Yu. 1995. "Infant Mortality in the United States: Trends, Differentials, and Projections, 1950 Through 2010." *American Journal of Public Health* 85, no. 7: 957–64.

Smedley, B.D.; A.Y. Stith; and A.R. Nelson, eds. 2003. *Unequal Treatment: Confronting Racial and Ethnic Disparities in Health Care.* Washington, DC: National Academies Press.

Smith, David B. 2005a. *Eliminating Disparities in Treatment and the Struggle to End Segregation.* The Commonwealth Fund, August 2005.

———. 2005b. "Racial and Ethnic Health Disparities and the Unfinished Civil Rights Agenda." *Health Affairs* 24(2): 317–24.

State Health Access Data Assistance Center (SHADAC) and Urban Institute. 2005. *Going Without: America's Uninsured Children.* Washington, DC: Robert Wood Johnson Foundation.

Sullivan, Louis W. 2005. *Setting Priorities for Health Disparities.* Washington, DC: Public Health Advisory Board.

Summer, L., and C. Mann. 2006. *Instability of Public Health Insurance Coverage for Children and Families: Causes, Consequences, and Remedies.* Washington, DC: Commonwealth Fund.

Teitelbaum, J.B. 2005. "Health Care and Civil Rights: An Introduction." *Ethnicity and Disease* 15: S2-27–S2-30.

Trivedi, A.N.; B. Gibbs; L. Nsiah-Jefferson; J.Z. Ayanian; D. Prothrow-Stith, (2005). "Creating a State Minority Health Policy Report Card." *Health Affairs* 24(2): 388–396.

U.S. Department of Health and Human Services. 2005. "Understanding Estimates of the Uninsured: Putting the Differences in Context." Office of the Assistant Secretary for Program Evaluation. Washington, DC.

Vladeck, B.C.; P.N. Van de Water; and J. Eichner. 2006. *Strengthening Medicare's Role in Reducing Racial and Ethnic Health Disparities.* Washington, DC: National Academy of Social Insurance.

White House. 2010. "Health Reform for Latinos: The Affordable Care Act Gives Latinos Greater Control over Their Own Health Care." Available at www.whitehouse.gov/files/documents/health_reform_for_latinos.pdf (accessed July 15, 2010).

Wilkinson, R.G., and M.G. Marmot. 2003. *Social Determinants of Health: The Solid Facts, Second Edition.* Geneva: World Health Organization.

Williams, D.R., and P.B. Jackson. 2005. "Social Sources of Racial Disparities in Health." *Health Affairs* 24, no. 2: 325–34.

Wong, M.D.; M.F. Shapiro; W.J. Boscardin; and S.L. Ettner. 2002. "Contributions of Major Diseases to Disparities in Mortality." *New England Journal of Medicine* 347, no. 20: 1585–92.

8

Social Equity in Criminal Justice

James R. Brunet

The administration of justice in the United States is carried out through coercive state action. By its very nature, government provision of criminal justice services involves government taking or diminishment of individual liberties. When the state arrests or incarcerates a person, it severely restricts that person's freedom of movement. Those prosecuted for crimes against the state, especially individuals branded with the "felon" label, stand to lose future employment prospects, privacy (e.g., sex offender registry), and the full prerogatives of citizenship (e.g., the franchise, jury service, gun ownership). In the most extreme form of taking, the state may execute a criminal defendant found guilty of a capital crime. Clearly, the actions taken by police, courts, and corrections officials have significant consequences for individuals and society at large. Implicit in this line of reasoning is the idea that the criminal justice function is administered in a lawful and equitable manner. Consider the opposite view. What results when the actions of the state are prejudiced or create disparate impacts? At the micro level, individuals may be wrongly accused of crimes, subjected to excessive force, or unjustly denied early release from prison. Individuals are not the only victims of arbitrary or biased state action. There are pernicious macro-level effects as well. These occur when subsets of the population are subjected to disparate and discriminatory treatment. Take, for example, a situation where members of a minority class, whether racial, ethnic, or economic, are denied due process protections typically afforded to the majority. Chronically disadvantaged groups may come to question a basic principle of American jurisprudence—a belief in "justice for all."[1] In the worst case, these questions may extend to the very legitimacy of the criminal justice enterprise or the state itself. The salve for this societal wound is the fair exercise of authority by all justice system actors.

If criminal justice administrators are to play an active role in establishing just organizational processes and outcomes, they first must gain an understanding of the social equity issues confronting their agencies. The social science literature is replete with empirical studies showing unfair treatment and unequal outcomes at different points in the criminal justice system. These will be considered later in discussions of racial profiling and drug sentencing. Absent the occasional academic study, there is little evidence to show that equity conditions are routinely monitored in criminal justice agencies. Many readers are no doubt familiar with the old management adage, "what gets measured, gets done." This bit of wisdom provides the starting point for all subsequent social equity efforts. Administrators need information about the nature and extent of inequities before setting out to fix them. The purpose of this chapter is to identify measures that may be used to track progress in achieving social equity in the criminal justice system.

The analysis is undertaken in six parts. First, a brief overview of performance measurement in criminal justice is offered. Second, the concept of social equity is defined and a case is made to justify its inclusion in performance measurement systems. Third, the current state of social equity in criminal justice agencies is presented by considering the equity concerns raised in contemporary criminal justice issues including racial profiling, immigration enforcement, and drug sentencing. Fourth, the barriers to social equity performance measurement are made explicit. Fifth, the history of social equity measurement and ideas for extending its use are discussed for each institution of justice (police, courts, and corrections). Social equity within criminal justice organizations (internal equity) also is addressed in this section. The chapter concludes with a discussion of the implications of this analysis for criminal justice administrators. The approach taken in this chapter is both descriptive and prescriptive. An effort is made to illustrate initiatives currently under way to measure social equity as well as offer suggestions to better measure the concept.

Performance Measurement in Criminal Justice

Performance measurement is an increasingly important part of public management. An entire cottage industry has grown up around the issue, instructing public managers on what to measure and how to report success. The methods for evaluating program efficiency and effectiveness are numerous and growing in level of sophistication. Agencies track their performance through benchmarks, scorecards, citizen satisfaction surveys, performance budgets, report cards, and dashboards, to name just a few. Performance measurement provides a vital role in the governance process. Policymakers rely on performance data to make critical resource decisions. The same results help agency executives to assess the progress made toward achieving strategic goals. Program managers use feedback information to better serve the public. And finally, performance measures keep public administrators accountable to political superiors and citizenry.

It may be a surprise to some that criminal justice agencies have been at the vanguard of the measurement movement. Since the mid-1930s, the FBI has collected data on the number of crimes reported to police departments throughout the country. Today, crime rates serve as the leading measure of municipal police performance. The advent of the professional era of policing in the 1950s brought another performance standard to policing—response time. The speed with which police officers arrive on the scene of a crime is a widely reported efficiency measure to this day. The other institutions of justice, courts and corrections, have their own long-established performance metrics. For decades, courts have tracked the amount of time to process civil and criminal cases. In the corrections area the U.S. Census Bureau began collecting and reporting changes in state prison incarceration rates in 1926. Criminal justice agencies have become quite adept at using workload, efficiency, and effectiveness performance measures.

What have been missing are performance measures, that gauge an agency's progress in promoting social equity, a distinctive value of American public administration. While good longitudinal information about crime rates, case processing times, and incarceration rates exist, little is known about disparities in the distribution and quality of criminal justice services delivered to different citizen groups. The goal here is to fill the gap and explore the possibility of measuring social equity at different stages in the criminal justice process.

What Is Social Equity and Why Should It Be Measured?

Since its scholarly introduction nearly thirty-five years ago (Marini 1971), social equity has gained legitimacy as a normative pillar supporting American public administration (Frederickson 1980; Svara and Brunet 2004). There is mounting evidence to support this view. For one, a large number of conference papers and journal articles have been produced on the subject.[2] Public administration organizations have formally recognized the importance of social equity in multiple ways. For example, the National Academy of Public Administration maintains a standing panel on social equity, one of only a handful of ongoing committees for this prestigious body. The code of ethics developed by the American Society for Public Administration (ASPA 1994) encourages its members to act according to principles that contribute to social equity.[3] Even introductory public administration textbooks provide some coverage of social equity themes (Svara and Brunet 2004). In sum, the concept has shed much of its "outsider" status and moved into the mainstream of public administration thought and practice.

It is good to begin with a definition of social equity. A leading text in the field describes it as "fairness in the delivery of public services; it is egalitarianism in action—the principle that each citizen, regardless of economic resources or personal traits, deserves and has a right to be given equal treatment by the political system" (Shafritz, Russell, and Borick 2009, 454). By this definition, social equity encompasses broad constitutional principles including fairness, justice, and equal treatment under the law. Svara and Brunet (2004) distinguish between four types of social equity. *Procedural fairness* requires administrators to ensure the due process rights of all individuals and to treat all equally (equal protection). Under this form of social equity, agency action is constrained by the rule of law and certain procedural safeguards (notice, judicial appeals). An individual who is stopped by a police officer solely on the basis of skin color has been denied procedural fairness. *Access or distributional equity* focuses on how services are provided to citizens. Services or benefits should be provided equally, or in a manner that benefits those who are disadvantaged. Administrative barriers that prevent those from receiving services (e.g., not providing forms in multiple languages, requiring fees for certain services) should be rectified under this form of social equity. *Quality* ensures that there is consistency in the quality of services provided to all groups of people. In a policing context, one would ask whether the quality of police services is the same in each part of a city. *Outcomes* focus on the results of government policies on groups of people. Are certain citizens more likely to be victims of crime? Does demography play a role in explaining differences in people's perceptions of the police, courts, and corrections? As demonstrated in the above examples, it is possible to assess agency performance on each aspect of social equity.

The call to incorporate social equity principles into existing performance measurement systems is not new. Over three decades ago, Chitwood (1974) lamented the lack of social equity content in productivity measures. An influential book on municipal performance measurement from this period acknowledged the important link between performance data and equity: "A major use of the data collected is to provide information on the effectiveness of services for various population groups in the community, in order to obtain a perspective on the need for, and equitableness of, services" (Hatry et al. 1977, 6). This suggests that the results generated from performance measurement systems can be used to achieve equity. Frederickson (1980) expressed a similar sentiment, "Social equity, then, would be a criterion for effectiveness in public administration in the same way that efficiency, economy, productivity, and other criteria are used" (36). For him, public administrators have an affirmative responsibility to not only include social equity content in performance measures, but to advocate for their inclusion and study their implications. In his own words, "It is incumbent on the public servant to be able to develop and defend criteria and measures of equity and to understand the impact of public services on the dignity and well-being of citizens" (46). Unfortunately, these arguments have had little impact on actual practice.

Why renew the push for social equity performance measures at this point in time? A confluence of factors has created a favorable environment for such action including: (a) civil rights cases requiring equal treatment of all; (b) changing public attitudes about the importance of equity; (c) the improved status of social equity within the academy; (d) the measurement mania sweeping through public organizations; and (e) recent events in New Orleans, which show government's failure to serve all of its citizens equally. This is an especially good time to investigate social equity as carried out in the institutions of justice. The public has low confidence in the criminal justice system as a whole, ranking it between organized labor and big business (Jones 2008). Individual institutions of justice, most especially the police, score very well in public opinion surveys. Public opinion does differ based on age, race, and education. Young African American men, for example, hold the police in extremely low regard and tend not to trust them to treat criminal defendants fairly (see National Research Council 2004, 300–301 for a review of research on this topic). This raises the question—do perceptions of unfair treatment have a basis in fact? Social equity measures may provide an answer.[4]

Social Equity in the Criminal Justice System: Three Examples

Social equity remains a salient issue for justice administration in America. A growing body of research finds racial and ethnic disparities throughout the criminal justice process from police stops (Warren et al. 2006) to prison victimization (Wolff, Shi, and Blitz 2008). It is not the intention here to offer up a detailed rendering of all inequities in the criminal justice system, as there are many excellent summations of the disparity literature (Kansal 2005; Spohn 2000; Walker, Spohn, and DeLone 2004). Instead, the status of social equity in criminal justice is assessed through a review of social equity themes embedded in three current policy issues. The topics are racial profiling, immigration enforcement, and sentencing disparities. For each topic, relevant data illustrating the extent of the equity/disparity issue are provided. Promising interventions for overcoming discriminatory practices and outcomes are also discussed.

Racial Profiling

Racial profiling occurs when the police use race as the sole or primary pretext for stopping or searching an individual. The most common manifestation of racial profiling, referred to as D.W.B., or *driving while black*, crashed onto the policy agenda in the mid-1990s. Several factors focused attention on the problem including increasingly frequent stops of prominent African American drivers (military personnel, judges), court rulings that liberalized the grounds for initiating traffic stops, and departmental policies that explicitly singled out minorities for enforcement (Harris 1999).[5] Fifteen years later, cases of racial profiling are still reported. Police officers in the small east Texas town of Tenaha stand accused of stopping African American or Latino motorists suspected of drug crimes and seizing their cash and property (Witt 2009).[6] A state asset-forfeiture law allows police departments to keep items including jewelry, cash, and cell phones seized during the commission of a crime. The implementation of the law by some police departments in Texas seems to violate a key tenet of social equity—procedural fairness.

In the face of mounting anecdotal evidence, researchers set out to ascertain the true extent of racial profiling by police. In the first nationwide survey of police traffic stops, researchers found that racial and ethnic minorities were pulled over at roughly the same rate as white drivers (Durose, Schmitt, and Langan 2005). This aligns with studies that uncovered little evidence of racial bias in police stops conducted in large (Alpert, Dunham, and Smith 2007) and suburban (Novak 2004) cities. Other studies find hints of minority overrepresentation in stops; however, disparate treatment is not consistently located across types of police units or departments (Gaines 2006; Warren et al. 2006). In short, the empirical evidence does not show widespread, systematic attempts by law enforcement to target minorities for traffic stops. This is not meant to imply that problems do not exist. Racial differences are more evident when looking at police–citizen interactions *after* the traffic stop. Black and Hispanic motorists were three times more likely to be physically searched or to have their vehicles searched (Durose, Schmitt, and Langan 2005). Additionally, officers were twice as likely to use force on minority drivers compared to whites. In situations where police used force against drivers, blacks and Hispanics were more likely to assert that the police acted improperly in their exercise of force (ibid.).

Strategies for reducing racial bias in police stops and searches are widely available (National Research Council 2004; Nellis, Greene, and Mauer 2008; Walker, Spohn, and DeLone 2004). Commentators agree that data (i.e., race or ethnicity of individuals) should be collected for all traffic stops, even those that do not result in formal police action (i.e., citation or arrest). These data should be monitored continuously by police managers to detect disparities in the treatment of citizens. Cultural competency and diversity training is also suggested as well as the hiring of more minority officers. Another strategy is to provide citizens with information on how to file a complaint against an officer suspected of racial profiling. The U.S. Customs Bureau significantly reduced the amount of disparity in its passenger searches by creating a clear set of factors that would trigger a search and requiring supervisor approval before initiating certain types of searches (Walker, Spohn, and DeLone 2004).

Immigration Enforcement

Section 287 (g) of the Immigration and Nationality Act allows state and local law enforcement officers to perform the role of federal immigration officials. Almost seventy such agencies have entered into agreements with U.S. Immigration and Customs Enforcement (ICE) to identify and deport individuals who are in the United States illegally. The original intent of the program was to disrupt serious criminal enterprises, including drug trafficking, human smuggling, and gang-related violence. The idea is to use state and local police as a force multiplier for federal immigration enforcement efforts. Since 2006, more than 70,000 individuals (mostly confined to jails) have been identified as in the country illegally (U.S. Immigration and Customs Enforcement 2008).

Many social equity concerns have been raised about the implementation of the 287 (g) program. A program review conducted by the U.S. Government Accountability Office (GAO) (2009) uncovered several troubling findings. In some jurisdictions, local law enforcement processed offenders caught for minor crimes, such as speeding, in contradiction to program intent. This introduces the possibility that members of certain ethnic groups will be targeted for stops in an attempt to locate illegal aliens. Additionally, ICE failed to provide consistent guidance on the types of data that should be collected and reported. Perhaps most disturbing are concerns expressed by community members that the 287 (g) program increases the likelihood of racial profiling and intimidation by the police. In a broadside against 287 (g) implementation in North Carolina, the University of North Carolina Law School determined that the program was "being used to purge towns and citizens of 'unwelcome' immigrants" (Weissman, Headen, and Parker 2009, 8). The negative implications identified in the report include reduced public safety due to the unwillingness of immigrants to report crimes to the police, marginalization of immigrants who are denied basic rights and liberty, and economic calamity in communities with large immigrant populations as undocumented individuals seek refuge elsewhere.

Several steps may be taken to reduce disparities resulting from immigration enforcement. The overriding problems identified in the GAO report (2009) concern ICE oversight of state and local partners; essentially, *quis custodiet ipsos custodes* (who regulates the regulators)? They suggest a return to the original goals of the program (i.e., focus on violent criminals) and improved data monitoring. The report notes that many departments have engaged in outreach efforts (radio spots, public meetings) to allay the immigrant fears about ethnic targeting and harassment. Others see the need for a clear process for filing complaints against officers and incorporating citizen input into local enforcement practices (Weissman, Headen, and Parker 2009).

Sentencing Disparities

Fueled by a "get tough on crime" philosophy and self-declared war on drugs, America's correctional institutions quickly filled to capacity. An incredible one in thirty-one adults is under some form of correctional supervision in the United States today (Pew Center on the States 2009). The rate for blacks is starker—one in eleven. Increasingly tough criminal sentences, especially those related to crack cocaine,[7] have had a disparate impact on certain social groups. In her comprehensive review of sentencing research, Spohn (2000) concluded that blacks and Hispanics, especially those who are young, male, and unemployed, were more likely to receive a prison sentence than white offenders. Minorities receive harsher sentences than whites if they are detained in jail before trial, are represented by a public defender rather than private counsel, or are convicted at trial rather than by plea. Young African American males (twenty-five to twenty-nine years of age) were seven times more likely to be imprisoned on December 31, 2004, than white males (Harrison and Beck 2005). Hispanic males were twice as likely to be incarcerated as their white counterparts. A similar racial/ethnic pattern exists with female prisoners. At the end of 2004, blacks and Hispanics made up 60 percent of all federal and state inmates (Harrison and Beck 2005) while representing only one-quarter of the entire American population.

There are signs that the number of black drug offenders in state prisons is dropping relative to the number of white offenders (Mauer 2009). From 1999 to 2005, black drug offenders declined from 58 percent to 44 percent of the total as whites increased from 20 percent to 29 percent. While blacks are still disproportionately represented among those convicted of drug crimes, the imbalance is less severe. The Sentencing Project credits the greater use of drug courts as alternatives to incarceration and the rise in crystal meth use by whites as factors contributing to reduced disparity. Irrespective of this recent trend, the body of evidence shows that young minorities are subjected to harsher sentences than similarly situated white offenders, a phenomenon now recognized as an "imprisonment penalty" (Spohn and Holleran 2000).

Does this punishment penalty contribute to racial and ethnic imbalances at other decision points in the prison admissions process? The latest research finds that blacks sentenced to probation, a community-based sanction offered in lieu of incarceration, are much more likely to have their probation revoked compared to other groups (Tapia and Harris 2006).[8] Young blacks had twice the odds of revocation as white probationers. In a somewhat surprising finding, Hispanic probation revocation rates mirrored those of whites. Race also seems to play a role in decisions regarding the revocation of parole. Parole is a postincarceration surveillance program that seeks to reintegrate offenders back into the community. In a study of parolees in four states (New York, Kentucky, Michigan, and Utah), Steen and Opsal (2007) found that blacks were more likely than whites to have their parole revoked for technical violations. The race differential is more pronounced in situations where administrative discretion is greatest. For example, 47.2 percent of black public order offenders had their parole revoked due to a technical violation compared to 26.6 percent of white parolees. In the continuum of crime types, public order crimes (e.g., drugs) are considered less serious than property and violent crimes. There is greater subjectivity at work in the parole revocation decision for minor crimes versus more serious ones. Additionally, revocation due to technical violation (e.g., drug use, firearm possession, and unknown whereabouts) is by its very nature more discretionary than revocation due to the commission of a new crime. A California study found that black parole violators were more likely referred to the parole board, the more discretionary sanctioning body, and ultimately returned to prison (Grattet et al. 2009). In sum, race does seem to influence probation and parole revocation decisions, thus contributing to disparities in prison populations.

Efforts have been made to ameliorate sentence disparity in the criminal justice system. Sentencing guidelines adopted by the federal government and a number of states sought to reduce judicial discretion and thereby create more consistent punishments based on legally prescribed factors such as an offender's prior criminal history and seriousness of the current crime. Studies show, however, that extralegal factors such as race, ethnicity, and educational levels still play an important role in sentencing decisions, despite the use of sentencing guidelines (Albonetti 1997; Steffensmeier and Demuth 2000). The guideline approach has been extended to other criminal justice contexts. Parole officials in some jurisdictions use a sanc-tioning grid/violation matrix to provide uniform reentry services and punishments to similarly situated parolees (Martin 2008). Guidelines have the dual purpose of reducing parole officer discretion and promoting procedural justice. While initial findings from Martin indicate some promise for the parole-sanctioning grid, further research is necessary before making a final determination as to the success of the program.

Barriers to Social Equity Measurement in the Criminal Justice System

Before exploring the current use of social equity measures in criminal justice agencies, it is instructive to identify barriers that may hinder the adoption of such measures. The paucity of social equity measures may be explained by several factors. One barrier relates to the fragmented nature of the American criminal justice system. Two other problems relate to the lack of data and limitations in statistical analysis. Organizational dynamics may also play a role in tamping down efforts to measure social equity. Finally, definitional ambiguity and lack of benchmarks for comparison contribute to the slow adoption of social equity metrics.

Fragmentation and Localization of Criminal Justice Responsibilities

Justice administration is primarily a state and local affair in the United States. The diversity of institutions and approaches involved in providing criminal justice services creates its own set of problems. Some states have a unified court system (North Carolina), while others have a decentralized system of lower courts (South Carolina, New York). Most police departments are extremely small (fewer than five sworn officers), so there is little or no staff to support data collection and presentation activities. It is difficult to locate responsibility for social equity measurement with so many different actors—elected sheriff, local court administrator, justice of the peace, and juvenile probation officer. This stands in stark contrast to the centralized (nationalized) approach to criminal justice administration found in many European countries.[9]

Data Availability

The federal government gathers a tremendous amount of data about criminal justice matters. Data are routinely collected about jails, prisons, victims, crimes reported to police, sentencing, and executions. This is just a sampling of federally sponsored data gathering efforts. Much more is done at the state and local levels. It is important to remember that these national data sources were not created to assess social equity. As such, they do not include key data elements useful for measuring social equity. For example, problems exist with racial/ethnic categories in federal data systems (Walker, Spohn, and DeLone 2004). In addition, no data are collected on the socioeconomic status of victims and criminal defendants. Oftentimes, state and local management information systems are created to meet federal data requirements. So, data gaps and inaccuracies experienced at the federal government are prevalent in subnational data systems as well. Smaller jurisdictions (the norm in the United States) have a different data problem. They may have too few crimes and offenders to make any meaningful comparisons or inferences about social equity.

Difficult to Disentangle Disparity from Discrimination

There are well-documented disparities in the criminal justice system. Members from racial and ethnic minorities, men, and the poor are overrepresented at nearly every stage of the criminal justice process (see Walker, Spohn, and DeLone 2004 for a full treatment of this issue). A good amount of the disparity may be explained by legitimate factors such as higher criminality within certain demographic groups. However, criminologists have concluded that a significant portion of disparity is due to racial bias, prior criminal history, policing practices, and sentencing legislation (Schrantz and McElroy 2000). This, perhaps, creates the most difficult barrier to overcome. One could make the argument that complex concepts such as discrimination, criminality, and social equity cannot be measured with simple benchmarks or metrics. Social scientists typically use higher order statistical techniques to uncover the factors that explain disproportionate arrests and sentences. In short, performance measures may identify conditions of apparent discrimination and unfair treatment at certain points in the criminal justice system, but they do not permit us to make conclusive statements about the existence of these problems. When social equity measures show troubling results, administrators should follow up with more rigorous (statistical) investigation. In this regard, social equity measures perform as an early warning system for managers.

Change in Organizational Culture Must Precede Social Equity Indicator Development

Before specifying measures, there has to be agreement within the organization to pursue social equity. This requires intensive organizational development work including a mission statement that recognizes the importance of social equity. Only after the organization has embraced the idea of social equity can you begin to measure and report your progress in achieving it.

Definitional and Operational Ambiguity

While the social equity concept has been around for some time, it is a somewhat difficult concept to grasp. There is no standard definition of social equity, and scholarly treatments have provided limited guidance on how to measure it. Definitional and operational ambiguity has likely contributed to the poor implementation of social equity measures. Without agreed-upon ways of measuring social equity, there are few opportunities for comparison between jurisdictions (benchmarking). The most vexing problem for researchers who study police racial profiling is in defining the comparison base rate, the so-called denominator problem (Blank, Dabady, and Citro 2004). In efforts to study differential traffic enforcement, for example, does one use the number of minorities in the study population, the number of licensed minority drivers, the number of minority licensed drivers observed on the particular stretch of highway under study, or the number of minority drivers exhibiting certain driving behaviors that may attract the attention of law enforcement (e.g., speeding)?

Social Equity Measurement in Criminal Justice Agencies

There is much discussion about social equity in criminal justice circles today. Attempts are under way within each institution of justice to incorporate social equity principles into existing performance measurement systems. In this section, progress toward this goal is detailed for each institution. Particular attention is given to historical factors that contributed to the adoption of social equity metrics. The goal is to create a list of existing and potential social equity measures by type for each stage of the criminal justice process. The police are considered first, followed by the courts and corrections.

Police

Historical Antecedents

Police organizations have a long history of measuring performance. Efforts to measure police outcomes first emerged in the 1920s and 1930s. As noted earlier, the FBI began collecting and reporting crime data from local police departments at this time. The Uniform Crime Report (UCR) is still used today to gauge police success in controlling crime. The International City/County Management Association (ICMA) was also very active early on in developing performance standards for police departments. The ICMA research director at the time suggested that police departments be judged on their ability to clear cases and restore stolen property (Maguire 2003). The ICMA began its annual survey of police departments in 1939. Currently, the ICMA collects information on several different dimensions of policing—outcomes (crime rate), processes (arrests, response time), and administration (staffing levels, expenditures).

Until the end of the twentieth century, police performance was closely linked to the efficiency and effectiveness values inherent in the professional model of policing (Alpert and Moore 1993). Performance measures were directed toward the primary objectives of policing during this era—preventing crime, catching criminals, responding to calls, improving citizen perceptions of safety, and providing services in a fair, honest, and courteous manner (Hatry et al. 1977). Equity considerations were secondary to crime-fighting concerns. This is not to say that equity was totally ignored. Citizens should be asked if the police were "generally fair in dealing with them" (86). Also, the number of complaints lodged against the officers and the number resulting in judgment against the government could also be tracked. The time for social equity in police performance systems had not yet arrived.

Social Equity Performance Measures

A paradigmatic shift in policing occurred in the 1980s and 1990s. This created the need for a different set of metrics to assess performance. The new approach to policing was based on closer, more sustained interactions with the community. The police were to strike up partnerships with citizens, businesses, and other governmental actors to solve community problems. The trust relationship between police and community became a primary focus. New measures, especially ones that focused on fairness and equal treatment, were in order.

Harvard professors Mark H. Moore and Anthony A. Braga (2003, 444–45) identify seven dimensions of police performance that should be measured under the new paradigm:

1. reduce criminal victimization;
2. call offenders to account (solve crimes, make arrests);
3. reduce fear and enhance personal security;
4. guarantee safety in public spaces;
5. use financial resources fairly, efficiently, and effectively;
6. use force and authority fairly, efficiently, and effectively; and
7. satisfy customer demands and achieve legitimacy with those policed.

The first four are consistent with a more traditional style of policing (compare to Hatry and colleagues' list above). The final three encompass important social equity ideals, and they do so in novel ways. Police departments are encouraged to become responsible stewards of public funds (item 5), reduce the use of force and authority (item 6), and gain the trust of all citizens (item 7). In this conceptualization of police performance, social equity shares an equal status with other police values (efficiency, effectiveness).

So, how can police departments measure social equity? Table 8.1 identifies a range of potential measures across several different types of equity described earlier (procedural, distributional, outcomes, quality). The source of data supporting these measures is also identified. The idea is to modify existing data systems and measures so as to reflect social equity values.[10] Violations of procedural equity—using excessive force, not investigating citizen complaints, and engaging in racial profiling—may be tracked using data collected by the Bureau of Justice Statistics (BJS) or through a review of local police records. Consistency in police response to calls and fairness in resource allocation are examples of distributional equity. Police records may show that police response is slower in some neighborhoods or

Table 8.1

Social Equity Measures for Police Organizations by Type and Data Source

Equity issue	Measure	Type of equity	Data sources
Are certain citizens subjected to greater uses of force by police?	Type of force used by race, ethnicity, and other demographics	Procedural	Police-Public Contact Survey (BJS); police records
Are complaints against the police handled differently according to complainant characteristics? Are all complaints investigated in a similar manner?	Complaints filed, investigated, and final disposition (sustained, unfounded) by demographics	Procedural	Sample Survey of Law Enforcement Agencies (BJS); police records
Do police engage in racial profiling?	Police stops by race and other demographics; final disposition (warning, citation, search, arrest) by race and other demographics	Procedural	State or local sources
Are police services provided equally? Based upon need?	Officers/patrols per neighborhood; officers per neighborhood crime rate	Distributional	Police records
Are the police consistent in how quickly they respond to calls for service?	Response time by neighborhood, district, or census tract	Distributional	Police records
Are groups of citizens more fearful of crime in their homes and neighborhoods?	Fear of crime by location and demographics	Outcomes	Citizen survey
Are certain groups impacted by crime at disproportionate rates?	Crime rates by location and demographics; victimization by location and demographics	Outcomes	Local crime reports; citizen survey
Are certain groups impacted disproportionately by police policies and practices (e.g., vice operations, aggressive enforcement of panhandling)?	Arrests by demographic variables	Outcomes	Police records
Are certain groups more or less satisfied with police services?	Satisfaction by neighborhood, district, census tract, age, race, gender, and ethnicity	Quality	Citizen survey
Do citizens view themselves as equal partners with the police in addressing community concerns?	Perceptions of relationship with police by demographics	Quality	Citizen survey

that fewer officers are assigned to an area with a greater need for police services. Outcome equity can be ascertained through citizen surveys (have you been victimized? are you fearful of crime in your neighborhood?). To ensure that there are no quality differences in police services, citizens may be asked about their level of satisfaction with the police.

Some commentators hypothesize that community policing has led to a shift in equity concerns (Eck and Rosenbaum 1994). They see a movement away from certain procedural and distributional forms of equity and a movement toward quality-type equity. Contemporary policing, with its focus on the quality of the relationship between police and community members, raises new questions for police administrators. For example, "Did the police ask us which problems are the most important for our community?" (12)

Performance measures are most useful if they are part of a larger strategic vision for the organization. Measures help to determine whether the organization is meeting its goals and objectives. In another sign of the growing acceptance of social equity, police organizations now often incorporate elements of social equity into their broad statements of purpose (vision or mission statements). By way of example, the vision statement for the Dayton (Ohio) Police Department notes that agency members are guided by three core values—integrity, respect, and fairness. The fairness value is expressed in the following statement: "We are consistent in our treatment of all persons. Our actions are tempered with reason, equity, and governed by the law" (Dayton Police Department 2005). There is a strong emphasis on procedural equity. According to its mission statement, the Virginia Beach (Virginia) Police Department "is committed to providing a safe community and improving the quality of life for all people. We accomplish this by delivering quality police services and enforcing laws with equity and impartiality" (Virginia Beach Police Department 2009). Here we see both distributional ("delivering services . . . with equity and impartiality") and procedural ("enforcing laws with equity and impartiality") types.

Courts

Historical Antecedents

The judicial system's experience with performance measures is quite different from the path followed by the police. For one, courts were slow to jump onto the measurement bandwagon. In fact, the courts did not begin to formulate performance indicators in earnest until the 1970s (Cole 1993). Police departments actively lobbied Congress to create the UCR almost fifty years prior to the court's initial foray into measurement. The courts also relied heavily on federal funding to support its efforts to build performance measurement capacity. In contrast, groups outside of the policing profession, including ICMA and the Urban Institute, facilitated the development of measures in law enforcement. The courts also took a more measured and centralized approach to setting up performance measures. With funding from the Bureau of Justice Assistance in 1987, the National Center for State Courts initiated a project (Trial Court Performance Standards Project) to develop performance standards for state trial courts. The idea was to develop measurable standards, field test them in a few locations, evaluate the results, and implement the new measures throughout all state trial courts. Police standards developed in a more ad hoc manner without a single, central coordinating entity. The early experiences of both institutions were similar in one regard—there was a lack of attention given to social equity measures. On this point, Cole (1993, 42) notes that initial court studies

> . . . stressed measures emphasizing process rather than results, efficiency rather than effectiveness, and program outcomes rather than policy outcomes. As a consequence, we know a lot about conviction rates, numbers of dismissals, percentages of guilty pleas, case processing times, and the use of various sentencing options—yardsticks that say little about the quality of justice. Few offices of prosecution, indigent defense, or courts have developed and incorporated performance assessments to evaluate the quality of behavior of officials as they interact with citizens—be they defendants, victims, jurors, or the general public.

Process and output measures were more highly valued than social equity measures during the early stages of indicator development. It would take the court's version of a paradigm shift to elevate the standing of social equity vis-à-vis other indicators.

Social Equity Performance Measures

After three years of study, the Trial Court Performance Standards Project identified five performance areas for state trial courts: access to justice; expeditiousness and timeliness; equality, fairness, and integrity; independence and accountability; and public trust and confidence. At least three of the five areas complement aspects of social equity. Several examples illustrate this point. To ensure that courts are open and accessible, the costs of access to proceedings and records must be "reasonable, fair, and affordable" (Standard 1.5). To ensure equality and fairness, jury lists should be representative of the jurisdiction from which they are drawn (Standard 3.1). The public should have trust and confidence that trial court proceedings are conducted "expeditiously and fairly and that its decisions have integrity" (Standard 5.3). The entire Trial Court Performance Standards and Measurement System is available online.[11] The Web site includes detailed instructions for collecting performance data as well as sample forms and questionnaires. The Access and Fairness Survey asks citizens to indicate whether they felt that their case was handled fairly (procedural equity) and whether they felt as if they were treated the same as everyone else. Unfortunately, the survey requests only a limited amount of background information (gender, ethnicity/race).

Social equity measures for courts, prosecution, and defense are presented in Table 8.2. There are a wide range of measures available covering all types of equity. Data to undertake these measures may be found in court records, direct observation of courtroom proceedings, and questionnaires available on the Trial Court Performance Standards and Measurement System Web site.

Corrections

Historical Antecedents

There is comparatively little information about the history of performance measurement in corrections. Based on Wright's (2005) brief overview, it would seem that corrections officials have only recently taken up the cause of performance management. Wright identified seven performance indicator models—two were from state correctional systems (Florida, North Carolina) while another was from the Federal Bureau of Prisons. Charles Logan (1993), a professor at the University of Connecticut, is responsible for perhaps the most complete set of indicators of the lot. All models were devised within the past dozen years.

Social Equity Performance Measures

Logan's extensive list of prison performance measures does have social equity content. "Justice" is one of the eight dimensions in his model. Justice can be determined by staff fairness (are inmates written up without cause?), limited use of force, fairness of the grievance and disciplinary processes, and access to law library. Interestingly, almost all data are collected from inmate surveys and prison records. Table 8.3 describes these and several other social equity measures in some detail. Procedural and outcome equity seem to predominate in corrections.

Internal Equity Concerns

Another form of equity looks at fairness and justice *within* organizations. Instead of focusing on the relationship between public servant and citizens, *internal* equity involves the relationship between employer and employees. It really operates as a form of procedural equity but with an internal constituency. It matches procedural equity closest, because many internal equity questions involve human resources issues, which are tightly regulated by laws and agency rules. Below, I briefly discuss several issues that have an internal equity component relevant to criminal justice agencies.

- There is some concern about the lack of diversity in criminal justice organizations, especially at the executive officer level. While blacks have significantly increased their numbers in law enforcement, women are still underrepresented

Table 8.2

Social Equity Measures for Courts by Type and Data Source

Equity issue	Measure	Type of equity	Data sources
Are there disparities in sentencing outcomes for different groups?	Length of sentence, type of punishment (probation v. incarceration, death penalty) by race, social class, and other demographics	Outcomes	Court records
Are there disparities in plea-bargaining outcomes for different groups?	Guilty pleas by demographics	Outcomes	Court records
Do all classes of citizens have equal access to quality defense counsel? Does jurisdiction offer adequate funding for indigent defense? Are defendants given access to legal adviser in a timely manner? Does defendant have repeat contacts with same legal adviser?	Compare public defender and ADA caseloads, pay, and education Compare public defense expenditures to community demographics	Distributional, Procedural, Quality	Court records
Are certain classes of individuals disproportionately detained prior to trial?	Pretrial detainees by social status and demographics, length of detention	Distributional	Intake information, probation officer report, pretrial service agency report
Does the complexion of the jury pool match that of the larger community? Are juror challenges biased against certain individuals?	Compare number and types of persons by demographics to census data Characteristics of jurors challenged by attorneys	Access, Procedural	Participant observation, jury questionnaires, census data
How do different groups view the fairness of court proceedings?	"The way my case was handled was fair"	Procedural	Access and Fairness Survey

Table 8.3

Social Equity Measures for Corrections Organizations by Type and Data Source

Equity issue	Measure	Type of equity	Data sources
Do inmates have access to quality treatment, vocational, and educational programs?	Compare inmate needs assessments to program hours completed	Distributional, Quality	Prison records, inmate survey
Access to law library	Library usage by inmate classification, proportion of inmates who are satisfied with information available in library		
Are certain inmates more likely to recidivate?	Recidivism by race, class, and other demographics	Outcomes	Local criminal justice records (jail, police, court)
Are correctional facilities overcrowded?	Inmate characteristics per correctional facility, rated capacity	Procedural	Jail census
Are certain offenders more likely to fail in community corrections?	Types of offenders in community corrections, failure rate per offender characteristics	Outcomes	Probation records
Is grievance process available to all? Is it considered fair?	Use of grievance process by offender characteristics	Procedural	Prison records, inmate survey
Are certain offenders subjected to greater uses of force than others?	Type of force used by race, ethnicity, and other demographics	Procedural	Incident reports, inmate survey
Are certain offenders subject to more violence in jail or prison?	Type and rate of victimization by race, ethnicity, and other demographics	Outcomes	Incident reports, inmate survey
How do offender groups perceive staff fairness?	"Inmates are written up without cause"	Procedural	Inmate survey

(National Research Council 2004). Schrantz and McElroy (2000) propose stronger affirmative action efforts to bring more racial minorities into positions of authority in the criminal justice system. In social equity terms, this is referred to as the principle of representativeness—do public servants share the characteristics of the citizens they serve?

- Brunet (2005) found that police agencies with racially diverse workforces were more likely to test officers for drugs than agencies with a racially homogeneous workforce. This finding may indicate a contextual form of bias at work in agency drug testing policies.
- There is some research indicating that female police officers may be subject to adverse disciplinary actions at a rate higher than their male counterparts.
- Other personnel issues including employee turnover, promotions, and grievances may have elements of social equity yet to be discovered.

Conclusion

This analysis of social equity measurement in the criminal justice system has important implications for all public administrators. First, one can conclude that it is indeed possible to add social equity measures into existing performance systems. The data sources used to collect other workload, efficiency, and effectiveness data (e.g., official records, client surveys) can also be called into service to measure social equity. Second, social equity has many dimensions. Administrators should use multiple types of social equity indicators so that important issues are not missed. What good is it to provide universal access to poor-quality services? Three, this study also reinforces the point that administrators have both external "customers" and internal ones. Social equity considerations apply to both. Fourth, in an environment where organizations have direct impacts on one another, it is extremely important not to let your equity problems pass downstream. There is a compounding effect that occurs when disparity in one part of the process is followed up with more disparity in the next institution. It is important to work with other system actors to monitor this phenomenon (perhaps necessitating the creation of interinstitutional social equity metrics). Finally, public administrators should realize that there might be factors creating disparities that are outside their control. Laws that require stiffer penalties for certain types of drug possession may be applied in a fair manner (i.e., arrest and prosecute all individuals consistently—procedural due process), but result in the disproportionate incarceration of racial minorities.

Notes

1. A broader rendering of this ideal, "Equal Justice Under Law," is enshrined on the West Pediment of the U.S. Supreme Court Building.

2. An entire issue of the *Journal of Public Affairs Education* (vol. 10, no. 2, 2004) explored ways of introducing students to social equity.

3. Tenet II, no. 7 of the ASPA Code of Ethics asks members to "Promote constitutional

principles of equality, fairness, representativeness, responsiveness, and due process in protecting citizens' rights" (1994).

4. Social equity measures could be incorporated into the Early Intervention System (EIS) suggested by Walker and Milligan (2005). These data-driven systems are meant to warn supervisors of problematic police officer behaviors before they escalate to more significant problems (e.g., lawsuit, excessive use of force complaint).

5. Profiles used by the U.S. Drug Enforcement Administration, New Jersey State Police, and Maryland State Police included racial or ethnic dimensions.

6. The Tenaha Police Department stands accused of shaking down minority drivers after stopping them for minor traffic violations. Officers threatened drivers with serious crimes such as money laundering or drug trafficking. Drivers were given the option to sign over their cash and property to the officer in return for the state's not pursuing prosecution. It appears that dozens of stops were handled in this manner.

7. Federal sentences for crack cocaine offenders are typically 50 percent longer than for powder cocaine offenders. Guidelines used by judges to sentence drug offenders have been modified recently to eliminate some (not all) of the disparity in punishment for different types of cocaine.

8. Probation revocation leads to the activation of the offender's prison sentence, thus serving as an additional pathway to incarceration.

9. This is not meant to imply that it is impossible to create a uniform method for evaluating criminal justice organizations. Ammons (2001) has put forth a set of benchmarks for municipal police agencies.

10. The Vera Institute of Justice (2003) suggests using indicators disaggregated by income, gender, religion, and ethnicity, among other variables.

11. The entire Trial Court Performance Standards and Measurement System is available online at http://www.ncsconline.org/D_Research/tcps/index.html (accessed March 6, 2011).

References

Albonetti, Celesta A. 1997. "Sentencing Under the Federal Sentencing Guidelines: Effects of Defendant Characteristics, Guilty Pleas, and Departures on Sentencing Outcomes for Drug Offenses, 1991–1992." *Law and Society Review* 31: 789–822.

Alpert, Geoffrey P., and Mark H. Moore. 1993. *Measuring Police Performance in the New Paradigm of Policing. Performance Measures for the Criminal Justice System: Discussion Papers from the BJS-Princeton Project.* Washington, DC: U.S. Department of Justice.

Alpert, Geoffrey P.; Roger G. Dunham; and Michael R. Smith. 2007. "Investigating Racial Profiling by the Miami-Dade Police Department: A Multimethod Approach." *Criminology and Public Policy* 6: 25–55.

American Society for Public Administration. 1994. Code of Ethics. Available at www.aspanet.org/scriptcontent/index_codeofethics.cfm.

Ammons, David N. 2001. *Municipal Benchmarks: Assessing Local Performance and Establishing Community Standards.* Thousand Oaks, CA: Sage.

Blank, Rebecca M.; Marilyn Dabady; and Constance Forbes Citro, eds. 2004. *Measuring Racial Discrimination.* Washington, DC: National Academies Press.

Brunet, James R. 2005. *Drug Testing in Law Enforcement Agencies: Social Control in the Public Sector.* New York: LFB Scholarly.

Chitwood, Stephen R. 1974. "Social Equity and Social Service Productivity." *Public Administration Review* 34: 29–35.

Cole, George F. 1993. *Performance Measures for the Trial Courts, Prosecution, and Public Defense. Performance Measures for the Criminal Justice System: Discussion Papers from the BJS-Princeton Project.* Washington, DC: U.S. Department of Justice.

Dayton (Ohio) Police Department. 2005. *Core Values*. Dayton: Self-published.

Durose, Matthew R.; Erica L. Schmitt; and Patrick A. Langan. 2005. *Contacts Between Police and the Public: Findings from the 2002 National Survey*. Washington, DC: U.S. Department of Justice.

Eck, John E., and Dennis P. Rosenbaum. 1994. "The New Police Order: Effectiveness, Equity, and Efficiency in Community Policing." In *The Challenge of Community Policing: Testing the Promises,* ed. Dennis P. Rosenbaum, 3–23. Thousand Oaks, CA: Sage.

Frederickson, H. George. 1980. *New Public Administration*. University: University Press of Alabama.

Gaines, Larry K. 2006. "An Analysis of Traffic Stop Data in Riverside, California." *Police Quarterly* 9: 210–33.

Grattet, Ryken; Joan Petersilia; Jeffrey Lin; and Marlene Beckman. 2009. "Parole Violations and Revocations in California: Analysis and Suggestions for Action." *Federal Probation* 73: 2–11.

Harris, David A. 1999. *Driving While Black: Racial Profiling on Our Nation's Highways*. New York: American Civil Liberties Union.

Harrison, Paige M., and Allen J. Beck. 2005. *Prisoners in 2004*. Washington, DC: U.S. Department of Justice.

Hatry, Harry P.; Louis H. Blair; Donald M. Fisk; John M. Greiner; John R. Hall; and Philip S. Schaenman. 1977. *How Effective Are Your Community Services? Procedures for Monitoring the Effectiveness of Municipal Services*. Washington, DC: Urban Institute.

Jones, Jeffrey M. 2008. Confidence in Congress: Lowest Ever for Any U.S. Institution. Gallup Poll. Available at www.gallup.com/poll/108142/Confidence-Congress-Lowest-Ever-Any-US-Institution.aspx.

Kansal, Tushar. 2005. *Racial Disparity in Sentencing: A Review of the Literature*. Washington, DC: Sentencing Project.

Logan, Charles H. 1993. *Criminal Justice Performance Measures for Prisons. Performance Measures for the Criminal Justice System: Discussion Papers from the BJS-Princeton Project*. Washington, DC: U.S. Department of Justice.

Maguire, Edward R. 2003. "Measuring the Performance of Law Enforcement Agencies." *CALEA Update,* no. 83 (September). Available at www.calea.org/online/newsletter/No83/measurement.htm.

Marini, Frank, ed. 1971. *Toward a New Public Administration: The Minnowbrook Perspective*. San Francisco: Chandler.

Martin, Brian. 2008. *Examining the Impact of Ohio's Progressive Sanction Grid, Final Report*. Washington, DC: National Institute of Justice.

Mauer, Marc. 2009. *The Changing Racial Dynamics of the War on Drugs*. Washington, DC: Sentencing Project.

Moore, Mark H., and Anthony A. Braga. 2003. "Measuring and Improving Police Performance: The Lessons of Compstat and Its Progeny. *Policing: An International Journal of Police Strategies and Management* 26: 439–53.

National Research Council. 2004. *Fairness and Effectiveness in Policing: The Evidence*. Washington, DC: National Academies Press.

Nellis, Ashley; Judy Greene; and Marc Mauer. 2008. *Reducing Racial Disparity in the Criminal Justice System: A Manual for Practitioners and Policymakers*. 2d ed. Washington, DC: Sentencing Project.

Novak, Kenneth J. 2004. "Disparity and Racial Profiling in Traffic Enforcement." *Police Quarterly* 7: 65–96.

Pew Center on the States. 2009. *One in 31: The Long Reach of American Corrections*. Washington, DC: Pew Charitable Trusts.

Schrantz, Dennis, and Jerry McElroy. 2000. *Reducing Racial Disparity in the Criminal Justice System: A Manual for Practitioners and Policymakers*. Washington, DC: Sentencing Project.

Shafrtiz, Jay M.; E.W. Russell; and Christopher P. Borick. 2009. *Introducing Public Administration.* 6th ed. New York: Pearson/Longman.

Spohn, Cassia C. 2000. "Thirty Years of Sentencing Reform: The Quest for a Racially Neutral Sentencing Process." In *Policies, Processes, and Decisions of the Criminal Justice System, Criminal Justice, 2000,* vol. 3, ed. Julie Horney et al., 427–501. Washington, DC: National Institute of Justice.

Spohn, Cassia, and David Holleran. 2000. "The Imprisonment Penalty Paid by Young, Unemployed Black and Hispanic Male Offenders." *Criminology* 38: 281–306.

Steen, Sara, and Tara Opsal. 2007. "Punishment on the Installment Plan: Individual-Level Predictors of Parole Revocation in Four States." *Prison Journal* 87: 344–66.

Steffensmeier, Darrell, and Stephen Demuth. 2000. "Ethnicity and Sentencing Outcomes in U.S. Federal Courts: Who Is Punished More Harshly?" *American Sociological Review* 65: 705–29.

Svara, James H., and James R. Brunet. 2004. "Filling the Skeletal Pillar: Addressing Social Equity in Introductory Courses in Public Administration." *Journal of Public Affairs Education* 10: 99–109.

Tapia, Michael, and Patricia M. Harris. 2006. "Is There a Penalty for Young, Minority Males?" *Journal of Ethnicity in Criminal Justice* 4: 1–25.

U.S. Government Accountability Office. 2009. *Immigration Enforcement: Better Controls Needed over Program Authorizing State and Local Enforcement of Federal Immigration Laws.* Washington, DC: U.S. Immigration and Customs Enforcement. Available at www.ice.gov/partners/287g/Section287_g.htm.

U.S. Immigration and Customs Enforcement. 2008. *ICE Fiscal Year 2008 Annual Report.* Washington, DC: U.S. Department of Homeland Security.

Vera Institute of Justice. 2003. *Measuring Progress Toward Safety and Justice: A Global Guide to the Design of Performance Indicators Across the Justice System.* New York.

Virginia Beach Police Department. 2009. Mission Statement and Core Values. Available at www.vbgov.com/dept/police/.

Walker, Samuel, and Stacy O. Milligan. 2005. *Supervision and Intervention Within Early Intervention Systems: A Guide for Law Enforcement Chief Executives.* Washington, DC: U.S. Department of Justice.

Walker, Samuel, Cassia Spohn, and Miriam DeLone. 2004. *The Color of Justice: Race, Ethnicity, and Crime in America.* 3d ed. Belmont, CA: Wadsworth.

Warren, Patricia; Donald Tomaskovic-Devey; William Smith; Matthew Zingraff; and Marcinda Mason. 2006. "Driving While Black: Bias Processes and Racial Disparity in Police Stops." *Criminology* 44: 709–38.

Weissman, Deborah M.; Rebecca C. Headen; and Katherine Lewis Parker. 2009. "The Policies and Politics of Local Immigration Enforcement Laws: 287 (g) Program in North Carolina." Available at www.law.unc.edu/documents/clinicalprograms/287gpolicyreview.pdf.

Witt, Howard. 2009. "Highway Robbery? Texas Police Seize Black Motorists' Cash, Cars." *Chicago Tribune*, March 10. Available at www.chicagotribune.com/news/nationworld/chi-texas-profiling_wittmar10,0,6051682.story/.

Wolff, Nancy; Jing, Shi; and Cynthia L. Blitz, 2008. "Racial and Ethnic Disparities in Types and Sources of Victimization inside Prison." *Prison Journal* 88(4): 451–72.

Wright, Kevin N. 2005. "Designing a National Performance Measurement System." *Prison Journal* 85: 368–93.

9

Racial Test Score Gaps

Leanna Stiefel, Amy Ellen Schwartz, and
Ingrid Gould Ellen

In our previously published article, "Disentangling the Racial Test Score Gap: Probing the Evidence in a Large Urban District," we discuss racial test score gaps in the United States—that is, the gap in the average performance of black or Hispanic and white students on standardized tests—based on data from New York City public schools (Stiefel, Schwartz, and Ellen 2006). For example, white fourth- and eighth-grade students score significantly higher than black or Hispanic students on the National Assessment of Education Progress (NAEP) in both reading and mathematics (U.S. Department of Education 2003). The gaps are typically 20 to 30 points on a test ranging from 0 to 500. In addition, these same patterns emerge for other grades and for tests in other subjects as well.

The discussion provided here provides an overview of the performance gaps and indicates possible changes in policy and practice that could be undertaken to reduce these disparities. We also include two additional analyses beyond those in the published paper, focusing on racial gaps among boys, where targeted resources could be especially useful, and among immigrants, where further study could be especially productive.

Why Do Differences in Achievement Test Scores Matter?

It is worth emphasizing that differences in achievement test scores matter. Many critical opportunities and outcomes are related to performance on early tests. The quality of future schooling, including access to special high school programs and college opportunities, depends in part on test scores. Put simply, getting off to a bad start is generally difficult to undo. In addition, there is evidence that test scores play an independent and possibly causal role in future labor market outcomes, leading to differences in earnings. For example, scores on math tests in high school have been shown to affect hourly earnings for individuals, over and above the impact of other characteristics and years of schooling (Murnane, Willett, and Levy 1995). Third, in the age of school accountability, especially after the passage of the federal No Child Left Behind Act (NCLB) in 2001, schools are judged and sanctioned on the basis of student test scores. When parents and students choose among public schools, they increasingly judge them in part by their test scores, and schools can be reconstituted if their test scores are not good. Finally, gaps in scores suggest that there is underlying inequality in schooling opportunities.

Unfortunately, test score distributions differ systematically across racial groups. While many black or Hispanic students perform better than many white students, on average the scores of black and Hispanic students are lower. Reducing this disparity in performance, then, is an important step toward racial equality in earnings and life chances for all children.

How Large Are the Racial Test Score Gaps?

The magnitude of racial gaps is strikingly consistent across many different types of tests. On average, black and Hispanic students tend to score between three-quarters and one standard deviation lower than white students on tests of academic performance (see Jencks and Phillips 1998). These "raw" differences are the ones that matter for many of the future outcomes outlined above. For example, Neal and Johnson (1996) calculate that a standard deviation difference in high school test scores is associated with about a 20 percent difference in hourly wages.[1]

On the other hand, these raw scores may provide less information than would first appear. For example, students of different races are not similarly situated with respect to income or English-language knowledge, or even the schools they attend. We find that controlling for student characteristics reduces the gaps as does controlling for school and classroom environments. Still, gaps persist. Moreover, we find that black and Hispanic students gain less in scores from one grade to the next than do white students. Thus, the gaps expand over time. The specifics of these findings for New York City public school students are reported in our previously published paper (Stiefel, Schwartz, and Ellen 2006).

Space constraints in the original publication prevented us from reporting on racial gaps among specific subpopulations. Two subgroups of particular interest are boys and foreign-born students. Table 9.1 displays these gaps for New York City public school fifth- and eighth-graders in 2000–2001. The first column in each pair presents the raw, unadjusted gaps, and the second column presents gaps that are "fully adjusted" for individual characteristics and schools attended. Only bolded numbers are significantly different from comparable numbers computed for the comparison group (e.g., foreign-born versus native-born, black versus white, fifth-, or eighth-graders).

Comparing black boys to white boys reveals larger differences in their scores than the gap between black and white girls, although the differences in the gaps are not statistically significant. For both boys and girls, the differences are large. The results for boys, however, are especially troubling because national data clearly reveal that black males have higher high school dropout rates and lower college attendance rates compared to both white males and black females. Improving the early performance of black boys (in elementary school) would be likely to have positive effects later in life.

Table 9.1

Racial/Ethnic Reading Test Score Gaps Between Girls and Boys and Between Foreign- and Native-Born, New York City Public School Students, 2000–2001, Difference from White Students

	Girls		Boys	
	(1)	(2)	(1)	(2)
Fifth grade				
Black	−0.705***	−0.285***	−0.752***	−0.299***
	(0.015)	(0.020)	(0.016)	(0.021)
Hispanic	−0.708***	−0.175***	−0.671***	−0.149***
	(0.015)	(0.019)	(0.016)	(0.019)
No. of students	33,103	33,103	31,825	31,825
No. of schools	664	664	666	666
R^2	0.10	0.30	0.10	0.29
Eighth grade				
Black	−0.793***	−0.413***	−0.778***	−0.425***
	(0.018)	(0.021)	(0.016)	(0.019)
Hispanic	**−0.844***	**−0.329***	**−0.717***	**−0.271***
	(0.018)	**(0.020)**	**(0.016)**	**(0.019)**
No. of students	26,833	26,833	25,363	25,363
No. of schools	277	277	276	276
R^2	0.13	0.39	0.14	0.38
	Foreign-Born		Native-Born	
Fifth grade				
Black	**−0.641***	**−0.079**	**−0.730***	**−0.307***
	(0.033)	**(0.052)**	**(0.012)**	**(0.015)**
Hispanic	−0.644***	−0.083**	−0.692***	−0.165***
	(0.031)	(0.040)	(0.012)	(0.015)
No. of students	7,217	7,217	57,711	57,711
No. of schools	623	623	666	666
R^2	0.08	0.36	0.10	0.29
Eighth grade				
Black	**−0.841***	**−0.307***	**−0.753***	**−0.425***
	(0.031)	**(0.041)**	**(0.014)**	**(0.015)**
Hispanic	−0.890***	−0.245***	−0.747***	−0.290***
	(0.029)	(0.035)	(0.014)	(0.015)
No. of students	9,170	9,170	43,026	43,026
No. of schools	274	274	277	277
R^2	0.13	0.43	0.12	0.39

Source: Stiefel, Schwartz, and Ellen (2006).

Notes: 1. Specification (1) is unadjusted from regression with no covariates. Specification (2) is fully adjusted from regression with sociodemographic and educational controls plus school fixed effects; 2. Robust standard errors in parentheses; 3. Only eighth-grade Hispanic girls compared to eighth-grade Hispanic boys differ from one another at a 10 percent or better level (5 percent in this case); 4. The differences between native-born black and white students compared to foreign-born black and white students are different from one another at the 1 percent level in both fifth and eighth grades, in both 1996–97 and 2000–2001. This is not true for Hispanic students in either year or grade; 5.

*Significant at 10 percent; **significant at 5 percent; ***significant at 1 percent.

An especially interesting pair of statistics compares the black–white gap for foreign-born to the gap for native-born students. Table 9.1 shows that the fully adjusted black–white gap (in column 2) in fifth grade falls to zero for the foreign-born (the reported number cannot be distinguished from zero, statistically), while the adjusted gap is 0.31 for native-born students in fifth grade.[2] Why should racial gaps disappear for foreign-born students? Are immigrants treated differently by the school system? Are their families affected differently by their racial classifications? The study of foreign-born black students may offer some clues about how to reduce the racial gaps among native-born students.[3]

What Can Be Done? Within, Before, Beyond, and Around Schools

Racial test score gaps are a prominent public concern, especially since they are now publicly reported pursuant to NCLB. In addition, since the 1998 publication of *The Black-White Test Score Gap* by Christopher Jencks and Meredith Phillips, many researchers have turned attention to studying how and why the gaps emerge and persist. As of now, there are neither clear-cut answers nor simple ways to reduce disparities, but the following are some suggestions that we take away from our own and others' research.

The emphasis of NCLB is on school accountability and on finding solutions to gaps within schools. Our work leads us to believe that there is a limit to what schools, at least as currently organized, can do to reduce gaps. But there do seem to be some promising steps that schools can take. These include decreasing school size, adopting longer grade spans, such as K–8, and obtaining better-qualified teachers. Without significantly more resources or radically different organizations, which are untested, it is hard to see how schools alone will be able to do the job.

To fully eliminate racial gaps, we may need to look beyond schools. There is much research on how gaps emerge before children even reach school age, leading many to suggest that good-quality preschooling and even infant–parent education efforts might be needed (Belfield et al. 2006; Heckman and Caneiro 2003). Others suggest that during the school years, parents and families play a central role in helping students achieve, and, thus, it might help to encourage more high-quality participation on their part. Finally, improving the neighborhoods where black and Hispanic students live could potentially improve their scholastic achievement.

Notes

1. These differences in wages hold constant race and age and highest grade attained.
2. As far as we know, only Fryer and Levitt (2004) have reported an insignificant racial gap, and in their case, it was among students entering kindergarten.
3. Note that in this same year, the eighth-grade foreign-born students do show a significant gap, and that the Fryer and Levitt research reveals that over time the gap reappears for the group of students who are followed from kindergarten through third grade.

References

Belfield, C.; Milagros Nores; Steve Barnett; and Lawrence Schweinhart. 2006. "The High/ Scope Perry Preschool Program." *Journal of Human Resources* 41, no. 1: 162–90.

Fryer, R.G., and S.D. Levitt. 2004. "Understanding the Black-White Test Score Gap in the First Two Years of School." *Review of Economics and Statistics* 68: 551–60.

Heckman, J., and P. Caneiro. 2003. "Human Capital Policy." In *Inequality in America: What Role for Human Capital Policy?* ed. J. Heckman and A. Krueger. Cambridge: MIT Press, 77–239.

Jencks, Christopher, and Meredith Phillips. 1998. *The Black-White Test Score Gap.* Washington, DC: Brookings Institution.

Murnane, R.J.; J.B. Willett; and F. Levy. 1995. "The Growing Importance of Cognitive Skills in Wage Determination." *Review of Economics and Statistics* 77: 251–66.

Neal, D A., and W.R. Johnson. 1996. "The Role of Premarket Forces in Black-White Wage Differences." *Journal of Political Economy* 104: 869–95.

Stiefel, Leanna; Amy Ellen Schwartz; and Ingrid Gould Ellen. 2006. "Disentangling the Racial Test Score Gap: Probing the Evidence in a Large Urban District." *Journal of Policy Analysis and Management* 26, no. 1: 7–30.

U.S. Department of Education. 2003. National Center for Education Statistics, National Assessment of Educational Progress (NAEP). Washington, DC.

10

Environmental Justice and Land Use Planning

Sylvester Murray and Mark D. Hertko

Environmental justice addresses the differential exposure of disadvantaged populations to ecological health hazards resulting from inequitable land use policies and administrative decisions.

In the early 1990s, the Congressional Black Caucus, a bipartisan coalition of academicians, social scientists, and political activists, met with U.S. Environmental Protection Agency (EPA) officials to discuss their findings of the EPA's unfairly implementing its enforcement inspections, and that environmental risks were higher in low-income populations with a high concentration of people of color. The EPA administrator, in response, created a work group on "environmental equity." The work group produced a final report titled "Reducing Risk in All Communities" in June 1992, which supported the risk allegations and made ten recommendations for addressing the problem. One of the recommendations was to create an office to deal with these inequities. The office was established in November 1992, and it was formally named the Office of Environmental Justice in 1994.

The majority of data used in this chapter come from recent studies conducted by the National Academy of Public Administration (the Academy) for the Office of Environmental Justice at the U.S. Environmental Protection Agency. Three studies were conducted looking at the relationship between environmental justice and local land use planning and zoning. The first study focused on EPA's programs for issuing air, water, and waste permits. The second study examined various state models for addressing environmental justice, with a particular focus on the permitting function. The third study focused on how local government decisions on land use planning and zoning have—or have not—been used to address environmental issues in five selected communities where concerns about inequities have been raised.

In conducting the three studies, the Academy used EPA's definition of environmental justice:

> Environmental justice is the fair treatment and meaningful involvement of all people regardless of race, color, national origin, culture, education, or income with respect to the development, implementation, and enforcement of environmental laws, regulations, and policies. *Fair treatment* means that no group of

people, including racial, ethic, or socioeconomic groups, should bear a dispro-portionate share of negative consequences resulting from industrial, municipal, and commercial operations or the execution of federal, state, local, and tribal environmental programs and policies. *Meaningful involvement* means that: (1) potentially affected community residents have an appropriate opportunity to par-ticipate in decisions about a proposed activity that will affect their environment and/or health; (2) the public's contribution can influence the regulatory agency's decision; (3) the concerns of all participants involved will be considered in the decision-making process; and (4) the decision-makers seek out and facilitate the involvement of those potentially affected (U.S. Environemntal Protection Agency 2011).

This chapter first gives a background of government policies in environmental justice. Next, we present findings and conclusions of the Academy studies. Then we discuss the relationship between environmental justice and land use plan-ning, its understanding by local government managers and land use planners, and available tools and approaches communities can use to mitigate or avoid harmful environmental justice situations.

Milestones in Environmental Justice Policy

Permits, licenses, and zoning are policy terms for prescribing what uses are autho-rized on specific land locations. Such authorizations have long been the purview of state and local governments. However, the federal government plays a prominent role in environmental regulation. As early as 1899, the United States adopted the Rivers and Harbors Act. The primary purpose of the act was to protect commercial shipping, but it also established a "permit system" that applied to dredge and fill projects. A permitting system that required written government permission and approval for dredge and fill projects eventually became a part of almost every environmental regulation enacted. Licenses and permits, often given by federal agencies, are required for most developments impacting air, water, and solid waste pollution. The federal agencies granting the majority of permits are EPA, Depart-ment of Energy, Department of Transportation, Department of Labor, the Army Corps of Engineers, and the Occupational Safety and Health Administration. All have promulgated regulations aimed at environmental protection and the control of environmental hazards.

The inauguration of zoning came at the beginning of the 1900s. Los Angeles launched the country's first "use" zoning ordinance in 1908 "to protect its expand-ing residential areas from industrial nuisances." In 1916, New York enacted the first comprehensive zoning ordinance, "separating and protecting residential uses from incompatible commercial and industrial uses." Local police powers for zon-ing were affirmed in the landmark 1926 Supreme Court decision *Village of Euclid v. Ambler Realty Corporation*. Euclid upheld the general principle of using police power to separate incompatible uses and to protect residential uses and residential environments from the pressures of growth and industrialization. Thus, the concerns over health, safety, and the general welfare that are embodied in the police powers of a municipality were properly extended through the device of zoning to protect residential uses from the encroachment of commerce and industry (National Academy of Public Administration 2003).

Federal policies have also played a role in establishing the legal framework for zoning laws. The Standard State Zoning Enabling Act of 1922, under the sponsorship of the U.S. Department of Commerce, served as the basic model for state zoning acts. Among other things, the 1922 act granted states the power to regulate land use for the "health, safety, morals, or the general welfare of the community" (U.S. Department of Commerce 1926, 4). This authority included regulating and restricting "the height, number of stories and size of buildings and other structures, the percentage of lot that may be occupied, the size of yards, courts and other open spaces, the density of population and the location and use of buildings, structures and land of trade, industry, residence, or other purposes" (4-5).

The National Environmental Policy Act (NEPA) was adopted in 1970. Primarily, NEPA establishes national policy, sets obtainable goals, and provides a means for implementing and enforcing environmental policy. It sets forth requirements for the inclusion of environmental-protection provisions in all actions of federal agencies. The act states that the goals and objectives of NEPA must be achieved through the use of federal plans, functions, programs, and resources. These objectives include the assurance of "safe, healthful, productive, and esthetically and culturally pleasing surroundings for all Americans [while] attain[ing] the widest range of beneficial uses of the environment without degradation, risk to health or safety, or other undesirable and unintended consequences" (NEPA 1970, Section 101). This NEPA goal and objectives statement is the genesis and measurement for environmental justice.

The environmental justice movement signaled the merging of two of the most significant social movements of the twentieth century: the civil rights and environmental activist movements. Three studies highlighted the problem:

1. In 1987, the United Church of Christ's Commission for Racial Justice published Toxic Waste and Race in the United States: A National Report on the Racial and Socioeconomic Characteristics of Communities Surrounding Hazardous Waste Sites (1987), which confirmed what many had already believed to be true: that race was the most significant factor nationwide in the siting of hazardous waste facilities.

2. In 1992, the National Law Journal published "Unequal Protection—The Racial Divide in Environmental Law: A Special Investigation," which found that penalties under hazardous waste laws and penalties for all federal environmental laws aimed at protecting citizens from air, water and waste pollution were significantly higher in white communities than in minority communities (Lavalle and Coyle 1992).

3. Studies by the American Planning Association have found that zoning has
    failed to deliver on its loftier promises of producing high-quality working
    and living environments; has been misused by suburban communities to
    exclude low-income and minority families; and has engendered corruption,
    because the basic concept of uniform treatment within and among zoning
    districts has been frequently undercut by issuance of variances, exceptions,
    and special permits (National Academy of Public Administration 2003).

The pursuit of social equity is the gold standard against which the actions of
effective public governance should be judged. Good governance should not only
seek to achieve efficiency and economy but also must be evaluated on how well
it manages to enhance fairness, justice, and equity in the outcomes of governance
processes. In the context of environmental justice, it is how we determine who
bears, or does not bear, the burden of exposures to involuntary risks from pollution. The scope of equity concerns has broadened in the past half century as public
administrators have moved beyond procedural approaches to equity to consider the
nature of resource allocation and the differential impact of government action on
individuals and groups in society. Nowhere is this shift more evident than in the
pursuit of environmental justice.

Connecting Environmental Justice and Land Use Planning and Zoning

Environmental justice presents many challenges and many opportunities for local
planning and zoning officials. The concerns of people of color and low-income
communities challenge local governments to find ways to prevent and solve problems that create disproportionate impacts. Although land use planning and zoning
are not the only reason for the environmental problems that currently exist, they
have, in some instances, continued to be significant barriers to addressing environmental justice concerns. However, planning and zoning are important tools for
making positive local changes, and some states and local governments are trying
to do just that.

The official recognition that environmental justice is an issue for concern by
government is evidenced in the 1994 Executive Order 12898, "Federal Actions
to Address Environmental Justice in Minority Populations and Low-Income
Populations." This order directly states that citizen participation, transparency, and
harmful-effects mitigation must be a part of projects that receive federal government financing.

The Role of Government in Providing Environmental Justice

The Academy has conducted a thorough examination of how federal, state, and
local government organizations have addressed environmental justice. The ex-

amination looked at how public administrators at federal, state, and local levels responded to environmental justice issues, what tools were available, and what tools were needed to provide equitable environmental conditions across communities. The examination found that the goal of environmental justice can be achieved by every level of government where there is a will to do so. There are a number of commonalities from successful environmental justice efforts that can be applied to all efforts at all levels.

In order to create positive changes, government officials must:

1. Exercise leadership by recognizing environmental justice as an important issue and by establishing accountability to address equity problems.
2. Judiciously enforce environmental regulations and requirements designed to protect citizens when giving siting, permitting, and zoning approval.
3. Set priorities to reduce risks caused by pollution and other hazards.
4. Engage the public early and proactively in substantive discussions about decisions that affect their health and welfare.
5. Adopt effective mechanisms for communicating with the public and provide the public with adequate information so they can make useful contributions prior to agency decisions.
6. Coordinate with other levels of government so that local citizens can benefit from the unique kinds of support that agencies at each level can provide.

At all three levels of government, the studies found encouraging progress toward environmental justice, but also two consistent and recurring problems: (1) the failure to integrate environmental justice initiatives fully into core agency programs, and (2) the lack of performance measures or accountability mechanisms to evaluate work efforts. A brief review of the government levels studied illustrates these recurring challenges.

The federal-level study—*Environmental Justice in EPA Permitting: Reducing Pollution in High-Risk Communities Is Integral to the Agency's Mission* (National Academy of Public Administration 2001)—focused on the environmental permitting process and the extent to which EPA has incorporated environmental justice concerns into its permitting programs by using its current legal authorities under the Clean Air Act, the Clean Water Act, and the Resource Conservation and Recovery Act. The study found that EPA had clearly articulated policy commitments to environmental justice and dedicated resources to the issue. However, EPA had not integrated its environmental justice initiatives into its core programs and functions, such as permitting, standard setting, and rule making. A recent EPA inspector general report found that "EPA senior management has not sufficiently directed program and regional offices to conduct environmental justice reviews in accordance with Executive Order 12898" (EPA 2006, 5). The study indicated that without such reviews, the agency could not determine whether its programs cause disproportionately high and adverse human health or environmental effects on minority and low-income populations. In *Models for Change, Efforts by Four States to Address Environmental Justice* (National Academy of Public Administration 2002), four states—California, Florida, Indiana, and New Jersey—were examined to see the variety of approaches they employed to address environmental justice problems, including:

- Enacting new legislation
- Proposing new regulations
- Issuing executive orders, policies, or other directives
- Launching in-depth public health studies
- Convening advisory committees composed of diverse stakeholders
- Implementing various management measures

While the variety of state approaches provides heartening evidence that at least a few states are attempting to address environmental justice concerns, the study also identified the need to strengthen accountability and integrate environmental justice into the states' core environmental protection and public health programs. For instance, in Florida, the leadership for environmental justice rose from outside the state's environmental agency, which did not believe it had legal authority to address their issues. The need for strengthened accountability was true for even the most expansive state programs. California adopted legislation requiring that state agencies address environmental justice issues, plus other innovative approaches and tools, some of which were based on risk reduction strategies. However, California's initiatives still lacked measurable program objectives and accountability measures.

Addressing Community Concerns: How Environmental Justice Relates to Land Use Planning and Zoning (National Academy of Public Administration 2003) is the topic of the third study, which concentrated on local-level environmental justice activities. The local level is the title and primary discussion of this entire report. The study found that state and local officials can make creative and aggressive use of existing legal authorities to resolve the environmental and public health concerns of community residents. They can take steps to eliminate existing nonconforming uses that present public health and environmental hazards by adopting more flexible zoning techniques, such as:

1. Setting up conditional uses that impose restrictions on certain actions that may affect environmental justice issues;
2. Establishing overlay zones that impose additional requirements to provide for additional environmental protection;
3. Using performance zoning to regulate the adverse impacts of nuisance-like activities, such as noise and odor;
4. Establishing buffer zones in transitional areas between incompatible land uses, especially for industrial uses adjacent to residential areas;

5. Training staff in how to conduct effective community outreach and how to analyze the environmental justice impacts of proposed land use plans and zoning ordinances;

6. Ensuring that state agencies adequately assess and address localized adverse impacts and that the state agencies solicit perspectives of community residents and address their concerns before approving permits;

7. Thoroughly reviewing their legal authorities to understand the full scope of their powers for addressing particular issues of concern to low-income and people-of-color communities, and ensuring that the citizens who are affected by environmental decisions receive fair treatment and are involved in a meaningful way.

These are just some of the options available to reduce risk that could be more fully utilized if planning and zoning officials were better informed and aware of how other jurisdictions have implemented these approaches.

Later in the chapter, we provide information on the five localities studied as case histories in the 2003 NAPA study.

Siting and Permitting: Two Sides of the Environmental Justice Coin

Intergovernmental coordination is very important for success at each level of government because agencies at each level have unique legal authorities, expertise, technical tools, and other resources to prevent or mitigate harmful neighborhood impacts from nearby pollution sources.

Environmental permit decisions at the state or federal level have direct linkages to local land use planning and zoning. Siting, approval of the exact location for a facility, is primarily a local land use decision controlled by comprehensive plans and zoning ordinances. Permitting, approval of the design and mechanisms associated with the operation of the facility, is primarily a state or federal responsibility controlled by acceptable levels of emissions and residues of the operation. The interaction between these two processes presents the intersection between environmental justice and land use planning and zoning. When the linkage between siting and permitting is ignored, localized impacts may not be adequately considered.

State governments issue major environmental permits for air emissions, water discharges, and land disposal under the authority delegated to them by the federal EPA. In some instances, states have, in turn, delegated permitting authority to local governments. Many states also adopt their own environmental protection laws for issues peculiar to their states. Where more specific authorities are not appropriate, general welfare or nuisance authorities under common law may be available to address particular problems. The decision to approve a permit will be influenced by the anticipated environmental impact.

Uncoordinated efforts at siting, permitting, and zoning have often led to decisions that failed to protect many residential areas and shield them from sources of pollution. Instead, they have created inequities among different communities' exposure to environmental and public health threats. Past approaches by local officials have left some communities, often people of color or low-income communities, without adequate protection for health and welfare, and in certain cases have deprived some citizens of opportunities for effective civic engagement. A legacy of actions that left citizens without meaningful involvement in decisions affecting their health, environment, and neighborhoods requires current public officials and administrators to conduct the business of land use planning and zoning with the goal of environmental justice in the forefront of their minds.

Importance of Local Government Authority

Local land use planning and zoning decisions made by local officials and administrators have had an important influence on environmental justice problems. The disproportionate exposures that often trigger environmental justice concerns are many and complex. They include racism, inadequate health care, low quality housing, high hazard workplace environments, limited access to environmental information, simple lack of political power, and willful noncompliance with environmental laws, among others. The argument is made not only that people of color or low-income residents are likely to live close to polluting industries with the resulting unequal distribution of environmental exposures but also that local zoning has sometimes created these disparities, and that local decision makers were often fully aware of the likely outcomes.

Local land use planning and zoning decisions shape the environment of a community. Yet, members of planning and zoning boards and local legislative bodies (such as city councils or county commissions), which make local land use decisions, commonly have had little or no formal training in planning, although they may be supported by a staff of professional planners. They define where potential pollution sources—such as businesses, industrial facilities, and highways—can be located, and zoning ordinance restrictions on noise, odor, and nuisances that can also affect neighborhood quality. The result has often been that land decisions tended to concentrate undesirable land uses in certain areas, often near neighborhoods that have significant minority or low-income populations. The lack of training to help local officials understand how land use decisions relate to environmental justice, and the steps they can take to prevent, reduce, or eliminate risks to neighborhoods facing disparate impacts, is a major stumbling block to achieving environmental justice.

Some local governments have taken action to correct these problems and to prevent future mistakes that expose local residents to nearby pollution sources. Some examples of effective mechanisms include:

- Revision of zoning ordinance to impose conditions in building/operating permits based on proximity to residential areas and the potential for adverse

environmental impacts. Permits can require advance mitigation and reduction of fume emissions.
- Revision of zoning ordinance to prohibit industrial facilities from producing a net increase in environmental pollution; adoption of a series of performance measures to mitigate environmental impacts from new facilities, including noise, glare, and air pollution.
- Adoption of ordinance requiring any new facility with operations more intense than an existing commercial use to obtain a special use permit and conduct an extensive process to notify local residents.

There are many encouraging signs that state and local governments are beginning to tackle environmental justice challenges and are starting to address them in more effective ways, utilizing both siting and permitting authorities. Some cities and counties have begun to use their land use planning and zoning authorities to prevent or resolve community environmental and public health problems, which can serve as useful models for other local governments. To resolve existing environmental justice problems and avoid future ones, critical partnerships across all levels of government must be enhanced; accountability to the public by local officials must be strengthened by creating greater participation of citizens in decision-making processes; and local government leaders must receive training on environmental justice, especially with regard to local land use planning and zoning authorities.

Local Government Case Studies

Austin, Texas

Findings

Mandated racial segregation, historic zoning patterns, and changing economies have created many of the environmental justice problems in East Austin. Segregation required nonwhites to live in East Austin, and cumulative industrial zoning focused economic growth in East Austin, allowing homes to be built next to factories.

The Texas Commission on Environmental Quality (TCEQ) has responsibility for environmental permits for all facilities in Austin. TCEQ does not believe it has authority to consider environmental justice concerns in the permitting process. Additionally, TCEQ and the city of Austin were not communicating regarding their separate duties—siting and pollution permitting—and where they overlap, namely, with regard to protection of public health and welfare.

Strong community pressure in the early 1990s motivated the city to address environmental justice. Using its planning and zoning authorities, the city of Austin responded to environmental justice concerns of its citizenry by rezoning incompatible uses in East Austin, adopting a neighborhood approach to planning, enacting overlay ordinances, expanding public participation, and addressing environmental and public health risks at city-owned properties.

Recommendations

The city of Austin needs clearly articulated policies, programs, and priorities for addressing environmental justice problems to ensure that, in the future, no group of citizens has to bear a disproportionate share of environmental burdens and that all citizens will have opportunities to be meaningfully involved in decisions that affect their environment and health.

TCEQ should look broadly at its existing legal authorities for addressing environmental justice concerns, including those related to environmental permitting. TCEQ's environmental justice program should include commitments to reduce risk, improve communication, and provide greater public access to information. TCEQ should also provide guidance and other assistance to local Texas governments to help them understand and address the potential public health and environmental implications of their land use decisions.

Chester, Pennsylvania

Findings

Chester's plan for economic development, including desired land uses, does not articulate goals for reducing pollution, achieving environmental justice, or reducing risks, except for lead exposure. Chester has adopted ordinances limiting the development of new heavy facilities and specifying performance standards designed to minimize environmental impacts, but the city's attempt to control where certain types of facilities are sited is severely limited by lack of enforcement.

Chester has not yet tackled the environmental justice issues associated with existing land uses, including inhabited but depressed housing stock located in close proximity to older industrial facilities that have toxic emissions. Chester lacks a formal process for addressing or tracking citizen concerns about environmental or public health hazards.

Recommendations

The city of Chester should enforce the 1994 changes to its planning and zoning code as well as its 1998 Performance Standards ordinance. These requirements were designed to ensure there would be no net increase in pollution from new industrial facilities, no violations of federal air quality regulations, no unlawful discharges of liquids or solid wastes, and no offensive odors beyond lot lines. Chester should take steps to increase public participation in local decision making and develop a formal process for tracking citizen concerns about environmental or public health hazards.

Altgeld Gardens—Chicago, Illinois

Findings

The environmental problems at Altgeld Gardens are the legacy of the region's 100-year history as an area for industrial and waste disposal and the more recent siting of nearby municipal waste treatment facilities. The environmental conditions reflect Chicago's failure to consider the potential implications of locating residential and industrial areas in close proximity to each other, because current pollution controls may not provide adequate protection to residents faced with multiple exposures. Much of the land near Altgeld Gardens is zoned for manufacturing uses. If the Calumet regional plan is implemented, some of the land will be preserved or reclaimed for open space and recreation. However, large tracts will remain zoned for manufacturing uses because the area, with it existing infrastructure for transporting goods, is considered vital to Chicago's economic redevelopment. The challenge is to reduce the adverse impacts on neighboring residential districts from existing and past facilities in the manufacturing districts.

Recommendations

Chicago should ensure that its current effort to adopt comprehensive zoning reforms addresses community and public health concerns, and should plan and carry out extensive public outreach and participation on the zoning reforms. The new zoning should require explicit consideration of public health and environmental impacts for all proposed land uses. The new zoning should strengthen controls on noise, odor, toxics, smoke, and traffic, and make them apply to both existing and future activities.

Chicago agencies should expand their public participation efforts and actively reach out to community-based and environmental justice organizations when making permitting, planning, and zoning decisions. The State of Illinois Environmental Protection Agency should fully implement its Interim Environmental Justice Policy, and help Chicago's planning and environmental agencies to develop and implement comparable policies and practices.

St. James Parish, Louisiana

Findings

Louisiana law does not require local governments to adopt comprehensive plans or zoning ordinances, and St. James Parish has no comprehensive plan or zoning ordinance. Louisiana law authorizes regional planning agencies to assist local governments that are interested in planning and zoning, but officials in St. James Parish have seldom used these services.

In 1990, the Louisiana Department of Environmental Quality (LDEQ) issued a memorandum to all local officials reminding them of their responsibility for protecting human health and welfare and of their existing authority to exercise that responsibility when making local siting decisions.

The government of St. James Parish does not identify environmental justice as either a problem or a priority, in large part because parish officials believe there are no environmental justice issues unless a polluting facility purposefully locates near a low-income or people-of-color community intending to harm residents.

Recommendations

LDEQ should develop a clear environmental justice policy, action agenda, and accountability measures that include commitments to reducing risk, improving communication, and providing public access to more information. LDEQ should also provide parish and town governments with guidance to help them understand the public health and environmental implications of their land use decisions.

St. James Parish should adopt an environmental justice policy, embracing an appropriate definition of environmental justice and acknowledging that all citizens should receive fair treatment and have opportunities for meaningful involvement in processes that affect their health and welfare.

Huntington Park, California

Findings

Early zoning decisions did not prohibit residences from being built in manufacturing zones. For a long period, residences and manufacturing facilities coexisted in the areas zoned for manufacturing. Over time the demographics of the area changed from predominately white to predominantly Hispanic; public agencies became increasingly aware of the health consequences of pollution; and by the mid-1990s, citizens organized to select remedies for the adverse impacts of excess pollution.

Huntington Park revised the zoning ordinance to enhance the city's ability to condition environmental permits based on the proximity of a facility to residences and the level of adverse impact it presents. As part of this effort, the city took action to reduce risks from diesel emissions, because they present the greatest health risk in the area. Additionally, the city developed an air quality task force to develop strategies to reduce air toxins.

South Coast Air Quality Management District (AQMD) has responsibility for issuing permits in Huntington Park. The district has demonstrated a commitment to environmental justice as evidenced by implementing a robust set of measures to reduce risks, by improving community access to information and public participation, and by developing tools to address concerns raised by people-of-color and low-income communities, as well as other communities that may have high levels of exposure to pollution.

Recommendations

City government should continue to improve public participation and share information on environmental and health impacts relating to redevelopment projects.

South Coast AQMD should consider how the policies, implementation strategies, accountability measures, and tools the district has developed could be shared more widely with other state air-planning and local government agencies.

Consolidated Recommendations for Environmental Justice Action

1. State, county, and city officials who are responsible for making planning, zoning, public health, and environmental protection policy and decisions should take immediate action to determine whether their residents in low-income and people-of-color neighborhoods are exposed to excessive levels of environmental and health hazards. If so, they should initiate appropriate actions to reduce risks and communicate to the public when and how these risks will be reduced or eliminated.
2. State, county, and city governments should incorporate consideration of potential environmental and public health impacts of land use decisions into the fabric of their planning and zoning activities. They should actively explore how they can use current authorities to prevent excessive levels of pollution and mitigate environmental and other impacts such as noise, odor, and traffic—especially in low-income and people-of-color communities.
3. Local governments should enhance opportunities for meaningful public participation in all government decisions that have environmental and public health impacts; and each level of government should improve public access to information about land use planning, zoning, siting, and permitting.

These case histories show the critical connections between environmental justice problems and local land use planning and zoning decisions. While there are significant challenges to incorporating environmental justice principles into the nation's planning and zoning system, there are many opportunities to do so, and the potential rewards are great. Given the magnitude of local land use planning and zoning efforts, environmental justice advocates should not ignore this critical step in community decision making and economic development. There is a growing network of public, private, and non-profit interests all committed to ensuring that environmental justice issues are taken into account through local planning and zoning. Increasing collaboration, cooperating, sharing resources, and working on joint efforts will help to remedy past environmental justice problems and prevent their repetition in the future.

Another Point of View

In his book *Environmental Justice Through Research-Based Decision-Making*, William Bowen argues, "environmental justice is largely a provocative political symbol, invoked to elicit citizen participation toward greater empowerment for selected social groups, independently of any empirical justification" (2001, xi). He argues that there appears to be a major gap between the political rhetoric and the empirical reality of environmental justice. He says the rhetoric refers primarily to concern with public health impacts in minority and low-income neighborhoods, but the reality is that relatively little serious research has been done on the issue.

In Bowen's view, very little is evidently known about the distribution of environmentally hazardous sites in terms of the socioeconomic characteristics of nearby neighborhoods. Similarly, little is known about the public-health risks posed by such sites, and even less is known about differences in these risks in terms of socioeconomic categories. He concludes with this assessment:

> Thus, while the prevailing discourse tends to refer to empirical factors related to environmental risk-related public health in low-income and minority neighbor-hoods, it can plausibly be argued that the real underlying concerns have more to do with access to power, community empowerment, social justice, and anxieties over public health (2001, 12).

Bowen's flawed premise is that no scientific evidence exists to support the environmental justice movement. The environmental justice movement does indeed include concern for citizen participation and empowerment in public decisions affecting their quality of life. Public health impact is a significant quality of life issue. There exists scientific, empirical evidence that toxic pollutants impact the health of people exposed to them. Toxic pollutants are those that, after discharge and upon human exposure, can cause death, disease, behavioral abnormalities, and poisoning.

The United Church of Christ study mentioned earlier found that three out of five African Americans or Hispanics lived in a community adjacent to an uncontrolled waste disposal. Other studies buttressed these findings, as summarized in the *National Law Journal* article (Lavalle and Coyle 1992):

- In New Jersey communities, the number of hazardous waste sites is associated with more poor, elderly, young, and African American residents.
- In Houston, Texas, most of the incinerators and private municipal landfill sites permitted by the state and all of the un-permitted municipal landfill sites were located in predominantly African American neighborhoods, even though African Americans were only 28 percent of the population in 1980.
- In the Baton Rouge area of Louisiana, minority communities had an average of one hazardous waste incineration facility for every 7,300 residents, while white communities had only one site per 31,100 residents.

A study of three counties surrounding Detroit found that people-of-color neighborhoods were almost four times more likely to be located within one mile of a waste facility than white neighborhoods (Mohai and Bryant 1992, 171).

Summary

Environmental justice presents many challenges and many opportunities for local planning and zoning officials. The concerns of people-of-color and low-income communities challenge local governments to find ways to prevent and solve problems that create disproportionate impacts. Although land use planning and zoning are not the only reasons for the environmental problems that currently exist in these communities, they have, in some instances, continued to be significant barriers to addressing environmental justice concerns. Planning and zoning are important tools for making positive changes, and when coupled with other tools and techniques for reducing risk, and achieving informed and effective community participation, their proper use by public officials and administrators can provide better health and quality of life to citizens.

References

Bowen, William M. 2001. *Environmental Justice Through Research-Based Decision-Making.* New York: Garland.

Environmental Protection Agency, Office of Inspector General. 2006. *EPA Needs to Conduct Environmental Justice Reviews of Its Programs, Policies, and Activities.* Report No. 2006-P-00034 (September 18): Washington, DC.

Lavalle, M., and M. Coyle. 1992. "Unequal Protection—The Racial Divide in Environmental Law: A Special Investigation." *National Law Journal* 21 (September): S1–S12.

Mohai, Paul, and Bunyan Bryant. 1992. "Environmental Racism: Reviewing the Evidence." In *Race and the Incidence of Environmental Hazards: A Time for Discourse,* ed. Bunyan Bryant and Paul Mohai. Boulder: Westview Press, 163–176.

National Academy of Public Administration. 2001. *Environmental Justice in EPA Permitting: Reducing Pollution in High-Risk Communities Is Integral to the Agency's Mission.* Washington, DC.

———. 2002. *Models for Change, Efforts by Four States to Address Environmental Justice.* Washington, DC.

———. 2003. *Addressing Community Concerns: How Environmental Justice Relates to Land Use Planning and Zoning.* Washington, DC.

National Environmental Policy Act. 1970. Public Law 91-190, U.S. Code. Vol. 42, Section 4321–4347.

United Church of Christ Commission for Racial Justice. 1987. *Toxic Waste and Race in the United States: A National Report on the Racial and Socioeconomic Characteristics of Communities with Hazardous Waste Sites.* New York.

U.S. Department of Commerce. 1926. A Standard State Zoning Enabling Act, Under Which Municipalities May Adopt Zoning Regulations. Washington, DC. Reprint available at http://www.planning.org/growingsmart/pdf/SZEnablingAct1926.pdf (accessed March 27, 2011).

U.S. Environmental Protection Agency, 2011. *Basic Information on Environmental Justice.* www.epa.gov/environmentaljustice/basics/index.html (accessed March 27, 2011).

U.S. President. 1994. "Federal Actions to Address Environmental Justice in Minority Populations and Low-Income Populations." Executive Order 12898.

Village of Euclid v. Ambler Realty Corporation 272 U.S. 365. 1926.

Part III

Leadership, Outreach, and Organizational Development

11

Using Framing Theory to Make the Economic Case for Social Equity: The Role of Policy Entrepreneurs in Reframing the Debate

Kristen Norman-Major and Blue Wooldridge

In 2005 the National Academy of Public Administration in its Strategic Plan elevated equity to be the fourth pillar along with economy, efficiency, and effectiveness. Definitions of the latter three terms are well known to members of the public administration community. The first definition of the word *economy* in the online dictionary is: Careful, thrifty management of resources, such as money, materials, or labor. With an example of: *learned to practice economy in making out the household budget* (Dictionary.com 2010).

In answer to the question, "what exactly do we mean by *efficiency*?" Wolff provides the following answer:

> In common use efficiency simply means non-wastage: getting the most output from the least input. However, two thicker notions are often used in economic contexts: utility maximization and Pareto efficiency. The former holds that the most efficient system is the one that produces the highest sum of utility, while the latter claims that a situation is Pareto efficient if and only if no one can be made better off without making someone else worse off. (Wolff 2003, 449)

Klingner and Nalbandian (2003, 95) suggest that *effectiveness* asks the question: "Are we accomplishing the goal we set out to accomplish?" Whereas Patton and Sawicki (1993, 220), using effectiveness as an evaluation criterion, say that it measures whether the policy or program has its intended effect.

The newer term, *social equity* has developed many variations on a basic definition, each providing different insights to this complex concept. The one used by the National Academy of Public Administration defines social equity as:

> The fair, just and equitable management of all institutions serving the public directly or by contract, and the fair and equitable distribution of public services, and implementation of public policy, and the commitment to promote fairness,

justice, and equity in the formation of public policy (National Academy of Public Administration, Standing Panel on Social Equity in Governance).

Other definitions include:

> Definitions (for social equity) can range from "simple" fairness and equal treatment to redistribution and reducing inequalities. (Svara and Brunet 2004, 100)

> A principle of justice as "fairness" in which "each person is to have an equal right to the most extensive basic liberty compatible with a similar liberty for all." (Rawls 1971, 250)

Stone (2002, 42) uses equity to denote distributions regarded as fair, even though they contain both equalities and inequalities.

As the newest member of this quartet, equity often struggles to gain significant consideration in the promotion of public policies. Equity can be considered the second question of policy analysis. The first is focused on effectiveness, "what is the most effective means of achieving 'what we set out to do'?" The second question asks "effective for whom?"

This tension between equity and effectiveness is also reflected in the contrast between equity and efficiency. As Patton and Sawicki (1993, 204) point out, "In many instances programs that prove to be very efficient also prove to be very inequitable. The two criteria are seldom both maximized in the same program." Usually in the promotion of social equity there is an assumed trade-off with efficiency at the least, and potentially economy as well, given that social equity programs are often assumed to be expensive. This perceived trade-off could lead to reduced emphasis on programs directed toward social equity, especially in times of tight public sector budgets.

Traditionally, social equity policies have been promoted using messages that stress social justice, morality, and ethics—it is the right thing to do. Increasingly, however, many advocates of policy that promote social equity are using arguments around economic investment to show the payoffs and return on investment (ROI) achieved through equity programming. This "reframing" of the argument is changing the face of debates around programs and policies that address equity issues, building a new audience of support from more fiscally and socially conservative decision makers who may in the past have been unwilling to accept the assumed trade-off between equity and efficiency.

In this chapter, after this discussion of definitions of social equity, we examine framing theory and how it might be used to reshape debate around equity. Next, examples of promotion of equity programs through economic arguments based on cost–benefit analysis and ROI, including a more detailed case study of early childhood development in Minnesota will be covered. Finally, the role of leadership in reframing social equity arguments will be discussed.

As noted earlier, traditionally, social equity has been defended on a social justice basis. For example, Charles Darwin, in *The Voyage of the Beagle* published in 1839 stated "If the misery of our poor be caused not by the laws of nature, but by our institutions, great is our sin" (quoted in Pogge 2006, 607).

Roger Wilkins in his keynote speech to the 2001 NAPA Leadership Conference on Social Equity in Governance states that public administrators have an obligation to find ways of strengthening the weak, poor, and in need of our society (Wilkins, 2001).

Robert Kennedy clearly supported the social justice basis of equity when in 1966 he said:

> We must recognize the full human equality of all people before God, before the law, and in the councils of government. We must do this, not because it is economically advantageous, although it is; not because the laws of God command it, although they do; not because people in other lands wish it so. We must do it for the single and fundamental reason that it is the right thing to do. (Kennedy 1966)

Recently, however, some advocates of social equity have suggested that its promotion might be more effective if it were "reframed" depending upon the intended audience. For example, as Roger Hughes said in his presentation at the Seventh Annual Social Equity Leadership Conference in Phoenix:

> For those who care deeply about issues of social equity—and I count myself among them—(social inequity) isn't right. It's not fair, it's not moral, it's not just. It needs to be addressed, and that means we need to become more proactive in addressing social equity issues.
>
> Well, I've learned the hard way that the language you use—or more precisely, how you frame your language in an argument to persuade somebody of something—makes all the difference in the world.
>
> To flourish, we will all need to become masters of rhetoric—the art of persuasion—and adapt our language accordingly. (Hughes 2008)

This new orientation calls for supporters of social equity to learn from the insights provided by "framing theory."

Framing Theory

Scholars in many disciplines have been intrigued by finding that decision makers respond differently to problem statements that are objectively equivalent but presented differently (Greenberg and Baron 2003). Framing theory attributes this phenomenon to the situation in which, when describing an issue or event, the incoming message emphasizes some particular aspect or subset of ideas rather than some others, thus leading the recipient to choose differently than he might otherwise (Druckman 2001). "A framing 'effect' occurs when individuals arrive at different positions on the issue, depending on the priority given to various considerations"

(Druckman and Nelson 2003, 730). While some suggest that research on framing is characterized by theoretical and empirical vagueness (Scheufele 2006), others, such as Kuhberger (1998), who conducted a meta-analysis of more than 130 empirical papers on framing effects, conclude that framing is a reliable phenomenon. Malarkey (2008) points out that an extensive body of literature has evolved in a number of disciplines, including advertising, market research, social psychology, medicine, education, and perception as well as other areas.

An example of this phenomenon in the policy arena is illustrated by the "marketing" of the African American Men Project in Hennepin County, Minnesota. This project was developed to address high rates of unemployment and other issues affecting African American men in the county, despite strong economic performance and low unemployment otherwise in the state and county. In their case study of the development of this project, Crosby and Bryson note that initially the steering committee members for the project looked at the problems affecting the male African American population in Hennepin County as a matter of "social injustice" (2005, 245). As time went on, however, leaders of the project reframed the debate from which social injustices were causing the problems for African American men to what could be done to help the men help themselves. The new frame became "What's good for African American men is good for Hennepin County" (ibid.). This reframing allowed the project leaders to open doors to new policy alternatives and a mindset of helping each other help the county versus having the county do all the work. The new frame was potentially less divisive and, as Crosby and Bryson note, opened the path to more creative problem solving.

As Malarkey points out (2008, 91), framing is distinct from persuasion.

> "The standard model of communication-based persuasion typically involves a source who presents a message about an attitude object to an audience with the goal of changing audience beliefs. If the audience member both understands and believes the message, then the new belief is adopted . . . frames operate by changing the relative importance of beliefs already stored in the decision maker's long-term memory."

However, there do appear to be some prerequisites of persuasion that carry over to framing theory. For example, Neidhardt suggests that persuasion strategies should have the following attributes: "Statements (that) must seem correct, explanations (that) must seem plausible, evaluations (that) must seem legitimate, and actions (that) must seem necessary and advantageous" (1994, 18). These attributes appear to be vital in convincing a skeptical audience as to the economic value of strategies used to promote social equity. These attributes would call for sophisticated economic analysis, including life-cycle costing and discounting to present value using a defensible discount rate. Life-cycle cost is the total cost of ownership of machinery and equipment, including its cost of acquisition, operation, maintenance, conversion, and/or decommission (Society of Automotive Engineers, 1995).

Discounting to present value is *necessary* because the consideration of the effects of time on both costs and benefits is essential to analysis, especially where there exist positive and negative cash flows exist, over an extended planning horizon. A present monetary unit is worth less than a future monetary unit, and it follows that procurement of that unit in the present will cost less in the future. Or resources on hand today are usually worth more than the identical resources delivered tomorrow. There is a special problem in estimating future costs and benefits. Somehow, one must compare future costs with today's costs. This equivalence value is determined through the concept of *discounting*.

Discounting has always been a controversial matter and even more controversial within the controversy is agreement on the appropriate rate to use for discounting. Mikesell (2003) points out that the "big three" of federal government finance— the Office of Management and Budget (OMB), the Government Accountability Office (GAO), and the Congressional Budget Office (CBO)—all do discounting, but the discount rates they use are not the same. Mikesell goes on to suggest that two important alternatives for discounting are the costs of borrowed funds to the government and the opportunity costs of displaced private activity.

Given these arguments concerning the importance of characteristics of a "reframed statement," reframing the argument for social equity from a social justice basis to an economic benefit–cost rationale would most likely appeal to those individuals who are interested in the "bottom line," or a combination of the effectiveness and economic efficiency of alternate public policy approaches. This approach could bring a new set of potential policy advocates and leaders to the debate on social equity and could alter the willingness of citizens to accept solutions that advance social equity.

Reframing in Action: Social Equity as Economic Investment

A close review of the research identifies several scholars and policy advocates whose work has begun to use the economic analysis of cost–benefit ratios or ROI to reframe arguments in support of programs that have social equity implications. Following are examples with more detailed description of policy around early childhood development in Minnesota.

A common focal point of research on the economic costs of social inequity is the cost of poverty to society. In one study conducted by the GAO, the researchers found that regardless of whether poverty is a cause or an effect, the conditions associated with poverty can limit the ability of individuals to develop the skills, abilities, knowledge, and habits necessary to fully participate in the labor force. The researchers also found that economic research suggests that individuals living in poverty face an increased risk of adverse outcomes, such as poor health and criminal activity, both of which may lead to reduced participation in the labor market. Finally, the study indicates that poverty can negatively impact economic growth by affecting the accumulation of human capital and rates of crime and social unrest (GAO 2007).

Another study builds on these research findings to clearly distinguish the differences between the social justice and the economic benefit–cost justification for reducing social inequities. While acknowledging that most arguments for reducing poverty in the United States, especially among children, rest on a moral case for doing so—one that emphasizes the unfairness of child poverty, and how it runs counter to our national creed of equal opportunity for all—the authors note that there is also an economic case for reducing child poverty. When children grow up in poverty they are somewhat more likely than nonpoor children to have low earnings as adults, which in turn reflects lower workforce productivity. They are also somewhat more likely to engage in crime (though that is not the case for the vast majority) and to have poor health later in life. Their reduced productive activity generates a direct loss of goods and services to the U.S. economy (Holzer et al. 2007). This research suggests that the costs to the United States associated with childhood poverty total about $500 billion per year, or the equivalent of nearly 4 percent of the gross domestic product (GDP). Specifically, the researchers estimate that each year childhood poverty reduces productivity and economic output by about 1.3 percent of GDP, raises the costs of crime by 1.3 percent of GDP, and raises health expenditures and reduces the value of health by 1.2 percent of GDP (ibid).

Yet another study on the same topic found that more than 4 million infants, toddlers, and preschoolers lived in poverty in the United States in 2005. Based on this fact, the researchers asked: What economic benefits would be provided by a policy that brought poor children's prenatal through age-five family incomes up to the poverty line but made no other concurrent changes in the socioeconomic status of those children's families? After looking at the outcomes for adults from varying economic backgrounds, the researchers found relative to children with early childhood incomes exceeding at least twice the poverty line, poor children complete nearly two fewer years of schooling, work 25 percent fewer hours, earn only about half as much, receive $750 more per year in food stamps, and are more than twice as likely to report poor overall health or high levels of psychological distress. Also, poor males are nearly twice as likely to be arrested, and their rates of incarceration are three times as high as those of males in higher-income families. Finally, they found that for females, early poverty is associated with a nearly $200 increase in annual cash assistance from the Aid to Families with Dependent Children (AFDC) or Temporary Assistance to Needy Families (TANF) programs (Duncan, Kalil, and Ziol-Guest 2008). As with the earlier cited GAO study, this research revealed a broader economic cost to society for economic inequity, thus reframing the debate away from the emphasis on the moral costs of poverty to society and toward the recognition of economic costs.

While the above study does not compare the cost savings by the reduction of childhood poverty against the cost of the intervention, other studies on the economic analysis of reducing social inequities do. For example, Chilton's testimony to a House of Representatives Committee (2007) identifies a recent U.S. Department of

Agriculture cost–benefit analysis that found that the Special Supplemental Nutrition Program for Women, Infants, and Children (WIC) saves $1.71 to $3.00 in direct and indirect medical costs for every dollar spent on WIC. The identification of both costs and benefits of social equity strategies is vital for making the economic case for the reduction of inequities.

The Economic Case for Supportive Shelter

In a completely different policy arena, studies suggest that providing "supportive shelter" for the homeless rather than the traditional approach to this social inequity can offer significant economic benefits to the community as well as to the individuals experiencing this dilemma. Research in this policy area includes contrasting the traditional treatment of the homeless with a newer concept of providing supportive shelter.

The traditional approach to responding to homelessness of one specific subpopulation is typified in the example of "Million-Dollar Murray" in Reno, Nevada. This study tracked three chronic inebriates in the downtown area who were arrested the most often. The first of those people was named Murray Barr. The researchers estimated if they toted up all his hospital bills for the ten years that he had been on the streets—as well as the costs of treatment for substance abuse, doctors' fees, and other expenses—Murray Barr probably ran up a medical bill as large as anyone in the state of Nevada. State officials concluded that "It cost us one million dollars not to do something about Murray" (Gladwell 2006, 97).

Another estimate of the costs of the traditional approach to responding to homelessness is provided by Dennis Culhane. Culhane estimates that in New York at least $62 million was being spent annually to shelter just 2,500 hardcore homeless. "It costs twenty-four thousand dollars a year for one of these shelter beds," Culhane said. "We're talking about a cot eighteen inches away from the next cot" (as cited in Gladwell 2006, 101).

Other examples of the costs associated with the traditional approach to responding to the homelessness experienced by alcoholics are also described by Gladwell:

> Boston Health Care for the Homeless Program, a leading service group for the homeless in Boston, recently tracked the medical expenses of 119 chronically homeless people. In the course of five years, thirty-three people died and seven more were sent to nursing homes, and the group still accounted for 18,834 emergency-room visits—at a minimum cost of a thousand dollars a visit. The University of California, San Diego Medical Center followed fifteen chronically homeless inebriates and found that over eighteen months those fifteen people were treated at the hospital's emergency room four hundred and seventeen times, and ran up bills that averaged a hundred thousand dollars each. One person—San Diego's counterpart to Murray Barr—came to the emergency room eighty-seven times. (101)

A different approach has been suggested for removing the shelter inequities of this population. This approach is known as supportive housing or supportive shelter.

Supportive housing has been defined as "permanent housing with services" (North Carolina Housing Coalition 2010). The type of services provided depends on the individual needs of the residents and may be available for a limited time, sporadically, or indefinitely. The cost of housing is usually set at the affordable level, or intended to serve persons who are on an SSI income.

Gladwell reports on a major study in Denver that demonstrates the benefit–cost ratio of using the supportive housing strategy for reducing housing inequities:

> The cost of services comes to about ten thousand dollars per homeless client per year. An efficiency apartment in Denver averages $376 a month, or just over forty-five hundred a year, which means that you can house and care for a chronically homeless person for at most fifteen thousand dollars, or about a third of what he or she would cost on the street. The idea is that once the people in the program get stabilized they will find jobs, and start to pick up more and more of their own rent, which would bring someone's annual cost to the program closer to six thousand dollars. (Gladwell 2006, 103)

While Gladwell does not provide sufficient data to be able to judge whether this analysis has used life-cycle costing, and identified all of the operating and maintenance costs associated with this strategy, he does cite homelessness scholar Dennis Culhane as suggesting that the kind of money it would take to solve the homeless problem could well be less than the kind of money it took to ignore it. The conclusion is that by reducing the inequities of permanent shelter between the homeless and those with shelter, the benefit–cost ratio to society would be significant.

Youth Intervention

In a report written for the Minnesota Youth Intervention Programs Association, Paul Anton and Judy Temple put forth a model to calculate the social return on investment (SROI) for youth intervention programs. Youth intervention programs according to this study are "community-based programs that help young people deal with a variety of challenges including crime, family violence, truancy, chemical dependency, child abuse, teen pregnancy, and homelessness. These programs serve a wide variety of youth who are often identified and/or referred by schools, law-enforcement agencies, courts, and families" (Anton and Temple 2007, 3). Such programs tend to focus on issues of crime prevention, truancy reduction, and increased school achievement.

Using cost–benefit analysis, Anton and Temple argue that intervention programs aimed at youth who are identified as "at risk" due to previous behaviors, can produce returns of up to $14 for every state dollar invested and between $5 and $8 per dollar for total dollars invested if private sector funding is added to total cost. These returns are both short-and long-term and include reduced costs to schools due to reduced truancy, reduced court costs, reduced school dropout rates that lead to long-term higher lifetime earnings, reduced cost of prosecuting adult crimes, and decreases in public assistance expenditures. Thus, the SROI reframes the outcomes of these youth intervention programs to provide not only socially just programming, but a significant ROI to both the public and private sectors.

Examples from the Copenhagen Consensus

Early in the first decade of 2000, the Copenhagen Business School began a system of commissioning research from economists to analyze the most cost-effective ways to address the world's biggest challenges. The results of these analyses of the challenges are presented at the annual conference of the Copenhagen Consensus. Using cost–benefit analysis, economists across the globe have analyzed various ways to address the ten top global issues, which the Consensus lists as: air pollution, conflicts, diseases, education, global warming, malnutrition and hunger, sanitation and water, subsidies and trade barriers, terrorism, and women and development (www.copenhagenconsensus.com).

For the Copenhagen Consensus Conference of 2008, a panel of eight economists, including five Nobel laureates, reviewed proposals submitted by dozens of other economists and set priorities among the proposals based on the following question: "What would be the best ways of advancing global welfare, and particularly the welfare of developing countries, illustrated by supposing that an additional $75 billion of resources were at their disposal over a four-year initial period?" (www. copenhagenconsensus.com).

Based on the cost–benefit analysis of each of the proposals considered, the panel of experts ranked the solutions, the top being the provision of micronutrient supplements (vitamin A and zinc) for children. According to economist Sue Horton, who wrote the proposal, providing micronutrients for 80 percent of the 140 million children who lack essential vitamins in the form of vitamin A capsules and a course of zinc supplements would cost just $60 million per year, but would provide a yearly ROI of over $1 billion. This means that each dollar invested provides benefits worth over $17. These benefits include better health, fewer deaths, and increased future earnings (www.copenhagenconsensus.org).

While the micronutrient proposal came out on top, several other proposals that address social equity around health and education on a global scale ranked high on the list of priorities. Other programs considered to be priorities include expanding immunization coverage for children, deworming and nutrition programs at schools, lowering the price of schooling, and community-based nutrition promotion.

The authors of the challenge papers submitted to the Copenhagen Consensus acknowledge the limits of using cost–benefit analysis, especially on a global scale, but argue that such analysis is critical to the formulation of cost-effective solutions to global challenges. This work further supports the need to analyze social equity from a cost–benefit analysis basis and thus reduce the assumed equity/efficiency trade-off, reframing the debate to one of productive economic investments by the public sector.

Early Childhood Development

Over the past ten years, an increasing amount of research has come out showing the importance of high-quality early education experiences in brain development and preparing children for school success (see Barnett and Belfield 2006; Kirp 2007; and Knudsen et al. 2005; Shonkoff and Phillips 2000). *From Neurons to Neighborhoods* (Shonkoff and Phillips 2000) was the watershed work in raising awareness and advocacy about the need to connect early childhood education and child care because of the need for quality experiences, especially between ages zero and three. This research began to reframe the early childhood policies debate from an assumption of providing day care while parents worked to providing educational experiences that helped prepare children for school success. Thus, what had previously been referred to as "child care" became "early childhood development" (ECD), and the emphasis shifted to providing safe and high-quality early education experiences for children.

At the same time that the research on brain development and quality early childhood experiences was gaining momentum, economists began to argue that dollars spent providing high-quality early education experiences for children from low-income families or those facing other risk factors, provided a public ROI between 9 percent and 17 percent. Most of this return would come in future savings on educational remediation, welfare, and criminal justice costs as well as value added to the economy by productive adults (Heckman 2006; Kirp 2007; Rolnick and Grunewald 2003, 2007; Grunewald and Rolnick 2003).

Much of the economic analysis of early childhood development programs started with the work of James Heckman, a University of Chicago economist and Nobel laureate who argues that investments in disadvantaged young children provide large gains that can be quantified (2006). Acknowledging that, traditionally, support for investments in early childhood development programs revolved around ideas of fairness and social justice, Heckman argues that longitudinal results from programs such as Perry Preschool, Abecedarian, and Chicago Child-Parent Centers show significant ROI, thus challenging the equity/efficiency trade-off. According to Heckman, "[i]t is a rare public policy initiative that promotes fairness and social justice and at the same time promotes productivity in the economy and in society at large. Investing in disadvantaged young children is such a policy" (2006, 2).

Heckman (2006) argues that for disadvantaged children, investment in ECD programs—such as high-quality preschool that improves school readiness—leads to both short- and long-term gains because such programs promote schooling, raise the quality of the workforce, enhance the productivity of schools, reduce crime, teenage pregnancy, and welfare dependency as well as raise long-term earnings and promote social attachment. Part of this long-term gain comes from the fact that in such ECD programs, children gain not just cognitive skills, but noncognitive skills such as motivation and emotional maturity that serve them better in the long run (Federal Reserve Bank of Minneapolis 2005; Heckman 2006). According to Heckman's review of earlier research on the long-term outcomes of intensive, high-quality early childhood programs, such programs produced a rate of return between 15 percent and 17 percent. He also argues that this ROI is much higher than anything gained through remediation or job training at an older age. According to Heckman:

> We have found that for severely disadvantaged children, there are no levels of later childhood skill investments that can bring the children to a level of social and economic performance attainable from well-targeted early investments. We find that both social and emotional skills are essential in producing successful people. These findings change the way economists think about the human capital formation process. If we don't provide disadvantaged young children with the proper environments to foster cognitive and noncognitive skills, we'll create a class of people without such skills, without motivation, without the ability to contribute to the larger society nearly as much as they could if they'd been properly nurtured from an early age. (Federal Reserve Bank of Minneapolis 2005)

Heckman's work started a wave of research on the economic benefits of investment in early childhood. In the past five years, literally dozens of reports and articles that use a cost–benefit or ROI approach to analyze the economic return of investments in programs that deal with social equity issues facing children have been produced. A review of a few of the most recent titles clearly illustrates the reframing of the debate to one of economic gains versus fairness and social justice:

1. Enriching Children, Enriching the Nation: Public Investment in High-Quality Prekindergarten (Lynch 2007)
2. Dynamic Estimates of the Fiscal Effects of Investing in Early Childhood Programs (Dickens and Baschnagel 2008)
3. The Economic Costs of Poverty in the United States: Subsequent Effects of Children Growing up Poor (Holzer et al. 2007)
4. Long-Term Economic Benefits of Investing in Early Childhood Programs: Proven Programs Boost Economic Development and Benefit the Nation's Fiscal Health (Partnership for America's Economic Success n.d.)
5. Reducing Poverty Through Preschool Interventions (Duncan, Ludwig, and Magnuson 2007)
6. Economic Costs of Early Childhood Poverty (Duncan, Kalil, and Ziol-Guest 2008)
7. The Economics of Early Childhood Policy: What the Dismal Science Has to Say About Investing in Children (Kilburn and Karoly 2008)
8. The Economic Promise of Investing in High-Quality Preschool: Using Early Education to Improve Economic Growth and the Fiscal Sustainability of States and the Nation (CED 2006)

The Minnesota Case for ECD

Building on the work of James Heckman, Art Rolnick and Rob Grunewald of the Federal Reserve Bank of Minneapolis began to dig deeper into the economic benefits of investment in ECD for at-risk children. In 2003 editions of the Federal Reserve Bank publications, *FedGazette* and *The Region*, Rolnick and Grunewald reported a potential 12–16 percent ROI should early education become a focus of change in Minnesota. Using the same reports as Heckman on the long-term results of early childhood programs, in particular the Perry Preschool Program, Rolnick and Grunewald calculated the benefit–cost and internal rate of return. These calculations showed an ROI of between 8 percent and 16 percent. Using calculations of the internal rate of return, the results yielded a 12 percent return to the public and a 4 percent return to the participant, for a total 16 percent ROI. Rolnick and Grunewald argued that such a return was higher than any other economic development programs in place and thus ECD should be moved to the top of the list of public investments. According to the authors:

> These disadvantaged children are not only shut out from Minnesota's famed high quality of life, but they also impose social costs on the rest of society. And that's where the budget and economic development come into play. Research has shown that investment in early childhood development programs brings a real (that is, inflation adjusted) public return of 12 percent and a real total return, public and private, of 16 percent. We are unaware of any other economic development effort that has such a public return, and yet early childhood development is rarely viewed in economic development terms. (Rolnick and Grunewald 2003, 2)

At the same time that Rolnick and Grunewald were releasing their work, the Minnesota Department of Education (MDE) was working on school readiness assessments, the results of which showed that fewer than 50 percent of Minnesota's kindergarteners were entering school fully prepared for success (MDE 2004). Early childhood policy advocates took this opportunity to reframe the ECD investment debate from a moral issue to a workforce and economic development issue. Rolnick and Grunewald's work was key in this reframing of the ECD debate in Minnesota. Rolnick soon became a leader on the national front on the issue of investing in early childhood and as followers of Rolnick, Minnesota business leaders began to come to the table around investments in ECD as a means of assuring a quality future workforce that will allow Minnesota to stay competitive.

The main proposal being pushed by Rolnick and Grunewald is the creation of an endowment that would provide scholarships to families of low-income or at-risk three- to four-year-olds to allow them to purchase high-quality early educational experiences either through child-care or preschool settings. This market-based model would create a partnership between the public and private sectors and be implemented through a foundation that would pilot programs and determine the most effective means of delivering high-quality early education to at-risk children.

In 2005, the Minnesota legislature established the Minnesota Early Learning Foundation (MELF) modeled on Rolnick and Grunewald's proposal that started the process of piloting best practices in ECD. While the seed money from the state for the pilot projects showed support for a new direction in Minnesota, there has been little progress otherwise. However, the debate has definitely been reframed. Rarely heard are arguments about "the right thing to do." Now the discussions revolve around investment, rate of return, and economic development.

Leadership in Reframing

Despite this reframing of the ECD debate in Minnesota, there have not been significant increases in early childhood programs in the state and most programs faced cuts in the years of tight budgets. What has been missing in the case of ECD in Minnesota is shared leadership on the issue. As scholars of the policy process note, policy entrepreneurs are a key to moving issues and alternatives for consideration by policymakers in the development of public policy. Traditionally, in the realm of policy around investment in early childhood development, the entrepreneurs have been advocates from nonprofit and service organizations that have taken on advocacy from a moral position—investing in our children is the right thing to do. However, as noted in the previous case, in the past few years the debate on early childhood policy both in Minnesota and nationally has been reframed and leadership has begun to shift as a new group of entrepreneurs from business interests have joined the debate. These new policy entrepreneurs have included CEOs from major companies and other community business leaders that have taken up the mantle of early childhood development, often leading the charge around new investments and expanded programs. This time these policy entrepreneurs are taking an economic argument—investing in our kids is an economic development issue and provides a high ROI. The question is whether or not this shift on its own is enough to spur additional public investments in ECD.

Kingdon's Model of Policy Development

In his classic work, *Agendas, Alternatives, and Public Policies* (1984/1995), John Kingdon lays out a model to describe how issues get in front of policymakers for decision. In the model, Kingdon argues that there are three streams, which, when coupled, provide a window of opportunity for policymakers to take action. In the first stream, or the problem stream, problems are identified, defined, and if deemed appropriate, put on the agenda for consideration by lawmakers. In the second or policy stream, policy communities made up of various players develop alternatives or policy proposals that address identified or potential problems. Finally, the politics stream contains the factors that affect political mood and political feasibility. The contents of this stream include indicators such as public mood and opinion, election results, changes in administration, partisan makeup of decision-making bodies, and other factors.

According to Kingdon's argument, when these three streams come together—that is, a problem is identified and clearly defined, an alternative or alternatives are available to attach to the problem, and the political climate is open for action—a policy window opens. This window provides an opportunity for action but does not guarantee action will be taken. Policymakers may or may not take action before the window closes. A key factor in opening windows and encouraging action is the work of policy entrepreneurs. Policy entrepreneurs, in Kingdon's argument, are advocates inside or outside of government whose defining characteristic is "their willingness to invest their time, energy, reputation, and sometimes money, in hope of a future return" (1984, 129). Interests that drive policy entrepreneurs include a desire to promote a personal interest, a desire to promote a particular set of values that will shape public policies, and being a policy "groupie" or what we might today refer to as a policy wonk. The work of policy entrepreneurs is critical in Kingdon's model. They are key actors in opening the policy window as well as in pushing action by policymakers once the window is open. Policy entrepreneurs can be successful according to this model because:

1. They have some claim to being heard such as:
   a. Expertise
   b. The ability to speak for others
   c. An authoritative decision making position
2. They are known for their political connections or negotiating skills
3. They are persistent and their tenacity pays off as they lie in wait for a policy window to open (Kingdon 1984, 189).

In their work, *Leadership for the Common Good*, Crosby and Bryson also emphasize the need for policy entrepreneurs in what they refer to as a "shared power world" where several groups must come together in efforts to make policy changes. In Crosby and Bryson's words, policy entrepreneurs are "inventive, energetic, and persistent in overcoming systemic barriers" (2005, 156). This need for shared leadership is especially important in cases of social equity where the assumed equity/efficiency trade-off makes selling the policies to fiscally conservative policymakers more difficult.

In the case of ECD in Minnesota, many hoped that having the business community come to the table as entrepreneurs in partnership with the traditional players would greatly increase the likelihood of increased investments in ECD programs. This, however, has not been the case. While the traditional providers and nonprofits did join with business on this issue, they did not win over key policy actors including the governor and other high-level policymakers. Even with the reframing of ECD to economic and workforce development, the programs could not compete in an arena dominated by a fiscally conservative governor, Tim Pawlenty, who had pledged not to raise taxes, and thus the extra dollars needed for increased investments were not available.

While adding business as policy entrepreneurs has not been sufficient in Minnesota to bring increases in investments to ECD to date, business leaders have played an important role in reframing the debate. In relation to Kingdon's three streams, in the problem stream the issue has clearly moved away from the traditional moral arguments to raising concerns about school readiness as it relates to workforce and economic development. Thus, the lack of investment in ECD has become an economic issue as well as a moral one. In the policy stream, the alternatives offered to address support for ECD now emphasize market-oriented programs run in partnership with public agencies. Public–private partnerships and competition to ensure quality have become a priority over simply providing more money for programs to do the same things they have been doing for years. Finally, in the politics stream, business has had less impact in Minnesota than hoped. Many of the traditional policy entrepreneurs who had for years been advocating for increased investments in children hoped that the presence of business at the table would bring with it increased public funding for programs. This, at least in Minnesota, has not yet been the case. While the state did provide $6 million for some pilot programs around ECD, this amount is less than half of what the private sector has provided MELF to carry out these policies. The money was seen as funding for pilot projects that could later be brought to scale if successful, but the amount is still limited given the scope of the proposed programs. Business leaders have also not been able to bring Minnesota's governor onboard in support of early childhood development in the way many hoped would happen.

What the case in Minnesota seems to highlight is that while the presence of business as policy entrepreneur can help reframe the debate in terms of how the problem is defined and what alternatives are considered, it is not in itself sufficient to influence the political stream in support of major investments. The presence of business as entrepreneur seems to have changed the shape of policies to more market-oriented models but investments are still small. In the states where large-scale universal programs have been implemented—for example, Florida, North Carolina, and Georgia—the combination of business and top state officials, particularly the governor, as policy entrepreneurs has been necessary.

Limitations and Conclusion

In this chapter the authors have tried to make the argument that reducing social inequities can also be justified on the basis of the resulting economic benefits as well as on the grounds of social justice. That is, social equity is the right thing to pursue both morally and economically. However, in reviewing relevant literature and discussing this approach with colleagues, several caveats have surfaced.

The first of these emerges from organizational behavior theory. Our interpretation of Deci's cognitive evaluation theory (1971) is that "tangible rewards given for doing interesting activities undermines intrinsic motivation for that activity" (Deci, Ryan, and Koestner 2001, 49). This leads to the fear that reframing the case for social equity by pointing out the economic benefits of reducing inequities might undermine the commitment of those who support social equity for social justice/moral reasons. This leads to a potential second concern about how to gain or maintain support for policies that reduce social inequities when there are no direct economic benefits to be realized. Do these policy issues get ignored as the policymakers and other key stakeholders become accustomed to focusing on the bottom line?

There are also some methodological considerations that must be addressed in promoting the economic benefits rationale for reducing social inequities. Such analysis involves the current and future value of costs and benefits. Public finance scholars such as Mikesell (2003) and Gruber (2005) discuss the uncertainty and the methodological issues associated with estimating the future costs and benefits of strategies, especially those of long durations. In spite of these difficulties, Burr and Grunewald (2006) describe their methodology in conducting cost–benefit analysis of four high-quality preschool programs, and using best principles of economic program analysis, estimated benefit–costs ratios of from $3 to $17 for every dollar invested, and total internal rates of return, adjusted for inflation, ranged from approximately 7 percent to as high as 20 percent. This study did identify the methodology that should be used in estimating the costs and benefits when conducting such studies. They conclude strategic investments in early childhood development can yield substantial results. However, poorly focused, modestly funded programs do little to improve the well-being and school readiness of young children. These researchers stress there is no guarantee that results from studies of small model programs or programs brought to scale can be replicated in another place (Burr and Grunewald 2006, 1–4). All of these cautions must be stated to skeptical and, sometimes, outright hostile audiences.

These concerns are legitimate, and the authors do not propose the reframing of social equity arguments around economic benefits as the sole solution to bringing increased investments in social equity programs. In fact, the case of early childhood development in Minnesota clearly illustrates that such reframing in and of itself is not sufficient to bring significant new public investments. Along with reframing comes the need for leadership from policy entrepreneurs willing to push policy change and investment. The benefit of reframing in these situations is the building of expanded bases of support that bring with them a larger pool of potential policy entrepreneurs. In the shared power world described by Crosby and Bryson, the expanded points of leadership create a greater likelihood of successful policy acceptance. Reframing also helps to reduce or remove traditional arguments claiming an efficiency/equity trade-off, thus opening the door to support from more fiscally and socially conservative policymakers and the public. However, reframing the debate should not replace valuing social equity for its own good. Instead, reframing brings to light new ways of evaluating social equity that bring potential new partners to the policy arena. New partners bring new policy entrepreneurs who can play a vital role in guiding policies around social equity successfully through the policy process.

References

Anton, Paul A., and Judy Temple. 2007. *Analyzing the Social Return on Investment in Youth Intervention Programs: A Framework for Minnesota.* St. Paul: Wilder Research.

Barnett, Steven, and Clive Belfield. 2006. "Early Childhood Development and Social Mobility." *The Future of Children,* 16:2, 73–98.

Burr, Jean, and Rob Grunewald. *Lessons Learned: A Review of Early Childhood Development Studies.* 2006. April. Available at www.minneapolisfed.org/publications_papers/studies/earlychild/lessonslearned.pdf (accessed May 24, 2009).

Chilton, Mariana. 2007. Cost Savings Associated with Investing in Children and Nutrition Programs. Before the Committee on Agriculture U.S. House of Representatives. March 22. Available at http://publichealth.drexel.edu/GROW/SiteData/docs/CHILTON_economics_childhealth/6e60ba9328ad8e9a520c9057bd9e2ace/CHILTON_economics_childhealth.pdf (accessed May 24, 2009).

Committee for Economic Development (CED). 2006. The Economic Promise of Investing in High-Quality Preschool: Using Early Education to Improve Economic Growth and the Fiscal Sustainability of States and the Nation. Washington, DC. Available at www.ced.org/library/reports/41/203-the-economic-promise-of-investing-in-high-quality-preschool/ (accessed July 11, 2008).

Crosby, Barbara C., and John M. Bryson. 2005. *Leadership for the Common Good: Tackling Public Problems in a Shared-Power World.* 2d ed. San Francisco: Jossey-Bass.

Deci, E.L. 1971. "Effects of Externally Mediated Rewards on Intrinsic Motivation." *Journal of Personality and Social Psychology* 18: 105–15.

Deci, Edward L.; Richard M. Ryan; and Richard Koestner. 2001. "The Pervasive Negative Effects of Rewards on Intrinsic Motivation: Response to Cameron." *Review of Educational Research* 71, no. 1 (Spring): 43–51.

Dickens, William T., and Charles Baschnagel. 2008. *Dynamic Estimates of the Fiscal Effects of Investing in Early Childhood Programs.* Washington, DC: Partnership for America's Economic Success.

Dictionary.com. 2010. "Economy." Available at http://dictionary.reference.com/browse/economy/.

Duncan, Greg J.; Ariel Kalil; and Kathleen Ziol-Guest. 2008. *Economic Costs of Early Childhood Poverty.* Washington, DC: Partnership for America's Economic Success.

Duncan, Greg. J.; Jens Ludwig; and Katherine A. Magnuson. 2007. "Reducing Poverty Through Preschool Interventions." *Future of Children* 17, no. 2 (Fall): 143–90.

Druckman, J.N. 2001. "Evaluating Framing Effects." *Journal of Economic Psychology* 22, no. 1: 91–101.

Druckman, J.N., and K.R. Nelson. 2003. "Framing and Deliberation: How Citizens' Conversations Limit Elite Influence." *American Journal of Political Science* 47, no. 4 (October): 729–45.

Federal Reserve Bank of Minneapolis. 2005. Interview with James J. Heckman. *The Region,* June. Available at www.minneapolisfed.org/pubs/region/05–06/Heckman.cfm (accessed July 11, 2008).

Gladwell, Malcolm. 2006. "Million-Dollar Murray: Why Problems Like Homelessness May Be Easier to Solve Than to Manage." *New Yorker,* February 13 and 20, 96–107.

Government Accountability Office (GAO). 2007. "Poverty in America: Economic Research Shows Adverse Impacts on Health Status and Other Social Conditions as Well as the Economic Growth Rate." Highlights of GAO-07-344. January. Available at www.gao.gov/new.items/d07344.pdf.

Greenberg, J., and R.A. Baron. 2003. *Behavior in Organizations: Understanding and Managing the Human Side of Work.* 8th ed. Upper Saddle River, NJ: Prentice Hall.

Gruber, Jonathan. 2005. *Public Finance and Public Policy.* New York: Worth.

Grunewald, Rob, and Arthur J. Rolnick. 2003. Early Childhood Development: Economic Development with a High Public Return. *Fedgazette*, March. Available at www. minneapolisfed.org/publications_papers/pub_display.cfm?id=3832 (accessed October 4, 2007).

Heckman, James J. 2006. "Investing in Disadvantaged Young Children Is an Economically Efficient Policy." Paper presented at the Committee for Economic Development/Pew Charitable Trusts Forum on Building the Case for Investments in Preschool.

Holzer, Harry J.; Diane Schanzenbach; Greg J. Duncan; and Jens Ludwig. 2007. *The Economic Costs of Poverty in the United States: Subsequent Effects of Children Growing Up Poor*. Washington, DC: Center for American Progress.

Hughes, Roger. 2008. "Framing Social Equity: Alternatives to the Language of Social Justice." Paper presented at the Seventh Annual Social Equity Leadership Conference: Social Equity and Urban Governance. Phoenix, Arizona. Cosponsored by the National Academy of Public Administration and the Arizona State University School of Public Affairs. February 8.

Kennedy, Robert F. "Day of Affirmation" Address (news release text version), June 6, 1966. http://www.jfklibrary.org/Research/Ready-Reference/RFK-Speeches/Day-of-Affirmation-Address-news-release-text-version.aspx (accessed March 17, 2011).

Kilburn, M. Rebecca, and Lynn A. Karoly. 2008. *The Economics of Early Childhood Policy: What the Dismal Science Has to Say About Investing in Children*. Santa Monica, CA: Rand Corporation.

Kingdon, John W. 1984/1995. *Agendas, Alternatives, and Public Policies*. 2d ed. New York: HarperCollins.

Kirp, David L. 2007. *The Sandbox Investment: The Preschool Movement and Kids First Politics*. Cambridge, MA: Harvard University Press.

Klingner, Donald E., and John Nalbandian. 2002. *Public Personnel Management: Contexts and Strategies*. 5th ed. Englewood Cliffs, NJ: Prentice Hall.

Knudsen, Eric I.; Judy L. Cameron; and Jack P. Shon Koff, 2005. "Economic, Neurobiological, and Behavioral Perspectives on Building America's Future Workforce." *PNAS* 103, no. 27: 10155–62.

Kuhberger, A. 1998. "The Influence of Framing on Risky Decisions: A Meta-analysis." *Organizational Behavior and Human Decision Processes* 75, no. 1: 23–55.

Lynch, Robert. G. 2007. *Enriching Children, Enriching the Nation: Public Investment in High-Quality Pre-kindergarten*. Washington, DC: Economic Policy Institute.

Malarkey, Robert Dennis. 2008. "The Influence of Differently Framed Information on Decision Making in the Public Budgeting Process: Does Budget Reform Mean a Damn?" Available at http://hdl.handle.net/10156/1359 (accessed January 19, 2009).

Mikesell, John L. 2003. *Fiscal Administration: Analysis and Applications for the Public Sector*. Belmont, CA: Wadsworth.

Minnesota Department of Education. 2004. "Minnesota School Readiness Year Three Study: Developmental Assessment at Kindergarten Entrance." Available at www.eric.ed.gov/ERICWebPortal/custom/portlets/recordDetails/detailmini.jsp?_nfpb=true&_&ERICExtSearch_SearchValue_0=ED493058&ERICExtSearch_SearchType_0=no&accno=ED493058 (accessed September 18, 2007).

National Academy of Public Administration, Standing Panel on Social Equity in Governance. http://www.napawash.org/fellows/standing, panels/standing-panel-on-social-equity-in-governance/ (accessed March 17, 2011).

Neidhardt, Friedhelm. 1994. Öffentlichkeit, öffentliche Meinung, soziale Bewegungen," in Friedhelm Neidhardt (ed.) Öffentlichkeit, öffentliche Meinung, soziale Bewegungen. Opladen: Westdeutscher-Verlag: 7–41.

North Carolina Housing Coalition. 2010. "Affordable Housing Terms." Available at www. nchousing.org/advocacy-1/messaging-strategy/what_is_affordable_housing/terms/.

Partnership for America's Economic Success. n.d. *Long-term Economic Benefits of Investing in Early Childhood Programs: Proven Programs Boost Economic Development and Benefit the Nation's Fiscal Health*. Issue Brief no. 5. Available at www.partnershipforsuccess. org/docs/researchproject_dickens_bartik_200802_brief.pdf.

Patton, Carl V., and David S. Sawicki. 1993. *Basic Methods of Policy Analysis and Planning*. Upper Saddle River, NJ: Prentice Hall.

Pogge, Thomas W. 2006. "Eradicating Systemic Poverty: Brief for a Global Resources Dividend." In *Ethics in Practice: An Anthology*, 3d ed., ed. Hugh Lafollette, 601–17. New York: Wiley-Blackwell.

Rawls, J. 1971. *A Theory of Justice*. Cambridge, MA: Harvard University Press.

Rolnick, Arthur, and Rob Grunewald. 2003. "Early Childhood Development = Economic Development" in *Fedgazette*, March 2003, available at http://www.minneapolisfed.org/ publications_papers/pub_display.cfm?id=1839 (accessed October 4, 2007).

———. 2007. "Early Intervention on a Large Scale." *Quality Counts*, January 4. Available at www.minneapolisfed.org/publications_papers/studies/earlychild/early_intervention. cfm (accessed December 13, 2007).

Scheufele, D.A. 2006. "Framing as a Theory of Media Effects." *Journal of Communication* 49, no. 1 (February): 103–22.

Shonkoff, Jack, and D. Phillips, eds. 2000. *From Neurons to Neighborhoods: The Science of Early Childhood Development*. Washington, DC: National Academy Press.

Society of Automotive Engineers (SAE). 1995. *Reliability, Maintainability, and Supportability Guidebook*, 3rd edition, Warrendale, PA.

Stone, Deborah. 2002. *Policy Paradox: The Art of Political Decision-Making*, rev. ed. New York/London: Norton.

Svara, J., and J. Brunet. 2004. "Filling in the Skeletal Pillar: Addressing Social Equity." *Journal of Public Affairs Education* 10, no. 2: 99–110.

Wilkins, Roger. 2001. "Keynote Speech" First Annual Social Equity Leadership Conference: Social Equity and Urban Governance. Cosponsored by the National Academy of Public Administration and Indiana University. July 20.

Wolff, Jonathan. 2003. "Economic Justice." In *The Oxford Handbook of Practical Ethics*, ed. Hugh LaFollette, 433–58. Oxford: Oxford University Press.

12

Assessing Agency Performance: The Wisconsin Experience

Susan T. Gooden

Examining racial disparities in welfare programs is not an easy task. As John Rohr states in his classic work *Ethics for Bureaucrats*, "It is perhaps no exaggeration to say that questions of race, in one form or another, have been the most important issues in American politics" (1989, 99). Having governmental agencies take an active role in researching racial disparities of their programs is an important, but complex, task. It is important because under Title VI, Section 601 of the Civil Rights Act of 1964, "No person in the United States, shall, on the ground of race, color or national origin, be excluded from the participation in, be denied the benefits of, or be subjected to discrimination under any program or activity receiving Federal financial assistance." This prohibition includes intentional discrimination, as well as procedures, criteria, or methods of administration that appear neutral but have a discriminatory effect on individuals because of their race, color, or national origin. It is important for governmental agencies not only to respond to allegations of racial discrimination but also to *routinely self-assess* whether racial disparities exist in the services they provide. Race analysis is an important dimension in gauging social equity within public policy. "Race analysis is the systematic application of the tools of historical and cultural analysis to understand the social and economic circumstances facing blacks and other racial minority group members" (Myers 2002, 170).

Assessing racial disparities is qualitatively different from assessing other outcomes, such as comparing agency performance by region or by subgroups (for example, single-parent families vs. married families). It is different because there is an important emotional and historical context that intervenes. Why would agencies want to self-assess racial disparities of their programs given the wide array of emotions such an assessment could invoke?

Agencies should initiate this type of an assessment because it promotes good government. As defined by Lawrence Mead, good government involves making and implementing effective policy (2004, 213). Therefore, "good government" should also include assessing the implementation of public policy for racial disparities. The behavioral aspects of good welfare reform policy cut both ways: Clients have behavioral expectations in terms of seeking employment and reporting earnings. Agency staff has behavioral expectations to not discriminate in the implementation of their programs. Good government should monitor both sets of expectations.

This chapter is focused on the following question: How can government agencies assess whether racial disparities exist in their programs? Specifically, what is the *process* they can use to facilitate such a study? After discussing the concept of social equity as it relates to public administration and establishing important historical context for why examining racial discrimination in welfare administration is important, this chapter analyzes the work of a steering committee tasked with assessing racial disparities in the sanctioning of Wisconsin's welfare clients. It offers an examination of how public policies can be assessed for racial disparities.

Public Administration and Social Equity

A fundamental component of the promotion of good government is the examination of social equity. Issues of equity and justice are fundamental concerns of public administrators. Public administrators face the constant struggle of evaluating the country's social climate and ensuring equity in governance (Akram 2004). Like the United States, public administration has moved slowly in applying principles of justice. In fact, equity or fairness in public services was the last established "pillar" of the field—and it still remains secondary in emphasis behind economy, effectiveness, and efficiency.[1]

Assessing Social Equity in Governmental Services

A core challenge to achieving social equity in the delivery of governmental services is to identify an approach to social equity assessment. A useful framework to launch this type of assessment (see Appendix 14.1 p. 287) includes five key actions: (1) identifying the purpose of the department, the services it provides, and for whom these services are provided; (2) providing an assessment of agency procedures to identify equity issues; (3) conducting an assessment of the nature and distribution of benefits and services externally; (4) conducting an assessment of the quality of services provided; and (5) assessing the outcomes impacted by the department's performance. This chapter offers a case study of how the Division of Workforce Solutions in Wisconsin conducted an assessment of racial disparities in its welfare program and offers a conceptual model, as well as lessons learned, that may be useful for other agencies concerned with assessing the social equity of their services.

Contemporary Welfare Policy and Race

The Personal Responsibility and Work Opportunity Reconciliation Act of 1996 eliminated Aid to Families with Dependent Children (AFDC) as an entitlement and created a block grant for states to provide time-limited cash assistance for needy families. These state programs are funded under the Temporary Assistance for Needy Families (TANF). States may use their TANF funding in any manner "reasonably calculated to accomplish the purposes of TANF" (U.S. Department of Health and Human Services, 1996). States have broad discretion under TANF to determine eligibility, method of assistance, and benefit levels. The discretionary setting of TANF is very different from that of AFDC, because (1) the Department of Health and Human Services must determine that a state's plan is legally complete, but does not otherwise have authority to approve or disapprove a plan, and (2) it is not clear whether there is any consequence if a state fails to follow its plan (Greenberg and Savner 1996).

Based on the historical relationship between race and welfare in the United States, several areas of TANF policy are particularly relevant and should be systematically evaluated to ascertain racial bias. These areas include, for example, case management including client assessment; access to training, community work experiences, and education; availability of support services such as child care and transportation assistance; the issuance of sanctions; labor market opportunities and earnings; time limits; and lack of uniformity in political subdivisions.

Case Management

Case management is a key component of any welfare reform plan. An analysis of clients' experiences with their case managers facilitates better understanding of the nature of a program's "treatment" in practice. Case managers become agents of the policymakers and give a program model its concrete meaning. They operationalize their relationship between the client and the program by applying, in specific situations, legislative and regulatory directions about who must participate, in what activities they should participate, and what support services they should receive (Doolittle and Riccio 1992). How case managers complete these tasks will have a great effect on the program outcomes experienced by their clients. In delivering policy, public-service workers or "street-level bureaucrats" have substantial discretion in their work. They are entrusted to make decisions about people that affect their life chances (Lipsky 1980). In this case, these chances involve the likelihood of self-sufficiency. A pilot research study that examined the promotion of education services by caseworkers among black and white clients in two rural Virginia counties found 41 percent of white clients reported that their caseworker continued to promote education, compared to none of the black clients (Gooden 1998, 28).

Sanctioning

Under TANF, caseworkers may issue a financial sanction for welfare clients who do not comply with program rules and work activities without good cause. Deciding whether to issue a sanction or to excuse nonparticipation based on good cause is an area of caseworker discretion. A study of five panhandle counties in Florida found blacks were much more likely to be sanctioned for noncompliance than their white counterparts (61 percent versus 48.4 percent) (Clarke, Jarmon, and Langley 1999, 130).

Exiting Welfare

Recent research on welfare leavers suggest racial differences also occur. Clarke, Jarmon, and Langley found a 35 percent differential in post-welfare poverty figures, with white respondents reporting a mean income of $10,403, compared with $6,736 for blacks (1999, 122). When examining employer demand for welfare recipients in four urban cities, Holzer and Stoll found that "relative to their white counterparts, black and Hispanic welfare recipients are less likely to be hired in suburban and/ or smaller establishments, and for blacks, in the retail trade industries" (2000, 26). Using employer survey data with 170 firms in the Chicago area, Wilson found that 74 percent expressed negative views of inner-city blacks (1996, 112).

There are also some studies that suggest favorable outcomes for minorities under TANF. Studies in Arizona, Georgia, and Ohio suggest that the percentages of blacks that are employed exceed the percentages of whites that are employed and even report somewhat higher quarterly earnings (Savner 2000). Holzer and Stoll (2000, 35) also report employer demand for all racial groups of welfare recipients is somewhat higher in minority-owned businesses and that contact with the relevant local agencies is associated with substantial increases in demand for white and black recipients when initiated by agencies and especially for Hispanics when initiated by firms.

The Case of Wisconsin

Wisconsin Works, commonly called "W-2," replaced Aid to Families with Dependent Children and was designed to promote economic self-sufficiency via labor market engagement. The Division of Workforce Solutions (DWS) in the Department of Workforce Development (DWD) administers W-2, although providers under state contract administer W-2 at the local level. As a response to a legal complaint to the U.S. Department of Health and Human Services filed in 2002 by the American Civil Liberties Union (ACLU) and the Milwaukee Branch of the National Association for the Advancement of Colored People (NAACP)[2] and external research[3] suggesting some racial groups may be sanctioned at a higher rate than others in the W-2 program, the Division of Workforce Solutions (DWS) issued a preliminary report "Analysis of W-2 Sanctions by Race 2001 and 2002."

Sanctioning is the reduction or discontinuation of financial support based on participant noncompliance with program rules and guidelines. The impact of sanctions is real because it affects the overall grant amount, duration of grant reduction, and overall remaining eligibility for benefit receipt. Agencies and caseworkers have considerable discretion in issuing sanctions.

The DWS report found differences in sanctioning rates by race/ethnicity across a number of agencies throughout the state. Prior to the release of the DWS study, a study by the Institute for Wisconsin's Future reported that 42 percent of black and 45 percent of Hispanic W-2 recipients were sanctioned, compared to 24 percent of white recipients (Mulligan-Hansel and Fendt 2002). Another study by the Wisconsin Legislative Audit Bureau (LAB) indicated that black W-2 recipients were sanctioned at twice the rate of white recipients (47 percent vs. 23 percent) (Wisconsin Legislative Audit Bureau 2002). The DWS analysis also found some racial differences in sanctioning rates, and the department decided to examine the issue more in-depth. In doing so, the department clearly articulated its commitment to a critical examination of the racial issue: "This is a very complex issue and will require additional research beyond the exploratory analysis presented here. However, based on this review, the [DWS] has determined that the issue warrants further study in order to identify potential problems with more precision. . . . The Department is committed to forthrightly addressing issues that may arise from this research" (DWS 2003).

The DWS established a steering committee to provide guidance to the study. The steering committee reflected a broad range of knowledge, technical skills, and perspectives on the W-2 program. It included W-2 agency administrators, representatives of client advocacy groups, state administrators, and academics with experience in research methods and knowledgeable of W-2.

The charge to the steering committee was to develop the research questions for the study, to approve an overall methodology that would be used to address those questions, to review the research products developed, to draw conclusions about the research results, and to make recommendations to the DWS administrator. The original scope of the study was threefold: (1) to develop more sophisticated measures of sanction rates and analytical techniques to better understand where racial/ethnic disparities exist and the magnitude of these disparities; (2) to determine whether policy or variations in the interpretation of policy may contribute to disparities in sanction rates by race/ethnicity; and (3) to determine if variations in placement type and assignment to activities may contribute to disparities in sanction rates by race/ethnicity (Department of Workforce Development 2004, 4).

Although the general task of utilizing a steering committee to guide the work the research was fairly standard, the explicit focus on race was not. Over the course of more than a year, the steering committee and its technical work groups provided guidance to the study and examined racial disparities through a very diverse committee of people who held differing perspectives on the issue at hand. The approach of DWS and the steering committee provides a useful case study to better understand how public agencies can self-assess racial disparities in their poverty programs.

Research Methodology

This is a qualitative study based primarily on interviews with DWD administrators and members of the steering committee conducted during March 2005. Most interviews were conducted individually and lasted between sixty and ninety minutes. Interviewing the members of the steering committee provides valuable information because the steering committee was a very broad and diverse group. Its membership included members of advocacy groups, local agency staff, state administrators, and academic researchers. The interview protocol included questions about how the study evolved and how the steering committee conducted its work, resolved disputes, and formulated its recommendations. All respondents were assured of confidentiality. Appendix 12.1 provides the interview protocol. A content analysis of these interviews was performed using a qualitative software data analysis package. From this data analysis, themes were identified that became the basis for a conceptual model to facilitate the analysis of racial disparities by state agencies.

Key Findings

Drawing on the results of the content analysis, eight key findings were identified. They are summarized here with supporting quotations from the staff interviews.

1. Advocacy groups were important in elevating racial analysis on the agency agenda.

By all accounts, a motivating force behind the DWD study was the formal complaint filed by the ACLU and the NAACP. It seems unlikely that DWD would have committed to a study of this magnitude absent this preceding event, suggesting a critically important role of advocacy groups. As a steering committee member reflected:

> The complaint to the Office of Civil Rights was originally a disability complaint. But, then we stumbled onto data that had racial issues. Our primary focus initially was on disabilities, then race secondarily. But, we had the Legislative Audit Bureau report, so there really was a converging set of events that led to this study.

Another member of the steering committee agreed:

> Having the NAACP at the table [steering committee member] has not allowed them to forget or brush away race. . . . The conversation is just different when a black person is there. I'm sorry but it makes a difference. It's one thing to talk about these things, but when a black person is there, there's a different reaction. Having that representation is important; otherwise, the conversation can slip into this "we're all the same" discussion. A voice from this group was important.

2. Examining racial disparities within a governmental agency is a "nervous area of government." However, over time, both the steering committee and agency administrators became more comfortable engaging issues of race.

There was universal consensus across agency administrators and other steering committee members that engaging issues of race is uncomfortable. Specific comments included:

What was interesting to me was to listen to the explicit conversations about race. It's interesting to see how nervous and uncomfortable people are talking about race. Their first reaction is, "You're accusing me of being a racist." Don't accuse me of being a racist. But, you have the data, so why the protest?

Many of the agencies were defensive. They kept saying, "You're calling me a racist." We had to ensure them that we are not talking about your specific [caseworker], we're talking about a policy structure that does not consider racial discrimination. How could anyone find this unimaginable?

Yes, we had to focus on the impact, rather than the source.

Yes, people were horribly uncomfortable talking about race.

The sanctions study was one of the most hot button topics studied. There is a lot of defensiveness when you start talking about race. . . . Sometimes the process was painfully laborious, but in the end it was a very positive process. We need to be public about this [analysis of racial disparities].

It forced more thinking about this. It's easy to describe devolution and discretion theoretically. But, to break it down to discreet decision-making, it brings home the wild west nature of the program—injustice can happen.

Perhaps a senior DWD administrator summed it up best:

Examining racial disparities is a "nervous area of government." There's a tension. You want to do a good job. In order to do that, you must do the analysis. But, it's hard because an agency doesn't want to look like it's doing a bad job.

It is not surprising that steering committee members and agency administrators felt uncomfortable engaging issues of racial disparities. However, an important additional finding was that as the months progressed, committee members became more comfortable engaging issues of race. An administrator commented:

The process took much longer than anyone anticipated. We began to form a common basis and form common ground. In the end, people just said what they thought. They didn't have to worry about having a department person there or whatever. State workers could criticize the state. We just all told it like it was. It became a much more comfortable process. . . . Discrimination is likely occurring at all levels—by the individual person, by the agency, or due to policy intent. We need to ferret all of that out and examine a lot of assumptions.

This suggests an important finding for public sector agencies that embark upon racial disparities analysis. If the agency administrators understand that there will initially be discomfort in discussing race but decide to stay committed to racial analysis over the long term, concrete progress in analysis can occur.

3. The composition of the steering committee was important. It gave legitimacy to the study.

The fourteen-member steering committee reflected a broad range of knowledge, technical skills, and perspectives on the W-2 program. It included W-2 agency administrators, representatives of client advocacy groups, state administrators, and academics with experience in research methods and knowledgeable of W-2. The committee met at least once a month, with several work group meetings in between, as well as distribution of materials to the full group by e-mail. Specific tasks of the committee included developing research questions for the study, overseeing the analyses that were conducted, reviewing the research products that were developed, drawing conclusions about the research results, and making recommendations to DWS. The steering committee was supported by technical work groups that were responsible for guiding the specific analysis and for presenting research findings to the committee.

There was a strong consensus that the composition of the steering committee gave legitimacy to the study. The agency intentionally selected solid people from the variety of perspectives represented on the steering committee.

> Having solid, well-respected people regardless of sector was important. We made sure we had solid advocates, solid W-2 agency people, solid researchers. We didn't want to have the charge that we selected solid members from one sector and put them in a setting with weak members from other settings. We had strong, solid people on the entire team.

Over time, the quality of the composition of the steering committee led to some appreciation of alternative viewpoints. Although original positions were not radically altered, alternative positions were better understood.

> The steering committee was cumbersome. There was grandstanding at some points. Someone would make some point and then someone else would rebut it. . . . But, people at the table had "ah-ha" moments. *Discretion is important.* (original emphasis)

4. Agency leadership is important. DWD's willingness to commit time and resources to a study involving racial disparities was critical to overall project success.

Respondents universally acknowledged that the DWD committed a significant amount of time and resources to the study. DWD's commitment was twofold. Senior leadership sent strong signals of the study's importance, and they assigned well-respected lower-level administrators to work more closely on the study. By all accounts, the chief administrator of the Division of Workforce Solutions had an unwavering commitment to this study. In conducting racial analysis of public policies and programs, senior leadership matters. Respondents offered positive comments regarding the agency's ability to show senior support, but to minimize politicizing the study.

> [A senior administrator] was very supportive in us taking a look at the facts and not to get involved in the political process. The top folks are always going to be strategizing politically. But, the line bureaucrat wants to do the best job they can. These folks have a strong vested interest in making improvements in their areas.

> Staff were assigned to the study with appropriate skills. They did not give this to the limelight [political staff], but rather to the real worker bees. The study had sufficient expertise.

> [A senior administrator] said you have to do something about this. Having a core person within the agency take ownership right away was important. Right away, she made sure the Secretary took a position and launched a study.

> In fairness, I think the state spent more time on this study than they do on most. It did exceed our expectations. It was given a lot of time and space. There was a real sense of commitment.

5. The steering committee agreed upon specific methodology, which increased buy-in of the results.

Initially, the steering committee had several discussions about the research design and specific research methodology. The committee considered case file review, matched-pair testing, caseworker observation, and analysis of administrative data. Ultimately, the committee agreed to examine administrative sanctioning data for the entire state, and to rely primarily upon regression analysis. Although there are myriad ways to analyze any phenomenon, it was important that the group worked through this process and collectively decided on a research approach.

> Within DWD there was considerable discussion about whether the methodology was legitimate. There is this tension they were working out internally. Some folks thought they had a finding—others insisted you guys just don't know how to read the numbers. It's good to have a clear understanding of the methods if you're planning to do the study.

> Lots of [methodological] decisions to make, setting up equations, figuring out interaction effects of variables.

Academic researchers were particularly helpful here.

> The academic research side was very useful. They were helpful in explaining methodological concerns to the advocates. They were willing to discuss these issues. The Department did not have to broker this discussion. The Department would not have been viewed as an appropriate broker of the data.

It was important that the group agreed upon the methodological approach prior to the presentation of findings. Once the agreed-upon methodological approach was in place, there was a consensus to accept the findings. This was important for several reasons. It avoided "analysis paralysis," which can ultimately serve as an inhibitor to reaching consensus on any findings. It did not allow people to pick and choose the methodology based on the final results, and it facilitated buy-in from the entire steering committee regarding the research findings. The transparent nature of the methodological discussion also allowed all committee members to participate in the discussion, be aware of the trade-offs, and eliminate the "I didn't agree with the methodology" excuse for not accepting the findings.

6. When developing recommendations, removing the messenger from the message yielded positive results.

A challenging task of the steering committee was to develop a core set of recommendations. This became challenging because both DWS and the steering committee felt that, for the recommendations to be taken seriously, it was important to have consensus around the recommendations. However, in developing the recommendations, it was apparent early on that it was difficult to disassociate the recommendation from the recommender.

The steering committee relied upon a facilitator who had not been involved with the project. The facilitator had three major objectives: (1) refine how the report findings, the summaries, and the policy recommendations were finally worded; (2) identify the priority recommendations that they could agree upon as a full committee; and (3) identify a second tier of recommendations that received a majority of the committee votes, and include them as a separate set of recommendations. As one person commented: "Concern about group sign off was a real concern. No one wanted two sets of recommendations going forward. First of all, what is the Secretary supposed to do with that?"

The facilitator relied upon Group Systems, a facilitation software package. The product allowed sixteen users to participate simultaneously anonymously. Although the members were in the same room together, each member had an individual computer that he or she could provide input on an anonymous basis. Multiple voting processes were used through the process of formulating final recommendations. These included yes/no votes, ranking, and recommendations by a particular sector (advocate, state employees, W-2 agencies, etc.).

The facilitator commented:

> One of the key aspects of the facilitation software is that people key in their comments on an anonymous basis. They also appreciate that Group Systems allowed them to capture their exact comments as they typed it in. They could state

things as they felt it should be stated. . . . At the end people were delighted. The process was long and their ideas were not always chosen, but their participation mattered. It was a valuable participation effort. I think everyone felt that their comments were fully considered.

She continues:

We used multiple methods to identify the priorities. As first we ranked them. People could see the rankings on a spreadsheet. They were quite intrigued with that. The group decided as a group not to use the first round of rankings. We also ranked by sector (advocates, state workers, W-2 agencies). Those fell out pretty much as expected. We also used the yes/no function. We used multiple methods to work on the recommendations.

The neutral, but guiding role of the facilitator was also very important.

I made every effort to remain neutral. The recommendation had to be based on the group's decision. And a key point was that this wasn't going to work if the facilitator was not neutral. It is key to make sure you don't allow people to take the floor for too long. I stressed that comments should be succinct. Group Systems could capture it. It's fine to state your issue, but you cannot take up the whole agenda.

The timing of the facilitator was also important. The facilitator was brought in at the end of the process, with a specific task of assisting the group in developing their recommendations. The facilitator had not been privy to or biased by earlier discussions of the Steering Committee.

Ultimately, the use of Group Systems and a facilitator forced the steering committee into making specific decisions.

In the end, after using several methods [to formulate recommendations], and doing several revisions, collecting comments back from e-mail, the final method we used was yes/no. You either had to say up or down whether you supported the recommendation. The voting structure we used took a long time. I can live with that. I think it helped people with the final product.

A senior administrator commented, "Group Systems provides an equal opportunity for input and mediates the chatty types. It eliminates the people who like to brow beat one way or the other." Through use of the Group Systems software, the steering committee ultimately agreed upon a core set of nineteen recommendations in the areas of case manager and supervisor training, changes in policy statute, changes in implementation practices, increased monitoring of agency behavior, and analysis (see Table 12.1). As a senior DWD administrator commented, "This establishes the research agenda."

Table 12.1

Wisconsin Works Sanction Study Recommendations

	Priority Recommendations (based on group consensus)
Training	• Provide training to case managers and supervisory staff to increase awareness of diversity issues. Identify, analyze, and share the results of research from other states that examines the impact of case managers' decision making on sanctioning, with the goal of reducing differential impacts.
	• Develop policy and staff training to emphasize the need for accommodations for participants with health conditions (or children with disabilities) that preclude full-time participation. Those accommodations can include but are not limited to reducing required participation hours.
	• Evaluate W-2 training curriculum to determine how discretionary aspects of W-2 policy are trained. Determine if training outcomes are consistent with stated law, administrative rule, and policy. Focus training to ensure that all FEPs [case managers] and supervisory staff understand policy and appropriately uses guidelines when exercising discretion.
Policy/Statute	• Provide more guidance through policy in the area of granting "good cause." Guidelines should include reasons similar to those specified in Learnfare. The "good cause" process should be made accessible to people with a variety of barriers, and specify documentation for "good cause" and time frame. Agency practice must comply with state policy guidelines.
	• Emphasize through policy that assessment, including formal assessment, is an ongoing process and not a one-time event. Establish a trigger that requires that additional assessments and intensive case management would be offered to participants who receive severe or repeated sanctions, or to establish if they are employed full-time.
	• Restore the fair hearing process (would require a statutory change).
	• Establish a definition of what activities can be sanctioned. Only work activities should be sanctionable. Activities related to health needs would not be sanctionable. Train staff to assist customers on compliance.

(continued)

Table 12.1 *(continued)*

Practice/ Implementation	• Identify best practices that reduce inappropriate sanctioning to be implemented with agencies statewide. Determine if there are case management strategies or practices that lead to inappropriate sanctions.
	• Develop an action plan of ways to improve case management, including targeted training, policy clarification, and system reporting tools that can help FEPs.
	• Hold periodic roundtables for FEPs and supervisory staff to review case scenarios and discuss as a group where the individual should be placed in W-2, with the goal of increasing uniformity in decision-making statewide.
Monitoring	• Monitor adverse actions by race and require agencies with a high level of disparities to provide explanations.
	• Continue to monitor "significant sanction" cases through the DWS BW-2 Regional Offices to assure appropriate outcomes for all participants.
	• Increase BW-2 regional staff to ensure adequate case management monitoring can be continued.
Analysis	• Analyze why people of color are much more likely to be placed in CSJs [community service jobs] than white participants.
	• Conduct a comprehensive study of sanctions, strikes, and other adverse actions by race in the [next] biennium.
	• Analyze the significant changes in racial disparities between 2001, 2002, and 2003 and seek to identify patterns or factors that may have contributed to the reduction or increase. This could be used to develop best practices that could be implemented in Wisconsin, as well as other states.
	• Examine the findings related to Native American participants, whose sanction rates are also much higher than white participants.
	• Approve the proposal to evaluate the W-2 screening and assessment process.
	• Create and release a standardized annual report of sanctions by race.

Source: Wisconsin Works (W-2) Sanctions Study, State of Wisconsin, Department of Workforce Development, December 2004, 32–35.

7. The study took a long time, but the process itself was viewed as a clear strength.

The steering committee and associated work groups worked intensively for over a year. As one may expect, some meetings were more productive than others.

However, ultimately, the commitment of time itself seemed to be an important variable in promoting study buy-in and acceptance. As committee members commented:

> I'm not a patient person. So, when I saw this concept of a slow process, I was not thrilled. But, I did appreciate that more. There are times when a slow process can be helpful.

> The entire process was very time consuming, but also extremely valuable.

> It was time consuming working through the recommendations. We realized that some people were against some of the recommendations based on a minor point. We were able to clarify some misunderstandings. It did shift my opinion on the use of a consensus project.

8. Ultimately agency administrators viewed the examination of racial disparities to be a very important undertaking. They encourage other agencies to not be afraid to engage in racial analysis.

Public sector agencies may be reluctant to embark upon racial disparities analysis of their programs for many reasons. At best, it can be an uncomfortable analysis to undertake. At worse, it can lead to public embarrassment or legal action by exposing internal agency shortcomings. Importantly, however, senior administrators at DWD recognized a larger, overarching concern of providing administrative justice, fairness, and equity. A senior administrator commented:

> I've been involved in government for many, many years and seen many, many studies. I've been through all types of investigations. The fallout never concerns me. What concerns me is that we do whatever we can to improve the integrity of our services and improving that—making a positive impact on people's lives— that we're helping them. If a report points something out that we are doing wrong, then so be it. To find there's discrimination in our program is not a surprise. I am very aware that discrimination exists. When a white male, convicted felon is more employable than an African-American male that has no negatives, there are major racial disparities. It has always amazed me that more people haven't taken to the street when it comes to racial disparities. Documented discrimination in W-2 and racial disparities is not a surprise. . . . Agency appreciation of research is critical. You can't work in a "no bad news" environment.

Other senior administrators agreed.

> I think we are in a better position having done the study itself. It shows a willingness of the agency to look at what it is doing.

Of course, we have had many, many studies. I've seen in years past when negative studies never saw the light of day. But, this isn't the case now. The agency understands the importance of this type of research.

Don't be reluctant to do a study. Get your stakeholders onboard and ensure them that it is not a witch-hunt. If there is a problem, let's see what we can do to fix it.

Conceptual Model for Racial Disparities Analysis Within Agencies

Findings from the Wisconsin case study offer an important understanding of one agency's experience in examining racial disparities. But, in order to reduce social inequities in the administration of public services and benefits more generally, a conceptual model is warranted. How might other agencies approach a similar type of racial disparities analysis? Figure 12.1 proposes a useful model.

First, and perhaps most important, the agency must be willing to examine racial disparities. Wisconsin's DWD analysis was preceded by a legal complaint by the Office of Civil Rights. This need not be the case. In order to advance good government and social equity, agencies should routinely assess whether the benefits and services they provide suggest racial disparities. Second, such a study of racial disparities must have solid support from senior agency administration. Administrators must send clear messages regarding their unwavering commitment to undertake such a study and to devote significant agency time and expertise to conducting race-related research in a rigorous and thoughtful manner. Third, it is important for the agency to rely upon multiple sources of expertise. In the case of DWD, the steering committee was composed of well-respected administrators, line-staff, policy researchers, and advocates. This gave the study credibility and fostered buy-in of the research findings. Fourth, the study's research design and overall methodology should be thoroughly vetted and decided in advance of the findings. Following careful consideration of the research design, the methodological approach should be considered valid. In the case of Wisconsin, input from external, academic public policy researchers was very helpful and reduced skepticism of the agency's methodological approach. Fifth, findings should be accepted. In a study of this type, employing a steering committee comprising multiple stakeholders with varying perspectives is helpful. In the absence of such a deliberative process, findings may be viewed as suspect. The deliberative and transparent process, coupled with a solid agreement upon the methodological approach, should result in acceptable findings. Sixth, utilizing software packages such as Group Systems to separate the message from the messenger can promote maximum participation, limit overbearing personalities, and provide a useful means to facilitate a consensus set of recommendations. Finally, developing consensus on a core set of recommendations is important for future agency action. Ultimately, two sets of recommendations are not valuable to agency decision makers in determining next steps.

Figure 12.1   Conceptual Model for Agency Examination of Racial Disparities

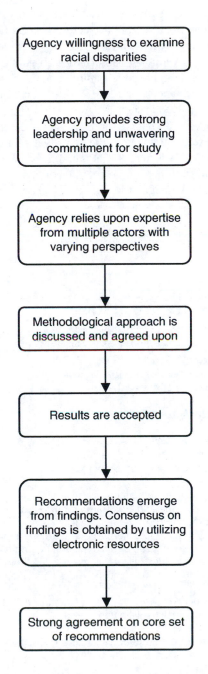

Conclusion

Examining racial disparities is important to the overall distribution of public services. Such an examination allows public sector agencies (and their contractors) to gauge the fairness of the benefits and services they provide. In order to promote social equity and good government associated with public service delivery, assessing racial disparities should become common practice. An examination of the work of the DWD welfare sanction study in Wisconsin provides a useful, close-up view of the processes involved in such an agency's undertaking. The lessons from Wisconsin should prove very valuable for other public sector agencies that decide to engage in similar research. Of course, the investigative process is only one step in assuring social equity. To reverse social inequities or maintain existing social equities, agency administrators also must implement core recommendations in a timely manner. Yet, an important first step is still an agency's willingness to embark upon the discovery process.

Appendix 12.1

Interview Protocol

Opening Question

1. The DWS has been examining racial disparities for the past three years. How has it generally been going?
2. How would you assess your overall level of involvement with this study? [probe: continuous, sporadic, specific areas]

Study Development (Background and Context)

3. Can you walk me through how the study evolved? Why did you decide to examine racial disparities in the sanctioning of welfare clients?
4. Who were the key people (or organizations) who were instrumental in getting this study on the map?
5. How did they decide to initiate the study?
6. What was the original scope and time frame for the study? How was the scope and time frame decided?
7. Originally, what did you hope to accomplish or learn from this study?
8. Did you encounter any obstacles or difficulties in getting this study initiated? If so, what were the difficulties? How did you resolve them? [Identify each difficulty and resolution technique until no more difficulties are named by the interviewee.]
9. In getting the study initiated, were there aspects that were easier (or went smoother) than you originally anticipated?
10. Overall, how would you evaluate the *initiation* phase of the study? What suggestions would you have for other agencies if they were seeking to develop a similar study?

How the Study Was Conducted (Implementation)

11. Once the decision was made to conduct a racial disparities study, how did you decide the research design (or how to conduct the study)?
12. What level of support did DWS internally provide to the study? [probes: departments/units, personnel, expertise, budget]
13. Did you find this level of support adequate? Why or why not?
14. How did it compare to the types of support DWS typically provides to internal research studies?
15. DWS established a steering committee to provide guidance on the study. Were there other approaches considered? If so, please describe them. Why were these approaches rejected?
16. How did you determine the membership of the steering committee? What role (or purpose) did you envision for the steering committee?
17. How did you decide which tasks would be performed by DWS and which tasks would be conducted by the steering committee?
18. What were the main contributions of the steering committee? How were they helpful?
19. What were the main weaknesses or shortcomings of the steering committee?
20. Did the scope and time frame originally envisioned for the study change over time? If so, why and how so?
21. In designing this study, did you encounter difficulties that you felt were unique to this study because the focus was on examining racial disparities? If so, what? How did you get through these challenges?
22. Overall, how would you evaluate the research design phase of this study?
23. What research design suggestions would you have for other agencies if they were seeking to conduct a similar study?

Anticipated Changes Resulting from Study [Impacts]

24. I have reviewed a draft of the final report resulting from this study. Did you feel the study offered accurate findings?
25. What do you feel are the most important findings from this study?
26. In what ways did the findings confirm what you initially thought?
27. In what ways were the findings surprising?
28. What did you learn from this study? Specifically, what do you know about racial disparities in W-2 sanctioning that you did not know before this study was conducted?
29. Are there any questions that you had hoped this study would address, that still remain? If so, what?

Overall Evaluation and Assessment

30. Wisconsin is widely viewed as an innovator in developing U.S. welfare policy. When this study is publicly released, other organizations, researchers, or advocacy groups may be interested in conducting a similar analysis. What advice would you give them? What can they learn from the Wisconsin experience? [Probe: If you had to design a "to do" and "not to do" list, what items would you place on each list?]

Notes

1. The National Academy of Public Administration's Board of Directors adopted social equity as the fourth pillar of public administration, along with economy, efficiency, and effectiveness. See National Academy of Public Administration, (2005).

2. American Civil Liberties Union and NAACP Complaint to U.S. Department of Health and Human Services, Office for Civil Rights, Docket No. 05023078, filed February 22, 2002.

3. See, for example, Mulligan-Hansel and Fendt (2002); Wisconsin Legislative Audit Bureau (2002, 5).

References

Akram, R. 2004. *Social Equity and the American Dream. Standing Panel on Social Equity in Governance.* Washington, DC: National Academy of Public Administration.

Clarke, Leslie L.; Brenda Jarmon; and Merlin Langley. 1999. "Qualitative Study of WAGES: People Who Have Left WAGES." Florida Inter-University Welfare Reform Collaborative, Fall.

Division of Workforce Solutions. 2003. "Analysis of W-2 Sanctions by Race 2001 and 2002." Madison, Wisconsin, March 6.

Gooden, Susan Tinsley. 1998. "All Things Not Being Equal: Difference in Caseworker Support Toward Black and White Welfare Clients." *Harvard Journal of African American Public Policy* IV: 23–33.

———. 1999. "The Hidden Third Party: Welfare Recipients' Experiences with Employers." *Journal of Public Management and Social Policy* (Summer): 69–83.

Greenberg, Mark and Steve Savner. 1996. "A Detailed Summary of Key Provisions of the Temporary Assistance for Needy Families Block Grant of HR. 3734: The Personal Responsibility and Work Opportunity Reconciliation Act of 1996." Center for Law and Social Policy: Washington, D.C.

Holzer, Harry J., and Michael Stoll. 2000. "Employer Demand for Welfare Recipients by Race." Institute for Research on Poverty, Discussion Paper no. 1213–00.

Lipsky, Michael. 1980. *Street-Level Bureaucracy: Dilemmas of the Individual in Public Services.* New York: Russell Sage Foundation.

Mead, Lawrence. 2004. *Government Matters: Welfare Reform in Wisconsin.* Princeton, NJ: Princeton University Press.

Mulligan-Hansel, Kathleen, and Pamela S. Fendt. 2002. *Unfair Sanctions: Does W-2 Punish People of Color?* Milwaukee: Institute for Wisconsin's Future, University of Wisconsin (October).

Myers, Samuel L. Jr. 2002. "Presidential Address: Analysis of Race as Policy Analysis." *Journal of Policy Analysis and Management* 21(2): 169–190.

National Academy of Public Administration. 2000. Standing Panel on Social Equity in Governance. Issue Paper and Work Plan, November.

———. 2005. Strategic Plan. Spring.

Rohr, John. 1989. *Ethics for Bureaucrats: An Essay on Law and Values.* New York: Marcel Dekker.

Savner, Steve. 2000. "Welfare Reform and Racial/Ethnic Minorities: The Questions to Ask." *Poverty and Race* 9, no. 4 (July/August): 3–5.

U.S. Department of Health and Human Services. 1996. Major Provisions of the Personal Responsibility and Work Opportunity Reconciliation Act of 1996 (P.L. 104–193). Washington, DC.

Wisconsin Legislative Audit Bureau. 2002. *Sanctioning of Wisconsin Works (W-2) Participants (Report 01–07).* December 10.

Wisconsin Works (W-2) Sanctions Study. 2004. State of Wisconsin, Department Workforce Development, December.

Wilson, William Julius. 1996. *When Work Disappears: The World of the New Urban Poor.* New York: Knopf.

13

Integrating Social Equity into the Core Human Resource Management Course

Susan T. Gooden and Blue Wooldridge

Issues of equity and justice are fundamental concerns of public administrators. Public administrators face the constant challenge of ensuring equity in governance (Akram 2004), and in certain respects the field of public administration has moved slowly in applying principles of justice. In fact, equity or fairness in public services was the last established "pillar" of the field—and it still remains secondary in emphasis behind economy, effectiveness, and efficiency.[1] Although the National Academy of Public Administration is not the decisive voice of the discipline—nor does such a decisive voice exist—this respected organization's adoption of social equity elevates its importance to our profession.

Social equity is generally identified as a post-1960s concern of public administration. As H. George Frederickson notes, "It was during the 1960s that it became increasingly evident that the results of governmental policy and the work of public administrators implementing those policies were much better for some citizens than for others" (Frederickson 2005). In 1974, *Public Administration Review* published a symposium on "Social Equity and Public Administration." This symposium helped build social equity theory, citing social equity as (1) the basis for a just, democratic society; (2) an influence on the behavior of organizational man; (3) the legal basis for distributing public services; (4) the practical basis for distributing public services; (5) operationalized in compound federalism; and (6) a challenge for research and analysis (Frederickson 1990, 229). In February 2000, the National Academy of Public Administration's Board of Trustees authorized the establishment of a Standing Panel on Social Equity. This panel defined social equity as "[t]he fair, just, and equitable management of all institutions serving the public directly or by contract, and the fair and equitable distribution of public services, and implementation of public policy, and the commitment to promote fairness, justice, and equity in the formation of public policy" (National Academy of Public Administration 2000).

It is important to assess how well we are educating our students about this fourth pillar of public administration. What do we teach MPA students about social equity? More important, what training to practice social equity do they receive in our programs? It stands to reason that we want our students to become equipped to and practice social equity in their jobs as public servants. But what formal training do our students receive to do so? This article suggests that the human resource management (HRM) area is one logical place to expand our focus on social equity by offering specific suggestions to educate students on the formal and informal social equity practices related to human resources.

Gooden and Myers (2004) coedited a symposium on social equity in public affairs education in the April 2004 volume of the *Journal of Public Affairs Education*. As part of his response to that volume, David Rosenbloom asked for an explanation of "the advantages, if any, of applying the term social equity to standard, longstanding subject matter in MPA education" (2005, 249). Rosenbloom's question is an important one, as it essentially asks about social equity's added value in our curricula.

Our response parallels the sentiments of Svara and Brunet when they state:

> A commitment to social equity prompts one to analyze and explore the activist limits of equal protection, whereas the absence of this commitment might cause one to tolerate instances of inequality out of concern that remedies might not pass the equal protection test. Although Rosenbloom is concerned that social equity will be "muddled when it is treated as a pillar built of sometimes incompatible concerns and concepts," an opposing view is that it is stronger because it is based on considering and balancing multiple forms of analysis reflecting the four dimensions [efficiency, economy, effectiveness, and equity]. (2004)

Our central response to Rosenbloom's question is that applying social equity MPA education—specifically in the HRM area—offers the opportunity to (1) introduce students to the concept of social equity; (2) allow them to analyze common formal and informal HRM practices through the concept of social equity; and (3) provide students with the tools and resources they need to actively apply the social equity pillar in their future professional work. The latter purpose is of particular importance. Ultimately, professors in HRM courses can integrate social equity for each HRM component by ensuring that their students understand how the formal context promotes or discourages social equity and how the informal "HR dialogues" promote or discourage social equity. In each instance, students need to carefully consider the role of the public sector manager.

Human Resource Management: A Promising Training Ground

The National Association of Schools of Public Affairs and Administration (NASPAA) is the accrediting body for graduate programs in public affairs and administration. The Standards for Professional Master's Degree Programs in Public Affairs, Policy, and Administration are proposed by its Standards Committee and adopted by NASPAA. The curriculum components are designed to produce professionals capable of intelligent, creative analysis and communication and action in public service (NASPAA 2005). Although NASPAA does not require specific courses, it does identify common curriculum components. As Table 13.1 shows, HRM is a key component in the management of public sector organizations.

Table 13.1

Public Administration Core Curriculum Areas

4.21 NASPAA Common Curriculum Components

The common curriculum components shall enhance the student's values, knowledge, and skills to act ethically and effectively.

In the Management of Public Service Organizations, the components of which include:
- Human resources
- Budgeting and financial processes
- Information management, technology applications, and policy

In the Application of Quantitative and Qualitative Techniques of Analysis, the components of which include:
- Policy and program formulation, implementation, and evaluation
- Decision-making and problem-solving

With an Understanding of the Public Policy and Organizational Environment, the components of which include:
- Political and legal institutions and processes
- Economic and social institutions and processes
- Organization and management concepts and behavior

These area requirements do not prescribe specific courses. Neither do they imply that equal time should be spent on each area or that courses must all be offered by the public affairs, public policy, or public administration programs.

Source: NASPAA (2005).

Issues of social equity should permeate the entire public affairs curriculum (Wooldridge 1998). This is especially true for HRM courses. Social equity issues are not exclusive to personnel management, but they do have a historical tie there. According to the National Academy of Public Administration (NAPA 2000), "[t]hese issues were front-and-center in the early years of affirmative action and were reflected in public administration practices such as hiring and promotion, the selecting of contractors and bidders, and the like."

In their textbook, Shafritz and Russell (2002) identify three qualities of social equity:

> All public administrators have an obvious obligation to advance social equity. However this obligation can be legitimately and honorably interpreted in several ways. First is the obligation to administer the laws they work under in a fair manner.
> The second way of interpreting obligations to advance social equity is to feel bound to proactively further the cause—to seek to hire and advance a varied

workforce. . . . The third aspect to advancing social equity is best illustrated by a story. In 1963 George C. Wallace, then governor of Alabama, dramatically stood in the doorway of the University of Alabama to prevent the entry of black students and the desegregation of the university. . . . As was arranged, the deputy U.S. attorney general, Nicholas Katzenbach, backed up by 3,000 federal troops, ordered Wallace to allow a black student, Vivian Malone, to enter. After a longwinded speech about federal encroachment on state's rights, Wallace stepped aside and Katzenbach escorted Malone to the university cafeteria. . . .

After Malone entered the cafeteria, she got her tray of food and sat alone. Almost immediately some white female students joined her. They sought to befriend her, as they would any new student. . . . Then, as now, government can go only so far in forcing social equity. But there is no limit to the amount of inspiration it can provide to encourage people to do the right, decent, and honorable thing. This encouragement has a name. It is called moral leadership. (10–11)

Each of these three qualities of social equity is directly related to HRM. First, public administrators must administer the laws fairly. Second, public administrators should proactively hire a diverse workforce. Third, public administrators should provide moral leadership to the fulfillment of social equity. At the crux of each of these normative qualities is the eminence of government workers. Human resource management essentially forms the base of social equity in public administration. Personnel and personnel policies matter. As Frank Thompson states:

Personnel policies lay the ground rules for position determination—the creation and allocation of formal roles within agencies (e.g., job design and classification). They shape human-resource flows—recruitment, promotion, transfer, demotion, removal. They specify an approach to performance appraisal—processes through which managers acquire and interpret information concerning the activities of subordinates. They seek to motivate subordinates to behave in certain ways through regulation, the establishment of incentive systems, and socialization that instills certain knowledge, perceptions, skills, and values. (1991, vii)

The human resource management area already has the most activity in connection with social equity. It provides a natural focal point upon which to increase the integration of social equity into public administrators' professional training. In their analysis of social equity coverage in public administration textbooks, Svara and Brunet (2004, 104) found "the most attention is given to procedural social equity concerns, including due process, discrimination, and equal employment opportunity."

Increasing Student Exposure to Social Equity Through Formal and Informal Personnel Policies and Practices

HRM refers to the comprehensive set of managerial activities and tasks concerned with developing and maintaining a qualified workforce—human resources—in ways that contribute to organizational effectiveness (DeNisi and Griffin 2001). HRM components include job analysis, human resource planning, recruitment,

placement, performance appraisal, compensation, training and development, organizational justice, and collective bargaining. Each component is shaped by formal
and informal personnel policies and practices. By formal, we mean technical and
legal policies. By informal, we mean what happens in reality. It is common for
HRM textbooks (and courses) to discuss the former. It is less common to discuss the
latter, *especially in terms of social equity*. This reality is characterized by conversations we call informal "HR dialogues" that affect all aspects of personnel. These
are the behind-closed-doors conversations that occur throughout each component
of personnel management. These dialogues include verbal and nonverbal actions
that can greatly affect personnel practices but are not routinely monitored.

Such dialogues are often complex and discomforting. As one external reviewer
noted, "Discussions of race, gender, religion, sexual orientation, and disability in
organizations are usually emotionally charged as each individual brings a unique set
of feelings, beliefs, experiences, and motivations. . . . We must provide students (and
ourselves) with the frameworks and practices of having these difficult conversations
in class to ensure adequate preparation for the workplace and community." As with
efficiency and effectiveness, there may not be one best way to promote social equity,
but clearly some decisions and practices are more equitable than others. We used
personnel textbooks, literature, federal policy and initiatives, and our own instruc-
tional and selection committee experiences to guide the suggestions formulated in
this chapter. However, this chapter is not intended to offer a systematic assessment
of HR textbooks, government resources, federal policy, or HR dialogues. Rather,
we describe our use of these dialogues to illustrate how public affairs educators can
enhance the social equity focus of their HRM courses. As stated earlier, multiple
aspects of human resource management are commonly covered in public affairs
programs. For illustrative purposes in this discussion, we limit our discussion to
three: job analysis, employee recruitment, and employee selection.

Job Analysis

Job analysis is the process of recording information about the tasks (job elements)
an employee performs. It results in a job description: a written statement of the
employee's responsibilities, duties, and qualifications. Typically, the information
described and recorded includes the purposes of a job, major duties or activities
required of job holders, conditions under which the job is performed, and the
competencies (i.e., skills, knowledge, abilities, education, experience) an employee
needs to perform the position's duties at a satisfactory level (Jackson and Schuler
2002).

Social Equity Lesson 1

Job analysis is shaped by a fluid legal context that is directly related to social equity
elasticity. Executive orders, laws passed by the legislative body, and court decisions

all affect the widening or constricting of social equity. In one of the landmark Equal Employment Opportunity law cases, *Griggs v. Duke Power*, Willie Griggs was an applicant for a job as a coal handler. The Duke Power Company required its coal handlers to be high school graduates, but "Griggs claimed this requirement was illegally discriminatory because it wasn't related to success on the job and because it resulted in more blacks than whites being rejected for these jobs" (Dresser 1997, 43). The 1971 *Griggs* decision is a clear example of how public employment laws can promote social equity: "For the first time, an employer would have to prove in court that its personnel practices were valid and job-related if the numbers showed that minorities were not succeeding in the same proportions of non-minorities" (Nigro and Nigro 2000, 33). Federal support of employment policies designed to promote social equity has declined since the 1980s, from which time "Presidents Reagan and Bush declared that remedial hiring ratios were a form of reverse discrimination . . . both also expressed their commitment to Equal Employment Opportunity (EEO) and 'color blind' personnel policies" (ibid.). Although the 1991 Civil Rights Act was a shift away from employment policies of the 1960s and 1970s designed to promote social equity, it remains a key component of human resource management.

As a current example, Title 41, Section 60, in the Office of Federal Contract Compliance Programs (OFCCP) in the U.S. Department of Labor's Code of Federal Regulations (1976, 2000) details the purposes of affirmative action and encourages public sector agencies to implement affirmative action programs beyond formal requirements.

Purpose
(1) An affirmative action program is a management tool designed to ensure equal employment opportunity. A central premise underlying affirmative action is that, absent discrimination, over time a contractor's workforce, generally, will reflect the gender, racial and ethnic profile of the labor pools from which the contractor recruits and selects. Affirmative action programs contain a diagnostic component, which includes a number of quantitative analyses designed to evaluate the composition of the workforce of the contractor and compare it to the composition of the relevant labor pools. Affirmative action programs also include action-oriented programs. If women and minorities are not being employed at a rate to be expected given their availability in the relevant labor pool, the contractor's affirmative action program includes specific practical steps designed to address this underutilization. Effective affirmative action programs also include internal auditing and reporting systems as a means of measuring the contractor's progress toward achieving the workforce that would be expected in the absence of discrimination.

(2) An affirmative action program also ensures equal employment opportunity by institutionalizing the contractor's commitment to equality in every aspect of the employment process. Therefore, as part of its affirmative action program, a contractor monitors and examines its employment decisions and compensation systems to evaluate the impact of those systems on women and minorities.

(3) An affirmative action program is, thus, more than a paperwork exercise. An affirmative action program includes those policies, practices, and procedures that the contractor implements to ensure that all qualified applicants and employees are receiving an equal opportunity for recruitment, selection, advancement, and every other term and privilege associated with employment. Affirmative action, ideally, is a part of the way the contractor regularly conducts its business. OFCCP has found that when an affirmative action program is approached from this perspective, as a powerful management tool, there is a positive correlation between the presence of affirmative action and the absence of discrimination.

Affirmative action obligations. The use of selection procedures that have been validated pursuant to these guidelines does not relieve users of any obligations they may have to undertake affirmative action to assure equal employment opportunity. Nothing in the guidelines is intended to preclude the use of lawful selection procedures that assist in remedying the effects of prior discriminatory practices, or the achievement of affirmative action objectives.

Encouragement of voluntary affirmative action programs. These guidelines are also intended to encourage the adoption and implementation of voluntary affirmative action programs by users who have no obligation under Federal law to adopt them; but are not intended to impose any new obligations in that regard. The agencies issuing and endorsing these guidelines endorse for all private employers and reaffirm for all governmental employers the Equal Employment Opportunity Council's "Policy Statement on Affirmative Action Programs for State and Local Government Agencies." (41 FR 38814, September 13, 1976; 41 CFR 60–2.10 and 41 CFR 60–2.17, November 13, 2000)

Formal requirements of job analysis are shaped by the current landscape of social equity. Human resource management students should critically analyze subtle and not-so-subtle changes in public employment policy for their effect on social equity. What do these formal changes mean for social equity? How do governmental agencies communicate their commitment to social equity? How can our students assess formal social equity dimensions of job descriptions? A primary way is to have students perform a social equity analysis of job descriptions. Does the job description contain a statement regarding its equal employment opportunity policy? Does it contain a reasonable accommodation statement? Where are these statements placed within the job description? Overall, after reading the job description, what impression would a job applicant have about this agency's commitment to social equity? What are the social equity implications of the specific enumerated job qualifications (knowledge, skills, and abilities)?

Job analysis is also influenced by informal HR dialogues. Table 13.2 presents an example of a social equity HR dialogue surrounding qualification requirements for a fiscal technician position.

The issue in this scenario is the agency's commitment to abiding by the qualifications listed in the position. Although the position description allows applicants with a college degree or four years of related work experience to apply, the HR dialogue captures the organization's practice of preferring individuals with a college

Table 13.2

HR Social Equity Dialogue: Job Analysis Scenario

Freda (manager): We've received eighteen applications for our fiscal technician position. I hope you've each had a moment to look over these applications. I'd like to leave our meeting today with an agreement on the candidates we'd like to bring in for an interview.

Maria: Yes, I've looked at these and I noticed that five of the applicants do not have a college degree.

Carlos: Our job ad clearly states that a candidate should have a four-year college degree or four years of related experience. The applicants who do not have a college degree have related experience.

Maria: Well, I wouldn't say this beyond this room, but I think—in this day and time—it would be a mistake to hire someone without the degree. We've received applications from several people who have a degree, so I think it's only practical that we focus our energies on this group.

Carlos: I have a real problem with that. Just look at our ad.

Maria: Carlos, I know you haven't been with our agency that long, but generally we try to hire people with a degree. We had to advertise the position that way to get it approved through HR. In practice, we try to hire people with degrees.

Freda: We need to look at all of the applications. But, Maria has a point. We do tend to hire people with degrees. When we're reviewing the applications, if someone without a degree really stands out, we can consider bringing that person in for an interview. Now, let's turn our attention to selecting the specific individuals we'd like to interview.

---

degree. This scenario raises several social equity concerns. How do the norms and practices of this agency compare with the specific language contained in the job description? What are the social equity implications of these differences? Older applicants, minority applicants, and individuals who live in or are from low-income families may be disproportionately affected. How could the manager handle this situation more effectively? If public managers wish to integrate social equity into areas where it has previously been ignored, what challenges will they face? How can they overcome these challenges?

Recruitment

Recruitment is the process of attracting individuals in a timely manner, in sufficient numbers, and with appropriate qualifications to apply for jobs within an organization. It is specifically the set of activities and processes used to legally obtain a sufficient number of the right people at the right place and time so that the people and the organization can select each other in their own best short-run and long-run interests (Schuler and Huber 1997). It is the process of developing a pool of qualified applicants who are interested in working for the organization and from which the organization might reasonably select the best individual or individuals to hire for employment (DeNisi and Griffin 2001). Recruitment has a direct relationship to social equity, because it is the initial step in placing more employees from protected groups in government jobs (Klingner and Nalbandian 1993, 142). For example, using the aforementioned lens of Shafritz and Russell's (2002) three qualities of social equity, how can public managers advance the second quality to aggressively "seek to hire and advance a varied workforce" within their agencies?

Writing in 1944, J. Donald Kingsley developed the concept of "representative bureaucracy," which asserts that all social groups have a right to participate in their governing institutions. This concept has been expanded to hold that the bureaucracies should reflect the demographic composition of the general public (Dolan 2000, 2002; Kranz 1976; Meier and Nigro 1976; Riccucci and Saidel 1997), so that the preferences of a heterogeneous population will be represented in organizational decision making (Riccucci and Saidel 1997). Public administrators should be alerted to seek out opportunities when turnovers, growth, the need for new competencies, and other circumstances can allow for currently underrepresented populations to be recruited, promoted, or developed to fill these anticipated vacancies.

Social Equity Lesson 2

Courses designed to enhance HRM competencies and to integrate social equity concepts would certainly stress the need for employers to generate and use innovative recruitment methods and locales. The disparate impact of high-tech job postings and recruitment methods, such as Web-based or Internet strategies, on ethnic/racial/religious minorities, individuals with disabilities, and low-income individuals must be assessed. Traditional recruitment practices that involve reliance on "word-of-mouth and employee referral networking; the use of executive search and referral firms in which affirmative action/EEO requirement were not always made known" (Riccucci 2002, 69) also serve as institutional barriers for some currently underrepresented groups. For some groups, nontraditional recruitment approaches such as religious organizations, social associations, and recreational outlets can be effective for reaching currently underrepresented groups.

Our MPA programs should familiarize students with formal social equity initiatives that are currently in place in governmental agencies. Nigro and Nigro's textbook, *The New Public Personnel Administration* (2000) offers a useful example of the formal relationship between social equity and recruitment through the Office of Personnel Management's Hispanic Employment Initiative (Table 13.3).

Students in our HRM courses should acquire competencies in recruitment practices designed to promote social equity. One such way is to have students engage

Table 13.3

OPM's Hispanic Employment Initiative

An example of minority-oriented recruitment is provided by OPM's Hispanic Employment Initiatives, which include helping to implement Executive Order 12900, the White House Initiative on Educational Excellence for Hispanic Americans. In addition to issuing guidance on recruiting strategies for Hispanic students, OPM works with federal agencies to identify job opportunities and institutions that offer training and educational opportunities that prepare Hispanic students to qualify for those jobs. Other OPM initiatives in this area are:
- Providing employment information to students, faculty, and the Hispanic community by sponsoring Employment Information (Touch Screen) Computer Kiosks and placing them in Hispanic-serving institutions.
- Expanding the Presidential Management Intern (PMI) recruitment program to include visiting more institutions that are graduating significant numbers of Hispanics.
- Providing assistance in coordinating the placements with federal agencies of Hispanic students under the National Internship Program of the Hispanic Association of Colleges and Universities (HACU). HACU interns are college students with grade point averages of 3.0 or better who work in federal agencies for 10 weeks over the summer.
- Using the flexibilities available under the federal Student Employment Program to bring Hispanic students into federal occupations where there are shortages of qualified applicants, as well as all other occupations.
- Developing mentoring programs to encourage and support young Hispanics' educational development and career progress.
- Encourage participation of Hispanics in agency career development programs, including intergovernmental rotational assignments for senior executives, management, and professional/technical occupations (U.S. Office of Personnel Management, 1997).

Source: Nigro and Nigro (2000, 90–91).

in group projects that require direct involvement with governmental agencies to propose similar employment recruitment initiatives for underrepresented groups. This allows students to take a social equity HRM concept (hiring a more diverse workforce) and apply it in a practical setting (working with a governmental agency to understand their diversity needs) with a real-world application (developing an agency-specific social equity proposal).

Our students also should become competent in the informal HR dialogues that affect social equity and recruitment. The HR dialogue recruitment scenario contained in Table 13.4 displays a common tension between efficiency and equity that emerges in the recruitment area. In performing an analysis of the recruitment scenario, students can assess the social equity implications of these dialogues. For example, Kevin, the manager, conveys an important message about the agency's values. This is a direct application of the tension of the public administration pil-

Table 13.4

HR Social Equity Dialogue: Recruitment Scenario

Kevin (manager): Well, we need to think about how we want to advertise our position. Typically, we post these positions on our agency's Web site, and the state's DOL's [Department of Labor] Web site. We'll also advertise this in the employment section of our local newspaper.

William: Yes, this sounds good. Perhaps we also should consider advertising our position in minority communities a bit more. There's the *Minority Tribune* [weekly newspaper with a readership base of African Americans], and we could also submit our posting to several listservs that have an excellent link to minority communities. There are three that come to my mind, right off hand.

Jennifer and Jack: [on recruitment committee, but remain quiet; body language suggests indifference and slight disengagement]

Kevin: [looks around at the committee] I agree, William, those are all good ideas. But, we also need to consider our overall budget and where we can get the most bang for our buck. And, we need to think about the overall workload involved. One of us will need to make sure all of these postings go out. And, I'm sure we all agree we need to fill this position quickly.

William: Well, the electronic venues I'm thinking of are free or involve minimal costs. It's just a matter of getting the information out.

Kevin: Sure, I'm not opposed to that at all. It seems like you've got some good leads there. So, you—and for that matter—any of us can forward this announcement to any group we'd like. How does that sound?

Jennifer: Yes, that sounds good to me.

Jack: Yes, we could try this and see where it gets us. Then, if we don't get a good group of applicants, we can considering advertising more broadly.

William: [disappointed] OK.

Kevin: Great. Well, I think that about wraps up our meeting for today.

---

lars. In this scenario, the manager's clear message is that efficiency—filling the application quickly—is more important than equity.

Kevin also conveys a value statement on how employees should spend their time. Engaging in social equity activities would distract from other, more important job tasks. As the manager, Kevin's comments convey a concrete statement on social equity. He is not opposed to it, but fundamentally views it as distractive. His comments suggest that promoting social equity in recruitment should be an individual employee activity rather than an agency-wide activity. William, an employee, tries to advance the public administration social equity pillar, but receives little support from either his coworkers or his supervisor. What implications does this have? What message does an organization send when social equity efforts are individually driven rather than agency driven? How is William viewed? What risks does William take? What are the trade-offs if William continues to push the issue?

Jack also makes an important value statement. In his view, the agency should not engage in strategies specifically designed to recruit minorities as a first step. Rather, this should be a secondary consideration. Jack and Jennifer appear neutral at first. They weigh in only after receiving cues from the manager, Kevin. A social equity analysis of this scenario raises many important questions. A follow-up assignment could require students to rewrite this dialogue displaying a stronger agency value of social equity, using insights from representative bureaucracy.

Selection

Selection is the process of gathering legally defensible information about job applicants in order to determine who should be hired for a long- or short-term position (Schuler and Huber 1997). The selection process is concerned with identifying the best candidate or candidates for jobs from the pool of qualified applicants developed during the recruiting process (DeNisi and Griffin 2001).

Social Equity Lesson 3

Professional public affairs programs should ensure that students are competent in formal, federal guidelines for employee selection. One excellent, practitioner-oriented resource is *The Uniform Guidelines on Employee Selection*, which provides a set of principles for determining proper test use and selection procedures, covering topics such as test fairness and adverse impact. Easily accessible from the Office of Personnel Management's Web site, these guidelines incorporate a single set of principles designed to assist employers, labor organizations, employment agencies, and licensing and certification boards to comply with requirements of federal law prohibiting employment practices that discriminate on grounds of race, color, religion, sex, and national origin. They are designed to provide a framework for determining the proper use of tests and other selection procedures (Office of Personnel Management, n.d.)

The assessment applied by public employers usually involves some combination of the following: minimum qualifications requirement; evaluations of training, education, and experience; written tests of knowledge and analytic skills; job performance tests and simulations; oral examinations by individual examiners or boards; background checks or investigations; and medical and physical examinations (Nigro and Nigro 2000, 97–98). Although public employment searches often use a combination of these methods, the job interview remains an important part of the process. Most organizations will not hire an applicant without an interview because they believe it provides them the opportunity to observe an applicant's appearance and interpersonal skills and to ask questions not adequately covered on the application (Klingner and Nalbandian 1993, 159).

Perhaps most relevant to social equity analysis, the body of research focused on interviews seems to be oriented toward the discovery of what irrelevant constructs are measured in the interview. Schmitt and Chan (1998, 171) contend that the interview decision comes out of the complex interplay among the situation and the characteristics and behavior of both interviewer and interviewee (Figure 13.1). Race (Parsons and Liden 1984), gender (Hitt and Barr 1989), physical attractiveness (Pingitore et al. 1994), and age (Avolio and Barrett 1987) have all been related to interviewer judgments. The two most important considerations to increase interview reliability and validity are to rely upon the use of multiple independent interviewers and to ask the applicants a similar set of structured or semistructured questions (Schmitt and Chan 1998). The situational interview is one particular development that avoids some of the pitfalls of conventional interviewing (Stohr-Gilmore, Stohr-Gilmore, and Kistler 1990). In particular, the situational interview structure avoids the possibility of including discriminatory questions that are unrelated to job performance (Hays and Kearney 1995, 100).

One critically important component of the selection process is the informal HR dialogue that occurs when selecting the final candidate. Klinger and Nalbandian (1993) include a case study that captures important behind-the-scenes HR dialogue that ultimately impacts candidate selection (Table 13.5). This scenario raises important questions regarding the role of politics in employee selection and what the statement "best-qualified candidate" really means. A typical application of this scenario is to have students decide whom to hire, and provide a justification of their reasoning. An important extension of the students' hiring decision is to consider the social equity implications if multiple candidates with similar backgrounds are always or nearly always hired. Ultimately, it is an organization's cumulative pattern of hiring decisions that alters or fails to alter the advancement of social equity in the public sector workforce.

Conclusion

What competencies will students gain from engaging in formal and informal social equity analysis in HRM courses? First, they increase their formal knowledge of personnel practices. For example, we have found when sharing the Office of Personnel Management's Hispanic Employment Initiative in our classes that many students are not aware of the initiative. A few even express surprise, thinking that such an initiative would be illegal. It is important that HRM courses provide a clear sense of the legal guidelines and the vast opportunities to formally include social equity in their managerial actions. Second, through the use of informal HR dialogues,

260

Figure 13.1   Representation of Various Influences on Interview Decisions

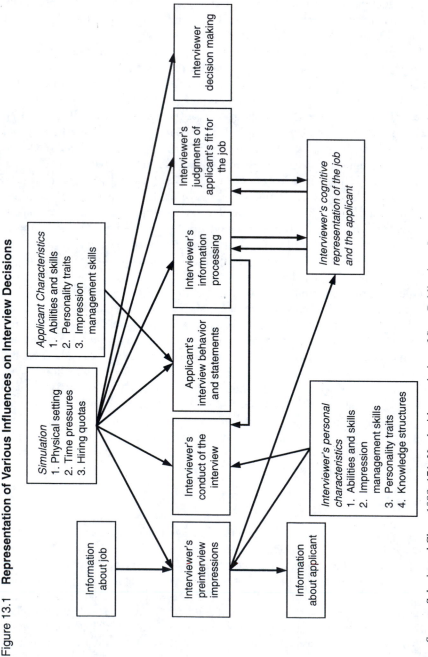

Source: Schmitt and Chan, 1988, 171. Used with permission of Sage Publications, Inc.

Table 13.5

HR Social Equity Dialogue: Employee Selection Scenario

Brenda: Well, I don't know about you two, but in my book this John Simpson seems to have enough experience to handle the job. I need someone who can take over the internal operations of the agency while we get this new program off the ground. But what really impressed me is his commitment to the policy direction we're headed in.

Mary: You know I admire your judgment, Brenda, but does he really have the skill to pull off the job? We know Don Johnson is doing a fine job now as a division director. He already knows the ropes around here, and I think he's ready for a bigger job. Besides, it's about time we get another minority into this sacred secretarial hut!

Brenda: Hold on, Mary. You know I supported our affirmative action program. I gave you a boost some time ago, I remember.

Mary: Now wait a minute! Let's not dredge up the history on that one. You know very well I was qualified for this job. This is now, and Don's qualified.

Brenda: Mary, Don may be able to do the job; I'm not as convinced as you, but this Simpson is on target when it comes to supporting the philosophy behind the new program. And the more I think about it, the more I need that commitment to make this thing go. There's a lot at stake in making the program a success. Don's pretty hardheaded when it comes to seeing us turn this agency into what he feels is a soft-hearted bunch of social workers.

Larry: Look folks, I hate to complicate things for you, but the governor's been getting pressure to find a spot for Jim Massington.

Mary: Jim who? I've never heard of him.

Brenda: Well, I have. He worked pretty hard in the governor's last campaign, didn't he?

Mary: Oh no! I can see it coming.

Larry: Don't get excited. Just give the guy some consideration. Brenda, you know the governor went out on a limb with the legislature to give you the chance to experiment with this new program, and he may need a favor here.

Mary: I just don't like the politics in all this.

Brenda: Look Larry, I want to help, but I need someone who is committed to this program.

Mary: And I think we'd better get someone who can manage the internal operations of this agency.

Larry: Well, I think you ought to look at Massington's application. You know that's all the governor is asking.

Brenda: Thanks, Larry. I want to think about this. Mary, let's get together on this tomorrow afternoon.

Mary: Politics!

Source: Klingner and Nalbandian (1993, 164–65).

students develop managerial competencies to handle the real-world social equity tensions and resistance they are likely to encounter. These competencies allow future managers to become better equipped to structure, manage, and influence such dialogues. Taken together, schools of public administration and public affairs will better prepare students to breathe agency life into the fourth pillar of public administration and to better implement the concept of social equity in their work as public administrators.

Editors' Note: This article is reprinted from *Journal of Public Affairs Education* 13, no. 1, 59–77 (Winter 2007) with permission of the National Association of Schools of Public Affairs and Administration. Some revisions were made to make the original article consistent with the formatting of this book, and some citations and references were corrected. The quote from Shafritz and Russell (2002) has been shortened to conform to fair use standards.

Notes

The authors express appreciation to our external reviewers for their comments and suggestions, as well as to Kasey Martin, graduate student at Virginia Commonwealth University, for her research assistance. This manuscript was presented at the National Association of Schools of Public Affairs and Administration (NASPAA) Annual Conference in October 2005.

1. See National Academy of Public Administration, (2005).

References

Akram, R. 2004. *Social Equity and the American Dream. Standing Panel on Social Equity in Governance*. Washington, DC: National Academy of Public Administration.
Avolio, B.J., and G.V. Barrett. 1987. "Effects of Age Stereotyping in a Simulated Interview." *Psychology and Aging* 2, no. 1: 56–63.
DeNisi, A.S., and R.W. Griffin. 2001. *Human Resource Management*. Boston: Houghton Mifflin.
Dolan, J. 2000. "The Senior Executive Service: Gender, Attitudes, and Representative Bureaucracy." *Journal of Public Administration Research and Theory* 10, no. 3: 513–31.
———. 2002. "Representative Bureaucracy in the Federal Executive: Gender and Spending Priorities." *Journal of Public Administration Research and Theory* 12, no. 3: 3–26.
Dresser, G. 1997. *Human Resource Management*. 7th ed. Upper Saddle River, NJ: Prentice Hall.
Frederickson, H.G. 1990. "Public Administration and Social Equity." *Public Administration Review* 50, no. 5: 228–37.
———. 2005. "The State of Social Equity in American Public Administration." Unpublished manuscript.
Gooden, Susan T., and Samuel Myers Jr. 2004. "Symposium: Social Equity in Public Affairs Education." *Journal of Public Affairs Education* 10, no. 2: 91–98.
Hays, S.W., and R.C. Kearney, eds. 1995. *Public Personnel Administration: Problems and Prospects*. 3d ed. Upper Saddle River, NJ: Prentice Hall.

Hitt, E.R., and S.H. Barr 1989. "Managerial Selection Decision Models: Examination of Configural Cue Processing." *Journal of Applied Psychology* 74, no. 1: 53–61.

Jackson, S.E., and R.S. Schuler. 2002. *Managing Human Resources Through Strategic Partnerships*. Mason, OH: South-Western.

Kingsley, J.D. 1944. *Representative Bureaucracy*. Yellow Springs, OH: Antioch Press.

Klingner, D.E., and J. Nalbandian. 1993. *Public Personnel Management: Contexts and Strategies*. 3d ed. Upper Saddle River, NJ: Prentice Hall.

Kranz, H. 1976. *The Participatory Bureaucracy: Women and Minorities in a More Representative Public Service*. Lexington, MA: Lexington.

Meier, K.J., and L.G. Nigro. 1976. "Representative Bureaucracy and Policy Preferences: A Study in the Attitudes of Federal Executives." *Public Administration Review* 36, no. 4: 458–69.

National Academy of Public Administration. 2000. Standing Panel on Social Equity in Governance Issue Paper and Work Plan. Available at www.napawash.org/aa_social_equity/papers_ publications.html.

National Association of Schools of Public Affairs and Administration (NASPAA). 2005. Standards for Professional Masters Degree Programs in Public Affairs, Policy, Administration. Available at www.naspaa.org.

———. 2005. Strategic Plan. Spring.

Nigro, L.G., and F.A. Nigro. 2000. *The New Public Personnel Administration*. 5th ed. Itasca, IL: F.E. Peacock.

Office of Federal Contract Compliance. 1976. U.S. Department of Labor, Code of Federal Regulations. 41 FR 38814, September 13.

———. 2000. U.S. Department of Labor's Code of Federal Regulations. 41CFR 60–2.10 and 41CFR 60–2.17, November 13.

Office of Personnel Management (OPM). n.d. Uniform guidelines on employee selection. Available at www.uniformguidelines.com/uniformguidelines.html (accessed September 15, 2005).

Parsons, C.K., and R.C. Liden. 1984. "Interviewer Perceptions of Applicant Qualifications: A Multivariate Field Study of Demographic Characteristics and Nonverbal Cues. *Journal of Applied Psychology* 69, no. 3: 557–68.

Pingitore, R.; B.L. Dugoni; R.S. Tindale; and B. Spring. 1994. "Bias Against Overweight Job Applicants in a Simulated Employment Interview." *Journal of Applied Psychology* 79, no. 5: 909–17.

Public Administration Review. 1974. "Symposium: Social Equity and Public Administration."

Riccucci, N.M. 2002. *Managing Diversity in Public Sector Workforces*. Boulder, CO: Westview.

Riccucci, N.M., and J.R. Saidel. 1997. "The Representativeness of State-Level Bureaucratic Leaders: A Missing Piece of Representative Bureaucracy Puzzle. *Public Administration Review* 57, no. 5: 423–31.

Rosenbloom, David. 2005. "Taking Social Equity Education Seriously in MPA Education." *Journal of Public Affairs Education* 11, no. 3: 247–51.

Schmitt, N., and D. Chan. 1998. *Personnel Selection: A Theoretical Approach*. Thousand Oaks, CA: Sage.

Schuler, R.S., and V.L. Huber. 1997. *Personnel and Human Resource Management*. St. Paul, MN: West.

Shafritz, J.M., and E.W. Russell. 2002. *Introducing Public Administration*. 3d ed. Boston: Addison Wesley Longman.

Stohr-Gilmore, M.K.; M.W. Stohr-Gilmore; and N. Kistler. 1990. "Improving Selection Outcomes with the Use of Situational Interviews: Empirical Evidence from a Study of Correctional Officers for New Generation Jails." *Review of Public Personnel Administration* 10: 1–18.

Svara, J., and J. Brunet. 2004. "Filling in the Skeletal Pillar: Addressing Social Equity in Introductory Courses in Public Administration." *Journal of Public Affairs Education* 10, no. 2: 99–110.

Thompson, F.J. 1991. *Classics of Public Personnel Policy.* 2d ed. Belmont, CA: Wadsworth.

U.S. Office of Personnel Management (1997). *Hispanic Employment Initiatives.* September. http://www.opm.gov/pressrel/9point.htm (accessed May 2, 2011).

Wooldridge, B. 1998. "Protecting Equity While Reinventing Government: Strategies for Achieving a 'Fair' Distribution of the Costs and Benefits of the Public Sector." *Journal of Public Management and Social Policy* 4, no. 1: 67–80.

14

Toward a More Perfect Union:
Moving Forward with Social Equity

Norman J. Johnson and James H. Svara

In any society, the equitable treatment of all regardless of membership in particular social groups is essential to support the democratic process. This is particularly important in the United States with its history of exclusion, and its explosion now in social diversity. Although we declared our right to independence because all men are created equal, we have not treated all men or all groups equally. Our ideals draw us forward as we seek to make the union more perfect, but old issues and old infrastructure linger and new challenges arise. From its initiation in 2000, the Standing Panel on Social Equity of the National Academy of Public Administration has sought to raise the salience of social equity and provide guidance about how to achieve it.

The panel issued a Call to Action in 2005 that stated the rationale for increased commitment to advancing social equity.

> The United States faces critical issues in the fair, just, and equitable formation and implementation of public policy, distribution of public services, and management of the organizations that do the work of the public. While many public programs are delivered equitably there are also:
>
> - Fundamental class, racial, and ethnic differences in access to basic services
> - Differences in the quality of programs provided and services received
> - Systematic differences across racial and ethnic lines in the way people are treated by public officials
> - Disparities in outcomes for population groups (e.g., by race or income) as a result of differences in social conditions and individual behavior as well as differential distribution, access, and treatment
>
> Not all Americans have an equal base level of opportunity and protection. Risk is not randomly distributed.
>
> (Standing Panel on Social Equity, 2005)

The ideas presented in this book help us to understand our shortcomings and identify the possibilities for positive action by those who seek to advance the public interest and serve the people in our society.

There are four broad approaches that can be used to measure social equity: access, procedural fairness, quality, and outcomes. They are useful as indicators of inequity because each suggests different kinds of governmental response to improving equity. The measures should be understood in human as well as analytical terms.

- Access in social equity is a commitment to reduce omission and neglect, which contribute to systematic inequality in access to services. In distribution of existing services and recommendations for policy change, access in social equity seeks to promote equality in the provision of services and benefits or to direct resources to address specific needs.
- Procedural fairness in social equity is a determination to eliminate acts of commission that deprive individuals of fair and consistent treatment and to act with urgency when members of groups are systematically treated unfairly.
- Quality in social equity ensures that those who receive services and benefits are not slighted and consigned to a level of quality that does not measure up to acceptable standards.
- The outcomes emphasis in social equity rejects systematic differences in life chances across groups in society. Social equity does not accept the idea that certain groups must be limited to poorer outcomes and promotes the idea of narrowing and eliminating disparities.

These four measures of social equity can be illustrated in the case of public education. Although the battle for equal access to schools has been won, there are continuing differences in the quality of educational services and the preparation of teachers in predominantly minority schools, and greater likelihood that minority children will be suspended or expelled in the enforcement of disciplinary policies. Minority children will achieve at lower levels and fewer will graduate. Their likelihood of attending college is less while being overrepresented in the pipeline to prison.

Now in 2010, the time has come for moving forward. In our introductory discussion, we stressed that the advancement of equality as a value in American society must move in tandem with our commitment to freedom, and our concern for justice for all social groups must rest on justice for all individuals. The values reinforce each other in some respects. All persons and all groups should be equally free to pursue life, liberty, and the pursuit of happiness, and fairness should be equally available to all. Freedom cannot, however, extend to oppressing others. We live in a society with uneven distribution of resources in which some groups are advantaged over others. The standards of a humane society assure that the disadvantaged have access to the minimum resources that make it possible to compete freely and experience a decent life if they have met their personal responsibility to advance themselves and contribute to society. Social equity also requires that efforts be made to remedy the effects of group discrimination and exclusion that limit the options of individuals.

Frank Fairbanks, city manager of Phoenix, Arizona, from 1990 to 2009 and recipient of a 2005 National Public Service Award,[1] summarized the social equity responsibility of a society in this way: "Government needs to help those who need the most help to succeed in building a great city" (Standing Panel on Social Equity 2005, 11)—or state, or nation.

Specific Findings and Recommendations from the Contributors

The framework for understanding social equity and seeking legitimate ways to advance it as public administrators and members of society has been advanced by the contributors to this volume. A brief summary that focuses on findings and recommendations follows, but it is no substitute for the rich and detailed discussion in each chapter.

Context and Background

Three of the chapters offer careful examination of inequality measured by the gap between the share of income and wealth available to the rich and the majority group, on the one hand, and the poor and minorities, on the other. They help us understand the complex nature of inequality and examine options for reducing it.

The fundamental difference in the treatment of whites and blacks in American society is Payton's focus. There is a tradition of extending the protections of the Constitution to whites in American history, and there has been substantial accomplishment in achieving the ideal of equality of opportunity and promoting economic self-sufficiency and the capability to function as informed citizens in the democratic process. If there was a set of principles to promote the ideal of the self-governing, enterprising, educated white man, there is substantial evidence of a set of regressive principles designed to keep the black man from becoming a fully functioning member of the public. The cumulative effect of these principles to deny education, restrict acquisition of property and benefits from owning property, and limit political participation and influence has been to stratify the society along racial lines. There is much here that links the current situation to the period of explicit racial separation that extended into the twentieth century. The American public and also public administrators must recognize the contribution that regulation has made to perpetuating the condition of separation and the importance of modifying regulation to promote true inclusion of all groups into American society.

Investment in people is the central concern of Robles, and she defines it broadly. Minority groups have had difficulty acquiring material goods, but these groups have other cultural and social assets that can be acknowledged and valued more highly in our society. The social, cultural, and institutional resources of the Native American, African American, and Asian American communities have also made important contributions to offsetting the governmental policies that have contributed to wealth erosion. The diverse Hispanic groups are characterized by strong bonds to family and community. Undocumented people are a segment of the Hispanic population, and they currently face the risk of deportation and loss of property. Admittedly, undocumented people are in the country illegally (although they may have family members who are citizens or legal residents, and they include children who may not know any society other than the United States), but European immigrants through the first two decades of the twentieth century did not face the same restrictions on entering the United States (DeLaet 2000).[2] By today's standards, people coming without papers or permission would be illegal immigrants. Nor did these earlier immigrants encounter the same disruption of family and community that results from deportation.

In recent decades, governmental programs and court rulings have tended to expand opportunities for marginalized minority communities. If governments at all levels commit to an inclusive economic prosperity for all, it is possible to offset the unequal economic opportunities through increased educational access with linkages to employment that offers a living wage. Governments can also contribute to wealth and asset building in distressed and faltering communities through an inclusive partnering process with community-based organizations and businesses that currently operate below the radar. Examples of such informal entrepreneurship are weekend mechanics, home-based food preparers selling in public venues during seasonal religious and cultural holidays, informal elderly care, and informal child care. These activities typically limit the benefits available to those who engage in them. For example, the persistence of the "nanny problem" means that domestic workers are paid in cash and cannot access family supports such as the Earned Income Tax Credit in the federal income tax and are not contributing to Social Security. Robles recommends that governments at all levels explore ways to bring left-behind and left-out entrepreneurs into the mainstream.

Buss and Ahmed provide a look abroad and in a sense a look back at events that occurred in the United States at earlier times. In many countries of the developing world, the principle of social equity is not recognized. All of the observations made earlier about the acts of omission and commission in the United States apply to the public administrators in these countries. A social equity commitment would require that they act in ways that will promote equality and check social exclusion, including oppressive treatment of groups that have been devalued. We must recognize from our own national experience how slow progress can be in dismantling the systemic patterns of disadvantage but at the same time how insistent administrators should be in applying the fundamental administrative values of fairness and equality to all individuals and groups.

It is also important for administrators in the United States and other developed countries to recognize the need to provide encouragement and assistance to the governments and nongovernmental organizations in developing countries. The administrators involved in the operation of aid and assistance programs are directly connected to equity action, but administrators generally can contribute to the improvement of conditions in developing countries. They have opportunities for exchange and professional development activities with professional colleagues abroad, and they can meet with and share their values and practices with officials who visit from other countries. Agency-to-agency and city-to-city exchanges can be promoted. These administrators in the United States can also help to broaden the understanding of the importance of foreign aid and support for multinational organizations.

There is an array of initiatives by multinational organizations and programs by nongovernmental organizations. The Millennium Development Goals (MDG), adopted by the UN Millennium Summit in 2000, encourage developing countries to accomplish ambitious development goals by 2015. Admittedly, efforts to advance these goals make little difference in those developing countries whose governments do not heed them and ignore appeals by multinational organizations, nongovern-mental organizations, and governments to accept basic standards of social equity. The national sovereignty of resistant countries makes it difficult or impossible to enforce international standards or universal moral principles, but the efforts should continue nonetheless to create pressures for breakthroughs when sources of resistance weaken or are challenged internally.[3]

Glaeser, Resseger, and Tobio examine the factors that contribute to variation in inequality across metropolitan regions in the United States. Against a backdrop of a lesser commitment to redistribution of resources that would increase equality in the United States compared to countries in Western Europe, inequality among regions reflects the results of competition. Building on historical patterns, some regions have attracted large numbers of highly skilled people who contribute to growth. These areas also attract large numbers of less-skilled workers. The distribu-tion of inequality across urban areas also reflects a tendency to more highly reward greater concentrations of skilled workers. Thus, the conditions for greater income disparity are present; there are more highly skilled people receiving relatively higher returns than in other regions. These trends have been apparent in recent decades when immigrants have been attracted to regions that provide economic opportunity and a socially comfortable milieu. As a consequence, the degree of inequality increases.

The authors assess the consequences of trying to reduce inequalities through actions at the regional level. Local attempts at redistribution can be counterproductive because taxpayers with resources can choose to relocate. Furthermore, efforts by regions to foster "industrial policies" to advance the local economy will not necessarily benefit workers and do little to directly benefit those with low income. More efficient ap-proaches to increasing equality come through the tax system, through programs such as the Earned Income Tax Credit. Another policy choice for reducing inequality is to improve education for disadvantaged Americans. If the aim is to decrease inequality, then it is necessary to invest in the education of the less fortunate. Increasing high school graduation rates is more likely to reduce the level of inequality in society by improving human capital, which should in time lead to greater income equality. As we see in the assessment of education achievement gaps, however, school reforms are complex. Furthermore, reforms will be costly and subject to variation in methods and results across the large number of locally directed school systems. The overall approach indicates that income inequality is part of the fabric of American society that is best reduced directly through actions at the national level and best reduced indirectly and over time by investment in human capital development.

The conceptualization of social equity is advanced by Myers's examination of the economics of diversity. After progressively stronger efforts in the postwar period to desegregate and expand opportunities for minorities that had been harmed by slavery, segregation, and historic discrimination, in 1989 retrenchment and limitations on affirmative action started. During the Clinton administration and expanding after 2000, there was an emphasis on diversity rather than affirmative action, and diversity was often justified in economic terms—diversity is "good for business" or provides other broad social benefits. Myers offers careful analysis of the research literature to reveal the complexity of the claim and the risk that "diversity" may not advance the same goals as social equity. Diversity is not always beneficial especially when it stimulates ethnic conflict that impedes the work process. It is possible that diversity improves performance but that the primary beneficiaries are the members of the majority group. The range of perspectives and options majority group members consider may be expanded by incorporating the views of others, but the rewards may not be shared fairly. Finally, if the rationale for diversity is too closely linked to advances in efficiency, is it subject to rejection if the gains are not forthcoming?

Diversity training designed to expand acceptance and appreciation of difference can help to reduce the disruptive effects of increased mixing of people with different backgrounds and perspectives. Consequently, training increases the likelihood that diversity pays off in better results. Increasing the representativeness of the staff who work in government (and nonprofits) is positive in two respects: it reflects both the expanding availability of jobs for all persons and it improves the ability of the staff persons who serve the public to relate to the public competently and empathetically (Rice 2005). Thus, diversity programs are likely to be a positive development, and diversity can promote the democratic process. It is important, however, to affirm that elimination of discrimination and expansion of opportunity are important for social equity reasons regardless of the economic consequences. Attention should be given to assessing whether the advantages in diversity are simply reinforcing the preexisting distribution of resources.

Measuring Social Equity

Health care remains segmented by race, ethnicity, and class in access, quality, procedural fairness, and outcomes. Former Surgeon General David Satcher and his colleagues report that there were more than 83,000 excess deaths among African Americans on an annual basis, and there are also disparities in health outcomes among Hispanics and Native Americans as well. There are policy questions that must be resolved to address disparities, but there are also improvements that can come from the way that existing health programs are administered. These include patient or provider education, greater integration of health care, cultural modification, the establishing of performance standards, and the addressing of disparities as a civil rights compliance issue. A Medicare study concludes that most of the recommended improvements could be implemented with current statutory authority, although most would require additional Medicare spending. Thus, policy change to increase access is important, but there are other factors that produce differences in how the health-care system operates that (a) could be addressed without a change in policy or (b) must be changed even though greater access to health-insurance coverage will be provided under the Affordable Care Act of 2010. Public administrators and social equity policy advocates have developed a large number of promising approaches to measuring the problem. The combined impact of these efforts along with outreach and education may start to reduce the current wide disparities in health outcomes.

Hug recommends a number of actions to improve the measurement of health equity. The gaps in procedural equity call for new procedures and civil rights approaches to addressing disparities. As in the other initiative areas, effective initiatives addressing procedural equity begin with data gathering. Federal and state health-care financing programs could use their buying power to require the collection of the data needed to identify disparities, enforce standards of cultural competence, and demand that providers monitor and reduce disparities in the provision of care. Congress could also establish a section on health care in the Department of Justice Office of Civil Rights to match existing sections that deal with discrimination in housing, employment, and education. The scope of inquiry should include racial and ethnic disparities in the *quality* of clinical treatment.

In the area of law enforcement and criminal justice, reducing racial bias in police stops and searches can be supported by collecting data on the race or ethnicity of individuals for all traffic stops, even those that do not result in formal police action, such as citation or arrest. As Brunet recommends, these data should be monitored continuously by police managers to detect disparities in the treatment of citizens. Cultural competency and diversity training are also suggested as well as the hiring of more minority officers. Another strategy is to provide citizens with information on how to file a complaint against an officer suspected of racial profiling. Several steps may be taken to reduce disparities resulting from immigration enforcement. A Government Accountability Office report in 2009 suggests a return to a focus on violent criminals and improved data monitoring. Whereas some departments have engaged in sweeps to apprehend undocumented people on suspicion of minor infractions, many departments have engaged in outreach efforts (radio spots, public meetings) to allay immigrant fears about ethnic targeting and harassment.

There are other ways to use existing data systems and measures to advance social equity values. Violations of procedural equity—using excessive force, not investigating citizen complaints, and engaging in racial profiling—may be tracked using data collected by the Bureau of Justice Statistics (BJS) or through a review of local police records. Consistency in police response to calls and fairness in resource allocation are examples of distributional equity. Police records may show that police response is slower in some neighborhoods or that fewer officers are assigned to an area that has a greater need for police services. Outcome equity can be ascertained through citizen surveys with questions such as "have you been victimized?" or "are you fearful of crime in your neighborhood?" To detect possible quality differences in police services, citizens may be asked about their level of satisfaction with the police. Other areas for monitoring are diversity in criminal justice organizations, especially at the executive officer level, increased use of drug testing when the workforce is diverse, adverse disciplinary actions for women at a rate higher than their male counterparts, and disparities in other personnel issues including employee turnover, promotions, and grievances. Finally, public administrators should realize there may be factors that create disparities that are outside their control. Laws that require stiffer penalties for certain types of drug possession may be applied in a fair manner, but result in the disproportionate incarceration of racial minorities.

Disparities in educational accomplishment continue to be a vexing problem. Like other researchers, Stiefel, Schwartz, and Ellen find significant disparities between the test scores of white and black students and those of white and Hispanic students in New York City's elementary and middle schools. These test score gaps are explained in large part by racial and ethnic differences in poverty rates and, for the Hispanic–white gap, differences in English proficiency. Part of the difference can be attributed to differences in the quality of schools they attend—an example of process inequity. Black and Hispanic students attend schools with significantly less-experienced and less-qualified teachers as compared to the schools attended by their white and Asian counterparts, although they have a somewhat higher number of teachers for the students served. There is some sorting at the classroom level as well. An even more important determinant, however, of the race gap in any year is the performance of students in prior years, which is lower for black and Hispanic students. Put simply, much of the performance gap "this year" is explained by the performance gap "last year," a factor beyond the influence of this year's schools and teachers.

Once prior-year test scores are taken into account, controlling for effects associated with the school or the classroom does little to explain racial test score gaps. Race/ethnicity and gender, however, are still important. Black and Hispanic students perform less well than their white and Asian peers, and boys perform less well than girls, even after controlling for their performance on tests in the prior year. In some schools, racial gaps are minimized or even reversed. More teachers with appropriate licenses and advanced degrees and more experience are related to higher test scores for some minority students at some points in their schooling. More teachers per pupil ratios do not seem to improve the performance of minority children, but in New York City the least-skilled teachers disproportionately teach in the schools with higher percentages of nonwhite students and more teachers per student. There are no simple school remedies without possible negative effects. Closing poorly performing schools would help but increasing the size of other schools would not because smaller schools are linked to better performance for minority students. Other reforms in curricula, school organization, and teacher expectations may be beneficial, but strategies that go beyond the standard educational programs and the scope of schools themselves may also be needed.

Murray and Hertko examine how state and local governments contribute to creating or solving environmental problems for minorities or politically powerless groups. Officials at these levels can make creative and aggressive use of existing legal authority to resolve the environmental and public health concerns of community residents. They can take steps to eliminate existing nonconforming uses that present public health and environmental hazards by adopting more flexible zoning techniques. These include conditional uses that impose restrictions on certain actions that may affect environmental justice issues, establishing overlay zones that impose additional requirements to provide for additional environmental protection, and creating buffer zones in transitional areas between incompatible land uses, especially for industrial development adjacent to residential areas. Local governments can train their staff in how to conduct effective community outreach and how to analyze the environmental justice impacts of proposed land use plans and zoning ordinances.

Their inaction, on the other hand, permits inequities to persist. In many communities, land decisions in the past tended to concentrate undesirable land uses in certain areas, often near neighborhoods that have significant minority or low-income populations. The lack of training to help local officials understand how land use decisions relate to environmental justice, and the steps they can take to prevent, reduce, or eliminate risks to neighborhoods facing disparate impacts, is a major stumbling block to achieving environmental justice. They must face up to a "legacy problem." Although there are measures to prevent future problems, some cities seem to lack the authority or will to correct the accumulated legacy problems.

Leadership, Outreach, and Organizational Development

According to Norman-Major and Wooldridge, the economic case for investments to advance social equity is based on the advantages of taking action early to solve a problem when it is small rather than waiting for intervention later when the costs are much higher. The logic applies to early childhood education for children, efforts to provide job skills and living wage to reduce criminal behavior leading to incarceration, and preventive health programs. The emphasis is on social return on investment (SROI), which calculates the differences between early and late costs. Furthermore, this approach can be used to "reframe" social equity issues. Although social equity action has traditionally been justified with normative arguments grounded in social justice, many advocates of policy that promote social equity are using arguments that stress the economic investment and return achieved through equity programming. This reframing of the argument is changing the face of debates concerning programs and policies that address equity issues, building a new audience of support from more fiscally and socially conservative citizens and decision makers who may in the past have been unmoved by moral arguments but are willing to consider the benefits of cost savings. Illustrative in this regard is a comparative analysis that looks at the cost of the pipeline to prison in contrast to the pipeline to college.

The change in rationale may also increase the likelihood that business leaders will step up as policy entrepreneurs who can in turn credibly reframe the debate in terms of how the problem is defined and what alternatives are considered. The presence of business supporters does not guarantee that major investments will be approved. It is also possible that stressing economic arguments could devalue the moral and ethical grounds for social equity action. Thus, reframing the debate should not replace valuing social equity for its own sake as a principle that should be pursued. It can be used to make a double argument that potentially brings new partners to the policy arena. It may be in our complex, conflicted society that inattention to these arguments dooms any social equity proposal to failure. The slow movement toward a more perfect union has always combined aspects of practicality and morality. This process of building support continues to be a challenge in a nuanced, complex society like the one America has become.

Looking inside public organizations, public agencies should also be committed to uncovering practices that deny social equity. Gooden examines an agency that was challenged by a legal complaint by the Office of Civil Rights. Instead of resisting, the organization used the complaint as an opportunity to examine how it operates and what racial inconsistencies might be present in its treatment of clients in the Wisconsin Division of Workforce Solutions, which handled the welfare to work program. Agencies may wish to avoid an uncomfortable investigation or public embarrassment or legal action by exposing internal agency shortcomings. In this case, however, senior administrators in the Department of Workforce Development undertook an investigation to determine whether there were shortcomings in providing administrative justice, fairness, and equity.

The study ensured that participants could fully and freely participate in assessment by using a group processing software system. Ultimately, the Steering Committee agreed to nineteen recommendations in the areas of case management and supervisor training, changes in policy statute, changes in implementation practices, increased monitoring of agency behavior, and analysis. The long study contributed to its credibility and acceptance of the outcomes. This experience demonstrates that agencies must be willing to look for racial disparities. They need not wait for legal complaints. In order to advance good government and social equity, agencies should routinely assess whether the benefits and services they provide show any evidence of racial disparities and, if so, what factors may be contributing to this outcome.

Increasing social equity within public organizations requires new approaches to personnel management. Gooden and Wooldridge suggest ways for administrators involved in human resources activities and for students in our graduate programs in public administration to become aware of social equity issues, more competent in dealing with them, and more committed to advancing social equity in personnel matters. This entails not only following the law and procedure that set forth equity standards but also better handling the "informal HR dialogues" that pertain to the social equity dimension of personnel analysis, recruitment, and selection. As with ethical behavior generally (Rest et al. 1999, 100–101), the crucial first step to making a sound decision is to recognize that an equity issue is at stake in the informal exchanges among staff that typically do not explicitly suggest excluding or denying opportunities to minorities. Public administrators need to see the opportunity to recruit, promote, or develop currently underrepresented populations when turnover, growth, and the need for new competencies recreate vacancies. If social equity is really a priority, staff and students should acquire knowledge and skills to know how to advance it in ways that are consistent with law and principle and to avoid practices that have the effect of reducing inclusiveness and equal opportunity. Our universities (and training divisions in public organizations) have an important responsibility to educate public administrators in fair and equitable personnel practices and to make them aware of the hidden pitfalls that may obstruct progress and the opportunities that may not be obvious to promote inclusion.

Steps to Take

Those in the public administration community must take a wide range of steps to help the executive and legislative branches of government reduce or eliminate the disparities in American society. While public administrators cannot erase all poverty or make every citizen color-blind, they can seek to understand why the disparities exist and how public programs can be improved and managed better to overcome them. Some see the involvement of public administrators as agents of social change as a departure from the established logic of administrative practice and call for public administrators to be "transformative" (King and Zanetti 2005) and engage in small acts of "radicalness" (Box 2008) in their dealings with elected officials, staff, and the public. Others see the involvement of administrators in shaping policy and sound practice as long-established elements of the practice of public administration (Svara 2001). In either case, the scope and the consistency of the commitment to advance social equity can be expanded in a variety of ways. The seven steps proposed here can be taken by "public administrators" defined in a broadly inclusive way to refer to all those who contribute to governing society.

First, as leaders and advisers on policy, public administrators can speak out, particularly in the areas of their expertise.[4] This does not necessarily mean shouting publicly about unfair policy, although there may be times when that is called for. But it does mean "speaking truth to power" in the corridors of policymaking, and clearly identifying the aspects of social equity problems that are attributable to policy commissions or omissions. The responsibility goes beyond the formal policy process. Shafritz and Russell (2002, 250) assert that public administrators need to provide "moral leadership" to encourage people generally "to do the right, decent, and honorable thing." Crosby and Bryson (2005, 158) identify the importance of entrepreneurs who are able to "catalyze systemic change." Viewed in this way, the entrepreneurs can come from many places and may be visible or work behind the scenes. Policy entrepreneurs from the business sector can help to reframe social equity choices as investments, as noted previously, and social entrepreneurs can harness the resources of companies or nonprofits to directly intervene in solving a social problem. Governmental administrators can be the advocates and entrepreneurs, but they will often be leading from behind, supporting the out-front leaders. A convener brings together individuals and organizations that can potentially be enlisted in a change effort, but the official who identifies and then enlists the convener makes a critical contribution that may not be widely perceived. The British Society of Local Authority Chief Executives (SOLACE 2005) identifies the local government top administrator as the "chief strategic officer" who organizes people and other resources to achieve key goals. Public administrators need to play the same role in promoting social equity strategies weaving together the contributions of a wide range of other leaders.

In formulating new policy, public administrators should promote equal distribution, compensatory redistribution, and efforts to correct past discrimination, depending on the nature of the problem being addressed. For some services, simple equality is the relevant standard to produce fairness; for example, there needs to be the same level of solid waste collection in all parts of a city and the same water pressure and water quality. For other services, however, equality of services does not lead to the same outcomes because of the differences in starting points. In these cases, equity requires higher service levels for low income groups and disadvantaged minorities in order to redress disparities. For example, in the seemingly straightforward case of solid waste collection, there are income differences in the ability of a household to compact and securely store debris. Once-a-week garbage pickup may work adequately in higher income areas but lead to unacceptable outcomes in poor communities in densely populated areas.[5]

Public officials should avoid creating barriers to access, such as service fees for essential services, which impose a disproportionate cost for those with fewer resources. For example, when towns charge for access to recreational programs without providing relief such as a sliding scale based on income, children and families that most need the services may be excluded.

In developing policy proposals that entail redistribution, public administrators should take into account the obligation to be accountable to the rule of law, respect individual rights, and make the best use of scarce resources (Rosenbloom 2005).

Second, within the range of their discretion, public administrators should work diligently to mitigate the unfair consequences of policy. For existing policies and programs, distribution and access should match the intended purpose. Imaginative and targeted outreach that makes affirmative efforts to reach underserved or high-need groups is imperative. Whether all are to receive a service or benefit or distribution is limited to those who meet eligibility criteria, it should be made available to all who qualify with appropriate outreach efforts that will reach diverse audiences. Since the late 1990s, the federal Food Stamp Program has been transformed from a public assistance program whose recipients were stigmatized and forced to overcome administrative restrictions to qualify into a safety net program for all people who have difficulty obtaining adequate food. After initial efforts during the Clinton administration to reframe the program as one that helps the working poor, the Bush administration with bipartisan support "led a campaign to erase the program's stigma, calling food stamps 'nutritional aid' instead of welfare and made it easier to apply" (DeParle and Gebeloff 2009, 1). This emphasis has been continued by the Obama administration, which sees the program as an important source of assistance during the economic crisis. There is a commitment to enroll more of the one-third of eligible people who are not currently covered, and many states have undertaken aggressive outreach campaigns to expand coverage (ibid., 25).

Public administrators should be committed to consistency in the quality of services and benefits delivered to all groups of people and strive to ensure that prevailing standards of acceptable practice are met for all groups. They cannot be satisfied to have dilapidated classrooms and a poor library in schools in one part of town while other schools in the same jurisdiction are in pristine condition. Effective administrators allocate maintenance resources based on need and pursue creative approaches to securing more books for schools with less community support.

Third, public administrators have the authority and obligation to promote process equity—equal access and opportunity, equal treatment and protection, and due process. They need to work constantly and consistently to achieve it in every agency at all levels of government. Any improper deviations in treatment should be corrected, and the factors that contribute to this behavior should be eliminated. The deviations may be commissions, as in the disproportionate use of suspensions to remove black males from schools, or omissions, as in the failure to protect women who are victims of domestic violence.

Fourth, public administrators can give to issues of fairness the same creativity and attention they give to measuring performance and improving productivity. Analytical approaches include social equity impact analysis of policy proposals, impact analysis of performance, and an equity inventory for agencies or local governments. An examination of a variety of performance management systems—including those of two federal agencies, two states, two cities, and two community-based quality-of-life report card initiatives—found that there is generally little attention to social equity in the results-oriented measurement systems of these entities (Jennings 2005a). A broader review of all federal agencies reporting under the Government Performance and Results Act found quite limited attention to social equity (Jennings 2005b).

Equity considerations are relevant to a wide range of administrative and management analyses. Attention to equity can be added to assessment of programs that may be contracted out and monitoring service delivery. For example, this factor is missing from current federal A-76 standards (OMB 2003; Radin 2005). Given the incentives that contractors have to cut costs, it is likely that clients with the fewest resources are more vulnerable to lapses in service. Policy research and program evaluation should examine specific groups rather than relying on aggregate data. Strategic planning should address differences among population groups. The development of new programs or major changes in existing programs could be accompanied by social equity impact analysis. In this approach, comparable to environmental impact statements, a government agency would assess and share with the public an assessment of a program or policy's impact on issues of income and resource inequality (Rosenbaum 2002).

Fifth, public administrators need to measure social equity and track progress in alleviating disparities. The concept that "what gets measured gets done" can be used effectively to assess progress toward goals and objectives. It can also be seen as simply counting data that do not relate to mission or goals, or as an added burden for managers. It is essential for public managers not only to develop tools to track progress but also to educate policymakers and the public as to why they are important and how the data collected can make decisions more fair to all. Given the reality that measurement shapes action, the failure of public agencies to measure equity in their processes, outputs, and outcomes means that they are less likely to pursue or produce equity through their actions.

Sixth, public administrators must take proactive and creative action to ensure that all people, regardless of resources or individual characteristics, have a place at the table when needs are identified, policy options discussed, and programs and services assessed (Box 1998). It is easy to ignore or assign a lower priority to the poor conditions of streets in a lower-income neighborhood when no citizens who live in the area with poor streets are at the hearing on the city's public works budget. It may not be customary to post signs about the meeting in local day-care centers or churches, but perhaps that is the best way to reach everyone affected by the public works budget. Proactive steps should be taken to ensure that representatives of all people impacted by programs are involved. The test is not who is informed or invited but who actually comes, and the outreach methods should be adapted until they succeed in getting effective participation from all parts of the community.

Finally, public administrators must build partnerships with other organizations and the community to address equity issues. Linkages can be intergovernmental as well as cross-sectoral. In urban regions, it is critical for cities, counties, school systems, and special districts to work together rather than attempt to address equity problems as single jurisdictions. Although regions cannot viably pursue redistribution programs on their own without threatening their competitive position, governments within regions can cooperate in providing low-income housing opportunities across the region, improving transportation, better linking jobs and the areas where low-income residents live, and sharing resources for educational improvement across all systems (Dreirer, Mollenkopf, and Swanstrom 2001; Rusk 1995).

Governmental resources alone are often not sufficient to address the full extent of need (Rusk 1999). Furthermore, private and nonprofit organizations and other governmental units can help achieve access, support citizen empowerment, and provide complementary services and assistance. For example, Our Healthy Community Partnership in Omaha brings together more than thirty state and local governmental, university, nonprofit, business, and community organizations to improve the health of Douglas and Sarpy counties through a community-driven process. The partnership works with neighborhoods to identify community assets, prioritize the issues, and develop solutions that rely on the assets of the community.

A guide to equity analysis at the agency and jurisdictional level is presented in Appendix 14.1 on pages 287–288. It provides steps to follow in examining all four measures of social equity. For example, school systems now assess children before they reach school age so that if there are impairments to learning the child receives help early, when, for example, speech therapy can have the most impact. But, do young children in poor or crime-ridden areas receive the same level of assessment—an equity access issue? Do they receive services that are performed as well as in other areas—an equity quality issue? If problems are detected, do they get the same referrals for therapy as children in other parts of the school system—a procedural equity issue? Finally, are their learning impairments alleviated at the same rates—an equity impact issue?

Whenever a "no" is encountered, administrators must take steps to correct the shortcoming through the efforts of their own staff and in partnerships developed with other organizations. Throughout the process, parents should be informed and involved in order to be empowered to effectively monitor actions taken and offer appropriate input. Assessments of this kind should be systematically conducted at the program level, the agency level, and the jurisdictional level to develop a social equity agenda. In her chapter, Gooden illustrates how an agency can identify discrepancies in treatment of clients for job training and then demonstrate a serious commitment to understanding why they are occurring and how they can be eliminated. The results of that internal study have implications for work in other spheres such as sentencing in the courts and racial profiling in police agencies. Such assessments of disparities by race or other characteristics promote social equity and good government, both of which are required to continue building a more perfect union in our complex, nuanced twenty-first-century society. Public administrators must conduct self-analysis on a continuing basis in order to catch problems early.

Going Further: New Forms of Partnership with the Public

Public administrators must act, and they must also involve others and include those who suffer inequities in the fight to advance social equity. George Frederickson offers this reminder:

> Like it or not, senior public administrators and those who study public administration are part of the elite, the privileged. In much of our literature and ideology there is a distinct patronizing tone to social equity. A commitment to social

equity obliges us to see after the interests of those who are denied opportunities or are disadvantaged regardless of their competence. At the intermediate and upper levels of public administration we tend to avoid the uncomfortable issue of competence, although street-level workers have no illusions about competence. I am partial to the blunt words of Lawrence M. Mead on this subject: "To recover democracy, government must assume greater competence in lower-income Americans than the elite finds comfortable. We would rather lay the burden of change on ourselves than on the less fortunate. We believe in our own abilities; we are less sure about theirs. But, unless some minimal capacities are expected of the less privileged, change becomes unimaginable, and a caste society will emerge" (Mead 2004, 674). . . . In much of social equity there is democratic rhetoric but aristocratic assumptions. We search still for versions of social equity that are truly from the bottom-up. (Frederickson 2010, 82–83)

The choice of methods to involve citizens must be matched with the ends to be accomplished (Roberts 2004; Thomas 2008). A bottom-up approach is needed when the success of social equity actions depends on the active engagement and commitment of the people who seek to improve their lives and overcome the problems they face. For example, to improve the educational accomplishment of low-income minority children, several actions by government are needed—particularly early childhood health and educational development programs to promote "better beginnings." As we noted earlier, Stiefel, Schwartz, and Ellen report that once children get into school the most important predictor of performance is how they performed the previous year. Starting behind creates a deficit that is hard to overcome. Other school improvements can be made as well. The critical additional needed component, however, is the engagement of a parent or parents in the intellectual development of children starting when they are infants. The Harlem Children's Zone, with its baby college, addresses the oft-noted parent engagement issue. Talking to them, reading to them, and expanding the store of words and images on which they can draw when they go to school is critically important. It is not just the parent, grandparent, uncle, or sibling who provides this enrichment, it is the community—the "village"—that supports the intellectual growth of each child.

The American Dream Academy conducted by the Center for Community Development and Civil Rights at Arizona State University has succeeded in dramatically expanding the involvement of parents in the schooling process and improving educational achievement.[6] The organizers reach out aggressively to inform parents about the program and to get them to attend orientation sessions. Each parent provides a description of his/her child and writes the child's name on a board at the front of the room. The session leader talks about the statistical likelihood of failure and dropping out if kids do not have the support of their family, and randomly crosses out the names of the children reflecting the proportion likely to fail. Parents immediately get the message and want to know what they can do to keep this from happening. Attitudes toward education and its importance begin early in a child's life. When parents instill the value of education in themselves, they also instill it in their children. The program has "graduated" more than 7,000 parents of students attending forty-one different schools, and indirectly impacted more than 24,000 youth of Title I schools throughout the greater Phoenix region since the program began three years ago.

The improvements in the health-care-delivery system must be supported by improved health practices by each person. Preventive care is an example of the early investment that has a favorable SROI, and it should be expanded. In addition, healthy practices with respect to diet, smoking, exercise, and so on, are just as important as the foundation for health. Other examples could be offered in crime prevention and environmental protection.

Taken together, it is important to advance self-determination and make it available to all people. All should equally have the ability to exercise the freedom to choose based on cognition—the combination of knowing, awareness, and judgment—and access to the essential resources. The agency approach discussed by Buss and Ahmed reflects the same orientation. The distinction is between socially excluded groups viewed as beneficiaries of the development process whose well-being it enhances—the welfare approach—and socially excluded groups viewed as agents of development, as movers and shapers of change that benefits themselves, others, and society as a whole as well—the agency approach (Hamadeh-Banerjee 2000, 7). For agency or self-determination to work, the most effective strategy involves facilitating the participation of those who were once treated as subjects or excluded from participation in responsible positions to help make plans and contribute to their own development.

The end result is not just more resources or services but increased human dignity. Dignity includes both having respected social standing and a personal sense of pride, voice, and contribution. Dignity links social equity by government with individual personal responsibility. It includes the attributes of both freedom—ability to make any choice—and equality—being treated the same as others. Public administrators should look for ways to advance dignity in their interaction with all citizens.

The Meaning of Social Equity

We conclude with a revised definition of social equity that builds on the version of the National Academy of Public Administration (NAPA) Social Equity Panel. It refers explicitly to the obligation to act that the term has always implied. Social equity is a commitment to attack disparity and advance equality for people in groups that have been (or in the future might be) subject to treatment that is inferior, prejudicial, or hostile. The definition incorporates dimensions of measurement. Beyond the actions that government can take for people to improve their conditions, the definition also refers to the responsibility of people involved in governance to enable all people to act for themselves. We offer the definition as a starting point for a new stage of dialogue and debate among those interested in advancing social equity.

> Social equity is the active commitment to fairness, justice, and equality in the formulation of public policy, distribution of public services, implementation of public policy, and management of all institutions serving the public directly or by contract. Public administrators, including all persons involved in public governance, should seek to prevent and reduce inequality, unfairness, and injustice based on significant social characteristics and to promote greater equality in access to services, procedural fairness, quality of services, and social outcomes. Public administrators should empower the participation of all persons in the political process and support the exercise of constructive personal choice.

The practices that support equity, for example, managing with fairness, should be reflected in the behavior of public administrators. This commitment is reflected in the original definition of social equity developed by the NAPA Social Equity Panel. Similarly, Shafritz and Russell (2005, 465) in their definition simply refer to "fairness in the delivery of public services" and "the principle that each citizen has a right to be given equal treatment."

Social equity as a value demands more in three respects. First, treating all *individuals*—pleasant and unpleasant, well-informed and confused, encountered early in the day or at the end of a shift—the same is an essential requirement for public administrators, but there must be explicit recognition that *group characteristics* are important to understanding how individuals fare in this society. Second, the tradition of social equity has stressed correcting shortcomings and advancing equality as well. It should also include explicit attention to expanding participation and self-determination. Third, there is emerging recognition, as Buss and Ahmed observe, that all persons deserve the "equality of voice" reflected in the ability "to influence and contribute to the political discourse and the development process" (International Monetary Fund 2007, 106). Public administrators need to support meaningful involvement by all persons in the governance process. This renewed commitment to political engagement is accompanied by emphasis on encouraging individual responsibility in personal life.

The targets of action and methods of practice evolve as progress is made. At one time, disseminating information to all persons or creating programs that address social needs would have been viewed as positive steps. Now there is recognition that the same words do not mean the same thing to all persons, and the impact of the same program differs depending on how well the delivery of the program matches the characteristics of the recipient. The attention to "cultural competence" opens up new meanings of fairness, justice, and equality. Furthermore, the concern for achieving greater equality in the impacts of programs and in the social outcomes that programs are intended to affect indicates a deepening and broadening of the commitment to social equity. The actors potentially involved in promoting social equity are also broadened beyond government to include nonprofits, businesses, and a variety of other organizations that contribute to governance. Thus, the relevant question is no longer simply "what do I do or what does my agency do?" It becomes "what do I do to engage other organizations in the promotion of social equity?"

The definition ends where personal initiative begins and links public administrators to members of society. Personal initiative has always been important. At all times in all conditions some individuals heroically overcame the forces that oppressed others. America has progressed to the point that engagement and self-renewal are widely required to achieve additional progress. For more than two centuries there was active exclusion and for another century systematic discrimination that held most members of marginalized groups in check and severely limited the possibility of individual advancement. Promoting social equity required removing barriers or ending oppression and is still the initial challenge in many countries of the world. Starting a half century ago, the opportunities expanded, but serious obstacles remained. Government policy, and more slowly the views of the favored majority, supported individual advancement, but many could rightfully claim that resistance restricted their options and resources were too limited to overcome accumulated deficits. Social equity required the protection of rights, affirmative efforts to expand opportunity, and the creation of a wide range of social support programs targeted to those in need. The programs that were developed lacked the integration and comprehensiveness of a "system" observed in European countries, but the United States of 2010 has a collection of resources to support the welfare of the poor and minorities that was unimaginable fifty years ago. The effort to move further in perfecting the union continues, but the challenges of each new stage must be confronted to open the way to the next.

Programs and services need to be improved in design, operation, and support, but at the same time greater action by individuals is needed as well to overcome adversity and strengthen capacity. The current and continuing challenge is to increase the mutual support of organized and individual action. Early childhood education must be reinforced by involvement of parents and relatives in encouraging learning. Educational support for students from low-income families must be matched by the efforts of students and support of the family and community. Health care needs to be enhanced by better diet and healthier habits. Ron Haskins (2009) explains the need for personal responsibility in this way:

> To begin with, society—from parents and teachers to celebrities and political figures—should send a clear and consistent message of personal responsibility to children. They should herald the "success sequence": finish schooling, get a job, get married, have babies. Census data show that if all Americans finished high school, worked full time at whatever job they then qualified for with their education, and married at the same rate as Americans had married in 1970, the poverty rate would be cut by around 70%—without additional government spending. No welfare program, however amply funded, could ever hope for anything approaching such success. (48)

Janita Patrick, a fifteen-year-old African American from Cincinnati, put it this way in a letter she wrote to Black Entertainment Television that circulated widely on the Internet.

I'm used to seeing the sagging pants, tattoos, lack of emphasis on reading and respecting women that makes up your videos. People in my class live this out every day, while teachers tell us that we're acting just like the people in your shows. . . . Guess who watches your network the most? Not those who are intelligent enough to discern foolishness from substance, but those who are barely teenagers, impressionable and believing. It's awfully cruel to plant seeds of ignorance in fertile minds. (Patrick 2009)

Her letter indicates that an alternate message is getting through, but it needs to be strengthened. The same could be said of the need for boys generally to be encouraged to pursue education and socially constructive activities in order to offset the growing gender gap in academic achievement and commitment.

Public administrators need to be committed to the basic social equity measures of access, fairness, and quality, and seek new ways to achieve them. Stated simply, public administrators need to treat all fairly and equally to prevent acts of commission and consider special needs to reduce instances of omission. They also need to consider the new strategies that will be needed to reduce disparate conditions and promote greater equality in outcomes.

There is a wide range of social equity imperatives for public administrators to consider. Here is an initial list expressed in a way intended to provoke action: Social equity is

- the relentless systematic instigation of inclusion and denigration of exclusion;
- the intentional and unyielding commitment to identify those eligible to receive targeted services and deliver those services in a culturally appropriate manner;
- the uncompromising adherence to equal treatment and fair process even when one's own agency is inconvenienced;
- the intentional and unbending commitment to quality of services, programs, and facilities for groups that lack the political clout to demand quality;
- the intentional and clear-eyed examination of impacts of programs and disparate outcomes and unflinching statements about what is needed and what is not working;
- the fearless formation of new relationships with other organizations and with members of the society to pursue social equity together.

In an era made new by the country's acceptance of a president from a group that was formerly at the bottom of society, there is an opportunity to expand the commitment and rethink the approaches to advancing social equity that combine organized and individual action. Bold efforts should be made to seize the promise of the opening words of the Constitution. It is "we the people" drawing on the talent and imagination of public officials but not dependent on their leadership alone that must take the significant next steps toward perfecting the union. Each generation must make its contribution. Advancing from where we are depends on the full involvement of the American public both contributing to sound collective choices and as taking actions as individuals to make their lives better.

Making progress and even holding ground in social equity is a constant challenge. Natural or economic catastrophes can produce setbacks that fall disproportionately on minorities and those already economically disadvantaged. Lacking comprehensive social, housing, or medical safety nets, those who lose jobs or cannot find jobs in the economic downturn face personal and family disaster. New technologies can create new divides. The global economy produces economic disruptions that fall more heavily on low-skill workers.

Although "equity" is a challenging goal in itself in a changing society and economy, it is the "social" that never rests. At the same time as progress is being made on some fronts, social equity is being rearranged and reversed on others. Longstanding divisions and disadvantages persist but take new forms with changing social, economic, and political conditions. For example, a larger proportion of young black men are in a pipeline to prison than in a pipeline to college, and changing that pattern will require an alteration of attitudes and practices in a wide range of governmental and social institutions. There is progress in expanding gender equity, but at the same time we become more aware of the mistreatment of women in terms of pay discrimination in employment and physical abuse that was long ignored. New lines of division emerge with the influx of immigrants, and changing policies and attitudes alter the salience of legal status. New sources of injustice enter the public consciousness as different gender orientations have come out of the closet and now are demanding equal recognition in law and policy. These continuous changes in social characteristics and dynamics produce imbalances in the wheel of social equity.

Failure to recognize change and make adjustments is a dangerous flaw that has the potential to undermine the enterprise that has created a great, though unfinished, constitutional democracy. Disparities of income, wealth, and access to opportunity and due process undermine the ideal of equal citizenship and government by the people. What is clear in this pursuit of the vision of a more perfect union is the requirement to continuously rebalance and recalibrate this wheel called social equity.

Some argue that the American society is post-racial. There is an abundance of evidence, however, that suggests that we as a nation are nowhere near this hoped-for aspiration. We are delusional to believe that racial differences no longer exist, that race no longer matters, or that prejudice has been eradicated. It should be noted that the society is neither post-gender nor post-gender orientation. American society has always been relatively diverse compared to most countries. The question has been whether the new group or the "other" would be ignored, left out, or even exploited for the benefit of the majority, on the one hand, or given a full role to contribute to expanded vibrancy and innovation in the larger society, on the other. The inclusion of groups in the past and expanded acceptance of other groups today does not offset the pain for people who are still excluded or denigrated because of their group identity. The group basis for differences in access, treatment, quality, and results is powerful and pervasive in American society and continuously takes on new forms. Public administrators must be attentive to new expressions of the social inequity challenge and creative in combating these inequalities.

Deciding whether and how to resolve social and economic disparities is influenced by the conflicting values of freedom and equality and our orientation to the political process. For example, in the debate over health-care reform, the equality principle argues for affordable coverage for all persons. Even with one party in control of the White House and Congress, however, it was extremely difficult to cobble together an acceptable approach. Some objected to altering a system that had given many the freedom to choose how (and whether) they will acquire their health care. In our individualistic political culture, reducing disparities may provoke the response that individuals are responsible for their own welfare. Furthermore, many individuals and groups are unlikely to be able to get beyond feeling that something is being taken away from me/us, and they organize to resist change. The attitude commonly heard in European countries that taxes are the price of a decent society is likely to be countered in the United States by many who argue that taxes take away the people's money. The opposing views reflect ideological differences and emphasis on self versus shared interests. The debate, however, has implications for social equity and can disturb the fragile balance in the wheel.

Public administrators are not on one side of the ideological debate in their official actions (despite their personal political preferences), but they operate within the context shaped by this debate and the complex intergroup dynamics that characterize American society. They are obligated by public administration values to advance social equity, and they do so by identifying problems and recommending policies and by using the policies and programs that are available to correct disparities and advance equality. They also promote social equity by their principled and intentional adherence to procedural fairness and by the way they manage the resources of their organizations. This work is not the final word in this continuing effort to assure justice for all, but hopefully it is a primer that clarifies the case for social equity and provides new methods that can be used to achieve it. Most important, it calls for us to be ever mindful of our vision and aspiration to build a more perfect union. In the twenty-first century, it will take new approaches and a renewed commitment to create one nation with liberty, equality, and justice for all.

Appendix 14.1. Conducting a Government Equity Inventory

Equity Inventory at the Departmental Level

1. What is the purpose of the department, what services does it provide, and whom does it serve? Identify any equity issues that have arisen recently. Meaningful citizen input should be included in the assessment process. What are the equity areas that are likely to be relevant to the department and its programs?
   - procedural equity (see definitions below.)
   - access and distributional equity
   - quality and process equity
   - equal outcomes

2. Assess agency *procedures* to identify any equity issues.
   - How well does the agency meet the procedural fairness standard in its current operations?
   - What changes are needed to improve procedural fairness?

3. Assess the nature and *distribution* of benefits and services distributed externally, for example, services, benefits, enforcement activities, and so on, or internally, for example, hiring, promotions, access to training, and so on.
   - What criteria for access/distributional equity are currently followed?
   - What criteria should be followed?
   - How well is the agency performing in terms of the preferred criteria?
   - What impact is the agency having on equity outcomes relevant to its purpose?

4. Assess the *quality* of services provided.
   - Are there differences in quality by area of the city or characteristics of the client?
   - What changes are needed to improve the uniformity in quality?

5. Assess the outcomes impacted by the department's performance, for example, sense of security, cleanliness of area, job placement, or health.
   - Are there systematic differences in outcome indicators?
   - What changes are needed to reduce disparities in outcomes?

Equity Inventory at the Jurisdictional Level

1. After reviewing departmental reports, what are the areas of strength and weakness in departmental equity results?
2. Are there systemic factors that explain the results across the city or county?
3. What factors produce success and shortcomings?
4. What policy and procedural changes are needed to promote social equity?

Background: Measures of Equity Developed by Social Equity Panel, National Academy of Public Administration

1. *Access and Distributional Equity.*
   Review access to and/or distribution of current policies and services. Measures of distributional equity include

(a) simple equality—all receive the same level and amount of service. Examples: solid waste, water.
(b) differentiated equality—services provided to persons who meet selection criterion or who have higher need. Examples: low-income housing assistance grants; concentrated patrolling in areas with more calls for service.
(c) targeted intervention—services concentrated in a geographic area. Examples: community center or health clinic in low-income area.
(d) redistribution—effort to compensate for unequal resources. Examples: housing vouchers and public assistance.
(e) In rare instances, services may be distributed in such a way as to attempt to achieve equal results, for example, equal cleanliness or equal test scores, or to achieve fixed results, for example, acceptable level in incidence of communicable disease.

2. Procedural Fairness.
Examination of problems or issues pertaining to groups of people in
- procedural rights: due process and participation
- treatment in procedural sense: equal protection
- determination of eligibility within existing policies and programs.

3. Quality and Process Equity.
Review of the level of consistency in the quality of existing services delivered to groups and individuals. Process equity requires consistency in the nature of services delivered to groups and individuals regardless of the distributional criterion that is used. For example, is garbage pickup the same in quality, for example, extent of spillage or missed cans, in all neighborhoods? Do children in inner city schools have teachers with the same qualifications as those in suburban schools? Does health care under Medicaid match prevailing standards of quality? Presumably, a commitment to equity entails a commitment to equal quality.

4. Outcomes.
Disparities in outcomes for population groups (for example, by race or income). The analysis should include consideration of how social conditions and individual behavior affect outcomes or limit the impact of government services, that is, what underlying conditions contribute to differences in outcomes?

Source: Svara 2005.

Notes

1. The award is presented by the American Society for Public Administration and the National Academy of Public Administration.
2. Chinese immigrants had been excluded in 1882 as well as persons who were criminals or morally or mentally deficient. In 1891, the list of excluded classes "included idiots, insane persons, and paupers. Any person who could become a public charge on society was also not allowed to enter. The immigrants who came to the United States carrying a contagious disease were also not permitted entry. Anyone who had been convicted of a felony, misdemeanor, or any other crime such as any activity deemed contrary to the beliefs and standards of society such as polygamy were not granted citizenship" (U.S. Immigration Legislation On-Line 2010).
3. For example, in the nineteenth century, the British Anti-Slavery Society supported the efforts of abolitionist groups in the United States.

4. Portions of this section are from Frederickson and Svara (2002) and Svara and Brunet (2005).

5. Example provided by Sylvester Murray in Gooden and Myers (2004).

6. American Dream Academy Web site is http://cdcr.asu.edu/news-1/american-dream-academy-education-academy.

References

Box, Richard C. 1998. *Citizen Governance: Leading American Communities into the 21st Century.* Thousand Oaks, CA: Sage.

———. 2008. *Making a Difference: Progressive Values in Public Administration.* Armonk, NY: M.E. Sharpe.

Crosby, Barbara C., and John M. Bryson. 2005. *Leadership for the Common Good: Tackling Public Problems in a Shared-Power World.* 2d ed. San Francisco: Jossey-Bass.

DeLaet, Debra L. 2000. *US Immigration Policy in an Age of Rights.* Westport: Praeger Paperback.

DeParle, Jason, and Robert Gebeloff. 2009. "Food Stamp Use Soars Across U.S., and Stigma Fades." *New York Times,* November 29.

Dreier, Peter; John Mollenkopf; and Todd Swanstrom. 2001. *Place Matters: Metropolitics for the Twenty-First Century. Lawrence*: University Press of Kansas.

Frederickson, H. George. 2010. *Social Equity and Public Administration.* Armonk, NY: M.E. Sharpe.

Frederickson, H. George, and James H. Svara. 2002. "Public Administration and Social Equity." *PA Times.* (March): 3.

Gooden, Susan, and Samuel L. Myers Jr. 2004. "Social Equity in Public Affairs Education." *Journal of Public Affairs Education* 10, no. 2: 91–97.

Hamadeh-Banerjee, Lina. 2000. "Women's Agency in Governance.: In *Women's Political Participation and Good Governance*, ed. UN Development Programme, 7–13. New York: UN Development Programme.

Haskins, Ron. 2009. "Getting Ahead in America." *National Affairs,* 1 (Fall), http://nationalaffairs.com/publications/detail/getting-ahead-in-america (accessed November 1, 2009).

International Monetary Fund (IMF). 2007. *Global Monitoring Report: MDG—Confronting the Challenges of Gender Equality and Fragile States.* Washington, DC.

Jennings, Edward T. Jr. 2005a. "Results-Based Governance and Social Equity." Paper presented at the Annual Conference of the International Association of Schools and Institutes of Administration, Como, Italy, July 11–15.

———. 2005b. "Social Equity and the Government Performance and Results Act." Paper presented at the Public Management Research Conference, University of Southern California, September 29–October 1.

King, Cheryl Simrell, and Lisa A. Zanetti. 2005. *Transformational Public Service.* Armonk, NY: M.E. Sharpe.

Mead, Lawrence M. 2004. "The Great Passivity." *Perspectives on Politics* 2, no. 4 (December): 671–75.

Office of Management and Budget (OMB). 2003. Categorizing Activities Performed by Government Personnel as Inherently Governmental or Commercial. OMB Circular no. A-76, Attachment A, May 29.

Patrick, Janita. 2009. "BET, Why Do You Hate Us?," August 3. http://www.seeingblack.com/printer_681.shtml(accessed May 5, 2011).

Radin, Beryl A. 2005. "Direct Administration and Questions of Equity." Paper presented at NASPAA Annual Meeting, October 15.

Rest, James; Darcia Navraaz; Muriel J. Bebeau; and Stephen L. Thoma. 1999. *Postconventional Moral Thinking: A Neo-Kohlbergian Approach*. Mahwah, NJ: Erlbaum.

Rice, Mitchell F. 2005. "Teaching Public Administration Education in the Post Modern Era." In Mitchell F. Rice (ed.) *Diversity and Public Administration: Theory, Issues, and Perspectives*, 87–103. Armonk, NY: M. E. Sharpe, Inc.

Roberts, Nancy. 2004. "Public Deliberation in an Era of Direct Citizen Participation." *American Review of Public Administration* 34: 315–53.

Rosenbaum, Allan. 2002. "Program Evaluation and Inequality: On the Need for Social Equity Impact Analysis." Paper presented at the Seventh International Congress of CLAD, Lisbon, October 8–11.

———. 2005. "Taking Social Equity Seriously in MPA Education." *Journal of Public Affairs Education* 11, no. 3: 247–52.

Rusk, David. 1995. *Cities Without Suburbs*. Washington, DC: Woodrow Wilson Center Press.

———. 1999. *Inside Game/Outside Game: Winning Strategies for Saving Urban America*. Washington, DC: Brookings Institution.

Shafritz, JM., and E.W. Russell. 2002. *Introducing Public Administration*. 3rd ed. Boston: Addison Wesley Longman.

———. 2005. *Introducing Public Administration*. 4th ed. New York: Pearson Longman.

Society of Local Authority Chief Executives (SOLACE). 2005. *Leadership United: Executive Summary*. London: Society of Local Authority Chief Executives and Senior Managers.

Standing Panel on Social Equity. 2005. *Sounding the Call to the Public Administration Community: The Social Equity Challenges in the U.S.* Washington: National Academy of Public Administration.

Svara, James H. 2001. "The Myth of the Dichotomy: Complementarity of Politics and Administration in the Past and Future of Public Administration." *Public Administration Review* 61: 176–83.

———. 2005. "Conducting a Local Government Equity Inventory." Presentation at the Annual Meeting of the International City/County Management Association, Minneapolis, Minnesota (September).

Svara, James H., and James R. Brunet. 2005. "Social Equity Is a Pillar of Public Administration." *Journal of Public Affairs Education* 11, no. 3: 253–58.

Thomas, John Clayton, 2008. "Involving the Public and Other Stakeholders in Public Management: A Practical Theory with Case Applications." Paper presented at the Minnowbrook Conference, Syracuse, New York (September).

U.S. Immigration Legislation On-Line, 2010. "List of Public Laws." Available at http://library.uwb.edu/guides/USimmigration/USimmigrationlegislation.html (accessed July, 2010).

About the Editors and Contributors

Usama Ahmed is a professor of public policy at Pakistan's Military College. Professor Usama is a graduate of Carnegie Mellon University in Australia's graduate program in public policy and management.

Terry F. Buss, PhD, is executive director of Carnegie Mellon University in Australia and distinguished professor of public policy at the Heinz College at CMU. He has published 12 books and more than 350 professional articles. He is the editor of the book series on "Transformational Trends in Governance and Democracy" (M.E. Sharpe), of which this book is a part.

James R. Brunet teaches administrative ethics and criminal justice courses in the School of Public and International Affairs at North Carolina State University. His research interests include public agency performance, police administration, and social equity. He is currently developing data visualization techniques to assist police managers in allocating resources and assessing program performance. His research has appeared in the *Public Administration Review, Review of Public Personnel Administration, International Journal of Public Administration,* and *Journal of Public Affairs Education*. Professor Brunet is an associate member of the National Academy of Public Administration's Standing Panel on Social Equity.

Ingrid Gould Ellen is professor of public policy and urban planning at New York University's Wagner School and codirector of the Furman Center for Real Estate and Urban Policy. Her research centers on neighborhoods, affordable housing, and racial and ethnic segregation. She is the author of *Sharing America's Neighborhoods: The Prospects for Stable Racial Integration* (Harvard University Press, 2000) and numerous journal articles relating to housing policy, neighborhood change, urban growth, and school and neighborhood segregation.

Edward L. Glaeser is the Fred and Eleanor Glimp Professor of Economics in the Faculty of Arts and Sciences at Harvard University, where he has taught since 1992. He is director of the Taubman Center for State and Local Government and director of the Rappaport Institute of Greater Boston. He regularly teaches microeconomic theory, and occasionally urban and public economics. He has published dozens of papers on cities, economic growth, and law and economics. In particular, his work has focused on the determinants of city growth and the role of cities as centers of idea transmission. He received his PhD from the University of Chicago in 1992.

Susan T. Gooden, PhD, is a professor and director of Graduate Programs in the L. Douglas Wilder School of Government and Public Affairs and executive director of the Grace E. Harris Leadership Institute at Virginia Commonwealth University. She has published numerous scholarly articles, book chapters, and technical reports in the areas of social equity, welfare policy, and postsecondary education. She has conducted several research studies for MDRC, as well as for other national research organizations. She is a fellow of the National Academy of Public Administration, a member of the Academic Advisory Council for the Congressional Black Caucus Foundation, and an elected member of the national policy council of the Association for Public Policy Analysis and Management (APPAM) and the executive council of the National Association of Schools of Public Affairs and Administration (NASPAA).

Mark D. Hertko is a project director and senior research analyst at the National Academy of Public Administration. He has worked extensively for environmental agencies across the federal government, providing program evaluation and management analysis, with an emphasis on community outreach and engagement. His experience includes engagements with the Department of Commerce, National Oceanic and Atmospheric Administration; Department of Interior, National Park Service; Environmental Protection Agency (EPA); Department of Energy, Office of Energy Efficiency and Renewable Energy; and others. He received his master's degree from the University of Illinois at Springfield and his bachelor's degree from The Monmouth College.

Richard W. Hug is associate professor of public and environmental affairs at Indiana University Northwest in Gary, Indiana, where he teaches courses in research methods and statistics, program evaluation, computer applications in the public sector, and nonprofit financial management. Besides social equity and health care, his research and public service interests include community development, public sector ethics, public affairs teaching methods, and child welfare policy and services (particularly child abuse prevention, foster care, adoption, youth mentoring, and residential child care). He is an associate member of the Panel on Social Equity of the National Academy of Public Administration.

Norman J. Johnson is vice president at Alisias, an Atlanta-based public affairs firm that serves corporate and public entities engaged in complex and/or controversial issues. This work extends his engagement in social equity that began with OEO Pittsburgh and included elected membership on the Atlanta School Board. His teaching and administrative work at the University of Pittsburgh, Carnegie

Mellon, Florida A&M, and Georgia Tech focused on expanding the pool of human capital and diversity among engineers, managers, researchers, and entrepreneurs. As a fellow of the National Academy of Public Administration, he is a founding member of the Social Equity Panel, long-serving member and currently chair of the Brownlow Book Panel, and member of the Board of Directors. He holds a master's and PhD from The Ohio State University.

Sylvester "Sy" Murray was appointed professor of government and public administration at Savannah State University (Georgia) in August 2008. He is also coordinator of SSU's Master of Public Administration Program. From 1990 to 2008, he was a professor, director of the Public Management Program, and acting department chair at the Levin College of Urban Affairs, Cleveland State University. His primary academic research areas are state and local government management, public finance and budgeting, and comparative public administration. Between 1970 and 1987, he was city administrator in Ann Arbor, Michigan, and city manager in the cities of Inkster, Michigan; Cincinnati, Ohio; and San Diego, California. He has served as president of the International City and County Management Association and as president of the American Society for Public Administration. He is a fellow and chair of the Africa Working Group of the National Academy of Public Administration.

Samuel L. Myers Jr. holds the Roy Wilkins Chair for Human Relations and Social Justice at the Hubert H. Humphrey Institute of Public Affairs, University of Minnesota. He received his PhD in economics from the Massachusetts Institute of Technology and has published extensively on various aspects of racial and ethnic economic inequality. He is a past chair of the National Science Foundation's Committee on Equal Opportunity in Science and Engineering, a past president of the Association for Public Policy Analysis and Management and the National Economic Association. He is a fellow of the National Academy of Public Administration.

Kristen Norman-Major is associate professor and chair of the Department of Public Administration in the Hamline University School of Business. Her areas of research and teaching include public policy process and implementation, social policy, diversity, social equity, and cultural competency. She has also done work on incorporating the teaching of social justice and cultural competency issues across the public administration curriculum.

Sallyanne Payton is the William W. Cook Professor of Law at the University of Michigan, where she has taught since 1976. Prior to that time, she was chief counsel for the Urban Mass Transportation Administration of the U.S. Department of Transportation and earlier served as staff assistant to the president on the Domestic Council staff. In the private practice of law she was associated with Covington & Burling. She teaches administrative law, and has served as a public member and

senior fellow of the Administrative Conference of the United States and as chair of
the Administrative Law Section of the Association of American Law Schools. She
has been active in the effort to reform federal health care financing and regulation.
She is a fellow of the National Academy of Public Administration and holds both
BA and LLB degrees from Stanford University.

Matthew Resseger is currently pursuing a PhD in economics at Harvard University,
where he is an NSF-IGERT Doctoral Fellow in Inequality and Social Policy. His
research focusing on urban inequality and human capital in cities has appeared in
the *Journal of Regional Science*. A graduate of Williams College, he worked at the
Urban Institute in Washington, DC, prior to coming to Harvard. He is originally
from Cleveland Heights, Ohio.

Bárbara J. Robles is senior research liaison with the Division of Consumer and
Community Affairs, Board of Governors of the Federal Reserve System. She holds
a PhD in economics with fields in money and banking and econometrics from the
University of Maryland-College Park. She is the author of *U.S. Latino Families,
Heads of Households, and the Elderly: Emerging Trends in Financial Services and
Asset-Building Behaviors* (2009), and of *Financial Services and Product Usage by
Latinos in the U.S.* (2007), and a coauthor of *The Color of Wealth: The Story Behind
the U.S. Racial Wealth Divide* (2006). Formerly, she has taught at Arizona State
University, the University of Texas-Austin, and the University of Colorado-Boulder.
Her research focuses on wealth inequality, community asset building, tax and financial education policies, and micro-businesses/entrepreneurship with a special
focus on policies promoting community development in low- to moderate-income
communities. She wrote the chapter during her tenure at Arizona State University
and has since moved to the Board. The views expressed do not in any way reflect
those of the Board or the Federal Reserve System.

Amy Ellen Schwartz is professor of public policy, education, and economics and
director of the New York University Institute for Education and Social Policy. She
teaches courses in public finance and policy at both the Wagner and Steinhardt
Schools of Education. Her research is primarily in applied econometrics, focusing
on issues in urban policy and education policy and finance. Current research in
K–12 education examines the education of immigrant children in New York City,
the race gap in test scores, and the impact of school organization and school size
on student performance. Her work on economic development in New York City
investigates the impact of Business Improvement Districts on property values.
Previous research has examined the cost of college, evaluated the role of public
infrastructure in determining state output, growth, and employment, and other issues in public finance. Her research has been published in the *American Economic
Review, Journal of Human Resources, National Tax Journal*, and *Journal of Public
Economics*. In addition, she has consulted on various issues of economic and tax

policy for nonprofit organizations and governments. She received her PhD in economics from Columbia University.

Leanna Stiefel, professor of economics and education policy at the Wagner and Steinhardt Schools, New York University, specializes in research on education finance and policy. She is author of *Statistical Analysis for Public and Non-Profit Managers* (1990) and coauthor of *Measuring School Performance and Efficiency* (2005) and of *The Measurement of Equity in School Finance* (1984). Currently she is studying student mobility, performance of small high schools, and school organization. Her published work has appeared in numerous journals such as the *Journal of Policy Analysis and Management, Journal of Human Resources, Education Evaluation and Policy Analysis, Education Finance and Policy,* and *Economics of Education Review.* She is past president of the American Education Finance Association, past policy council member of the Association of Public Policy Analysis and Management, and a governor of the New York State Education Finance Research Consortium.

James H. Svara is a professor in the School of Public Affairs at Arizona State University and director of the Center for Urban Innovation. He specializes in local government politics, management, innovation, and ethics, and examines the conceptual, normative, and empirical aspects of political-administrative relations. Major publications include *Official Leadership in the City, Leadership at the Apex, The Ethics Primer for Public Administrators in Government and Nonprofit Organizations,* and *The Facilitative Leader in City Hall.* He previously taught at the University of North Carolina at Greensboro, and North Carolina State University. He is a fellow of the National Academy of Public Administration and an honorary member of the International City/County Management Association. He is a member of the board of the Alliance for Innovation.

Kristina Tobio is the assistant director of the Taubman Center for State and Local Government at the Harvard Kennedy School. She started working at the center as a senior research assistant in 2006, after spending a few years in the consulting industry. She received her bachelor's degree in economics from Harvard University, and is the coauthor of several articles with Edward L. Glaeser.

Blue Wooldridge is a fellow of the National Academy of Public Administration, a member of the NAPA Board of Directors, and chair of the Standing Panel on Social Equity in Governance. He is also a professor in the L. Douglas Wilder School of Government and Public Affairs at Virginia Commonwealth University. His current research interests include management education and training, trends in local government revenues, criteria for improving schools and institutes of administration, strategies used to improve productivity and innovation, workforce diversity, and ways to integrate social equity into the study and practice of public administration. His publications have appeared in a wide range of journals including the *International Review of Administrative Sciences, International Journal of Public Administration, Public Administration Review, Public Fund Digest, Review of Public Personnel Administration,* and *Public Productivity and Management Review*, as well as journals in Denmark, Italy, and Lithuania.

Index

Village of Euclid v. Ambler Realty Corporation (1926), 193–94
Violent crime, 58–59
Violent uprisings, 59–60
Virginia, 178
Voting Rights Act (1965), 44–45
Voyage of the Beagle, The (Darwin), 211

W
Wahhabism, 67
Wallace, George C., 250
War on Poverty, 11, 45, 47
Washington, 111
Washington, George, 28
Welfare sanctions
  government policy, 229–32
    case management, 230
    exiting welfare, 231
    sanctioning, 230–31
  racial/ethnic populations, 228–32, 233–45
    conceptual model, 242, 243*f*
  research overview, xvii–xviii
  research summary, 274
  social equity, 229
  Wisconsin Works (W-2), 231–45
Welfare system, 14, 23n6
Wilson, Woodrow, 5
Wisconsin Legislative Audit Bureau (LAB), 232
Wisconsin Works (W-2)
  Department of Workforce Development (DWD), 231, 232–37, 242
  Division of Workforce Solutions (DWS), 231–32, 235

Wisconsin Works (W-2) *(continued)*
  Group Systems, 237–38, 242
  racial/ethnic disparities
    conceptual model, 242, 243*f*
    welfare sanctions, 231–45
  staff interviews
    interview findings, 233–38, 241–42
    interview protocol, 233, 244–45
  steering committee, 232–38, 241–42
  welfare sanctions, 231–45
    procedural recommendations, 239–40*t*
Women
  abortion, 60–61
  affirmative action, 103–5
  criminal justice system, 180, 183
  global social exclusion, 60–61
  human rights conventions, 68–69
  infanticide, 60–61
  Islamic law, 61
  marital rape, 61
  maternal health, 141, 156
  missing girls, 60–61
World Bank, 56, 69, 71
World War I, 43
World War II, 40, 43, 47, 49, 50*f*, 53n1

Y
Yemen, 68
Youth intervention, 216–17

Z
Zana, Leyla, 63
Zimbabwe, 71
Zoning ordinances, 192, 193–95, 197–204